T. S. ELIOT: THE CRITICAL HERITAGE

VOLUME 1

THE CRITICAL HERITAGE SERIES

GENERAL EDITOR: B. C. SOUTHAM, M.A., B.LITT. (OXON.)
Formerly Department of English, Westfield College, University of London

For a list of books in the series see the back end paper

T. S. ELIOT

THE CRITICAL HERITAGE

VOLUME 1

Edited by
MICHAEL GRANT
Lecturer in English and American Literature
The University of Kent at Canterbury

820120

ROUTLEDGE & KEGAN PAUL
LONDON, BOSTON, MELBOURNE AND HENLEY

First published in 1982
by Routledge & Kegan Paul Ltd
39 Store Street, London WC1E 7DD,
9 Park Street, Boston, Mass. 02108, USA,
296 Beaconsfield Parade, Middle Park,
Melbourne, 3206, Australia, and
Broadway House, Newtown Road,
Henley-on-Thames, Oxon RG9 1EN.
Printed in Great Britain by
The Thetford Press Ltd, Thetford, Norfolk
Compilation, introduction, notes, bibliography and index
© Michael Grant 1982

Library of Congress Cataloging in Publication Data

T. S. Eliot, the critical heritage.

(Critical heritage series)
Bibliography: p.
Includes index.
1. Eliot, T. S. (Thomas Stearns), 1888-1965—
Criticism and interpretation—Addresses, essays,
lectures.   I. Grant, Michael 1940-
II. Series.
PS3509.L43Z8732   821'.912   82-3842

ISBN 0-7100-9224-5 (v. 1)   AACR2
ISBN 0-7100-9225-3 (v. 2)

General Editor's Preface

The reception given to a writer by his contemporaries and near-contemporaries is evidence of considerable value to the student of literature. On one side we learn a great deal about the state of criticism at large and in particular about the development of critical attitudes towards a single writer; at the same time, through private comments in letters, journals or marginalia, we gain an insight upon the tastes and literary thought of individual readers of the period. Evidence of this kind helps us to understand the writer's historical situation, the nature of his immediate reading-public, and his response to these pressures.

The separate volumes in the *Critical Heritage Series* present a record of this early criticism. Clearly, for many of the highly productive and lengthily reviewed nineteenth- and twentieth-century writers, there exists an enormous body of material; and in these cases the volume editors have made a selection of the most important views, significant for their intrinsic critical worth or for their representative quality—perhaps even registering incomprehension!

For earlier writers, notably pre-eighteenth century, the materials are much scarcer and the historical period has been extended, sometimes far beyond the writer's lifetime, in order to show the inception and growth of critical views which were initially slow to appear.

In each volume the documents are headed by an Introduction, discussing the material assembled and relating the early stages of the author's reception to what we have come to identify as the critical tradition. The volumes will make available much material which would otherwise be difficult of access and it is hoped that the modern reader will be thereby helped towards an informed understanding of the ways in which literature has been read and judged.

B.C.S.

For Theresa

Contents

Contents

*'The Elder Statesman' (first produced 25–30 August 1958
and published April 1959)*

'Collected Poems 1909–1962' (September 1963)

Acknowledgments

I should like to express my gratitude to my colleague
Professor R.A. Foakes, whose advice and encouragement have
proved invaluable. I should also like to acknowledge my
debt to the Library at the University of Kent and especially to Miss Enid Dixon. My thanks are due also to my
secretary, Mrs Freda Vincent.

It has not always proved possible to locate the owners
of copyright material. However, all possible care has been
taken to trace ownership of the selections printed and to
make full acknowledgment for their use. For permission to
reprint, and for answering queries, thanks are due to the
following: The Trustees of Amherst College for No. 100;
Edward Arnold (Publishers) Ltd for No. 156, from E.M.
Forster, 'Two Cheers for Democracy'; 'Atlantic Monthly'
for No. 40 (Copyright © 1923, by The Atlantic Monthly
Company, Boston, Mass. Reprinted with permission);
Brandt & Brandt for Nos 7 and 57, reprinted from 'Col-
lected Criticism of Conrad Aiken' published by Oxford
University Press; Cambridge University Press for Nos 138,
139 and 160; Carcanet Press Ltd for No. 50, from Edgell
Rickword, 'Essays and Opinions 1921-31', ed. Alan Young;
Chatto & Windus Ltd for Nos 83, 101 and 137, from D.W.
Harding, 'Experience into Words'; The Christian Century
Foundation for No. 91 (Copyright 1935 Christian Century
Foundation. Reprinted by permission from the 2 October
1935 issue of 'The Christian Century'); 'Commonweal' for
No. 73; Contemporary Review Company Ltd for No. 163; J.M.
Dent & Sons Ltd for No. 80; Dodd, Mead & Company for No.
25; The University of Durham for No. 171 by Nicholas
Brooke, from 'Durham University Journal', March 1954,
xlvi, 66-70; Farrar, Straus & Giroux, Inc., for No. 30
(reprinted with the permission of Farrar, Straus & Giroux,
Inc. Copyright 1922 by Edmund Wilson); George Firmage and
Nancy T. Andrews for No. 22, from E.E. Cummings, 'A

Miscellany' (Copyright © 1958 by E.E. Cummings); Helen
Ransom Forman for No. 38; Dame Helen Gardner for No. 127;
Horace Gregory for No. 115; the 'Guardian' for Nos 45 and
151; A.M. Heath & Company Ltd and Mrs Sonia Brownell Orwell
for No. 128; David Higham Associates Ltd for No. 142;
Hodder & Stoughton Ltd for No. 64; 'The Hudson Review' for
No. 162, English Verse Drama (II): 'The Cocktail Party', by
William Arrowsmith, reprinted by permission from 'The
Hudson Review', vol. III, no. 3, Autumn, 1950 (Copyright ©
1950 by The Hudson Review, Inc.); Hutchinson Publishing
Group Ltd for Nos 9 and 51; John Johnson for No. 72; James
Kirkup for Nos 118 and 135; James Laughlin for No. 87; 'The
Nation' (New York) for Nos 23, 31, 89, 98, 145 and 181;
'New Blackfriars' for Nos 81 and 133; New Directions Pub-
lishing Corporation for Nos 13 and 155, William Carlos
Williams, Prologue, 'Little Review', vol. 6, May 1919, and
It's About 'Your Life and Mine, Darling', 'New York Post',
12 March 1950 (All rights reserved. Reprinted by permis-
sion of New Directions, New York, Agents); New Directions
Publishing Corporation and Faber & Faber Ltd for Nos 2
and 8, Ezra Pound, Drunken Helots and Mr. Eliot, 'Egoist',
vol. 4, June 1917, and A Letter from Remy de Gourmont,
'Little Review', vol. 4, December 1917 (All rights
reserved. Reprinted by permission of New Directions
Publishing Corporation, New York, Agents for the Ezra
Pound Literary Property Trust, and Faber & Faber Ltd);
'The New Leader' for Nos 146 and 177, reprinted with permission from 'The New Leader', 14 August 1943 and 11 May
1959 (Copyright © The American Labor Conference on International Affairs, Inc.); 'The New Republic' for Nos 10,
20, 26, 34, 54, 56, 62, 97, 109 and 144; 'New Statesman'
for Nos 5, 15, 16, 19, 42, 46, 49, 53, 59, 67, 95, 105,
117, 134, 153, 167 and 172, from the 'Athenaeum', the
'Nation and Athenaeum' and the 'New Statesman'; 'New
Statesman' and Carcanet Press Ltd for No. 179, from Donald
Davie, 'The Poet in the Imaginary Museum'; 'New York Post'
for Nos 33 and 39, reprinted from the 'New York Post';
'The New York Times' for Nos 28, 60, 143 and 164 (© 1922,
1930, 1943, 1952 by The New York Times Company. Reprinted
by permission); Mrs Diana M. Oakeley for No. 93; 'The
Observer' for Nos 18 and 106; Ohio University Press and
Allen Tate for No. 68, Allen Tate, Irony and Humility, from
'Collected Essays' (© 1959); 'Partisan Review' and William
Barrett for No. 158 (Copyright © April, 1950, by Partisan
Review); 'Partisan Review' and Cleanth Brooks for No. 112
(Copyright © July, 1939, by Partisan Review); A.D. Peters
& Co. Ltd for Nos 116 and 119 (reprinted by permission of
A.D. Peters & Co. Ltd); 'Poetry' for Nos 11, 21, 36, 69,
74 and 103 (Copyright 1918, 1920, 1923, 1931, 1933, 1937 by

The Modern Poetry Association); 'Poetry' and the Trustees
of Amherst College for No. 126 (Copyright 1942 by The
Modern Poetry Association); 'Poetry' and Brandt & Brandt
for No. 84, first published in 'Poetry' (Copyright 1934
by The Modern Poetry Association), reprinted from 'Collected Criticism of Conrad Aiken' published by Oxford University Press; 'Poetry' and Mrs John Gould Fletcher for No.
147 (Copyright 1943 by The Modern Poetry Association);
'Poetry' and Helen Ransom Forman for No. 114 (Copyright
1939 by The Modern Poetry Association); 'Poetry' and Hugh
Kenner for No. 178 (Copyright 1959 by The Modern Poetry
Association); 'Poetry', New Directions Publishing Corpora-
tion, and Faber & Faber Ltd for No. 6, Ezra Pound, T.S.
Eliot, from 'Poetry', vol. 10, August 1917 (Copyright 1917
by The Modern Poetry Association. All rights reserved.
Reprinted by permission of the Editor of 'Poetry', New
Directions Publishing Corporation, New York, Agents for the
Ezra Pound Literary Property Trust, and Faber & Faber Ltd);
'Poetry' and Mrs Alta Fisch Sutton for Nos 63 and 70
(Copyright 1930, 1932 by The Modern Poetry Association);
'Poetry' and James Johnson Sweeney for No. 140 (Copyright
1943 by The Modern Poetry Association); The Poetry Society
for Nos 121 and 123; Kathleen Raine for No. 129; 'Saturday
Review' for Nos 65, 90, 165, 173 and 180; the 'Sewanee
Review' for No. 170, Bonamy Dobrée, 'The Confidential
Clerk', from the 'Sewanee Review', 62 (Winter 1954) (Copy-
right 1954 by the University of the South, reprinted by
permission of the Editor); Janet Adam Smith for No. 108;
The Society for Promoting Christian Knowledge for No. 78;
The Society for Promoting Christian Knowledge and M.C.
Bradbrook for Nos 125 and 136; The Society of Authors as
the literary representative of the Estate of John Middle-
ton Murry for No. 52; 'Southern Review' for Nos 99, 120
and 122; 'Spectator' for Nos 86, 94, 159, 166 and 175;
Father E.J. Stormon, S.J., for No. 150, from 'Meanjin';
'Studies' for No. 176; 'The Tablet' for Nos 79, 132 and
154; Times Newspapers Ltd for Nos 82 and 96, reproduced
from 'The Sunday Times', and for Nos 3, 14, 17, 27, 41,
76, 85, 104, 131, 157 and 161, reproduced from 'The Times
Literary Supplement' by permission; Louis Untermeyer for
Nos 24 and 32; Weidenfeld & Nicolson Ltd and A.P. Watt and
Son for No. 169; John Weightman for Nos 168 and 174; 'The
Yale Review' for Nos 92 and 111, from 'The Yale Review'
(Copyright Yale University Press); 'The Yale Review' and
Louis Untermeyer for Nos 102 and 148, from 'The Yale
Review' (Copyright Yale University Press).

Abbreviations

'Bibliography'	Donald Gallup, 'T.S. Eliot: A Bibliography' (London, 1969).
Browne	E. Martin Browne, 'The Making of T.S. Eliot's Plays', second impression (Cambridge, 1970).
CPP	'The Complete Poems and Plays of T.S. Eliot' (London, 1969).
Unger	'T.S. Eliot: A Selected Critique', edited with an introduction by Leonard Unger (New York, 1966).

Introduction

Eliot's career was influential in many fields, poetry and
drama, literary criticism, religious and social thought.
However, his importance as a critic and as a religious
and social thinker was and still is felt in so diffused
and oblique a manner that it seemed fitting, from the
point of view of this series, to confine the area of
interest to the poetry and plays. This means that a
wider selection of material can be given for each work
than would have been the case had more of Eliot's output
been covered. It seemed right, also, to concentrate on
the immediate reviews, since there have been a large number of collections of essays, most of which are still in
print, that consider at a more general level, and in a
more extended way, Eliot's achievement. To offer to reprint this material seemed out of place and unnecessary.
For this reason, and because of difficulties concerning
availability, the material gathered here is of varied
quality. Yet the very ephemerality and speed of response
evident in some of the reviews justify reprinting them.
Our own ideas as to what constitutes Eliot's lasting
importance, or even of what kind his importance may be,
are in continual change and almost two decades after his
death there is no final judgment on his work. Many of
Eliot's critics have recognised a profoundly unsettling
and baffling quality about his writing, a quality also
felt in the relation between the writing and the life.
It may be that Eliot was in a special way the kind of
writer whose work precludes any satisfactory classification, whose work undermines classification. However that
may be, there is more than one type of immediacy, and the
peculiar quicknesses of Eliot's poetry invoke that logic
of the imagination which may be discerned as clearly in a
review as in a full-length study.

1

THE EARLY YEARS

Thomas Stearns Eliot was born in St Louis, Missouri, on
26 September 1888. He was the seventh and youngest child
of Henry Ware Eliot and Charlotte Chauncey Stearns. The
Eliot family was of English origin, the American branch
descending through Andrew Eliot, who came to Massachusetts
from East Coker, Somerset, in the middle of the seventeenth century. Of the family influences upon him,
Eliot's mother would appear to have been the strongest.
Not only was she a woman of compelling moral passion and
eloquence, but the images and themes of her own poetry
recur in the work of her son. Beatific light, fires of
lust and purgation, the pilgrimage across the desert
waste, all these were to provide focal points in Eliot's
poetry, from the early days until 'Little Gidding'.
     His childhood and adolescence were spent in St Louis,
though in 1896 Eliot's father built a large house for the
family at Eastern Point, overlooking Gloucester harbour,
in Massachusetts. It was upon his memories of visits to
this New England coast that Eliot was to draw for many of
the images that pervade his work. In 1905, his earliest
poetry and prose were published in the school magazine of
Smith Academy, St Louis, and in 1906 he entered Harvard
as a student of philosophy. He took courses with teachers
such as George Santayana and Irving Babbitt. He was to
remain at Harvard, with periodical visits abroad, as
undergraduate, post-graduate and assistant, until 1914.
During his undergraduate years, which lasted from 1906
until 1910, early poems appeared in the 'Harvard Advocate',
a student literary journal of which he became editor.
These poems were reprinted in 'Poems Written in Early
Youth' (compiled by John Hayward and printed in 1950), and
collected again at the end of 'The Complete Poems and
Plays of T.S. Eliot' (1969).
     It was during the writing of these poems that Eliot
effected the transition from conventional, late romantic
verse to something very different. The first five poems
printed in the 'Harvard Advocate' between May 1907 and
January 1909, the group comprising 'Song' ('When we came
home across the sea'), 'Before Morning', 'Circe's Palace',
'Song' ('The moonflower opens to the mouth') and 'On a
Portrait', exhibit those features of vagueness, flowing
musicality and literariness that both Eliot and Pound were
so strongly to attack a few years later. None the less,
portents of the later work were already present. 'On a
Portrait', for example (the portrait in question was
Manet's 'La Femme au Perroquet', which hung in a friend's
drawing-room), anticipates the mature poetry both in

phrasing and in self-consciousness of perception.

During the December of 1908, Eliot first read Arthur Symons's 'The Symbolist Movement in Literature' (1899), a revised edition of which had appeared that year. Symons's discussion of the late nineteenth-century French poets drew Eliot's attention to the work of Laforgue, whose 'Oeuvres Complètes' he immediately ordered. Eliot read Laforgue over the summer of 1909, and the effect can be seen in the poems he wrote at this period. 'Nocturne', 'Humoresque', 'Spleen' and 'Conversation Galante' (the last poem was included in 'Prufrock and Other Observations') all date from this time. In the next year, 1910, the first two parts of 'Preludes' and 'Portrait of a Lady' were written; in 1911 Eliot composed 'The Love Song of J. Alfred Prufrock'.

In this new poetry, written under the influence of Laforgue, it is as though Eliot were examining his earlier procedures in a spirit of critical self-scrutiny, as though he could see that what formerly he had taken for an unquestioned and unquestionable meaning was without meaning, an illusion of meaning, a world whose meaning lay merely in the assertion that it has a meaning. If one compares 'The moonflower opens to the mouth' with 'Nocturne', the contrast and the connection are both apparent. Romeo's 'tune / Banal' might well be 'Whiter the Flowers, Love, you hold'. The poetic consciousness of 'Nocturne', as of other later poems, can participate in an experience that it is, simultaneously, alienated from. For Laforgue, this attitude was still essentially romantic. His personae, trapped within themselves and separated from truth and beauty, from the ideal, can do no more than mourn the fact in eloquent and ironic self-regard. Eliot, however, went beyond this by addressing himself to the question of the subject, the controlling 'I' of poetry, as a problem in its own right. Whereas Laforgue's ironic laments never undercut the identity and authority of the ego, of the imaginary, as the centre of the poem, it is precisely this that Eliot, with extraordinary genius, did effect. For Laforgue, the poem remains fixated upon the voice, upon the coherence of the lyric utterance, however debilitated and ironic this utterance may be. Eliot on the other hand, saw that the lyric subject of poetry was not constituted by some putative psychological and romantic condition, some presence, that pre-existed the poem. The subject, for Eliot, was constituted by writing, and specifically by a tradition of writing that reached back to the Renaissance and which had entered upon its death throes in the late nineteenth century. Peter Ackroyd has argued that it is the overt technical order of the poem and the literary

tradition of which it is a part that locate the voice of
the poem and at the same time displace it.(1)   In Prufrock, Eliot was able to create a persona who exists both
as formal device, as creation of the formal allusiveness
and resonance of the poetic language, and as a zone of
'consciousness', a moral 'I' that takes form only through
the substance of the poem's language. In the poem as a
whole, this process recognises itself as such and thereby
the 'character', Prufrock, retains upon experience (of a
highly attenuated order) an ironic hold, a hold continuously in process of being displaced by language. Eliot's
early work dwells in this uncertainty, and it is his
ability to sustain this almost impossible dwelling between two worlds that constitutes his genius at this
period.

From the autumn of 1910 to the summer of 1911, the
year in which 'Rhapsody on a Windy Night', the third part
of 'Preludes' and 'The Love Song of J. Alfred Prufrock'
were written, Eliot was in Paris, studying French literature and philosophy at the Sorbonne. Although this remo-
val to Europe was against the wishes of his mother, Eliot
had settled at a pension on the Left Bank in the autumn
of 1910. In the early part of 1911, he attended lectures
by Henri Bergson at the Collège de France. Though
initially he was much taken with Bergson's ideas, he found
that ultimately they would not suffice. Bergson's notion
of the *durée réelle*, Eliot wrote in a philosophy essay of
1911, was 'simply not final'. Despite his attraction to
France, and to French culture, an attraction that was to
prove life-long, Eliot had decided by the summer of 1911
that he should continue his philosophy studies at Harvard,
and, after a visit to Munich in the autumn, he enrolled as
a post-graduate student at his old university. Upon his
return to Harvard, he immediately took up the study of
Eastern philosophy: Sanskrit under Charles Lanman and
Patanjali's metaphysics under James Woods. In 1913, he
entered Josiah Royce's advanced seminar in Comparative
Methodology. Royce was Harvard's leading idealist philosopher, and had just published 'The Problem of Christianity'. During this period, lasting from 1911 to 1914, the
earliest of the material that was to form 'The Waste Land'
was drafted.

In the summer of 1914, Eliot visited Paris and then
went on to Marburg, where he had intended to participate
in the university's summer programme for foreign students.
The Harvard authorities regarded him as a future teacher
in the philosophy department, and were encouraging him to
complete his training in Europe, a training undertaken by
many leading American teachers of philosophy before him.

However, the outbreak of war in August brought him to
Merton College, Oxford, where he was officially to spend
the year on a Sheldon Travelling Fellowship, studying
Aristotle under Harold Joachim, a disciple of
F.H. Bradley's (Bradley himself had become virtually a
recluse in his rooms overlooking Christ Church meadow).
Eliot stayed in Oxford until his marriage to Vivien
Haigh-Wood on 26 June 1915.

It was during this period that the meeting between
Eliot and Ezra Pound took place. Conrad Aiken, one of
Eliot's Harvard friends and a fine poet in his own right,
had been impressed by Eliot's early poems, and at a poetry
gathering in London in 1912 had shown 'The Love Song of
J. Alfred Prufrock' to Harold Monro, editor of 'Poetry and
Drama', whose initial reaction was that the poem was
'absolutely insane'. Undeterred, Aiken wrote to Pound in
the summer of 1913 to alert him to Eliot's work, 'a guy
doing funny stuff at Harvard'. Eliot himself, when in
England over a year later, called on Pound in September
1914, at Pound's flat in Holland Park Chambers, where they
took tea. On 22 September Pound wrote to Harriet Monroe,
editor of 'Poetry', of which Pound was foreign editor, to
say that an American by the name of Eliot had called and
appeared to have 'some sense'. He wrote to her again on
30 September: 'I was jolly well right about Eliot. He has
sent in the best poem I have yet had or seen from an
American. PRAY GOD IT BE NOT A SINGLE AND UNIQUE
SUCCESS'. Eliot was getting the poem ready for the press
and Pound would sent it on to her in a few days. Pound
was overcome by the fact that Eliot had 'actually trained
himself *and* modernized himself *on his own*. The rest of
the *promising young* have done one thing or the other but
never both (most of the swine have done neither)'. Pound
was pleased not to have to tell him to wash his face, wipe
his feet, and remember the date (1914) on the calendar.
On 3 October, Pound wrote to H.L. Mencken, one of the editors of 'Smart Set': 'I enclose a poem by the last intelligent man I've found....' Eliot's mind was 'not
primitive', and the poem in question, 'Portrait of a
Lady', was 'very nicely drawn'. However, the poem did not
appear in Mencken's journal.

In October, Pound sent 'The Love Song of J. Alfred
Prufrock' to 'Poetry', with a covering letter stating that
it was 'the most interesting contribution I've had from an
American'. None the less, it took nine months for Pound
to beat down Harriet Monroe's resistance to a poem of such
strangeness. It did not finally appear in 'Poetry' until
June 1915. Pound had been obliged to defend Eliot with
vigour. The two letters of 9 November 1914, the letter of

31 January 1915 and that of 10 April 1915 ('*Do* get on with that Eliot') chart the course of a protracted struggle on Pound's part to convince Harriet Monroe of the poem's value. The letter of 31 January 1915 even gave her an explanation of what was happening in the poem:

> 'Mr Prufrock' does not 'go off at the end'. It is a portrait of failure, or of a character which fails, and it would be false art to make it end on a note of triumph. I dislike the paragraph about Hamlet, but it is an early and cherished bit and T.E. won't give it up, and as it is the only portion of the poem that most readers will like at first reading, I don't see that it will do much harm.

He went on to say that, since the poem was a satire on futility, it could not end by turning 'that quintessence of futility, Mr P, into a reformed character breathing out fire and ozone'. Pound's influence in securing the first publication of 'The Love Song of J. Alfred Prufrock' was decisive, and his efforts on Eliot's behalf continued. No sooner had 'Prufrock' appeared in 'Poetry' than Pound returned to the attack, pressing 'three gems of Eliot for September, and "Cousin Nancy"' on Harriet Monroe in a letter in August 1915. Three of the poems appeared in 'Poetry' for October 1915. The poems printed were 'The Boston Evening Transcript', 'Aunt Helen' and 'Cousin Nancy'; the fourth poem, 'The Death of St Narcissus', was set up in type, apparently for publication, but not printed. Not only did Pound expend his powerful energies on getting Eliot's work published in those magazines over which he had some influence, but he also introduced him to the world of the avant-garde in London, peopled by figures such as Wyndham Lewis, Harriet Shaw Weaver, H.D. and Richard Aldington. From the middle of 1915 onwards, Eliot attended the Thursday night gatherings of the group in Soho and Regent restaurants, in the company of writers like Arthur Waley and Ford Madox Hueffer. Furthermore, Pound took it upon himself to look after the material details of Eliot's life. In Lyndall Gordon's words, 'it was as though Eliot was a precious plant to be watered and tended with care'.(2) Pound even went so far as to borrow money, without Eliot's knowledge, for the publication of 'Prufrock and Other Observations'. Pound's care and concern for Eliot's work was to show itself in very active and practical ways for a number of years to come. Pound was influential in other ways as well. Eliot left Oxford in 1915 and in June married his first wife.

After a visit home that summer, he took up school teaching, initially a High Wycombe Grammar School at £140 a year plus one meal a day, and later at Highgate Junior School where he received a stipend of £160 plus dinner and tea. Between 1916 and 1918 he delivered a series of extention lectures on English and French literature at Oxford and the University of London and evening lectures on Victorian literature at the County Secondary School, in Sydenham, South London, under the auspices of the London County Council. He also continued his philosophical studies, and in April 1916 completed his doctoral dissertation. 'Experience and the Objects of Knowledge in the Philosophy of F.H. Bradley', which was submitted in partial fulfilment of the requirements for doctoral candidates at Harvard. Two months after he had sent it to the Philosophy Department he heard that the department had accepted it 'without the least hesitation', and that Josiah Royce considered it 'the work of an expert'. Despite all this, Eliot remained in London and gave himself over to poetry and literary criticism, abandoning the academic career for which he had been marked out. This decision was clearly influenced by Pound, whose encouragement and help with editors, and whose example of a man wholly dedicated to poetry, must have strengthened Eliot's determination to pursue a similar course.

In July 1915, the complete 'Preludes' and 'Rhapsody on a Windy Night' appeared in 'Blast', edited by Wyndham Lewis, while 'Portrait of a Lady' appeared in 'Others', edited by Alfred Kreymborg, in September of the same year. 'Portrait of a Lady' appeared again in '"Others": An Anthology of the New Verse', edited by Kreymborg, and published in New York by Knopf on 25 March 1916. In a letter to Harriet Monroe of 25 September 1915, Pound regretted that 'Portrait of a Lady' had gone to 'Others', but, as he put it, 'I was in a hurry for it to come out before the "Anth." as you know'. By this he meant the 'Catholic Anthology', which he edited for Elkin Mathews and which was published in November 1915. It included 'Prufrock', 'Portrait of a Lady', 'The Boston Evening Transcript', 'Hysteria' and 'Aunt Helen' (under the title 'Miss Helen Slingsby'). This was the first appearance anywhere of Eliot's poetry in book-form. Harold Monro's opinions had undergone a change since his meeting in 1912 with Aiken. According to Pound, Monro had 'discovered "Prufrock" on his unaided own', and Pound, on 25 September, considered that 'Harold is dawning'. Monro was also glad to see that Eliot was in the forefront of the 'Catholic Anthology'. (Shortly after publication, Elkin Mathews received protests from Francis Meynell and other Roman

Catholics concerning the anthology's title: however
'catholic' denoted its eclecticism, not its religious
persuasion.)

The year 1915 saw the publication of most of Eliot's
important poetry to date, while in September 1916 'Poetry'
published 'Conversation Galante', 'La Figlia Che Piange',
'Mr. Apollinax' and 'Morning at the Window'. During 1916,
Eliot's philosophical reviews started to appear in the
'International Journal of Ethics', while his literary
reviews appeared in the 'New Statesman', the 'Manchester
Guardian' and 'Poetry', a trend that continued as the
volume of work he undertook increased, with reviews, in
1917, in the 'Egoist' (of which he was assistant editor
from 1917 to 1919) and the 'Little Review', as well as in
the journals already mentioned. Eliot's dialogue on
poetry, Eeldrop and Applepex, a work of considerable
importance for gauging his thought at this time, appeared
in the May and September issues of 'Little Review' for
1917. By early 1917, when he entered the Colonial and
Foreign Department of Lloyds Bank in the City of London,
Eliot was in the process of gaining a considerable place
for himself in the world of letters.

'PRUFROCK AND OTHER OBSERVATIONS'

'Prufrock and Other Observations' was published in an
edition of 500 copies by the Egoist Press in June 1917.
The book comprised the poems by Eliot that had already
appeared in 'Poetry', 'Others' and the 'Catholic Anthology'.

The more traditional critics were dismayed and puzzled
by Eliot's work, foremost amongst these being Arthur
Waugh, poetry critic of the 'Quarterly Review'. In October 1916 Waugh had already opened the attack on both
Pound and Eliot in a review of the 'Catholic Anthology',
in which he asserted the connection between political
disruption and what he called the 'banalities of these
literary "Cubists"' (No. 1).

He went on to compare Pound and Eliot with the drunken
slaves exhibited in the households of antiquity as a
dreadful warning by example to the younger generation.
It should be remembered, however, that Waugh was considering not only the 'Catholic Anthology' in this review,
but two anthologies of Georgian poetry, of which also he
disapproved. C.K. Stead has provided an admirable account
of the critical presuppositions underlying this review
in particular and the period generally in 'The New
Poetic' (1964). Describing Waugh as belonging 'to the

school of critics who read poetry for the "ideas" it
expressed', Stead has shown that Waugh's objections to
the Georgians were based on his bewilderment at their
refusal of generalization and large statement.(3) None
the less, compared with this attitude towards the Georgians, disapproving though it may have been, Waugh's dislike of Pound and Eliot was total.

Other reviewers sustained their attacks along the same
lines. The anonymous critic of the 'Literary World',
writing in July 1917 of the published volume, was disturbed, like Waugh, by the 'revolutionary' quality that
seemed to lie behind Eliot's work (No. 4). Resentment of
Eliot's intelligence was also a feature of this review, as
it was of other adverse reviews, the 'New Statesman'
critic, for example, remarking that Eliot's poetry was
'all decidedly amusing', though much of it was 'unrecognisable as poetry at present' (No. 5). The 'Times Literary Supplement' reviewer wrote, with bland superiority,
that 'the fact that these things occurred to the mind of
Mr. Eliot is surely of the very smallest importance to
any one - even to himself' (No. 3). The assumption
behind this kind of response was that wit and poetry
were antithetical categories.

In reaction to these attacks it was chiefly Eliot's
friends, Ezra Pound and Conrad Aiken, who defended his
work in these first years. The violence of Waugh's prejudice in favour of the native tradition began what has
proved a continuing feature of the English reaction to
modernism, and it was this that Pound turned against in
his 'Egoist' article of June 1917 (No. 2). He pointed
up Waugh's ignorance of Laforgue, De Régnier and Corbière,
showing how Eliot had drawn on French poetry and achieved
a 'comparable finesse'. The main drive of Pound's review
was to situate Eliot's work in that tradition of Elizabethan English and modern French that much of the later
criticism of Eliot has taken for granted. Pound also
emphasised the uniqueness of Eliot, and spoke of his own
joy in 'the freshness, the humanity, the deep quiet culture' of Eliot's work. It was a violent essay, with
Pound's attention divided equally between Eliot's poetry
and 'this stench of the printing press', the 'Quarterly
Review'. One can see that for Pound the defence of the
modern entailed a corresponding attack on the institutions, especially the literary institutions, of the day,
an attack that lent credence to the political unease of
the more traditional man of letters. Waugh's failure to
respond to Eliot was, in Pound's eyes, a revelation of
the rottenness of the civilisation of which Waugh could be
seen as a symptom, a civilisation attacked so bitterly in

'Hugh Selwyn Mauberley' (1920). This connection between
literary and social values was to have far-reaching
consequences for Pound, as it was for Eliot, and it
figured as a central theme in the essay.

Pound returned to Eliot's defence in 'Poetry', August
1917 (No. 6). This essay was a more considered version of
his earlier 'Egoist' piece and restated his conviction
of the necessity, or at least the advisability, of comparing English and American poetry with French work. He
pointed to Eliot's 'two sorts of metaphor: his wholly
unrealizable, always apt, half ironic suggestion, and his
precise realizable picture'. He suggested also that
Eliot's mingling of subtle observation with unexpected
cliché was a further clue to the methods of the poetry.
Pound was very careful to locate Eliot's superiority in
his language and to assert what it was as an artist that
made Eliot unique. This was in contrast to the dominant
mode of critical reviewing at that time, which concerned
itself instead with emotions and content. For this reason
Pound's exposition led him into a lengthy consideration of
versification and *vers libre*. Referring to a recent essay
by Eliot in the 'New Statesman' (3 March 1917) on *vers
libre*, he said that Eliot assumed in that essay that all
metres were measured by accent. However, citing the
famous remark, 'no *vers* is *libre* for the man who wants to
do a good job', Pound argued that what was important in
poetry was a sense comparable to the musical recognition
of what he called the 'shape' of the rhythm in a melody
rather than the bar lines. It was the faculty of rhythmic
invention that mattered in a poet, as in a musician.
Pound would seem here to be running together both the
reading and the writing of poetry into the one act of
rhythmic recognition. In any event, it was for this personal rhythm that he valued Eliot so highly: 'Confound it,
the fellow can write - we may as well sit up and take
notice.'

This essay was the first important attempt to describe
the value of Eliot's contribution: it was a judicious endeavour to establish, early in Eliot's career, his true
value in relation to his contemporaries and to poetry
since Laforgue and Browning. It made clear Eliot's debt
to the French and compared his work with that of Joyce.
Pound was not afraid to measure Eliot against classical
literature, in this case Ovid and Theocritus, or to compare his use of contemporary detail with that of Velasquez, in 'Las Meninas'. In other words, the essay put
forward the claims of the moderns, at least as Pound saw
the matter, to represent the tradition in the best sense,
that modern poetry was alive with the true life of all

art, of what ever medium or period. The effect of this
insistence on the notion of tradition was to turn it
against critics like Waugh and to claim it for the new art.
Eliot himself was to take up the idea and give it a resonance that would be felt in nearly all subsequent criticism. For Pound himself, however, a vision, at once unique
unique and universal, had been made palpable in the
rhythmic 'shape' of Eliot's poetic language.

If Pound was the most vigorous and prophetic of Eliot's
early defenders, then Conrad Aiken was his most persistent. In his review of Pound's 'Catholic Anthology', a
review that appeared in 'Poetry Journal' for April 1916,
Aiken stressed that it was the inclusion of poems by
ELiot that gave the anthology its value. Of 'The Love
Song of J. Alfred Prufrock' and 'Portrait of a Lady' he
wrote:

> These are remarkable. They are individual to a degree.
> Mr Eliot uses free rhyme very effectively , often
> musically; and with the minimum of sacrifice of form
> conveys a maximum of atmosphere. Both poems are psycho-
> logically character-studies, subtle to the verge of
> insoluble idiosyncracy, introspective, self-gnawing.

In a later review for the 'Dial' in November 1917 (No. 7),
of the 'Prufrock' volume, Aiken again emphasised the
psychological subtlety of the poetry. The poems dealt
with the reactions of an individual to a situation for
which his own character was responsible, and this,
according to Aiken, made of the poetry something 'autobiographic' and thereby idiosyncratic, with the attendant
dangers of incomprehensibility. Perhaps because of this
reiterated sense of Eliot's idiosyncrasy Aiken appeared
somewhat wary of Eliot's work at this stage, though he
acknowledged the technical ability and general accomplishment of the verse. He emphasised Eliot's skill again
in the 'Dial' for 31 January 1918, when reviewing
'"Others": An Anthology of New Poetry', edited by Alfred
Kreymbourg in 1916. Compared with the rest of the anthology it was 'Preludes' and 'Rhapsody on a Windy Night',
together with Wallace Stevens's 'Thirteen Ways of Looking
at a Blackbird', that were 'more apparently, and more
really, works of art':

> It is significant in this connection that Mr Eliot uses
> rhyme and metre, a telling demonstration that the use
> of these ingredients may add power and finish and speed
> to poetry without in any way dulling the poet's tactile
> organs or clouding his conspicuousness - provided he
> has the requisite skill.

In this, for Aiken, Eliot surpassed the Poundian aesthetic, in which mood or sensation were expressed as briefly and pungently as possible, with or without the aid of rhyme, metre, syntax or punctuation. In the rest of the review Aiken discussed the work of the Flemish poet Jean de Bosschère, whose volume, 'The Closed Door', had been translated in 1917 by F.S. Flint. Aiken suggested that Eliot had learnt extensively from de Bosschère:

> Mr. Eliot's 'Love Song of J. Alfred Prufrock' would not have been the remarkable thing it is if it had not been for the work of Jean de Bosschère: in several respects de Bosschère seems like a maturer and more powerful Eliot.

Pound again returned to the attack a month after Aiken's piece in 'Poetry', this time in the 'Little Review' for December 1917 (No. 8). He ridiculed 'the incredible stupidity, the ingrained refusal of thought!!!!!' of the English intelligentsia, referring, as he had done in the two earlier pieces, to the 'Quarterly Review's' obtuseness on the subject of Keats which was now being repeated in Waugh's 'senile slobber against Mr. Eliot'. May Sinclair, also in the 'Little Review' for December 1917, summarised the positions of the contestants and herself joined in on the side of Pound and Eliot (No. 9). She suggested that it was Eliot's 'realism' that had offended the comfortable minds of the adverse reviewers, though it was precisely this realism that she herself saw as Eliot's major strength: 'Reality, stripped naked of all rhetoric, of all ornament, of all confusing and obscuring association, is what he is after.' In fact, by comparing Eliot with Balzac, she was drawing upon a tradition that held little or no importance for Eliot's work, and yet Balzac was none the less a name sufficiently impressive for the purpose of beating down the obtuse stupidity of the English reviewers. An American critic, Babette Deutsch, described Eliot as an 'impressionist' (No. 10), in a further attempt at finding categories in which to place Eliot's work and so relate it to already existing ideas about what literature should or should not be. Marianne Moore also attempted to find painterly equivalents to Eliot's method of presenting the city scene, citing Whistler's post-impressionist studies, but again she returned to the criterion of realism, saying that Eliot remained true to the objects he portrayed (No. 11).
　　There was in this line of criticism little or no recognition of Eliot's concern for his medium or of the obvious consciousness the poems exhibit of the poetic

process itself. Eliot's opponents and his admirers were
equally agreed about one thing, that the poetry was to be
justified or not in terms of its portrayal of certain
aspects of modern life, that the important considerations
were those of clarity and obscurity, of truth or falsity
to life. Even his more sympathetic critics exuded an
atmosphere of bafflement and no one was able to pin-point
the problematic qualities of 'The Love Song', that for
Eliot language and experience were both fragmented, that
the realism so confidently assumed by the critics was
exactly what Eliot's poetry did not, and could not,
endorse.

It is worth noting also the reaction of William Carlos
Williams to 'Prufrock and Other Observations', a reaction
initially sparked off by a review of Edgar Jepson's. In
May 1918, Jepson, an English literary critic and novelist,
had written an adverse account of contemporary American
poetry in the 'English Review' (No. 12). He made an
exception for Eliot, however, saying that 'Mr. T.S. Eliot
is United States of the United States; and his poetry is
securely rooted in its native soil'. He pointed to the
Americanness of 'The Love Song of J. Alfred Prufrock',
'in very truth the lover of the real, up-to-date United
States', and approved vehemently of 'La Figlia Che Piange'.
To all this Williams took violent exception a year later,
in the 'Little Review' (No. 13). 'And there is always
some everlasting Polonius of Kensington forever to rate
highly his eternal Eliot.' Apart from the direct assault
on Jepson, Williams had a more serious end in view, the
attempt to dislodge what he saw as Eliot's 'conformity' in
rhythm and beauty, and beyond that, to insist upon the
importance of locality, of place, which should give life
to the new art, and which Eliot seemed to have eschewed.
Williams expanded on his opposition to Eliot in his
'Autobiography' (1951), where, over thirty years later, the
the charge remained the same, that Eliot had turned his
back on America and the American place in preference for
the dead culture of the Old World, and England in particular, a country Williams intensely disliked. Many of
the most important poets of post-1945 America took over
from Williams that same distrust and dislike of Eliot and
his work, their sense being that Eliot was the poet of the
academic mind ('Eliot returned us to the classroom') and
was thereby dead, an impertinence to any new and living
poetry that might arise.

BEFORE 'THE WASTE LAND'

Eliot's poetry continued to appear in the small magazines
during the last three years of the decade. The 'Little
Review' published 'Le directeur', 'Melange adultere de
tout', 'Lune de Miel' (all in French) and 'The Hippopotamus' in July 1917. Next year, the same journal, in its
September issue, published 'Sweeney Among the Nightingales', 'Whispers of Immortality', 'Dans le Restaurant'
(a poem in French) and 'Mr. Eliot's Sunday Morning Service'. These poems, with the exception of 'Dans le
Restaurant', comprised Eliot's second book of verse,
'Poems' (1919). 'Coterie' published 'A Cooking Egg' in
its issue of May Day 1919, while 'Burbank with a Baedeker:
Bleistein with a Cigar' and 'Sweeney Erect' appeared in
'Art and Letters' (Summer 1919). Early in January 1918,
Eliot's 'Ezra Pound: His Metric and Poetry' appeared
anonymously from Knopf in an edition of 1,000 copies, timed
to coincide with the publication of Pound's 'Lustra'
(1917).
    The relations between the two men at this time were
close. In Eeldrop and Appleplex, Eliot gives a witty
account of the differences in temperament between Pound
and himself:

    Appleplex who had the gift of an extraordinary address
    with the lower classes of both sexes, questioned the
    onlookers, and usually extracted full and inconsistent
    histories: Eeldrop preserved a more passive demeanor,
    listened to the conversation of the people among
    themselves.... (4)

In reaction against the looseness of free verse, both men
decided that they would write in rhymes and regular
strophes, in a style based on Gautier's 'Émaux et
Camées'. In Pound's case this resulted in 'Hugh Selwyn
Mauberley' (1920), while for Eliot it resulted in the
Sweeney poems, 'The Hippopotamus', 'A Cooking Egg' and the
other quatrain poems of this period.
    Pound continued to promote Eliot's poetry. A year
after 'The Hippopotamus' had appeared in the 'Little
Review', he wrote an article on The New Poetry in the
June 1918 issue of 'Future', in which he spoke of 'a new
French vitality among our younger writers of poetry'.
Of these, Eliot was 'the most finished, the most com-
posed'. The cold sardonic statement of 'The Hippopo-
tamus' was of the school of Gautier, and 'Conversation
Galante' was in the manner of Laforgue. None the less,
Pound argued, there was much that was personal in Eliot's

work, derived neither from the French nor from Webster
or Tourneur, just as in 'The Hippopotamus' there was much
that was not derived from Gautier. Eliot with his book on
Pound, and Pound with his articles on Eliot, were engaged
in mutual promotion, employing all their resources of wit
and abrasiveness to that end.

On 15 November 1918, Eliot met Virginia Woolf for the
first time. In May 1919, she and her husband, Leonard,
published Eliot's 'Poems' at the Hogarth Press. Though
in a small edition, of less than 250 copies, the book
sold briskly. 'Poems' was composed of the work published
in 1917 and 1918, with the exception of 'Dans le Res-
Restaurant', which appeared in 'Ara Vos Prec', published
by John Rodker at the Ovid Press early in February 1920,
in an edition of 264 copies. 'Ara Vos Prec' was composed
of the poems that had been included in 'Prufrock and Other
Observations' (with the exception of 'Hysteria', which was
omitted) and in 'Poems', together with 'Dans le
Restaurant', 'Ode' and 'Gerontion'. 'Gerontion' had not
appeared separately prior to its publication in 'Ara Vos
Prec'. In late February 1920, Knopf published 'Poems' in
New York, which was made up of the poetry in 'Ara Vos
Prec', except that 'Hysteria' was substituted for 'Ode'.
The number of copies in which 'Poems' was published is not
now known. In addition to all this activity, the journals
accepting reviews from Eliot had increased to include the
'Athenaeum' and the 'Times Literary Supplement'. By the
end of 1920 he had contributed about ninety articles and
reviews to a dozen journals. His first book of critical
essays, 'The Sacred Wood', appeared from Methuen on
4 November 1920. Again, the number of copies is not
known. In other words, as Robert Nichols and Desmond
MacCarthy show in their reviews of 'Ara Vos Prec' (Nos 18
and 19), Eliot's reputation as poet and man of letters was
by this time firmly established. The problem was not one
of recognition, but of giving a coherent account of why it
was that Eliot so justly merited the attention he had
received.

For MacCarthy himself, what was distinctive about
Eliot's poetry was its method of conveying elusive emotion
or languid feeling by the evocation of vivid objects and
scenes. There was no attempt at logical progression:
rather, the reader should feel the emotion appropriate to
each object as it was presented. In all of this MacCarthy
would appear to be following Eliot's own theories in his
essay on 'Hamlet', with its famous formulation of the
'objective correlative', which had appeared in September
1919 in the 'Athenaeum', and again, in revised form, in
'The Sacred Wood'. MacCarthy was making the effort to

establish connections between the prose and the poetry in
order to see Eliot's work as a whole.

Little sense of the seriousness of this approach
emerges, however, from the flippant tone of the 'Times
Literary Supplement' review of the 1919 'Poems' (No. 14),
with its mixture of condescension and confusion, though
in the 'Athenaeum' a more thoughtful response was offered
(No. 15). However, the 'Times Literary Supplement'
(22 May), in a review of the first issue of 'Coterie'
(May Day 1919) which contained 'A Cooking Egg', later
published in 'Ara Vos Prec', did make an attempt to relate
Eliot's prose ('his elegant wit finds its best expression
in prose') to the 'superior irony' of the poetry, recognising the sheer vivacity of Eliot's writing in this poem.
In February 1920 Middleton Murry reviewed 'Ara Vos Prec'
in full assurance that Eliot would be a familiar name, at
least to readers of the 'Athenaeum', suggesting that the
real interest would be to see what emerged from Eliot when
the Eternal Footman, the super-ego of irony and self-
limitation had been displaced (No. 16). Murry's review
seems evasive and obscure, trying as it does to imply
something about Eliot's psychology that never quite gets
said.

In America at about this time it would appear that
Eliot's name had taken on the proportions of a myth, since
the fact that he published in England made it difficult
for the American audience to get their bearings. Louis
Untermeyer, therefore, welcomed 'Poems' (No. 24) since
the book gave the American public a chance to judge Eliot
for themselves, and thus to get some idea of his influence, especially the influence of the quatrain poems on
writers as diverse as Osbert Sitwell, Herbert Read and
Robert Nichols. None the less, Untermeyer finally concluded that Eliot's work was essentially *vers de société*,
lacking that 'exaltation which is the very breath of
poetry'. For Raymond Weaver, Eliot was 'laboured and
dull' (No. 25), while the anonymous reviewer in 'Booklist'
(June 1920) dismissed the collection as 'blurred and
meaningful as any post-impressionist artist could wish'.

On the other hand Padraic Colum, in a review of 'Poems'
and Pound's 'Instigations' (April 1920) together, reacted
more sympathetically, seeing Eliot, like Yeats, in the line
of the Symbolists, though instead of taking his symbols
from the natural world Eliot drew them from the urban
world, learning from Laforgue how to make use of these
settings as well as to parade 'a mockery of the literary
allusion' (No. 26). For E.E. Cummings, 'Poems' showed
that Eliot was his own man, not a product of Pound's
propaganda, for Eliot had a quality of intensity that put

aside the comforts of ordinary reality (No. 22). Cummings responded with enthusiasm to 'Poems', though he was less happy with 'The Waste Land'.

Notwithstanding these two more favourable pieces on him, the American response to Eliot just prior to the publication of 'The Waste Land' was less interesting and less comprehending than the English. Eliot's residence in England and his publishing in London obviously played a great part in this, though Eliot's sophistication and wit, the quality of his self-consciousness and his awareness of cosmopolitan irony, evoked distrust. Even Colum found Eliot to be a poet of decadence: 'the shadows of a long decay are upon it all'.

As opposed to this, Richard Aldington, writing in London for 'Outlook' early in 1922, defended Eliot passionately against charges of incomprehensibility and heartlessness:

His desire for perfection is misrepresented as puritan and joyless, whereas it is plain he discriminates in order to increase his enjoyment. But, of course, refinement will not be applauded by those who cannot perceive it, nor will intelligence by appreciated by those who cannot understand it; literary criticism is not the only human activity wherein ignorance is made a standard.(5)

Aldington placed Eliot's work in a tradition of French poetry that ran through Laforgue and Verlaine, Rimbaud and Corbière (though making no mention of Baudelaire), and back to Villon and the goliards. At the same time Eliot, like the Elizabethan dramatists, aimed at density of thought. The poetry, therefore, was neither heartless nor obscure, but was instead a healthy reaction against shallowness and the 'affectation of simplicity'.

'THE WASTE LAND'

On the evening of Sunday, 18 June 1922, Eliot dined with the Woolfs, and read a new poem, 'The Waste Land'. Virginia Woolf gave an account of the reading and the poem in her diary entry for 23 June: 'He sang it & chanted it rhythmed it. It has great beauty & force of phrase: symmetry; & tensity. What connects it together, I'm not so sure.' She was left with 'some strong emotion', while Mary Hutchinson, a close friend of Clive Bell's, considered the poem to be 'Tom's autobiography - a melancholy one'.

With the publication of 'The Waste Land' facsimile by
Mrs Eliot in 1971 and Lyndall Gordon's biography of Eliot
in 1977, it can now be seen that the process of composition of the poem extended back at least as far as 1914.
The poem drew together for Eliot many of the preoccupations of the previous decade, preoccupations that in the
poem's final form as altered by Pound are not so evident
as in the early drafts and fragments. None the less, it
was with the final form that the early reviewers were
concerned, and in its final form 'The Waste Land'
appeared, as Gallup puts it, 'almost simultaneously
(i.e. ca. 15 October)' in the first number of the 'Criterion' and in the 'Dial', without the dedication to Pound
and also without the Notes. The poem appeared as a book
on 15 December that same year, 1922, published by Boni &
Liveright in an edition of 1,000 copies, with the Notes,
that 'remarkable exposition of bogus scholarship',(6) at
the end. A second impression was published early in 1923,
with a further 1,000 copies printed. The first English
edition appeared on 12 September 1923. About 460 copies
were hand-printed by Leonard and Virginia Woolf at the
Hogarth Press.

On 7 September 1922 Gilbert Seldes, managing editor of
the 'Dial', met John Quinn and Horace Liveright in Quinn's
office, where it was decided that Eliot should receive the
annual 'Dial' award of $2,000, a turn of events that would
seem to have come about through Pound's energetic prompt-
ings.(7) On 26 November the 'New York Times Book Review'
noted that the 'Dial' award had been given to Eliot in
recognition of his able work which had established new
currents among younger poets (No. 28). In London, the
'Times Literary Supplement', noting the appearance of the
first number of the 'Criterion', remarked especially upon
'The Waste Land's' purgatorial quality and asserted unequivocally that here was a great poem (No. 27).

The predominant impression one gets when reading
through the early criticism of 'The Waste Land' is of a
response that is both serious and questioning. In
America the tone was set very much by the 'Dial', whose
comments on the award were written presumably by Seldes,
and by Edmund Wilson's review (No. 30), which Seldes
commissioned. After the earlier incomprehension and distrust in American criticism, the 'Dial' took its tone from
Eliot himself, who had demanded of the good critic 'a
creative interest, a focus upon the immediate future'.
Further, the 'Dial' recognised and approved in Eliot that
absence of 'localism' and provincialism, shown in his lack
both of apology and of aggression, which allowed him to
take his place in a European as well as an American

context (No. 29). It has been suggested that Seldes himself understood very little of the poem,(8) and yet he
saw a clear connection between the impersonality
theory expressed in 'The Sacred Wood' and the poetry of
'The Waste Land', a connection many later critics were to
take up. The language of 'The Waste Land' enacted, for
Seldes (No. 31), the cultural effects of the decentering
and fragmentation that had followed on the Renaissance.
The poem was not a romantic idealisation of the past, but
the recognition of an imaginative life whose loss it had
been Eliot's peculiar genius to present and explore.
Seldes was alert to the discontinuous and interrupted
quality of Eliot's writing, though he was none the less
drawn towards the search for some inner unity, some
'hidden form' which the text concealed. It is worth
noting also that Seldes saw Eliot's pre-eminence as beyond
question and fully established. As a critic, Eliot was a
man of the living tradition, and no purely American sense
of values could do justice to him, a theme taken up by
Allen Tate in the first issue of 'Fugitive' (December
1922). Tate considered that 'The Waste Land' raised
precisely the same questions about representation as did
the work of Picasso or Duncan Grant. Using Eliot's own
terminology, he wrote:

> It is patent, for instance, that the art of Duncan
> Grant and of Picasso has no objective validity and
> *represents* nothing; but perhaps the world as it is
> doesn't afford accurate correlatives of all the
> emotional complexes and attitudes; and so the painter
> and, it may be, the poets are justified in not only
> re-arranging (witness entire English Tradition) but
> remaking, remoulding in a subjective order, the stuff
> they must necessarily work with - the material world.

It was this remaking that justified Eliot's 'aberrant
versification' in 'The Waste Land'. Yet, for Tate, there
still seemed to be life in the old modes, and the question
for the American was to decide which tradition, the old
or the modern, he was to accept. Clearly, Tate was not
yet certain as to the meaning of tradition for Eliot, nor
could he see any connection between the idea of tradition
expressed in 'The Sacred Wood' and the poetic procedures
of 'The Waste Land'.
    In the same month, December 1922, Edmund Wilson pub-
lished in the 'Dial' his important review, The Poetry of
Drouth (No. 30). After describing the poem in terms of a
spiritual drought and the failure of fertility, Wilson
went on to comment that Eliot's work seemed the product of

a constricted emotional experience, though as a poet he
'belongs to the divine company'. Wilson saw the poem as a
triumph in spite of its lack of structural unity, each
fragment being an authentic crystal, in contrast to the
bewildering mosaic of the 'Cantos' of Pound. This comparison moved Eliot to write to both Seldes and Wilson to
say that he had no wish to be praised at Pound's expense,
since he was deeply in Pound's debt, and was also a personal friend. 'I sincerely consider Ezra Pound the most
important living poet in the English language.'(9)

    That Wilson gave considerable thought to Eliot at this
time is amply demonstrated by three of his letters to John
Peale Bishop. On 22 September 1922, he described 'The
Waste Land' as 'the great knockout up to date', while on
29 November he explained his understanding of 'A Game of
Chess', Tiresias and Phlebas, considering the quotation
from 'The Spanish Tragedy' 'a miracle of ingenuity'. He
recommended Bishop to read his essay in the 'Dial', which,
he said, he had just completed. On 13 December, he dis-
agreed with Bishop's view of 'Ode' as being entirely concerned with Eliot's marriage. The style of these letters
is free and candid, and he confessed that he found Eliot
on the basis of Pound's gossip as relayed by Bishop, 'a
dreary fellow'. Furthermore, Wilson considered Eliot's
influence too pronounced in Bishop's poetry, an opinion he
also held of Tate's work. On 3 January 1923, he wrote to
Tate: 'I look forward to something extraordinary from you.
But do try to get out of the artistic clutches of T.S.
Eliot.'(10)

    Another important review was that of Conrad Aiken,
An Anatomy of Melancholy, in 'New Republic', February
1923 (No. 34). The Casebook reprint of this review is
prefaced by a note dated 1966, in which Aiken recalled his
longstanding friendship with Eliot and also Eliot's doubts
about himself a month or two before his departure for
Lausanne. Aiken noted that he had seen passages from 'The
Waste Land' as pieces in their own right before the
publication of the finished work and felt that he should
have mentioned this fact in his review, in order to draw
the conclusion that such passages as 'A woman drew her
long black hair out tight' were 'not *organically* a part of
the total meaning' (Aiken's italics).(11) In the review
itself, Aiken made two important points, first, that
Eliot's literary roots were in the French poetry of 1870
to 1900, and, second, that the body of Eliot's work presented the consciousness of the twentieth-century poet as
very complex and very literary, 'a poetry not more actuated by life itself than by poetry'. This led on to the
recognition that allusion was the fundamental method of

the poem, yet Aiken read these allusions as symbols in the usual sense, as concentrations of meaning in an image or images. But what it was that kept these symbols together and guaranteed their unity, Aiken was unable to say, beyond positing a 'dim unity of "personality"' or consciousness that sustained the whole assemblage of frag- ments. In other words, he was not prepared to re-examine that identification of meaning with unity that his reviews consistently imply and which, it might well be argued, it was Eliot's purpose to displace.

The problem of unity and disunity was raised again by John Crowe Ransom in July 1923 (No. 38). Ransom con- sidered that Eliot was engaged in the destruction of the philosophical and 'cosmical' principles by which we form our usual picture of reality, and that Eliot wished to name cosmos Chaos. 'The Waste Land' was an unnatural in- version of a divinely constituted order, that order of which Wordsworth should be seen as the avatar. Ransom thought of Eliot's problems as essentially American and used the more conservative forms of English poetry, such as those of Robert Graves, as a stick to beat him with, accusing Eliot of what Yvor Winters later called the 'fallacy of imitative form', the attempt to express a state of uncertainty by uncertainty of expression. Ransom's review provoked a letter of reply from Allen Tate, who began by attacking Ransom's romantic assumptions about the creative process, assumptions about imagination and inspiration which Tate found 'superannuate' (No. 39). Ransom had attacked Eliot because of his failure to achieve a philosophy and because of his discontinuities of form. However, for Tate, it was precisely in the incon- gruities, labelled as 'parody' by Ransom, that the 'form' of 'The Waste Land' resided, in the ironic attitude of the free consciousness that refused a closed system.

One can see in this debate the fundamental terms of a controversy concerning the significance of Eliot's enter- prise that is still far from dead. For Ransom, there was, or should be, a 'natural' cohesion between the form of the work and the order of things: the imagination, as Coler- idge understood it, was the faculty by which such an order revealed itself in the forms of art. For Tate, the possibilities of such 'natural' discourse were over. A much later critic, Michael Edwards, put forward in 1975 a reading of the poem that may enable us to see the issues at stake more precisely.(12) 'The Waste Land', so Edwards argued, displaces discourse centred upon the individual subject through a refusal of linearity and continuous syn- tax, creating instead through an uncentred writing an act of ascesis that is both personal and, through cultural

allusiveness, simultaneously more largely representative.
The poem enacts a movement of spirit that is fundamentally
Christian, in its ambiguous and self-contradictory
language revealing language itself as fallen, so that the
poem's scrutiny of itself becomes, at many levels, an act
of exemplary recognition, 'a babble of dissonant voices
which registers the most intimate loss that the poem is
concerned with, the loss of a just, single speech'.

Certainly, the antipathy the poem aroused was strong
and violently felt. Clive Bell, for example, an admirer
of Eliot's earlier poetry, could react to 'The Waste Land'
only by way of polite maliciousness, comparing Eliot to
Landor in terms that seem calculated in their spite and
pettiness (No. 42). The stridency of tone in reviewers
such as Squire, Powell and Lucas, or Helen McAfee in
America, seems out of proportion to their consciously
asserted devaluation of the poem. Humbert Wolfe, on the
other hand, though not claiming to understand the poem,
was prepared to accept it for its beauty and the thrill
induced by that beauty (No. 47), while Gorham B. Munson
saw the poem as the 'funeral keen' of the nineteenth
century and an aberration from the realities of the
twentieth century, which were to be found in America,
not Europe (No. 48).

The conflict of views over 'The Waste Land' seems to
bear out Gabriel Josipovici's judgment in 'The Lessons
of Modernism' (1977) that Eliot's earlier work resists
that fundamental temptation, the temptation to ascribe
meaning, and derives its power instead from 'its embodiment of a sense of awakening', an awakening 'that is
always frightening'. There was no doubt, however,
amongst the hostile reviewers, of Eliot's importance, and,
as George Watson put it in 1965, 'admirers and detractors
were equally agreed about the reality of his reputation'.
(13)

In the autumn of 1922, on 15 November, Eliot wrote to
Aldington: 'As for "The Waste Land", that is a thing of
the past so far as I am concerned and I am now feeling
toward a new form and style."

'POEMS 1909-1925'

'Poems 1909-1925' appeared on 23 November 1925, in an
edition of 1,460 copies, published by Faber & Gwyer, and
containing 'Prufrock and Other Observations', 'The Waste
Land' and 'The Hollow Men'. Poems making up the final
version of 'The Hollow Men' had appeared in 'Commerce' and
'Chapbook' the previous year.

Commenting on Eliot's reputation at this point in his career, Edgell Rickword, editor of the 'Calendar of Modern Letters', was in no doubt that Eliot's position was un-rivalled, at least amongst those awake to the reality of the art (No. 50). It was as the poet who had come closest to the distresses of a post-war generation that Rickword valued him, an exploration that Eliot had achieved through his struggle with technique, a finer realisation of language which reached its height in 'The Waste Land', only to become 'gnomically disarticulate' in 'The Hollow Men'. It was the sense of emancipation afforded by Eliot's work that was valuable, since it allowed an essen-tial complexity of reaction.

Edwin Muir was less certain about the value of the poetry, though he admired Eliot's criticism unequivocally. Muir's essay appeared in the 'Nation' (New York) for 5 August 1925, shortly before the new collection of poems was published. He found a separation between the critic and the poet, in that Eliot aimed to restore the fullness of Elizabethan poetry, in accordance with his critical insights, but succeeded only in producing 'a diversity of rich effects':

Mr Eliot's poetry is in reality very narrow, and in spite of its great refinement of sensibility, very simple. In the main it is a statement of two opposed experiences: the experiences of beauty and ugliness, of art and reality, of literature and life. To Mr Eliot in his poetry these are simple groups of reality; their attributes remain constant; they never pass into one another; and there is no intermediate world of life connecting and modifying them.

In Muir's view, Eliot aimed at violent contrasts, as in his contrasts between 'formal beauty and psychological obscenity', that achieved an effect of horror. His poetry was inconclusive and fragmentary, lacking serious-ness. Muir attacked Eliot for taking up poses and atti-tudes, not expressing principles and truths, and yet he admitted the work to be unique. This essay was reprinted twice, once that same year in the 'Nation and Athenaeum', 29 August, and in 'Transition', a collection of Muir's essays published in New York in 1926.

Like Muir, Middleton Murry emphasised Eliot's critical achievement at the expense of the poetry. Comparing 'Jacob's Room' and 'The Waste Land' in an essay spread over the February and March issues of the 'Adelphi' for 1926, Murry found 'The Waste Land' the more impressive, being 'the more complete and conscious failure' (No. 52).

Both Woolf and Eliot he considered fine critics, tormented
by the longing to create, whose intellectual subtleties
gave rise only to futilities. Eliot, so far from being a
classical writer, voiced 'a cry of grinding and empty
desolation' no classical art could possibly give order to.
Murry's sense of Eliot's fragmentariness was so strong
that he described it as 'self-torturing and utter nihilism', which only the Catholic Church could understand.
One is forced to recognise that Murry's notion of classicism was limited and that he thought of Christianity
mainly in terms of metaphysical certitude, despite his
disclaimer in his final footnote. Thus he failed to see
the elements of parody and burlesque in Eliot, taking for
personal anguish, like many critics at this time and
later, what was rather the exploration of new artistic
possibilities. What Murry saw in Eliot's work was a
symptom of the breakdown of civilisation, an expression of
the sterility and loss of meaning in modern life.

    That Eliot's poetry at this stage provoked bewilderment,
either of irritation or enthusiasm, is witnessed to by
I.A. Richards. In his 'New Statesman' review for 20 February 1926 (No. 53), he attacked Murry's essay for its
insistence on unambiguous writing as the canon for good
style and adduced the concept of a 'music of ideas' to
explain the misunderstandings engendered by the verse,
ideas so arranged that they do not tell us about something
but instead combine in their effects upon us to create a
coherence of feeling and liberation of the will, such as
we experience in listening to music. This technique was
increasingly evident in Eliot's verse, and at its most
extreme in 'The Hollow Men'. In 'Science and Poetry'
(1926) Richards was led to assert that Eliot had
effected 'a complete severance between his poetry and all
belief', a view challenged by Eliot himself in 1933, in
chapter 7 of 'The Use of Poetry and the Use of Criticism'.
At the end of the 'New Statesman' review, however, Richards
seemed confident that in the articulation of a generation's sense of impotence Eliot had set healing energies
free, and that to realise one's plight was not thereby to
succumb to it. This account of Eliot's significance was
added as an appendix to 'Principles of Literary Criticism'
when it was reprinted that same year.

    In the USA, Eliot's indigenous and religious characteris-
tics were emphasised. For Edmund Wilson, Eliot's real
significance was less as a prophet of European disintegration than as a poet of the American puritan sensibility,
the waste land being the emotional waste land of deprivation and chagrin. He saw in Eliot's characters figures
comparable to those of James and Hawthorne and at the same

time insisted that Eliot was a poet 'of the first order' (No. 54). These comments come at the end of an essay on the first performance of Stravinsky's 'Les Noces', a context in which thoughts about Eliot seemed not inappropriate. For Allen Tate, the new collection was a spiritual epilogue to 'The Education of Henry Adams', though in Eliot the puritan sense of obligation had withdrawn into private conscience (No. 56). Eliot, in returning to the source of his own culture in Europe, had been forced to confront that source with a degree of general theoretical understanding no European found necessary. As a critic and as editor of the 'Criterion' Eliot had proposed as a rememdy for the disorder of the times that critical awareness he envisaged in The Function of Criticism (1923). Tate regarded the 'progressive sterilisation' of the poetry as due to a rationalisation of attitude carried over from the critical endeavour, the agony of the earlier poetry being reduced to the chaos of 'The Hollow Men', the inevitable result of a poetry whose fundamental ground was the idea of chaos itself. Tate saw this as a poetry of ideas, in contrast to Richards, and for him poet and critic were one. Both Wilson and Tate tried to see Eliot in context, relating the whole oeuvre to larger considerations of American history and culture.

In 1927, a number of important studies of Eliot appeared. For example, A.L. Morton's Notes on the Poetry of T.S. Eliot (an attempt to relate Eliot's spiritual sensibility to his writing) was published in 'Decachord' (March-April), while in 'Sewanee Review' for July George Williamson's The Talent of T.S. Eliot linked Eliot to Donne and argued for the unity of his theory and practice. This essay formed the basis of Williamson's book, 'The Talent of T.S. Eliot', published in 1929. Laura Riding and Robert Graves, in 'A Survey of Modernist Poetry', devoted considerable space to Eliot, especially to 'The Waste Land'. An attack by Henry Newbolt, in 'New Paths on Helicon' (1927), on Eliot's 'triviality' was repudiated the next year by an anonymous reviewer in the 'Times Literary Supplement' (19 January). Eliot's importance was by this time beyond all doubt, and in the thoughtful seriousness of his better critics one sees the fact emphasised.

'ASH-WEDNESDAY'

On 29 June 1927 Eliot was received by baptism into the Anglican Church, at Finstock in Oxfordshire. At the end of that year, 'Salutation', later to be reprinted as

Part II of 'Ash-Wednesday', appeared in the 'Saturday
Review of Literature', while Part I and Part III appeared
in 'Commerce' in 1928 and 1929 respectively. The poem was
published as a book in April 1930, with three further
parts added, by Faber & Faber.

The question of Eliot's religious beliefs was immediately broached by the reviewers. For Gerald Heard, the
poem raised the question of to which tradition in English
religious writing Eliot should be ascribed, that of the
'sanctified commonsense' of the Authorised Version, Milton
and Dryden, or of the iconographic tradition, found in
Crashaw and Donne, and traceable back to 'Pearl' (No. 58).
The former commended itself to Heard as the main English
Protestant tradition and it was to this that he felt Eliot
was returning. Eda Lou Walton considered that the religious search had begun for Eliot in 'The Waste Land', and
she saw the intensity of pain in the earlier work muted in
'Ash-Wednesday' into the desire for belief (No. 60). For
Edmund Wilson, the imagery was more artificial, because
more literary, than in the earlier work, and this seemed
to him a 'definite feature of inferiority' (No. 62).
Wilson recognised Eliot's honesty, but obviously had
little sympathy with Eliot's religious strivings, as his
review of 'For Lancelot Andrewes' in the 'New Republic'
for 24 April 1929 makes clear.

In an extended review for 'Poetry' (September 1930),
taking in not only 'Ash-Wednesday', but also 'Journey of
the Magi' (1927), 'A Song for Simeon' (1928), 'Animula'
(1929) and the essay on Dante (1929), M.D. Zabel attempted
to assess Eliot's career to date (No. 63). The last lines
of 'The Hollow Men' represented the conclusion of Eliot's
Inferno, while the new volume, with the three pamphlet
poems, could be seen as his Purgatorio. In the profound
simplicity and visual imagination of the writing Zabel
perceived the influence of Dante made manifest upon the
poetry, while in Eliot's conversion he recognised the
guidance of Dante upon the life. None the less, a feeling
of disappointment was expressed in the review, a feeling
that of 'profound conviction and the absolute creative
certitude of which the early poems partook' there was
little to be found here. In his first phase Eliot spoke
with an authority lacking in the 'conciliatory' attitude
of his later, religious, period. As with Edmund Wilson,
Zabel's assumption would appear to have been that Eliot's
expression of faith was less authentic than his earlier
disillusionment. No attempt was made to show that 'Ash-
Wednesday' was poorer than the earlier work, nor was it
made clear why Eliot's faith, according to Zabel's own
argument implicit in the earlier work, should have had

less 'authority' than his uncertainty or doubt.

It is, of course, easy, with the benefit of hindsight, and with new material available, especially 'The Waste Land' drafts, to see in Eliot's career a continuity that contemporary reviewers could not have recognised. And yet implicit or explicit denigration of Eliot for his reception into the Anglican Church was common. William Rose Benét accused Eliot of 'a new Pharisaism' and, implicitly, of 'spiritual snobbery', even though Eliot was one of the few modern poets capable of presenting the evidence of his own soul (No. 65). Brian Howard, though he recognised Eliot's technical skill, felt that 'Ash-Wednesday' lacked the power to transport the reader, which the earlier poetry had possessed in full measure (No. 67). Doubts about Eliot's religious position were mainly focused on 'For Lancelot Andrewes' (1928), by critics such as F.L. Lucas, in 'Life and Letters' for November 1929, Desmond MacCarthy, in the 'Sunday Times' (3 February 1929), and Middleton Murry, in 'New Adelphi' (March-May 1929). An extensive attack on Eliot's influence and reputation was was launched by Sherry Mangan in 'Pagany' (Spring 1930), i, 23-36, in an article entitled 'A Note': On the Somewhat Premature Apotheosis of Thomas Stearns Eliot, of which the following is characteristic:

> The logical result of this constant desire for right-
> ness and impersonality is the settling on some agree-
> able form of exterior authority. In Mr. Eliot's case
> this seems to be 'royalism, classicism, and Anglicanism'
> - truly an imposing triad. But it is ipso facto a
> retrogression, a confession of failure to create any
> personal standards.... If certain Anglo-French circles
> in Paris which are in close touch with the English
> scene still consider the best joke of the past three
> years Mr. Eliot's 'daring' in proclaiming himself a
> royalist in politics (and after all, for England, it
> is pretty funny), of how much less interest to our
> present generation in America are Mr. Eliot's however
> sincere preoccupations with out-cocteauing M. Cocteau
> in what is to American-born eyes the so much swankier
> English Church.

Though pronounced in its ridicule, this attack on Eliot for his presumed betrayal of America is by no means a lone voice in the history of Eliot's reputation.

It was in part to redress these assumptions that Allen Tate wrote his review of 'Ash-Wednesday' in 1931, saying that for Eliot's critics all forms of human action were legitimate for salvation, the historical religious mode

alone being disallowed (No. 68). The quality of the poem
had been ignored since it had been seen as biography and
without social or political use. For these critics,
according to Tate, to approve the poem would have been
tantamount to accepting the Church of England. They
assumed that the poetry was the same kind of formulation
as the doctrines acceded to on his reception. For Tate,
the seduction scene in 'The Waste Land' pointed up the
difficulties. Many critics saw in it evidence of romantic
disillusionment on the part of the poet, in which he
showed what love really was, a brutal and meaningless act,
designed only for procreation. And yet, Tate argued, the
scene was not concerned with disillusionment but with
irony, with showing what modern man for a moment thought
himself to be, with his secularisation of humane and
sacramental values. Achieving, by means of this irony,
insight into the folly of urbanised, dominating man, Eliot
allowed the reader to experience the meaningless repetition and aimless pride of an overweening and purely secular faith. According to Tate, it was this irony that
induced humility in the reader, out of the self-respect
that proceeded from 'a sense of the folly of men in their
desire to dominate a natural force or situation'. The
fact that the character, the clerk, the modern mind, could
not appreciate his or its own position was what constituted in Tate's sense irony, and the insight into it was
humility. While, in moral terms, irony and humility were
one, in artistic terms they had important differences. The
recognition of this difference Tate saw as the essentially
poetic attitude and one that Eliot, throughout his career,
had been approaching with increasing purity. The verse that
followed 'The Waste Land' was less spectacular, since Eliot
had less frequently objectified his leading emotion, humility, into irony. Only in the opening stanza of 'Ash Wednesday' was there irony of the earlier kind, whereby the poet
presented himself as he might think himself to be, in the
pose of a Titan too young to be weary of life and yet
weary of it none the less. The opening lines, far from
being a naive confession, were a technical performance
establishing the poet's humility towards his own capabili-
ties. Tate went on to argue that Eliot reduced conventional religious imagery from abstraction to sensation, while
at the same time pushing images of his own invention over
into abstraction, relating the two in such a way that the
idea of the Logos itself took on through the broken and distracted rhythms almost an illusion of presence. In this,
Tate tried to point up the subtlety and profundity of
the connection between Eliot's understanding of poetic
language and the specific nature of his Christian profession.

In the next year, 1932, F.R. Leavis published 'New Bearings in English Poetry' and devoted a lengthy study to Eliot's work, in which he discussed 'The Waste Land' and 'Ash-Wednesday'. In the opening lines of the latter poem Leavis also saw the irony of the self-dramatisation that Tate had pointed to, an irony that Leavis called 'a self-admonition against the subtle treasons, the refinements, of egotism that beset the quest of sincerity in these regions'. A little earlier in the essay Leavis had cited Eliot's remarks to the effect that Proust represented 'a point of demarcation between a generation for whom the dissolution of value had in itself a positive value, and the generation that is beginning to turn its attention to an athleticism, a *training*, of the soul as severe and ascetic as the training of the body of a runner'. Leavis recognised in this the asceticism that informed the devotion and concentration of Part II, and that turned renunciation into something positive:

> As I am forgotten
> And would be forgiven, so would I forget
> Thus devoted, thus concentrated in purpose.

Leavis saw this as a spiritual exercise which in its visionary imagery of leopards and unicorns could best be described as a 'disciplined dreaming' of a kind Eliot found in Dante but believed lost to the modern world. In Part III Leavis noted that blending of the conventional and literary that Tate had already recognised, while in the fourth poem he saw how Eliot had created out of ambiguity the precarious base of a rejoicing that turned into doubt and fear in Part V. The breathless circling movement of Part V, with its repeated play upon 'Word', 'world' and 'whirled', was suggestive both of the agonised attempt to seize the unseizable and of the elusive equivocations of what was grasped. Of the sixth poem, Leavis wrote:

> In the last poem of the sequence the doubt becomes an adjuvant of spiritual discipline, ministering to humility. But an essential ambiguity remains, an ambiguity inescapable
> > In this brief transit where the dreams cross.

What had been striven for was realised, for Leavis, in 'Marina' (1930), in the image of the girl who had been lost and then found. And yet even this recognition was an oversimplification: there was in this poem an ambiguity of even greater subtlety than in 'Ash-Wednesday'. The

indeterminate syntax of the poem intimated the kind of
relation that existed between the various elements, and
in that elusiveness was suggested at one and the same
time the 'felt transcendence of the vision and its pre-
cariousness'. Leavis recognised that this poetry was more
'disconcertingly modern' than 'The Waste Land', and
argued that the preoccupation with Christianity and the
use of the Prayer Book should not blind the reader to
the fact that here were modes of feeling found nowhere
earlier. In 'Scrutiny' (Summer 1942) Leavis returned to
the question of 'Marina', in which he found a 'tentatively
defining exploration' of the apprehension of a reality that
was in time, though not of it. In this he recognised Eliot's
spiritual discipline, his ascesis, his 'technique for
sincerity'. With extraordinary precision and gentleness
Leavis expounded Eliot's achievement in the poem:

> Thus, in the gliding from one image, evocation or sug-
> gestion to another, so that all contribute to a total
> effect, there is created a sense of a supreme signifi-
> cance, elusive, but not, like the message of death,
> illusory; an opening into a new and more personal life.

The influence of Leavis in making Eliot into perhaps the
most powerful literary figure of the 1930s cannot be over-
estimated. In 'Scrutiny', begun in 1932, and in his
critical writings generally, Leavis saw in Eliot's poetry
and criticism the modern literature on which the sensibilities of a critical elite could be formed. In later
years Leavis became less certain of Eliot's place, pre-
ferring to Eliot's ambivalence the more direct and realistic procedures of D.H. Lawrence, and yet to the end of his
life he remained preoccupied with the nature of Eliot's
lasting significance.

THE 1930S

In 1929 E.M. Forster asserted unequivocally that Eliot was
the poet of a generation, 'those men and women between the
ages of eighteen and thirty whose opinions one most respects and whose reactions one most admires'. Eliot was
the most important author of their day, 'they are inside
his idiom as the young of 1900 were inside George
Meredith's...'.(14) In 1930 William Empson, a pupil of
I.A. Richards at Cambridge, used a passage from 'The
Waste Land' in 'Seven Types of Ambiguity', thereby putting
Eliot's centrality to a modern understanding of literature
beyond question. As we have seen, Leavis, also lecturing

at Cambridge, devoted considerable attention to Eliot in
'New Bearings', and as early as 1929 had defended 'For
Lancelot Andrewes' in the 'Cambridge Review' against a
disparaging piece in the 'New Statesman'. Also in 1929
Bonamy Dobrée devoted some space to 'The Waste Land' in
'The Lamp and the Lute', while George Williamson's 'The
Talent of T.S. Eliot' appeared that same year. By 1930,
then, Eliot's position as a major, if controversial,
figure was fully established.

During this period argument arose concerning Eliot's
'classicism' and his relation to the Humanism of Irving
Babbitt and Paul Elmer More. Eliot was sympathetic to
Babbit and More, and in an essay for the American 'Bookman' in November 1929 Eliot stated: 'The various attempts
to find the fundamental axioms behind both good literature
and good life are among the most interesting "experiments"
of criticism of our time.' He certainly included amongst
such experimenters the American Humanists, the French
critic Ramon Fernandez, in Britain, Herbert Read, and
perhaps F.R. Leavis. In 1930 critics as various as
Rascoe Burton, Seward Collins, Franklin Gary, Bernard
Heyl and Rebecca West debated the nature of Eliot's
intellectual position, while in 1932 More himself,
acknowledging that Eliot was 'perhaps the most distinguished man of letters today in the British-speaking
world...', commented on what he saw as the split between
the earlier and the later Eliot:

There it is, the dilemma that confronts those who
recognise Mr Eliot's great powers; somehow they must
reconcile for themselves what appears to be an
inconsequence between the older poet and the newer
critic, or must adjust their admiration to what cannot
be reconciled.... And now against this lyric prophet
of chaos must be set the critic who will judge the
world from the creed of the classicist, the royalist,
and the Anglo-Catholic, who sees behind the clouds of
illusion the steady decrees of a divine purpose....(15)

More went on to question whether or not the modern form
of 'Ash-Wednesday' was suitable for an experience born of
Anglo-Catholic faith, since the metre and punctuation of
the poem were designed to present life as being without
form and as a void.

Eliot's status was thus assured on several fronts, the
appearance of 'Thoughts After Lambeth' (1931) and
'Selected Essays 1917-1932' (September 1932) only serving
to confirm his position. Academic criticism had already
made much of Eliot, and this was to continue, with

F.O. Matthiessen's 'The Achievement of T.S. Eliot' (1935)
and Cleanth Brooks's 'Modern Poetry and the Tradition'
(1939), while Eliot's influence was felt in the high
valuation given to Donne and the 'line of wit', as, for
example, in Leavis's 'Revaluation' (1936), in itself an
enormously influential work. The only important critic
to stand out against these developments was Yvor Winters.
In 'Primitivism and Decadence' (1937) he attacked modern
poetry generally and Eliot in particular, though with
little or no immediate effect on Eliot's reputation, sustained as it was on both sides of the Atlantic and pro-
mulgated in periodicals such as the 'Southern Review',
'Hound and Horn' and 'Scrutiny'.

During this period Eliot turned his attention towards
drama, and in 1932 published 'Sweeney Agonistes', which
ahd appeared previously in the 'Criterion' for the issues
of October 1926 and January 1927. The play was received
with little enthusiasm. D.G. Bridson was disappointed
with the undertaking, on the grounds that Eliot had
satirized dullness by writing dully (No. 71). Likewise,
M.D. Zabel doubted whether Eliot's obviously sincere concern with spiritual matters could justify the dullness of
the emptiness and sterile horror of the life presented,
and he felt that 'Sweeney Agonistes' was a tactical error
after the profundity and beauty of 'Ash-Wednesday'
(No. 73). George Barker admired the work for its
'exquisite, and perfectly lucid, decay' (No. 72), while
Marianne Moore pointed to the significance of the juxtaposition of Orestes and Sweeney, without saying what
exactly the significance of that juxtaposition was
(No. 74).

In 1933, after his lecture tour in America, which
resulted in 'The Use of Poetry and the Use of Criticism'
(1933) and 'After Strange Gods' (1934), Eliot wrote to
Paul Elmer More of a new project:

Now that these two bad jobs are off my hands, I am
working on something which amuses me more: the writing
of some verse choruses and dialogues for a sort of
play to be given to advertise the campaign for raising
money for 45 new churches in London dioceses. If I
have a free hand I shall enjoy it. I am trying to
combine the simplicity and immediate intelligibility
necessary for dramatic verse with concentration under
the inspiration of, chiefly, Isaiah and Ezekiel.(16)

This was 'The Rock', and it was performed at Sadler's
Wells from 28 May to 9 June 1934. It was a collaboration,
as a prefatory note makes clear, Eliot working with

E. Martin Browne, Bonamy Dobrée, the Rev. R. Webb-Odell,
Frank Morley and the Rev. Vincent Howson, who wrote some
of the scenes and played the part of Bert. Eliot himself
wrote only one of the scenes, together with the choruses
that are reprinted in 'Collected Poems'. The pageant was
published by Faber & Faber on 31 May 1934.

The reviews were, on the whole, favourable, though
certain critics raised questions as to how Eliot's
development as an artist was being influenced by his
Christian beliefs. 'The Times' reviewer wrote on 29 May
of how Eliot had made use of liturgy for his dramatic
form, 'though wisely imitating also the ready and popular
stage modes, such as music-hall, ballet and mime...'.
The reviewer considered that Eliot had 'created a new
thing in the theatre and made smoother the path towards
a contemporary poetic drama'. Derek Verschoyle, in the
'Spectator' (1 June), passed strictures on Eliot for not
dealing more adequately with the reasons for contemporary
dissatisfaction with the Church, such as the Church's
attitude to social questions. Eliot replied to this
review a week later. In contrast to this, Francis Birrell
in the 'New Statesman' (2 June) wrote an enthusiastic
account of Eliot's work, saying that Eliot 'shows himself
a greater master of theatrical technique than all our
professional dramatists put together'. As E. Martin
Browne, in 'The Making of T.S. Eliot's Plays', points out,
this review was 'excessively laudatory', and a more re-
strained, though no less approving, note was sounded in
the 'Listener', which was happy to see so great a poet
writing for a popular audience (No. 75). An editorial in
'Theology' (No. 78) expressed relief at finding a real
faith expressed in living language, though the 'Tablet'
found the language of the cockney working men tiresome in
the extreme (No. 79). In an important review in 'Scrutiny', D.W. Harding found the prose dialogue distressing,
the parody of a class by a class, but in the verse he
found innovations of 'tone' that allowed Eliot to remain
humble while being impersonally superior to those whom he
upbraided. There was here a movement towards a more personal poetry and 'The Rock' represented a stage in Eliot's
development that had not yet defined itself (No. 83).
Conrad Aiken also felt that Eliot's career was at a
transitional stage, but was less happy than Harding with
the direction it was taking (No. 84). His review considered 'After Strange Gods' as well as 'The Rock', and
together the two works suggested that the original poetic
impulse in Eliot was formalised. Even 'Ash-Wednesday',
supreme though it was, had to be taken to mark a diminution of vigour and inventiveness, and though he would not

want to suggest that Eliot's views had anything to do with
this, Aiken's conclusion was unmistakably that Eliot's
conversion had undermined his poetic genius.

Among the audience for 'The Rock' had been the Bishop
of Chichester, George Bell, who had invited Eliot to stay
at the palace in Chichester in December 1930. At that
time he had urged Eliot to write for the stage and as a
result of seeing 'The Rock' he was convinced that his
decision had been the right one. As a consequence, soon
after 'The Rock' closed, he offered Eliot a commission to
write the first new play for the Canterbury Festival, to
be staged the following year, 1935. As Browne puts it,
'the purpose of the play was to be the same as that of
most Greek tragedies – to celebrate the cult associated
with a sacred spot by displaying the story of its origin'.
The first performance of 'Murder in the Cathedral' was in
the chapter house of Canterbury Cathedral on the evening
of 15 June 1935, the first (acting) edition of the play
appearing from Faber & Faber on 10 May 1935, for sale at
those early performances. The complete edition of the
play was published on 13 June 1935.

The general opinion amongst the critics was that Eliot
had successfully entered upon a new phase in his career.
Browne cites the reaction of an American critic, whose
London Letter for the 'New Yorker' (3 July 1935) gave an
account of the first night:

> It is a triumph of poetic genius that out of such
> actionless material – the mere conflict of a mind with
> itself – a play so deeply moving, and so exciting,
> should have been written; and so rich, moreover, in
> the various language of *humanity*. That is perhaps the
> greatest surprise about it – in the play Eliot has
> become human, and tender, with a tenderness and human-
> ity which have nowhere else in our time found such
> beauty of form.(17)

The 'Times Literary Supplement' reviewer, writing, like
the other reviewers considered below, of the published
version, was of the opinion that Eliot had assimilated
the chorus, so self-consciously used in 'The Rock'
(No. 85). I.M. Parsons made a similar point, considering
that Eliot's religion, so far from harming his art, as
many critics had thought, was in fact the source of its
renewal (No. 86). In an interesting and very favourable
piece, James Laughlin suggested that Eliot's faith, as
expressed in the play, was Thomist, and that he had
attempted, at the level of the dramatic writing, a fusion
of medieval and classical formulae (No. 87). Edwin Muir

analysed at some length the theological significance of
the play, and the meaning of martyrdom that it propounded,
finding Becket's line 'I shall no longer act or suffer, to
the sword's end' crucial, for it declared Becket's purification of will and his freedom from the wheel of life
(No. 88). Mark Van Doren found the play a masterpiece, of
a seeming simplicity that was not, in fact, simple, and
asserted that Eliot had written no better poem (No. 89).
    The unity of the work was emphasised by F.O. Matthies-
sen, who compared it to 'Samson Agonistes', and to
Hawthorne and James (No. 90). He considered that Eliot's
mode of vision was that characteristic of Dante, whereby
not only a part of life was acutely realised but also the
total pattern informing life. Matthiessen, unlike some
other of the play's critics, approved of the speeches
given to the Knights, since these showed men who deferred
always to social circumstances and to the State, against
which Becket was called to reassert the value of the idea
rising above the value of the event. Philip Rahv ('Partisan Review' (June 1936), iii, 11-14) also noted the importance of Eliot's social views to a reading of the play,
though he doubted the reality of Eliot's political vision:

> We do not feel the 'joyful consummation' heralded as
> the play ends. The formal cause of the horror
> expressed by the chorus - the crime of murder absolu-
> tized in 'an instant eternity of evil and wrong' -
> remains an abstraction. The horror is not realized as
> such, its language is nowise equivalent to the peculiar
> logic of its indicated motivation. History, ever
> determinate, will not be cheated of its offspring;
> though the poem recoils from history, only history can
> give it life.

Rahv wondered what had become of the Christian vision of
man in the singular:

> Why does the chorus harp upon the image of the 'common
> man', the 'small folk'? Throughout the action Eliot-
> Becket, the clerical philosopher, answers the com-
> plaints of those who acknowledge themselves the type of
> the 'common man' in contrast to those who walk 'secure
> and assured' in their fate. Who hatched this heresy of
> a plural man, veritably a class conception in disguise?
> Has Eliot heard of the role of the masses in history,
> of their refusal to become the fodder of eternity?

Rahv saw in the chorus, chanting the doom of man, a language far in excess of the dogma of Original Sin and of

Eliot's conscious ideas about man. It was in Eliot's
vision of the disintegration of civilisation, a prophetic
sense of the modern age, that reality could be felt. Rahv
recognised a creative contradiction in Eliot's work, which
those who could only see in terms of their ideology were
blind to. Out of the choruses, out of the self-portrayal
of the plebeians, burdened with oppression, taxes, failed
harvests and so on, emerged a genuine poetry of surprise
and humility, that further dislocated the poet's conscious
intentions. In all this, Rahv had no doubt that 'Murder
in the Cathedral' contained Eliot's finest poetry since
'The Waste Land'.

Criticism of a more formalist nature attempted to see
Eliot's play in relation to his general literary development. In 'The Double Agent' (1935), which included a
lengthy study of Eliot's work from 'Ash-Wednesday' to
'Murder in the Cathedral',(18) R.P. Blackmur argued that
one could see over the years a growth in technique aimed
at appealing to more levels of response and at reaching
the widest possible audience:

> Applying Mr Eliot's sentences about levels of signifi-
> cance, we can say that there is for everyone the
> expectation (we can hardly call it a plot) and ominous
> atmosphere of murder and death; for others, there are
> the strong rhythms, the pounding alliterations, and the
> emphatic rhymes; for others the conflict, not of
> character, but of forces characterised in individual
> types; for others the tragedy or triumph of faith at
> the hands of the world; and for others the gradually
> unfolding meaning in the profound and ambiguous
> revelation of the expense of martyrdom in good *and* evil
> as seen in certain speeches of Thomas and in the
> choruses of the old women of Canterbury.

Blackmur considered that the play presented a supreme form
of human greatness, the greatness of the martyr, of good
and evil and suffering, and that no representation of it
could fail of terrible humility and terrible ambiguity.
The fundamental question was how the representation of
divine realities was to be undertaken in an age without a
tradition of such representation. It was only through
the chorus, the common denominator of all experience, that
the extraordinary experience of Thomas could be seen and
made real.

'Mr Eliot steps so reverently on the solemn ground that
he has essayed, that austerity assumes the dignity of
philosophy and the didacticism of the verities incorporated
in the play becomes impersonal and persuasive.' So

Marianne Moore concluded her review for 'Poetry' for
February 1936,(19) while for John Crowe Ransom, on the
other hand, writing in the 'Southern Review' (Winter
1936), Eliot was unable to sustain the religious tone and
the play, still bearing the marks of fragmenting moderni-
ism as it did, could not really stand comparison with
drama of the older tradition.(20) Ezra Pound had become
increasingly doubtful about Eliot over this period, as his
letters show, and 'Murder in the Cathedral' provoked him
too far. Writing to James Laughlin in January 1936, he
exploded: 'Waal, I heerd the "Murder in the Cafedrawl" on
the radio lass' night. Oh them cawkney voices, My Krizz,
them cawkney voices. Mzzr Shakzpeer *still* retains his
posishun. I stuck it fer a while, wot wiff the weepin and
wailin.... My Krrize them cawkney voyces!————.' (21) (The
play was broadcast by the BBC on the evening of 5 January.)
The direction Eliot was taking, though in one way aimed at
a wider response, had alienated his oldest ally, and for
Pound the split between the earlier and the later Eliot was
too vast to be overcome. Eliot's separation from the avant-
garde, in Pound's view, was total.

'COLLECTED POEMS 1909-1935'

This collection of poems not only included what had been
in earlier collections up to 1925, but also 'Ash-
Wednesday', 'Ariel Poems' (published separately a few
years earlier), 'Sweeney Agonistes' and 'Coriolan',
together with 'Minor Poems' and 'Choruses from "The
Rock"', and 'Burnt Norton'. It was published in England
by Faber & Faber on 2 April 1936, and in America by Harcourt, Brace on 21 May 1936. 'Burnt Norton' had not
appeared before and did not appear as a book in its own
right until 1941, when the other poems of 'Four Quartets'
were also coming out as separate publications prior to the
appearance of the complete poem in 1943 and 1944.
    The reviewers placed their emphasis mainly on the later
works, especially 'Burnt Norton'. For John Hayward,
friend of Eliot and closely associated with the writing
of 'Four Quartets', 'so much that once seemed obscure now
presents only occasional difficulties' (No. 93). Edwin
Muir stressed, as did Hayward, the beauty of 'Burnt
Norton', finding in Eliot's poetry after 'The Hollow Men'
a new kind of obscurity, one that was finally more comprehensible (No. 94). In the 'New Statesman' Peter Quennell, in a survey of Eliot's career, implied a preference
for the earlier period, concluding that as far as the
poetry was concerned Eliot's religious faith had added to
the delicacy while detracting from the breadth and variety

of his work (No. 95). Other critics also took the
opportunity to survey Eliot's career, Malcolm Cowley
rather dismissively (No. 97), M.D. Zabel recognising
Eliot's movement towards a more accessible style (No. 99),
while for Rolfe Humphries Eliot's work, great though it
was, indubitably sounded the elegy of an age that was
passing (No. 100).

In these poems, 'the underlying experience remains one
of suffering, and the renunciation is much more vividly
communicated than the advance for the sake of which it was
made', wrote Harding, in a brilliant attempt to suggest
the nature of Eliot's 'maturity' in his later work
(No. 101). Harding argued that in 'Burnt Norton' the
poetry was the creation of a new concept, that the words
of the poetry could take the place of our usually
accepted ideas about 'love' and 'eternity'. Through the
subtleties of rhythm and verbal suggestion Eliot had
orchestrated a rich collection of latent ideas, at the
same time as he had put forward 'pseudo-statements' in
highly abstract language for the purpose of revealing the
inadequacy of any ready-made concept that might move towards what the poem allowed, in its elusiveness, to be
shown forth. Harding here took up the complexity of
Leavis's response to Eliot's language and suggested modes
of approaching the poetry that later critics, such as
Kenner and Davie, were to employ on 'Four Quartets'.
Harding pointed to those qualities in Eliot's writing
that forbade the following of 'natural' ways of thought
whereby concepts might be formed that would usurp the
place of spiritual realities. This, for Harding, was
the fundamentally Christian quality of Eliot's art,
especially of 'Burnt Norton'. Blackmur also saw the
crucial importance of 'Burnt Norton' to an understanding
of Eliot's whole work, though he felt there was a problem
in the poem, of the relation between the abstract and the
concrete, a problem which he, Blackmur, was as yet unable
to resolve (No. 103). A wholly opposing view was put
forward by W.B. Yeats. In his Introduction to the 'Oxford
Book of Modern Verse: 1892-1935' (1936), of which he was
editor, Yeats found Eliot's art, especially the earlier
work, 'grey, cold, dry'. Not until 'The Hollow Men' and
'Ash-Wednesday', where Eliot was helped by the short
lines, did the poetry show any rhythmical animation.
Yeats did not consider Eliot's religion an enrichment,
since it 'lacks all strong emotion; a New England Protestant by descent, there is little self-surrender in his
personal relation to God and the soul'. None the less,
Yeats did give Eliot good coverage in the 'Oxford Book',
both in the Introduction and in the amount of his poetry
included.

In December 1938, writing for the 'Harvard Advocate',
Wallace Stevens found Eliot's 'prodigious reputation' a
'great difficulty'. While the complete acceptance of a
poet's work, which Stevens saw in Eliot's case, can help
to create the poetry of any poet, 'it also helps to
destroy it'.

'THE FAMILY REUNION'

'The Family Reunion', Eliot's first play conceived of in
terms of existing dramatic convention, was presented at
the Westminster Theatre on 21 March 1939, and published
by Faber & Faber the same day. As Browne points out, this
was the last time Eliot was to publish a play at the moment
of production. This procedure had involved a great deal of
alteration to later editions of the text of 'Murder in the
Cathedral', and though 'The Family Reunion' was not so
altered Browne tells us that Eliot regretted not being
able to make changes based on the experience of rehearsal
and audience-reaction. Eliot himself expected very little
in favour of the play after the first night, though he
hoped that the acting and production would get the recognition they deserved.
The response of the critics of the daily press was
mixed, Charles Morgan recognising Eliot's verse skill,
but finding an impression of lifeless smoothness in
the second part, W.A. Darlington in the 'Daily Telegraph'
faulting the dramatic effectiveness while approving the
literary qualities, and Lionel Hale, in the 'News
Chronicle', confessing himself 'vexed and exhausted' by
the effort demanded of him.(22) It was dessicated and
intellectual, according to the 'Times Literary Supplement'
reviewer, who threw Eliot's own words about 'Hamlet's'
lack of an 'objective correlative' back in his face
(No. 104).
Other critics commented on the introduction of choric
and hieratic effects into the context of a realistic
drama. Desmond MacCarthy was strongly critical (No. 105),
feeling that Eliot had been led astray from his Christian
concerns by the introduction of figures from Greek mythology, though for Michael Roberts the verse itself was
subtle and flexible enough to sustain great variations in
tone and subject matter (No. 108). Frederick Pottle, like
MacCarthy, compared the play to Ibsen and to O'Neill's
'Strange Interlude', though he approved of the device for
the chorus, whereas MacCarthy did not (No. 111). The
play's connection with Eliot's earlier work, especially
'The Waste Land' and 'Burnt Norton', was Cleanth Brook's

theme, and he suggested that Eliot's problems in presenting a religious vision of life to a secularised and
rationalistic audience were similar to Harry's in con-
fronting his family's incomprehension (No. 112). Brooks
also approved of Eliot's verse, saying that the closeness
of texture of the writing allowed shifts of intensity to
take place without strain, shifts that were the expression
of the central dramatic fact of the play. Another American critic, Philip Horton, felt that 'The Family Reunion'
failed, unlike 'Murder in the Cathedral', because there
was no adequate motivation to render the action convincing
(No. 113). Horton argued that Eliot had used the play as
a vehicle for his own speculations about sin, speculations
which would have been more effective dramatically if presented through the consciousness of the hero, as in
'Hamlet'. Horton regretted this central weakness, since
the verse, in its richness and flexibility, was a considerable advance on contemporary poetic drama.

Horace Gregory drew on Eliot's Dialogue on Dramatic
Poetry (1928), with its plea for the restoration of the
unities, in order to argue that Eliot's drama violated
these same unities, in 'Murder in the Cathedral' when the
Knights turn to address the audience, and in 'The Family
Reunion' when Harry sets off to pursue the Eumenides in
his car (No. 115). The more general question of unity, as
opposed to the specific problem of the unities, was dwelt
on by practically all the play's critics, not least by
John Crowe Ransom, who was sure that the Eumenides would
not appear believable to a modern, hardboiled audience
(No. 114). Ransom did not consider the play to be particularly Christian, and the play's success lay in its
giving an impression of a reality deeper than the visible
world. In 1940, writing for the 'Southern Review', vi,
no. 2, 387-416, C.L. Barber found that Eliot had failed
to overcome the cleavage between the modern setting and
the supernatural action. As a consequence, the religious
meaning of the symbols, of the Furies, remained abstract
or vague and obscure, too much a matter of dark hints and
furtive suggestions. Eliot had failed to make irrational
symbolic significance part of a socially meaningful
action, so that 'The Family Reunion' appeared more as a
work of fantasy than as a work of art. In an earlier
piece that year ('Southern Review', v, no. 3, 562-4),
Francis Ferguson had also argued much the same case,
though more briefly.

None of the critics, except perhaps Brooks, was prepared to allow that Eliot's use of the mythological figures might be related to his use of myth in his poetry,
that the play might be about the relation between the

image and the experience of expiation, and that this relation was not susceptible of dramatic unification. The
fissures in the play, it could well be argued, are the
'meaning' of the play, since it is here, precisely in the
dislocation of unity, that the elusiveness and the problem
of meaning are most strongly felt.

'FOUR QUARTETS'

'Burnt Norton' was composed towards the end of 1935, from
'bits left over from "Murder in the Cathedral"', before
Eliot began work on 'The Family Reunion', which play he
read in draft to the Brownes on the evening of 14 November
1937. Eliot composed 'Burnt Norton' quickly, finishing it
only a few weeks before its inclusion in 'Collected Poems
1909-1935'. 'East Coker' was published in a supplement to
the 'New English Weekly' Easter number, on 21 March 1940, in
the dark days of the war. Hayward wrote to Frank Morley,
one of the directors of Faber & Faber, 'Tom's "East Coker"
has been received with the greatest possible applause by
the few people who knew, or who were told that it could be
found in that obscure weekly in which Tom is interested.'
The supplement was reprinted in May and June, and in September the poem was published in pamphlet form by Faber &
Faber at one shilling. 'Burnt Norton' appeared as a pamphlet from Faber & Faber on 20 February 1941, in a printing of 4,000 copies. 'The Dry Salvages', written, like
the other two poems, at high speed, was published in the
'New English Weekly' for 27 February 1941, and by Faber &
Faber in pamphlet form on 4 September that same year, with
over 11,000 copies being printed. The writing of 'Little
Gidding' proceeded with less rapidity. Eliot was weakened
by exhaustion occasioned by his wartime duties and by ill-
ness, especially bronchitis and feverish colds. At this
time also he suffered the extraction of his teeth and the
painful adjustment to dental plates. Dame Helen Gardner
suggests that, beyond these afflictions, a further reason
for Eliot's difficulties

> was his realization that the three earlier poems that
> he had written so easily had grown into a unity, and
> that the fourth and concluding poem was to be more than
> a fourth poem of the same kind as its predecessors. It
> had to gather up the earlier ones and be the crown and
> conclusion of the series.

The poem finally appeared in the 'New English Weekly' on
15 October 1942 and appeared as a pamphlet on 1 December,

in a printing of 16,775 copies. It had taken Eliot just
over a year to complete 'Little Gidding'.

'Four Quartets' first appeared in America, published
by Harcourt, Brace on 11 May 1943, in two impressions, the
first of which was so badly done, as the result of un-
skilled wartime labour, that all but 988 copies of the
4,165 printed were destroyed. All would have been
destroyed, but for the need to meet the publication date
and so preserve copyright. The English edition did not
appear until 31 October 1944, and bore on its dust-jacket
the statement: 'The four poems which make up this volume
have all appeared separately.... The author, however, has
always intended them to be published as one volume, and to
be judged as a single work.' As Dame Helen has shown,
however, this scheme was not present in Eliot's mind when
he wrote 'Burnt Norton', nor when he wrote 'East Coker'.
It should be noted also that in 'Four Quartets' the Greek
epigraphs were printed on the reverse of the Contents page,
thus making them seem to refer to the whole poem. In
'Collected Poems 1909-1962' they were returned to being
epigraphs for 'Burnt Norton' alone.

Thus it was 'East Coker', the second poem of the
sequence, that first appeared singly, as a pamphlet. The
general response was to emphasise yet again Eliot's com-
manding position in the world of letters. Two days after
publication, G.W. Stonier was moved to assert that Eliot's
authority seemed even more powerful and exclusive than
Arnold's had been; it was rather of Claudel that he was
reminded (No. 117). 'Mr. Eliot is the only great English
poet living', was the opinion of James Kirkup, who found
the calm resignation of the poem comparable to that of the
aged Goethe or to the visionary humility of Rilke's
'Duino Elegies' (No. 118). On the other hand, the 'Times
Literary Supplement' (14 September 1941) was decidedly
cool:

> [Eliot's] poetry is the poetry of disdain - disdain of
> the tragic view of life, of the courageous view, of
> futile sensualists, of poetry, and now even of himself.
> He is becoming more and more like an embalmer of the
> nearly dead; he colours their masks with expert fingers
> to resemble life, but only to resemble.

As Bernard Bergonzi remarks, it was still possible as late
as 1940 for doubts to be expressed about the ultimate
worth of Eliot's achievements.(23) This review provoked
a sharp reply in the correspondence columns on 21 September 1940, from F.R. Leavis,(24) though the 'Times Literary
Supplement' remained distinctly unsympathetic towards

Eliot at this time. Leavis himself reviewed the poem in the 'Cambridge Review' (21 February 1941), lxii, 268, 270, finding it superior to 'Burnt Norton'.

In America, the 'Southern Review' devoted considerable coverage to Eliot. In the issue for Spring 1941, James Johnson Sweeney wrote a long study of 'East Coker' (No. 120), meriting Eliot's praise in a letter to H.W. Eliot jr, that it was 'an excellent detective article', following up every clue, and even discovering source material that Eliot had not read. The essay is an expanded exegesis, which three years later was supplemented by Curtis Bradford ('Southern Review' (Winter 1944), lii, 169-75), both writers treating the poem as a paraphrasable prose discourse and paying little or no attention to the variations in tone and rhythm that work so elusively to give 'East Coker' its life. In the issue of the 'Southern Review' that printed Sweeney's piece, Andrews Wanning reviewed 'Burnt Norton', finding it superior to 'East Coker': '"Burnt Norton" is a poem of suggestion, "East Coker" a poem of argument and explanation' (No. 122).

'The Dry Salvages' revealed, for J.P. Hogan (No. 124), Eliot's humility. Like Kirkup, Hogan compared Eliot to Rilke and saw in the work of both poets a turning inward, a reaching towards an inner kingdom which was not a condition of stasis or passivity but vigilance, not the absence of struggle, but the absence of uncertainty and confusion.

The 'Times Literary Supplement' had reviewed 'Burnt Norton' disparagingly in a short notice on 12 April 1941, finding it difficult to say precisely what Eliot's symbolism meant. This same attitude continued later that year, in a review headed Mr T.S. Eliot's Progress (4 September). Addressing itself with greater emphasis to 'Points of View' (July 1941) than to 'The Dry Salvages', it attacked Eliot's views of the past and tradition, finding in them not a sense of history but despair of the present. Eliot's attitude towards discipline was considered to point to Maurras, whereas the only man fit to rule was 'crowned, indeed, but on a Cross'. As for 'The Dry Salvages', a 'note of quiescence, even of bleak resignation' was in it. It had 'lost that spice of wit which was woven into the logic of the earlier poems'.

The attack on Eliot's ideas of tradition was taken up by other critics. Van Wyck Brooks, in 'Opinions of Oliver Allston' (1941), accused Eliot of being a 'destroyer of tradition', while George Orwell, in late 1942, in 'Poetry London', accused him of a negative acceptance of defeat and a half-hearted conservatism which Orwell, at that date,

called 'Pétainism' (No. 128). Kathleen Raine struck back
in the same issue of the journal, saying that Eliot, as a
poet and Christian, had shown a deeper respect for the
ordinary man than could ever be found in the simplifica-
tions Orwell offered to a public he inwardly despised
(No. 129).

In February 1942, Muriel Bradbrook's The Lyric and
Dramatic in the Latest Verse of T.S. Eliot appeared in
'Theology', a long study of Eliot as a Christian poet
(No. 125), while Helen Gardner's The Recent Poetry of
T.S. Eliot appeared in 'New Writing and Daylight' the same
year (No. 127). In 'Scrutiny' (Summer 1942), F.R. Leavis
published a study of the first three poems of the
'Quartets', a study which was reprinted next year in
'Education and the Idea of the University'. Leavis
emphasised not the Christian side of Eliot but the way in
which the poetry 'makes its explorations into the concrete
realities of experience below the conceptual currency', in
this consciously following Harding's earlier formulation
of the 'creation of concepts'.

On the publication of 'Little Gidding' in December
1942, Muriel Bradbrook presented in 'Theology' (March 1943)
what was the conclusion to her essay of the year before.
Taken together, the two essays make a sustained study of
Eliot's work (Nos 125 and 136). She saw, in the changing
use of the 'I' in Eliot's work, an index of Eliot's growing understanding of the theme of renunciation, the *via
negativa*. In 'Little Gidding' what emerged was not dogma,
but the dramatisation of Christian experience, an experience one felt in the act of reading to be both highly personal and genuinely representative. These essays are
early attempts to see Eliot's work in terms of the tradition of Western spirituality. The Anglican literary
revival, associated with Charles Williams, C.S. Lewis and
Dorothy Sayers, with Kathleen Raine and David Gascoyne on
the poetic fringes of the movement, was making itself felt
in this work, as well as in that of Helen Gardner.

The 'Scrutiny' group also saw the religious implications of Eliot's work and yet did not accede to them in
expressly Christian terms. Harding, writing in 'Scrutiny'
for Spring 1943 (No. 137), recognised in 'Little Gidding'
a double movement of repulsion and affirmation, repulsion
in Section II from the desolation of a life without
spiritual values and affirmation of love in Section III
and onwards. The pentecostal fire was noted as central to
this experience, but Harding made no attempt to relate it
to Eliot's Christian belief, nor did he attempt any analytical justification for his high valuation of the poem.
It was this lack of close analysis that led a

correspondent, R.N. Higinbotham, to disagree with Harding's
estimation of 'Little Gidding' (No. 138). Higinbotham
pointed to what he saw as cliché and stock response in
Eliot's writing, and argued that the poetry failed to
reconcile emotion and thought. In a reply printed immediately after Higinbotham's letter, Leavis came to the
defence of 'Four Quartets' and insisted that the intellectual material emerged from the experiential matrix in ways
that rendered Higinbotham's distinctions and sense of
thought as 'syllogism' altogether too imperceptive
(No. 139). The difficulties of the poem lay in its imposing a discipline of self-knowledge and readjustment: in
other words, the poem was itself an active force in trans-
forming the reader's life. James Johnson Sweeney, writing
for 'Poetry' in July 1943 on the appearance of 'Four Quartets', but with specific regard to 'Little Gidding',
traced Eliot's use of a tradition of contemplative writing
that reached back to the pseudo-Dionysius, and included
Dame Julian of Norwich, 'The Cloud of Unknowing', and St
John of the Cross (No. 140).

With the publication of 'Four Quartets' in New York on
11 May 1943, certain American critics responded warmly.
Horace Gregory gave an enthusiastic reception to the poem,
comparing it to 'The Prelude' less as an autobiographical
poem than as a work that recapitulated all that Eliot had
written since 'The Waste Land' (No. 143). In the 'New
Leader' (19 June 1943), after a survey of the current
critical writings on Eliot, Melvin J. Lasky considered
that 'as yet no professional reader has adequately conveyed the poem's elements of tragic wisdom and lyrical
power, its range of mood and idea and masterly self-
consciousness'. F.O. Matthiessen published a lengthy and
important analysis of the work as a whole, in the issue
for Spring 1943 of the 'Kenyon Review', which later he
incorporated into editions of 'The Achievement of T.S.
Eliot' from 1947 onwards. The essay was a sustained and
sympathetic exegesis of the religious themes, the images
and symbols that developed them, and the interconnections
between the poems. Like other critics, Matthiessen concluded on an affirmative note:

> Essential evil still constitutes more of Eliot's
> subject-matter than essential good, but the magnifi-
> cent orchestration of his themes has prepared for that
> paradisal glimpse at the close, and thereby makes it
> no decorative allusion, but an integrated climax to
> the content no less than to the form. Such spiritual
> release and reconciliation are the chief reality for
> which he strives in a world that has seemed to him
> increasingly threatened with new dark ages.

The essay did not concern itself with Eliot's linguistic inventiveness or with his artistic self-consciousness. Nor did Matthiessen hint at those elements in the poem that made it seem to later critics one of the great and problematic achievements of modernism in English. It was rather the religious themes that predominated, both in Matthiessen's work and in that of other early reviewers.

Other American critics were less wholehearted in their reception. Such a critic was Malcolm Cowley, in June 1943, who saw the poem as a mystical work and spoke of the ways in which Eliot had presented a sense of ecstatic oneness with the divine (No. 144). For Cowley, however, this seemed to point to qualities that were less Catholic or Anglican than Calvinist and Buddhist, the consequence of which was to take Eliot beyond poetry. Cowley saw the whole as a mixture of prosaic passages, together with some fine poetry in which Eliot was at his best. Delmore Schwartz also reacted with mixed feelings, disturbed by the 'falsity of tone' in passages such as 'East Coker', Section V, while the Dante section in 'Little Gidding' struck him with admiration. He pointed to the 'Buddhist' quality of Eliot's mind, stating that the Incarnation was present to Eliot for the sake of renunciation, not renunciation for greater closeness to God (No. 145). For Paul Goodman, Eliot's despair of the material world and emphasis on the emerging pattern had led towards a despair of Creation itself, and therefore he denied that Eliot was a Christian poet (No. 146). For all Goddman's admiration of Eliot's rhythms and cadences, this review was as doubtful as the others of Eliot's final significance. Again, for John Gould Fletcher, it was Eliot's musical abilities with language that were his only abiding value. Eliot's negative way to salvation was without significance in the face of the world's real problem, to create a true democracy (No. 147). Louis Untermeyer considered that the poem would not be to everyone's taste. Few would doubt the beauty of the poem, but its mysticism would not be easy to comprehend (No. 148). The American response, therefore, was mixed and ambiguous, the main emphasis falling on Eliot's musical effects, with a concomitant distrust of his religious explorations.

On the appearance of 'Four Quartets' in England in October 1944, the response was altogether more admiring, even though the 'Times Literary Supplement' (9 December 1944) carried no review, only a notice of publication. Reginald Snell, however, saw the triumph of an artist who had achieved universality and who by putting off individuality had none the less achieved it. 'Four Quartets' was Eliot's vindication, the poem being a true part of the

English tradition. The poem was a meditation on the
theme of the incarnation, the finest poem of the four
being 'Little Gidding' (No. 149). Snell's review, in the
'New English Weekly', sounded no note of doubt, and unlike
some of the American reviews accepted Eliot's religious
beliefs without demur. Eliot himself wrote to the 'New
English Weekly' on 25 January 1945, adding a few.points
about the text. Snell's review, taken together with those
on individual poems of the sequence by Helen Gardner,
Muriel Bradbrook, and the 'Scrutiny' critics, suggests
that Eliot was more respectfully received in England than
in America, with less willingness amongst the English to
criticise Eliot on either poetic or religious grounds.

'THE COCKTAIL PARTY'

In 1948 Eliot published his 'Selected Poems' and 'Notes
Towards the Definition of Culture'. In the same year he
received the Nobel Prize for Literature, as well as the
Order of Merit. It was during this period that 'The
Cocktail Party' was composed, and on 22 August 1949 was
performed for the first time as part of the Edinburgh
Festival, at the Lyceum Theatre.
    'The Times' reviewer on 24 August found the play 'bril-
liantly entertaining', since Eliot had dispensed with the
ritual and artifice of his earlier work and in return
achieved a 'lucid, unallusive verse'. Other newspaper
critics were divided, the 'Daily Telegraph' (23 August)
finding it 'one of the finest dramatic achievements of our
time', while Ivor Brown, of the 'Observer' (28 August),
disliked it totally.
    On the basis of the Edinburgh production, the weeklies
and periodicals generally approved of 'The Cocktail
Party'. Eliot in general and his play in particular were
both defended passionately in the first issue of 'Nine' by
its editor, Peter Russell, who recognised, as few of
Eliot's critics were prepared to do, that the principle of
diversity was as important to his work as that of innovation. Russell, who had clearly seen the play in production, found it excellent theatre (No. 152). In the 'New
Statesman', Desmond Shawe-Taylor also approved of the
theatrical quality of the play, especially the acting of
Alec Guinness as Sir Henry, and yet he found Eliot incapable
of love towards his characters (No. 153). A certain condescension towards Eliot's more serious preoccupations is
quite clearly perceptible in Shawe-Taylor's tone. Robert
Speaight, in the 'Tablet' for 3 September, saw the play in
the longer perspective of Eliot's career, and spoke

professionally of it as a dramatic production, praising
the actors and the director, E. Martin Browne (No. 154).

After the Edinburgh performances, the play opened in
Brighton on 19 December 1949, with two changes in the
cast. Harold Hobson's 'Sunday Times' review on 8 January
1950 referred to this production and to the fact that no
theatre could be found to stage the play in London.
Although Eliot was at first perturbed by the idea, he
finally agreed that the play should open in New York, and
in fact it opened there on 21 January 1950, where it
proved a success. The play was published in London and
New York in March 1950.

It is of this published version that William Carlos
Williams wrote in the 'New York Post', on 12 March, with
a degree of approval (No. 155).   E.M. Forster, in England,
found Celia's martyrdom hard to take (No. 156), while
Helen Gardner in 'Time and Tide' (25 March 1950) considered the play finally unconvincing, despite its brilliance, because the Guardians were not credible:

> In their exchanges with each other the Guardians appear
> as interfering busybodies, Buchmanite conspirators with
> classy connections throughout the world, spotters of
> winners. Their libations and the final toast to
> Lavinia's aunt are embarrassing evasions. The failure
> to render the central conception except in terms of
> fantasy invades the treatment of Celia.... The comedy
> of manners and the divine comedy fail to coalesce, for
> the same reason, I believe, which causes 'Murder in the
> Cathedral' and 'The Family Reunion' to fall apart.
> Mr Eliot's 'fatal Cleopatra' is his romantic conception
> of sanctity. What seems needed here is the classic
> idea of holiness.

William Barrett, in the 'Partisan Review', found the play a
a disappointment, weak as drama and as poetry, and suggested that the play's American success was due in large
part to the actors, in that American playgoers could for
once hear English well and naturally spoken (No. 158).
Barrett objected to what Carlos Williams had approved of,
the fact that the verse was not recognisable as verse.
Like other critics, though with greater passion, Barrett
contended that Eliot had never shown in his poetry the
fullness of love and joy, or that he believed in the possibility of such fullness. At the height of his reputation, Eliot's creative powers seemed at their lowest ebb.
Barrett saw himself as speaking for a new generation,
which, in Freudian terms, had first to kill its own
father. In 'Scrutiny' John Peter found the figures of the

Guardians preposterous, since the contrast between the
human figures of Julia and Alex in Act I and their spiritual transformation in Acts II and III was so gross as to
tear the play apart. He found the verse flaccid, doing
nothing to make the concepts it dealt in real or interesting (No. 160). Bonamy Dobrée wrote more favourably, finding the play a disturbing experience and one that caused
the reader to feel that some barb had pierced beneath his
skin (No. 159).

The play opened in London on 3 May 1950, at the New
Theatre, with a new cast, and ran until 10 February 1951,
assured of a large audience due to its Broadway success
and to its appearance in print. Philip Hope-Wallace in
'Time and Tide' (13 May 1950) found that the question
which had angered critics was whether or not the psychiat-
rist was right to advise Celia to follow the course that
led to a martyr's death:

> But really Mr Eliot is not the first to return a dusty
> answer to those who are hot for certainty. I don't
> myself like particularly the ambiguous figure of the
> doctor-priest, or the way his 'helpers and servers',
> the guardians, are incarnated in the apparently silly
> and therefore unsuspect cocktail party gossips. But
> that does not mean I do not find it the most fascinating
> and exciting piece of drama.

In a long study of the play for the 'Hudson Review'
(No. 162), William Arrowsmith argued that Eliot could only
give real emotional credence to the ascetic part of the
Christian tradition, not to the way of the common life,
the Chamberlaynes, a point that can be compared with Helen
Gardner's opinion of Eliot's ideas on sanctity. Arrowsmith recognised that Eliot's problem was to write a
Christian drama for a world that was secular and distrust-
ful of poetry, and to write in a way that would invite
notice and make its point. For this reason he did not
condemn Eliot's verse or his use of domestic, marital
comedy. It was in this way that Eliot had attempted to
repossess popular forms for his greater purpose. This is
a sympathetic and important review, dealing with all the
issues raised against Eliot by the contemporary critics,
including William Barrett. Middleton Murry also thought
well of 'The Cocktail Party', since the scheme of salvation and the dramatic contrast worked well and satisfyingly together, though Murry believed that there was more
to love than emerged from Eliot's sense of it (No. 163).

The reception of 'The Cocktail Party' was therefore
muted, with one or two exceptions, much of the passion

having subsided from the critical debate. One or two
critics suggested that the play was as important to drama
as 'The Waste Land' had been to poetry, though no one was
moved to any larger revaluation of Eliot's importance or
meaning.

'THE CONFIDENTIAL CLERK'

After the success of 'The Cocktail Party', which had
played, according to 'The Times' for 21 December 1952, to
close on a million and a half spectators, 'The Confidential Clerk' opened on 25 August 1953 at the Lyceum, as
part of the Edinburgh Festival.
     The critics were more or less agreed that the play was
flawed in various important ways. For Henry Donald, in
the 'Spectator' (No. 166), it was no comfort to be told
'The Confidential Clerk' was based on the 'Ion' of Euripides: Eliot's play was broken-backed, though the evening
itself was saved by the excellence of the acting. Donald
also noted the sets, designed by Hutchinson Scott to give
a sense of mysterious depth. Browne links this break with
naturalistic convention to the changes that were generally
taking place in the theatre, highlighted and developed by
George Devine with the English Stage Company in 1954. In
Browne's view, Eliot forestalled these developments, so
that the set designs, by creating an effect of strangeness
and by displacing naturalistic perspective, were intended
to emphasise Eliot's own aesthetic purposes.
     T.C. Worsley saw the play as more than a Gilbertian
comedy of manners, though he believed it to be confused,
mainly because of Eliot's abrogation of control over the
verse. Eliot would be well advised to emphasise more
strongly his poetic powers (No. 167). For John Weightman,
reporting on the Edinburgh Festival for 'Twentieth Century' the verse and the acting were excellent: the failure
lay in the content, especially in the third act. Eliot
seemed unable to establish the level at which the play was
to be taken and the result was a confusion both of convention and of tone (No. 168). Richard Findlater, in the
same issue of 'Twentieth Century', after dismissing the
usual comparisons with Wilde, gave an account of the play
as religious drama, but religious drama that failed because it lacked 'emotional unity', whereby the two levels,
of religion and farce, might have been mutually illuminating (No. 169). Findlater thought the time had come for
Eliot to impose himself more strongly upon the theatre, a
view shared by other critics at that time.
     For Bonamy Dobrée, if Eliot's purpose had been to make

each member of his audience examine his or her life, then
he had succeeded; if it had been to promote any sort of
doctrine, then he had failed. Eliot was perhaps the Kyd
or Tourneur of his day, and men of letters should recognise and support his 'valiant originality' (No. 170).
Dobrée would seem to have reviewed the performance of the
play in London, where it opened at the Lyric on Shaftes-
bury Avenue on 16 September 1953. Nicholas Brooke, also
reviewing the play in performance and not the published
text, found the work a bitter disappointment. Eliot
seemed to have been concerned only to write a West End
comedy (No. 171). Helen Gardner's review (No. 172), on
the other hand, was concerned with the published version
of the play, which appeared from Faber & Faber on 5 March
1954. She found that Eliot had achieved a unity which he
had not achieved in his drama before. By setting
Mr Eggerson at the spiritual centre of the play Eliot had
eschewed the heroics of Celia Coplestone, and instead
located his meaning in the whole design of his plot. That
romantic presentation of sanctity which had flawed 'The
Cocktail Party' so profoundly was no longer apparent.

The anonymous reviewer of 'The Confidential Clerk' in
the 'Times Literary Supplement' (19 March 1954) considered
that the incidents were organised into an amazingly complex whole, but that the underlying implications of the
action were left comparatively unorganised. The connection could only be found with some difficulty beneath the
comic surface:

> When found, the root of the matter would seem to be
> that until we know what we really are — and to reach
> this knowledge we shall usually need the help of others
> - we cannot expect to make the best of the terms which
> life offers us and rightly choose the way to self-
> fulfilment.

The play worked with great comic dexterity on the stage
and when read, but left the reader in a state of uncertainty as to its final meaning.

During the latter part of 1954 there was controversy
over the value of Eliot's achievement in the 'Times Literary Supplement', centred on a review (10 September) of
Aldington's 'Ezra Pound and T.S. Eliot', published in
1954 by the Peacock Press, Reading, but originally given
as a lecture fifteen years previously in America. The
review spoke of Aldington voicing a contemporary (1954)
criticism of the negative emotions in 'The Waste Land',
and went on to argue that modernism was superseded, Empson
and Graves being the models for a non-modernist poetry of

more modest pretensions. On 1 October Graves wrote in to
attack Eliot and Pound: '...Pound-Eliot modernism of the
twenties is already as dated as a stream-lined pogo-stick
with decorative motifs from Tutan-Khamen's tomb.' On 15
October the reviewer argued that Eliot was a great poet,
and that Pound also had written great poetry, to which
Graves replied (29 October): 'Can the "Four Quartets" be
called good? They are far from good, and their chief
appeal is perhaps a macabre one, as when one sees zombies
still working posthumously in the old sugar plantation.'
Gordon Wharton defended the 'Cantos' on 12 November, Graves
attacking them, especially Canto 79, a week later
(19 November). During this controversy Pound and Eliot
were lumped together as modernists, a term which, in
England in the period of the 'Movement' poets, had become
a term of abuse, in striking contrast to America where a
revitalised modernism was beginning to make itself felt,
under the influence of Olson and others. On both sides of
the Atlantic, however, Eliot's kind of modernism was being
discounted by the poets themselves, even though his reputation amongst critics and the world at large stood very
high indeed.

'THE ELDER STATESMAN'

During the early part of 1954 Eliot fell ill with the bron-
chial complaint that made it difficult, even dangerous, for
him to winter in England. None the less, he began a new
play during 1956, basing it on 'Oedipus at Colonus'.
During the composition of this work, on 10 January 1957, he
married Valerie Fletcher, who for seven years had been his
secretary.
    As a result, the rehearsal period prior to the first
production at Edinburgh on 25 August 1958 was plagued by
gossip writers. Eliot had become news, the expectation
being that Eliot would provide a 'human' play, which on
26 August was precisely what 'The Times' reviewer found.
The play was a 'realistic psychological drama of self-
revelation', touched with 'a gleam of extramundane meaning'.
    The general impression given by reviews of the first
performances of 'The Elder Statesman' was that the play
lacked vitality, being old-fashioned and even suggesting
Pinero. A strong attack came from Kenneth Tynan in the
'Observer' on 31 August:

    One's conclusion must be that, out of the wisdom of his
    years and the intensity of his cerebration, Mr Eliot

has come up with a gigantic platitude. Towards the
end, to be sure, he casts over the play a sedative,
autumnal glow of considerable beauty, and here and
there a scattered phrase reminds us, by its spare precision, that we are listening to a poet. On the whole,
however, the evening offers little more than the mild
pleasure of hearing ancient verities tepidly restated.

Henry Hewes, of the 'Saturday Review', also found Eliot
'more human' than before, and followed his review with the
report of an interview with Eliot in Edinburgh, to mark
Eliot's approaching seventieth birthday on 26 September
1958 (No. 173). In the same issue of 'Saturday Review'
Padraic Colum reviewed 'T.S. Eliot: A Symposium for his
Seventieth Birthday', edited by Neville Braybrooke, saying
that what characterised Eliot as a poet was wisdom, 'a
wisdom that has its roots in the perception that to have
integrity people have to take on burdens', the desolate
people in his poems being those who refuse that burden.
'The price to be paid', according to Colum, 'is the theme
of his plays.' John Weightman also considered 'The Elder
Statesman' old-fashioned, as something that could have
been written fifty years before (No. 174). Denis Donoghue
wrote a lengthy study of the play, based on watching performances at Edinburgh, and insisted that Eliot was not
concerned to present a comedy of manners. Donoghue suggested, reminiscent perhaps of a point made earlier by
Arrowsmith about 'The Cocktail Party', that Eliot had
written an 'ideal comedy', in which love and community
were drawn forth from ambiguity. The play pointed, in a
mood that was optative rather than indicative, towards an
order, but an order based on piety and love. This was
the wisest of Eliot's plays, and in it love was defined,
not by good deeds, but by a genuinely won illumination.
Even so, for Donoghue the play was not without faults, the
most important being Eliot's niggardliness in providing
a dramatic climax, by which Lord Claverton's recognition
of his own emptiness might have been acknowledged with
greater theatrical evidence (No. 176). This is a sympathetic review, making an effort to justify Eliot at least
at the thematic level.

Frank Kermode, reviewing the first edition, published
by Faber & Faber on 10 April 1959, found that Eliot's
drama had not succeeded in bringing together his Symbolist
poetic inheritance and the demands of the middle-class
'groundlings' for whom he had decided to write. It was
Yeats who took the right decision, rejecting the larger
audience and writing only for a small elite (No. 175).
The subtlest account, the one most attentive to Eliot's

understanding of language, was Kenner's in 'Poetry'
(No. 178). Kenner proposed that the characters of the play
play were functions of their language, the tension of
which was located in the very idea of privacy, as something held behind a role and as something that could give
itself into communion with another person precisely
because it was privacy and not that domination which
insisted on making its presence felt. In its simplicity,
the play, like medieval music, at once intimate and
formal, was Eliot's most personal work, so that the lyric
dedication to his wife at the beginning of the book was
perfectly in keeping. In this review Kenner succeeded in
bringing together with great tact Eliot's personal happi-
ness and the accomplishment of his final writing.

'COLLECTED POEMS 1909-1962'

'Collected Poems 1909-1962' was published by Faber &
Faber on 25 September 1963, the day before Eliot's
seventy-fifth birthday. The publication was noted with
satisfaction by the 'Times Literary Supplement', also on
25 September. On 11 October, in the 'New Statesman',
Donald Davie identified the crucial characteristic of
Eliot's language as 'symboliste', in which, as in Mallarmé, language revealed itself, not as the expressive
instrument of some individual or subject, but as pre-
existing any user of it. The only 'events' in Eliot's
poetry were the events of language, as words erupted into
consciousness manifesting and criticising the linguistic
system by which the 'world' was created (No. 179). Davie
elaborated this view in a later essay, but here, emphasising Eliot's modernism, he gave concrete examples of
Eliot's 'symboliste' poetry in operation, distinguishing
it from the work of Yeats and Pound. Eliot's poetry fore-
grounded its language, unlike the work of other poets, who
justified their language by its referential content and
who therefore regarded their language as transparent to
realities beyond it. For Eliot, according to Davie, there
was no such access to non-verbal reality, and none sought
for. However, Eliot had closed off this particular line
of development, and Davie, speaking out of his own experience as a poet, considered Eliot's influence on poetry to
be at an end.
    Like Davie, John Frederick Nims surveyed the whole
career, finding Eliot to be a great poet, but a 'moderately' great one. Eliot's greatest creation was 'Mr
Eliot', who now made it difficult for the reader to free
the poetry from the heavy-handed seriousness of the

commentators. Eliot showed himself, expecially in 'Four
Quartets', to have moved beyond humanity into prosaic
abstractness, confusing the colourless with the spiritual.
Nims found only Eliot's earliest poetry fully alive,
his later work lacking excitement (No. 180). For Kermode,
Eliot was matched only by Yeats and Pound, and the reader
who took up 'Collected Poems 1909-1962' should forget
Eliot's place as a classic of the modern and try to read
the poems as though he had never seen them before. In
this way the crystalline purity of language, the true
reward of a lifetime's effort, would become visible.
On this valedictory note Kermode concluded his review
(No. 181).

ELIOT'S POSTHUMOUS REPUTATION

Eliot died on 4 January 1965. The next day 'The Times'
spoke of his achievements, noting that his works had been
translated into almost every European language, and that
he had been the subject of more books and articles than
had ever before been published about an author during his
lifetime. On 6 January, tributes flowed in from American
writers, including Robert Lowell and Allen Tate. On
4 February, a memorial service was held in Westminster
Abbey, at which the choir sang the anthem 'The dove
descending breaks the air', set to music by Stravinsky and
dedicated to Eliot. A further homage to Eliot was held at
the Globe Theatre, London, on 13 June, when certain of his
poems were read by Laurence Olivier, Paul Scofield, George
Devine and others. Groucho Marx introduced and read 'Gus:
The Theatre Cat', and there was a performance of 'Sweeney
Agonistes' which included an unpublished last scene.
    On 8 January, the 'New Statesman' appeared with a Vicky
drawing of Eliot on the front page, and the words The Age
of Eliot across the lower edge of the drawing. It was the
opinion of the anonymous writer of the obituary, Eliot and
the Age of Fiction, that Eliot had held the same authority
in our age as Dryden, Johnson, Coleridge and Arnold had in
their respective ages. What made Eliot's achievement
notable, however, was the character of the age: 'That
Eliot, who was neither novelist nor a critic of fiction,
should have had such authority in what seems the age of
the novel makes his achievement at once more vulnerable
and more impressive.' Many of the obituaries, reminis-
ences and essays published immediately after his death
were understandably eager to stress Eliot's kindness and
generosity to younger writers and to those who knew him,
and there was general concurrence in the view that his

place in literature was beyond challenge. W.H. Auden, for
example, considered him a great poet and a good man
('Listener', 7 January). Eliot's achievement, however,
was not that of a classical, but an idiosyncratic, poet.
He was idiosyncratic both in subject matter and technique,
and, like Wordsworth, 'his inspiration for nearly all he
wrote arose out of a few intensely visionary experiences,
which probably occurred quite early in life'. Brand
Blanshard, in the 'Yale Review' (Summer 1965), recalled
memories of Eliot at Oxford, where as graduate students
they had been contemporaries. Blanshard considered that
Eliot had not only been a great man, but also a good one.
The chief failure of his life had been that he had never
found anything to lift men up as in his earlier writings
he had flattened them. He had not succeeded in making
Christianity attractive or intelligible, and his greatest
success had always lain in his attacks on the 'decent,
godless people'. Spender's article, Remembering Eliot, in
the Spring issue of 'Encounter', combined anecdote with a
moving sense of what Eliot's poetry had meant to his
readers.
    There were many attempts to give the essence of Eliot's
career. The reviewer in the 'Times Literary Supplement'
(7 January) saw the whole sequence of the serious and non-
dramatic poems as 'a kind of spiritual autobiography', in
which 'Ash-Wednesday' and 'Four Quartets' recorded a process of acceptance of religious belief 'and slow and painful disciplining of the self'. Philip Toynbee, in the
'Observer' (10 January), presented Eliot's career in terms
of an orderly and harmonious development, without any deep
change in stance or attitude from 'The Love Song of J.
Alfred Prufrock' to the last plays. Reed Whittemore
('New Republic', 16 January) saw Eliot as the poet of
death, of a sense of death that lodged in the basic
intellectual and emotional stance that the poems projected. Whittemore, 'a reluctant long-time admirer',
summed Eliot's work up thus:

> A poetry of death like his is no more a stance in the
> bad sense than the surge of the sea may be said to be a
> stance, the sea to which, to paraphrase the man, there
> is no end, no beginning - and certainly at the heart of
> it no contriving. To his admirers Eliot was a great
> poet of the sea.

For Hugh Kenner, writing in the 'National Review' (26 January), Eliot had effected almost single-handed our
century's most massive revolution in taste. Like William
Carlos Williams, the poet with whom he had been most
usually contrasted, Eliot had performed an operation on
English idioms similar to that performed by Williams on

the idioms of the New Jersey streets. It was Eliot, who,
with Pound, had stood for tradition in an age of revolution and universal literacy and had thus prevented a
civilisation from becoming 'lobotomised'.

Frank Kermode, in an essay headed Eliot's Dream,
written first for the 'New Statesman' of 19 February 1965,
compared Eliot to Milton, seeing their similarity in their
relation to their respective ages. Eliot was an imperial-
ist poet, 'The Waste Land' being an image of imperial
catastrophe wherein disaster, rather than the timeless
pattern of history, was to be found. Kermode saw the
function of 'The Waste Land' in terms of 'decreation', an
idea taken over from Simone Weil, through which the self
was purged by suffering of what was merely natural and
human. It was a process of clearing the world of 'its
stiff and stubborn man-locked set', and characterised the
great art works of the early 1920s.

Leonard Unger, editor of 'T.S. Eliot: A Selected Cri-
tique' (1948), an important collection of articles, paid
tribute to Eliot in the 'Southern Review' (Summer 1965):

> The poetry gave Eliot's reader a feeling of excitement
> and a sense of fulfilment different not only from poets
> of the past but from other poets of the present. No
> other poet had given voice so truly to the deepest and
> most intimate qualities of the modern sensibility - and
> it is my impression that no poet of our time has
> equalled Eliot in this particular aspect.

At the end of the year, the 'Sewanee Review' devoted a
special number to Eliot, which included reminiscences by
I.A. Richards, Herbert Read, Stephen Spender, Bonamy
Dobrée, Robert Speaight, Frank Morley and E. Martin
Browne, with essays on aspects of Eliot's work by such
critics as Helen Gardner and Leonard Unger. Essays on
Eliot continued to appear throughout the next year in the
same journal, and in 1966 in America and in 1967 in Eng-
land the whole collection was published as 'T.S. Eliot:
The Man and his Work' under the editorship of Allen Tate.
Worthy of note is Pound's comment, 'His was the true
Dantescan voice.'

In the years since his death, Eliot's reputation has
undergone a rapid change that has coincided with the
emergence of an insistently American tradition of writing.
The attacks made on Eliot by William Carlos Williams
during the 1920s, and taken up again in his 'Autobiography', were echoed by Charles Olson in the 1950s, so
that those writers who owe their allegiance, by way of
Olson, to Williams, Pound and the Objectivists could be
said to have taken Eliot as their main enemy, against whom
they defined their own aims and priorities. This was due

in part to their rejection of the dominant American academic ideology of the 1950s and 1960s, which owed, in the
teaching of English, a great deal to Eliot. The rejection
of the New Criticism involved also a rejection of Eliot.
But clearly, to poets who saw their first priority as the
return to, and care for, the American place in all its
specificity, Eliot's concern for European tradition and
English history would seem at best irrelevant and at worst
treachery. In 1972 Charles Tomlinson gave an account of
the relations between Eliot and Williams in his Penguin
anthology, 'William Carlos Williams', saying that Eliot's
and Williams's view of place were antithetical and that
while Williams thought in terms of new beginnings Eliot
thought in terms of the end. Tomlinson suggested that it
was not a matter for us to take sides in, and yet the
issue has been joined in a spirit that is extremely partisan. Robert Creeley and also, at least in 1959, Robert
Duncan, rejected Eliot completely. Jack Spicer's 'Book of
Magazine Verse', poems rejected by 'reputable' magazines
and published in 1966 by White Rabbit Press, opens with
the following lines:

> Pieces of the past arising out of the
>   rubble. Which evokes Eliot and
>   then evokes Suspicion. Ghosts
>   all of them. Doers of no good.

George Oppen, in the final poem of 'Primitive' (1978), dis-
sociated himself and his career from all that Eliot represented. Olson concluded his influential early manifesto,
'Projective Verse' (1951), with an extended attack on
Eliot: '...it is because Eliot has stayed inside the non-
projective that he fails as a dramatist – that his root is
the mind alone, and a scholastic mind at that (no high
intelletto despite his apparent clarities)...' For Olson,
Eliot's work was secondary and, in a derogatory sense,
classical: a poetry of repression.

Despite, or in ignorance of, this disapproval, however,
work has continued in many fields on Eliot. Donald
Gallup's 'T.S. Eliot: A Bibliography' appeared in 1969, a
revised and extended version of the 1952 original.
Mildred Martin's 'A Half-Century of Eliot Criticism: An
Annotated Bibliography of Books and Articles in English,
1916-1965' (Lewisburg, Pa., Bucknell University Press,
1972) is, like Gallup's bibliography, indispensable.
Donald Gallup's article, The 'Lost' Manuscripts of T.S.
Eliot, 'Times Literary Supplement' (7 November 1968),
1238-40, and Mrs Eliot's facsimile edition of 'The Waste
Land' drafts and fragments (1971), both drawing on
material in the Berg Collection in the New York Public

Library, are evidence of a growing need to establish the
basis of Eliot's texts. Dame Helen Gardner's 'The
Composition of "Four Quartets"' (1978) continued this
work.

Biographical studies have also been undertaken.
Lyndall Gordon's 'Eliot's Early Years' (1977) places
Eliot's work in the context of his life, drawing on material hitherto unavailable. Lyndall Gordon acknowledges her
debt to Dame Helen. Work by Ronald Schuchard emphasising
the personal nature of Eliot's poetry should also be seen
as forming part of the revaluation Dame Helen and Lyndall
Gordon have proposed.(25)

Further biographical material has become available with
the publication of 'The Autobiography of Bertrand
Russell', volumes i and ii, (1967-9), the second volume of
Michael Holroyd's 'Lytton Strachey' (1968), and Leonard
Woolf's 'Downhill All the Way' (1967). Full details of
further printed sources can be found in Gordon's biography. The 'Letters' of Conrad Aiken (1978) also contain
glimpses of Eliot at various times in his career. Eliot's
early reputation was summarised in a brief but telling
article, The Triumph of T.S. Eliot, by George Watson,
('Critical Quarterly' (Winter 1965), vii, 328-37).
Richard M. Ludwig gave a concise account of Eliot's reputa-
tation up to 1974 in 'Sixteen Modern American Authors: A
Survey of Research and Criticism', edited by Jackson R.
Bryer (1974).

More general studies of Eliot have appeared frequently
since his death. First printed in 1969 and reprinted in
1970, E. Martin Browne's 'The Making of T.S. Eliot's
Plays' proceeded from 'The Rock' to 'The Elder Statesman', studying in each case Eliot's drafts, alterations
after performance, and correspondence, and giving a wealth
of reminiscence. Browne also gives a good account of the
newspaper reception of each play on its first appearance.
John D. Margolis's 'T.S. Eliot's Intellectual Development:
1922-1939' (1972) was another guide to Eliot's context,
this time political and historical, with an extended
examination of the 'Criterion'. Another invaluable guide
to Eliot's general view of the world and its importance
for his poetry was Roger Kojecky's 'T.S. Eliot's Social
Criticism' (1971), which established the importance of
Eliot's membership of the Moot, a group including Karl
Mannheim, W.H. Moberly and H.A. Hodges. Eliot was one of
the most regular attenders at the group's meetings, and
Kojecky printed as an appendix a paper, On the Place and
Function of the Clerisy, written by Eliot for discussion
in December 1944.

In the public arena, the University of Kent at Canterbury named its first college, opened in 1965, after Eliot
and established the annual T.S. Eliot Memorial Lectures

through the generosity of Mrs Eliot. The first set of
lectures was given by Auden in 1967. Eliot's work has
appeared on school syllabuses and has become a standard
item on university courses devoted to modern poetry. In
response to this growing educational interest, the Casebook series, under the general editorship of A.E. Dyson,
published volumes of essays on 'The Waste Land' (1968,
reprinted 1972 and 1975), 'Four Quartets' (1969, reprinted
1975), and '"Prufrock", "Gerontion", "Ash-Wednesday" and
Other Shorter Poems' (1978).

Critical debate about Eliot's significance has continued. J. Hillis Miller, in 'Poets of Reality' (1966),
placed Eliot in relation to other modern poets as one
whose work was a recovery of immanence, of the God imma-
nent in reality and revealed by the musical patterns of
poetry: 'Like Yeats, Eliot begins in exclusion and
deprivation, then expands outward to include all space and
time, and finally narrows again to the concrete moment
which concentrates everything in the radiant presence of
the present.' Leavis, too, addressed himself to the question of Eliot's ultimate value and meaning. In 1968, he
gave the opening address at the Cheltenham Festival,
T.S. Eliot and the Life of English Literature, which was
reprinted in the 'Massachusetts Review' (Winter 1969).
The text of a previously unpublished lecture Leavis
delivered at the Catholic University of Milan on 18 April
1969, Eliot's Permanent Place, appeared in the 'Aligarh
Journal of English Studies' (October 1977). In 'The
Living Principle', published in 1975 and subtitled
'English' as a Discipline of Thought, Leavis devoted the
last third of his book to 'Four Quartets'. This essay
entered a number of reservations about the strength of
Eliot's achievement and should be seen as part of
Leavis's continual rethinking of Eliot, especially in
relation to Blake and Lawrence, and to English civilisation and culture more generally. For Leavis, Eliot never
achieved anything of the order of the best parts of 'Four
Quartets' again, the battle over the issues having been
fought, so that Eliot was able to sink back into a world
of settled and earned assumptions. For the first time,
Leavis's interest seems more concentrated upon Eliot's
ideas than upon his language.

A more general attack on 'Four Quartets', and by
implication on Eliot's whole oeuvre, was launched in
1976 by Eric Mottram in an essay on Jacques Derrida, in
'Curtains' (numbers 14-17, 38-57). Mottram's essay approved
of the work of Pound, Williams and Olson, and he set against
Eliot's very different undertaking the poetry practised by
Robert Duncan and others, a poetry of myth which, Mottram

asserted, Christianity denounced as vehemently as the
rationalists of Cambridge, the New Critics and the 'Movement' poets of the 1950s.

'Eliot in Perspective' (1970), edited by Graham Martin,
contained essays by critics such as F.W. Bateson, Donald
Davie, Gabriel Pearson, Ian Gregor and Terry Eagleton.
Davie's essay, Pound and Eliot: A Distinction, took up the
theme of 'symboliste' poetry from his 1963 'New Statesman'
essay and gave it more extensive treatment, distinguishing
between Pound's poetry of external reference and Eliot's
of linguistic self-consciousness. Davie's work here drew
on and extended that of Kenner's 'The Invisible Poet:
T.S. Eliot' (1959), and as a result it should no longer be
possible to confuse Pound's kind of modernism with that of
Eliot, or to separate Eliot's 'personal' Christian concerns from those of his modernist poetry. In an essay
entitled Anglican Eliot in the 'Southern Review' (January
1973), Davie considered Eliot's language as an embodiment
of the Anglican tradition. Davie also contributed to
'"The Waste Land" in Different Voices' (1974), edited by
A.D. Moody from papers given at the University of York in
honour of the poem's first publication fifty years before,
and considered his own relation as a poet to Eliot's work,
concentrating on the question of diction.

The question of Eliot's modernism was further discussed
by Hugh Kenner in 'The Pound Era' (1972), where he elaborated on the theme of Eliot as 'symboliste' poet, while in
1975 Stephen Spender's 'Eliot' appeared in the Fontana
Modern Masters series. Gabriel Josipovici also considered the same question of Eliot's modernism in 'The
World and the Book' (1971), 'The Modern English Novel'
(1976) and 'The Lessons of Modernism' (1977), placing
Eliot in relation to the modernist practices of writers
such as Blanchot, Kafka, Proust, Beckett and Borges, as
well as Wallace Stevens. These essays are important
developments in the understanding of Eliot, in that they
are not simply about Eliot but in themselves manifest
Eliot's own modes of thought and perception. Peter
Ackroyd's 'Notes for a New Culture' (1976) drew on Eliot,
as the title suggests, for a view of English cultural
history, as did Josipovici in 'The World and the Book'.
In an attempt to understand the failure of contemporary
England to develop a major modernist literature, Ackroyd
brought the work of Lacan and Derrida to a consideration
of poets such as Roche, Ashberry and J.H. Prynne in the
light of his reading of Eliot and Joyce. One contemporary
poet, however, Peter Riley, denounced Ackroyd for his
approval of Eliot, considering the displacement of the
self, seen by Ackroyd in 'Four Quartets', a 'complete

subterfuge' ('Poetry Information', no. 17). Eliot's
modernism was emphasised by the late Veronica Forrest-
Thomson, both in her articles and in her poetry, as well
as in 'Poetic Artifice' (published in 1979). (26) Like
Ackroyd, she saw Eliot as the presence who was to determine the writing to come. Michael Edwards, in 'Eliot/
Language' (1975), reading Eliot's work in terms of ideas
derived ultimately from contemporary French criticism,
persuasively aligned Eliot's poetry with a Christian
understanding of language, whose Fall was explored in
'Gerontion' and 'The Waste Land', and whose redemption was
evoked in 'Ash-Wednesday' and in parts of 'Four Quartets'.
Edwards's essay, suggestive of a post-modernist revaluation of Eliot's work, can be compared to Denis Donoghue's
'The Sovereign Ghost' (1976). In a chapter reprinted
from 'Studies' and Moody's collection, Donoghue also used
concepts taken from French criticism, on this occasion
that of Roland Barthes, to present 'The Waste Land' as a
text, the play of whose meanings was created by the fore-
grounding of language itself. A.D. Moody, on the other
hand, in 'Thomas Stearns Eliot: Poet' (1979), was concerned to present Eliot's poetry by means of sustained
elucidations of a more traditional kind. He set out
Eliot's position thus: 'Mallarmé's ideal was to create the
ultimate Word and Book; but Eliot's book remained the
Bible, and his ideal was that his words should conform
totally to the Word of God'.
    Theodore Weiss, discussing M.L. Rosenthal's 'Sailing
Into the Unknown' (1978) in the 'Times Literary Supplement'
(1 February 1980), gave a view of Pound, Yeats and Eliot
in relation to certain poets and critics of the last few
years. The current elevation of Hardy and Carlos Williams,
he argued, had led to a confusion of life and art, to an
idea of the artist as prostrate before life, victim of his
own confusions. As against this sense of 'openness', in
its current usage derived from Olson, he emphasised the
ability of Yeats, Pound and Eliot to exploit their whole
beings, 'their minds no less than their instincts, memory
and learning no less than the local and the immediate...'.
This argument will undoubtedly continue, involving as it
does not only the achievement of the early moderns in
itself but also the direction and meaning of most subsequent writing.
    Recent criticism of Eliot, then, would seem to have
divided into either a biographical reading and placing of
the poetry, or a criticism that takes its stand on its
attitude towards modernism itself, whether for or against.
With the exception of Moody's book, little attention has
been given to the drama. The publication of Eliot's early

criticism, letters and an authorised biography is anticipated as is a properly edited version of his works. The
most important criticism seems likely to come from a study
of Eliot's understanding of language in terms of his most
crucial beliefs, through an illumination of his poetic
language by an understanding of his sense of tradition.
Eliot is now a possession of the consciousness of the
people, his words and phrases entering into daily use as
part of the common currency by which we live and think.
Yet because of this we should not judge that the issues
raised by his poetry and drama are dead. In many ways
they are more urgent now than when first he wrote. His
art challenges us to re-examine the processes by which we
create and ascribe those meanings on which our world is
founded. That to which Eliot, in all love and humility,
offered his response is still, for us as for him, 'The
hint half guessed, the gift half understood'.

NOTES

1   Peter Ackroyd, 'Notes for a New Culture' (London,
     1976), pp. 48-9. I am also deeply indebted, through-
     out this early section, to A.D. Moody's 'Thomas Stearns
     Eliot: Poet' (Cambridge, 1979).
2   Lyndall Gordon, 'Eliot's Early Years' (Oxford and New
     York, 1977), p. 68. Gordon gives a disenchanted view
     of Pound's relation to Eliot, and points to the fun-
     damental differences that lay between the two men,
     especially on religious matters.
3   C.K. Stead, 'The New Poetic' (London, 1964), pp. 81-2.
4   T.S. Eliot, Eeldrop and Appleplex, 'Little Review'
     (May 1917), iv, 7.
5   Richard Aldington, The Poetry of T.S. Eliot, 'Out-
     look' (London) (7 January 1922), xlix, 12-13.
     Reprinted in the 'New York Evening Post Literary
     Review' (14 January 1922), 350; in 'Literary Studies
     and Reviews' (New York and London, 1924), pp. 181-91;
     and Unger, pp. 4-10.
6   A remark by Eliot concerning 'The Waste Land' in
     'The Frontiers of Criticism' (Minneapolis, 1956),
     p. 10. Cited in 'Bibliography', p. 31.
7   For an account of these transactions, see Mrs Eliot's
     Introduction to her edition of '"The Waste Land":
     A Facsimile and Transcript of the Original Drafts'
     (London, 1971), pp. xxiii-xxiv, and B.L. Reid, 'The
     Man from New York: John Quinn and His Friends' (New
     York, 1968), pp. 533-40. See also Noel Stock, 'The
     Life of Ezra Pound' (London, 1970), pp. 248-9, and
     Daniel H. Woodward, Notes on the Publishing History
     and Text of 'The Waste Land', 'Papers of the

Bibliographical Society of America' (third quarter
1964), lviii, 252-69.

8   C.B. Cox and Arnold P. Hinchcliffe make this comment
in their Introduction to 'T.S. Eliot: "The Waste
Land"', a Casebook (London, 1968), p. 12.

9   Stock, op. cit., pp. 249-50.

10 Edmund Wilson, 'Letters on Literature and Politics:
1912-1972', edited by Elena Wilson (London, 1977),
p. 101.

11 'T.S. Eliot: "The Waste Land"', a Casebook edited by
C.B. Cox and Arnold P. Hinchliffe (London, 1968),
p. 93. Reprinted from 'Collected Criticism of Conrad
Aiken' (1968).

12 Michael Edwards, 'Eliot/Language' (Isle of Skye, 1975),
pp. 18-26. This book is Number 4 of 'Prospice', of
which Edwards is editor.

13 George Watson, The Triumph of T.S. Eliot, 'Critical
Quarterly' (Winter 1965), vii, 328-37.

14 E.M. Forster, T.S. Eliot and His Difficulties, 'Life
and Letters' (June 1929), ii, 417-25. The essay was
reprinted in 'Abinger Harvest' (London 1936), pp. 87-
93, and in Unger, pp. 11-17.

15 Paul Elmer More, The Cleft Eliot, 'Saturday Review'
(12 November 1932), ix, 233, 235. Reprinted in Unger,
pp. 24-9. For a discussion of Eliot's relation to
'Humanism', see Roger Kojecky, 'T.S. Eliot's Social
Criticism' (London, 1971), pp. 72-8.

16 Cited by Kojecky, op. cit., p. 103.

17 Browne, pp. 63-4.

18 R.P. Blackmur, 'The Double Agent' (New York, 1935),
pp. 184-218. Reprinted in Unger, pp. 236-62.

19 Marianne Moore, If I Am Worthy, There is No Danger,
'Poetry' (February 1936), xlvii, 279-81.

20 John Crowe Ransom, Autumn of Poetry, 'Southern
Review' (Winter 1936), i, 619-23.

21 Ezra Pound, 'Selected Letters, 1907-1941', edited by
D.D. Paige (New York, 1971), p. 277.

22 For a detailed account of the newspaper response, see
Browne, pp. 148-51.

23 'T.S. Eliot: "Four Quartets"', a Casebook edited and
introduced by Bernard Bergonzi (London, 1969), p. 13.

24 Reprinted in F.R. Leavis, 'Letters in Criticism',
edited and introduced by John Tasker (London 1974),
pp. 31-3.

25 See Ronald Schuchard, 'Our Mad Poetics to Confute':
The Personal Voice in T.S. Eliot's Early Poetry and
Criticism, 'Orbis Litterarum' (1976), xxxi, 208-31.
For further work by Schuchard, see the select biblio-
graphy.

26 Veronica Forrest-Thomson's 'Poetic Artifice: A Theory
   of Twentieth Century Poetry' has been published by
   Manchester University Press (1979). Her posthumous
   collection of poems, 'On the Periphery' (Cambridge,
   1976), draws on Eliot's poetry with great brilliance
   and originality. She died in 1975.

Note on the Text

Apart from the silent correction of spelling errors and
other minutiae which it seemed pointless to reproduce, the
texts are printed verbatim. Deletions within the documents are marked by the use of ellipsis and square
brackets. Numbered notes are those added by the editor;
notes keyed in by letters of the alphabet are those of the
original text.

Poetic texts cited in reviews have been corrected where
necessary as follows: citations from 'The Waste Land' have
been checked against the 1922 edition, given by Mrs Eliot;
citations from 'Four Quartets' have been checked against
the first English edition (1944) as given by Helen
Gardner; all other citations have been checked against CPP.
For the sake of convenience, however, all references for
deleted material, whether poetic or dramatic, have been
made to CPP.

'Prufrock and Other Observations'

London, June 1917

1. ARTHUR WAUGH, THE NEW POETRY, 'QUARTERLY REVIEW'

October 1916, 226

Waugh (1866-1943), English critic, publisher and editor,
was the author of 'Reticence in Literature' (1915) and of
'Tradition and Change: Studies in Contemporary Literature'
(1919). He was the father of the novelists Alec and
Evelyn Waugh. This is an extract from a longer piece and
is concerned with the 'Catholic Anthology 1914-1915',
edited by Pound and published by Elkin Mathews in 1915.
The anthology contained 'The Love Song of J. Alfred Prufrock', reprinted from 'Poetry' (June 1915), and other
poems by Eliot. Pound's vigorous defence of Eliot against
Waugh can be found in No. 2.

Cleverness is, indeed, the pitfall of the New Poetry.
There is no question about the ingenuity with which its
varying moods are exploited, its elaborate symbolism
evolved, and its sudden, disconcerting effects exploded
upon the imagination. Swift, brilliant images break into
the field of vision, scatter like rockets, and leave a
trail of flying fire behind. But the general impression
is momentary; there are moods and emotions, but no steady
current of ideas behind them. Further, in their determination to surprise and even to puzzle at all costs,
these young poets are continually forgetting that the
first essence of poetry is beauty; and that, however much
you may have observed the world around you, it is impossible to translate your observation into poetry, without

the intervention of the spirit of beauty, controlling the
vision, and reanimating the idea.

The temptations of cleverness may be insistent, but its
risks are equally great: how great indeed will, perhaps,
be best indicated by the example of the 'Catholic Anthology,' which apparently represents the very newest of all
the new poetic movements of the day. This strange little
volume bears upon its cover a geometrical device, suggesting that the material within holds the same relation to
the art of poetry as the work of the Cubist school holds
to the art of painting and design. The product of the
volume is mainly American in origin, only one or two of
the contributors being of indisputably English birth. But
it appears here under the auspices of a house associated
with some of the best poetry of the younger generation,
and is prefaced by a short lyric by Mr W.B. Yeats, in
which that honoured representative of a very different
school of inspiration makes bitter fun of scholars and
critics, who

> Edit and annotate the lines
> That young men, tossing on their beds,
> Rhymed out in love's despair
> To flatter beauty's ignorant ear.

The reader will not have penetrated far beyond this
warning notice before he finds himself in the very strong-
hold of literary rebellion, if not of anarchy. Mr Orrick
Johns may be allowed to speak for his colleagues, as well
as for himself:

> This is the song of youth,
> This is the cause of myself;
> I knew my father well and he was a fool,
> Therefore will I have my own foot in the path before
>   I take a step;
> I will go only into new lands,
> And I will walk on no plank-walks.
> The horses of my family are wind-broken,
> And the dogs are old,
> And the guns rust;
> I will make me a new bow from an ash-tree,
> And cut up the homestead into arrows.

And Mr Ezra Pound takes up the parable in turn, in the
same wooden prose, cut into battens:

> Come, my songs, let us express our baser passions.
> Let us express our envy for the man with a steady job
>   and no worry about the future.

You are very idle, my songs,
I fear you will come to a bad end.
You stand about the streets. You loiter at the
    corners and bus-stops,
You do next to nothing at all.
You do not even express our inner nobility,
You will come to a very bad end.
And I? I have gone half cracked.

It is not for his audience to contradict the poet, who for
once may be allowed to pronounce his own literary epitaph.
But this, it is to be noted, is the 'poetry' that was to
say nothing that might not be said 'actually in life –
under emotion,' the sort of emotion that settles down into
the banality of a premature decrepitude:

I grow old.... I grow old ...
I shall wear the bottoms of my trousers rolled.
Shall I part my hair behind? Do I dare to eat a peach?
I shall wear white flannel trousers, and walk upon the
    beach.
I have heard the mermaids singing, each to each.
I do not think that they will sing to me.

Here, surely, is the reduction to absurdity of that school
of literary license which, beginning with the declaration

I knew my father well and he was a fool,

naturally proceeds to the convenient assumption that
everything which seemed wise and true to the father must
inevitably be false and foolish to the son. Yet if the
fruits of emancipation are to be recognised in the un-
metrical, incoherent banalities of these literary
'Cubists,' the state of Poetry is indeed threatened with
anarchy which will end in something worse even than 'red
ruin and the breaking up of laws.' From such a catastrophe the humour, commonsense, and artistic judgment of
the best of the new 'Georgians' will assuredly save their
generation; nevertheless, a hint of warning may not be
altogether out of place. It was a classic custom in the
family hall, when the feast was at its height, to display
a drunken slave among the sons of the household, to the
end that they, being ashamed at the ignominious folly of
his gesticulations, might determine never to be tempted
into such a pitiable condition themselves. The custom had
its advantages; for the wisdom of the younger generation
was found to be fostered more surely by a single example
than by a world of homily and precept.

2. EZRA POUND, DRUNKEN HELOTS AND MR. ELIOT, 'EGOIST'

June 1917, vol. iv, 72-4

Pound (1885-1972), American poet and critic, was educated
at the University of Pennsylvania and at Hamilton College
in New York State. He met Eliot after the outbreak of war
in 1914, and was instrumental in getting Eliot's early
poetry into print. Pound also worked on the drafts of
'The Waste Land', profoundly influencing the ultimate
shape of the poem. Pound's defence of Eliot was strong-
minded and generous, and the two men remained life-long
friends.

Genius has I know not what peculiar property, its manifestations are various, but however diverse and dissimilar
they may be, they have at least one property in common.
It makes no difference in what art, in what mode, whether
the most conservative, or the most ribbald-revolutionary,
or the most diffident; if in any land, or upon any floating deck over the ocean, or upon some newly contrapted
craft in the aether, genius manifests itself, at once some
elderly gentleman has a flux of bile from his liver; at
once from the throne or the easy Cowperian sofa, or from
the gutter, or from the oeconomical press room there
bursts a torrent of elderly words, splenetic, irrelevant,
they form themselves instinctively into large phrases
denouncing the inordinate product.

   This peculiar kind of *rabbia* might almost be taken as
the test of a work of art, mere talent seems incapable of
exciting it. 'You can't fool me, sir, you're a scoun-
drel,' bawls the testy old gentleman.

   Fortunately the days when 'that very fiery particle'
could be crushed out by the 'Quarterly' are over, but it
interests me, as an archaeologist, to note that the firm
which no longer produces Byron, but rather memoirs, letters of the late Queen, etc., is still running a review,
and that this review is still where it was in 1812, or
whatever the year was; and that, not having an uneducated
Keats to condemn, a certain Mr. Waugh is scolding about
Mr. Eliot.

   All I can find out, by asking questions concerning Mr.
Waugh, is that he is 'a very old chap,' 'a reviewer.'
From internal evidence we deduce that he is, like the rest
of his generation of English *gens-de-lettres*, ignorant of

Laforgue; of De Régnier's 'Odelettes'; of his French
contemporaries generally, of De Gourmont's 'Litanies,'
of Tristan Corbière, Laurent Tailhade. This is by no
means surprising. We are used to it from his 'b'ilin'.'
   However, he outdoes himself, he calls Mr. Eliot a
'drunken helot.' So called they Anacreon in the days of
his predecessors, but from the context in the 'Quarterly'
article I judge that Mr. Waugh does not intend the phrase
as a compliment, he is trying to be abusive, and moreover, he in his limited way has succeeded.
   Let us sample the works of the last 'Drunken Helot.'
I shall call my next anthology 'Drunken Helots' if I can
find a dozen poems written half so well as the following:

[Quotes 'Conversation Galante', CPP, p. 33.]

   Our helot has a marvellous neatness. There is a comparable finesse in Laforgue's 'Votre âme est affaire
d'oculiste,' but hardly in English verse.
   Let us reconsider this drunkenness:

[Quotes 'La Figlia Che Piange', CPP, p. 34.]

   And since when have helots taken to reading Dante and
Marlowe? Since when have helots made a new music, a new
refinement, a new method of turning old phrases into new
by their aptness? However the 'Quarterly,' the century
old, the venerable, the praeclarus, the voice of Gehova
and Co., Sinai and 51A Albemarle Street, London, W. 1, has
pronounced this author a helot. They are all for an
aristocracy made up of, possibly, Tennyson, Southey and
Wordsworth, the flunkey, the dull and the duller. Let us
sup with the helots. Or perhaps the good Waugh is a wag,
perhaps he hears with the haspirate and wishes to pun on
Mr. Heliot's name: a bright bit of syzygy.
   I confess his type of mind puzzles me, there is no
telling what he is up to.
   I do not wish to misjudge him, this theory may be the
correct one. You never can tell when old gentlemen grow
facetious. He does not mention Mr. Eliot's name; he
merely takes his lines and abuses them. The artful dod-
ger, he didn't (*sotto voce* 'he didn't want "people" to
know that Mr. Eliot was a poet').
   The poem he chooses for malediction is the title poem,
'Prufrock.' It is too long to quote entire.

[Quotes 'Prufrock', CPP, pp. 14-15, 'For I have known
them' to 'leaning out of windows'.]

Let us leave the silly old Waugh. Mr. Eliot has made
an advance on Browning. He has also made his dramatis
personae contemporary and convincing. He has been an
individual in his poems. I have read the contents of this
book over and over, and with continued joy in the freshness, the humanity, the deep quiet culture. 'I have tried
to write of a few things that really have moved me' is so
far as I know, the sum of Mr. Eliot's 'poetic theory.'
His practice has been a distinctive cadence, a personal
modus of arrangement, remote origins in Elizabethan
English and in the modern French masters, neither origin
being sufficiently apparent to affect the personal
quality. It is writing without pretence. Mr. Eliot at
once takes rank with the five or six living poets whose
English one can read with enjoyment.

The 'Egoist' has published the best prose writer of my
generation. It follows its publication of Joyce by the
publication of a 'new' poet who is at least unsurpassed by
any of his contemporaries, either of his own age or his
elders.

It is perhaps 'unenglish' to praise a poet whom one can
read with enjoyment. Carlyle's generation wanted
'improving' literature, Smile's 'Self-Help' and the rest of
it. Mr. Waugh dates back to that generation, the virus is
in his blood, he can't help it. The exactitude of the
younger generation gets on his nerves, and so on and so on.
He will 'fall into line in time' like the rest of the
bread-and-butter reviewers. Intelligent people will read
'J. Alfred Prufrock'; they will wait with some eagerness
for Mr. Eliot's further inspirations. It is 7.30 p.m. I
have had nothing alcoholic to-day, nor yet yesterday. I
said the same sort of thing about James Joyce's prose over
two years ago. I am now basking in the echoes. Only a
half-caste rag for the propagation of garden suburbs, and
a local gazette in Rochester, N.Y., U.S.A., are left
whining in opposition.

(I pay my compliments to Ernest Rhys, that he associates with a certain Sarolea, writer of prefaces to cheap
editions and editor of 'Everyman.' They had better look
after their office boys. I like Ernest Rhys personally, I
am sorry to think of him in such slums, but it is time
that he apologized for the antics of that paper with
which he is, at least in the minds of some, still associated. His alternative is to write a disclaimer. Mr. Dent,
the publisher, would also have known better had the passage been submitted to his judgment.)

However, let us leave these bickerings, this stench of
the printing-press, weekly and quarterly, let us return to
the gardens of the Muses,

Till human voices wake us and we drown,

as Eliot has written in conclusion to the poem which the
'Quarterly' calls the *reductio ad absurdum:*

I have seen them riding seaward on the waves
Combing the white hair of the waves blown back
When the wind blows the water white and black.

We have lingered in the chambers of the sea
By sea-girls wreathed with seaweed red and brown
Till human voices wake us, and we drown.

The poetic mind leaps the gulf from the exterior world,
the trivialities of Mr. Prufrock, diffident, ridiculous,
in the drawing-room, Mr. Apollinax's laughter 'submarine
and profound' transports him from the desiccated new-
statesmanly atmosphere of Professor Canning-Cheetah's.
Mr. Eliot's melody rushes out like the thought of
Fragilion 'among the birch-trees.' Mr. Waugh is my bitten
macaroon at this festival.

3. UNSIGNED REVIEW, 'TIMES LITERARY SUPPLEMENT'

21 June 1917, no. 805, 299

Mr. Eliot's notion of poetry - he calls the 'observations'
poems - seems to be a purely analytical treatment, verging
sometimes on the catalogue, of personal relations and
environments, uninspired by any glimpse beyond them and
untouched by any genuine rush of feeling. As, even on
this basis, he remains frequently inarticulate, his
'poems' will hardly be read by many with enjoyment. For
the catalogue manner we may commend 'Rhapsody on a Windy
Night': -

[Quotes CPP, p. 244, 'Half-past one' to 'a crooked pin'.]

This recalls other twisted things to the mind, and later
the street lamp said:-

[Quotes CPP, p. 25, 'Remark the cat' to 'which I held
him'.]

Among other reminiscences which pass through the rhapso-
dist's mind and which he thinks the public should know
about, are 'dust in crevices, smells of chestnuts in the
streets, and female smells in shuttered rooms, and
cigarettes in corridors, and cocktail smells in bars.'

  The fact that these things occurred to the mind of Mr.
Eliot is surely of the very smallest importance to any
one - even to himself. They certainly have no relation to
'poetry,' and we only give an example because some of the
pieces, he states, have appeared in a periodical which
claims that word as its title.

4. FROM AN UNSIGNED REVIEW, 'LITERARY WORLD'

5 July 1917, vol. lxxxiii, 107

Mr. Eliot is one of those clever young men who find it
amusing to pull the leg of a sober reviewer. We can
imagine his saying to his friends: 'See me have a lark out
of the old fogies who don't know a poem from a pea-shooter.
I'll just put down the first thing that comes into my
head, and call it "The Love Song of J. Alfred Prufrock."
Of course it will be idiotic; but the fogies are sure to
praise it, because when they don't understand a thing and
yet cannot hold their tongues they find safety in praise.'
We once knew a clever musician who found a boisterous
delight in playing that pathetic melody 'Only a Jew' in
two keys at once. At first the effect was amusing in its
complete idiocy, but we cannot imagine that our friend
would have been so foolish as to print the score. Among a
few friends the man of genius is privileged to make a fool
of himself. He is usually careful not to do so outside an
intimate circle. Mr. Eliot has not the wisdom of youth.
If the 'Love Song' is neither witty nor amusing, the other
poems are interesting experiments in the bizarre and
violent. The subjects of the poems, the imagery, the
rhythms have the wilful outlandishness of the young revolutionary idea. We do not wish to appear patronising, but
we are certain that Mr. Eliot could do finer work on traditional lines. With him it seems to be a case of missing
the effect by too much cleverness. All beauty has in it
an element of strangeness, but here the strangeness over-
balances the beauty.

5. UNSIGNED REVIEW, 'NEW STATESMAN'

18 August 1917, vol. ix, 477

Mr. Eliot may possibly give us the quintessence of twenty-
first century poetry. Certainly much of what he writes is
unrecognisable as poetry at present, but it is all
decidedly amusing, and it is only fair to say that he does
not call these pieces poems. He calls them 'observations,'
and the description seems exact; for he has a keen eye as
well as a sharp pen, and draws wittily whatever his capri-
cious glance descends on. We do not pretend to follow the
drift of 'The Love Song of J. Alfred Prufrock,' and therefore, instead of quoting from it, we present our readers
with the following piece:

[Quotes 'The Boston Evening Transcript', CPP, p. 28.]

This is Mr. Eliot's highest flight, and we shall treasure
it.

6. EZRA POUND, T.S. ELIOT, 'POETRY'

August 1917, vol. x, 264-71

This review was reprinted in 'Literary Essays of Ezra
Pound', edited with an introduction by Eliot, and first
published by Faber & Faber, London, 1954. It also appeared
in 'Instigations', New York, 1920.
    Padraic Colum's opinion of Pound's view of Eliot is
given in No. 26.

    Il n'y a de livres que ceux où un écrivain s'est
raconté lui-même en racontant les moeurs de ses
contemporains - leurs rêves, leurs vanités, leurs
amours, et leurs folies. - Remy de Gourmont (1)

    De Gourmont uses this sentence in writing of the incon-
testable superiority of 'Madame Bovary', 'L'Éducation
Sentimentale' and 'Bouvard et Pécuchet' to 'Salammbô' and

'La Tentation de St. Antoine'. A casual thought convinces
one that it is true for all prose. Is it true also for
poetry? One may give latitude to the interpretation of
rêves; the gross public would have the poet write little
else, but De Gourmont keeps a proportion. The vision
should have its place in due setting if we are to believe
its reality.

The few poems which Mr. Eliot has given us maintain
this proportion, as they maintain other proportions of art.
After much contemporary work that is merely factitious,
much that is good in intention but impotently unfinished
and incomplete, much whose flaws are due to sheer ignorance which a year's study or thought might have remedied,
it is a comfort to come upon complete art, naive despite
its intellectual subtlety, lacking all pretence.

It is quite safe to compare Mr. Eliot's work with anything written in French, English or American since the
death of Jules Laforgue. The reader will find nothing
better, and he will be extremely fortunate if he finds
much half as good.

The necessity, or at least the advisability of comparing
English or American work with French work is not readily
granted by the usual English or American writer. If you
suggest it, the Englishman answers that he has not thought
about it - he does not see why he should bother himself
about what goes on south of the channel; the American
replies by stating that you are 'no longer American', and
I have learned by long experience that this is the bitter-
est epithet in his vocabulary. The net result is that it
is extremely difficult to read one's contemporaries. After
a time one tires of 'promise'.

I should like the reader to note how complete is Mr.
Eliot's depiction of our contemporary condition. He has
not confined himself to genre nor to society portraiture.
His

> lonely men in shirt-sleeves, leaning out of windows

are as real as his ladies who

> come and go
> Talking of Michaelangelo.

His 'one night cheap hotels' are as much 'there' as are his

> four wax candles in the darkened room,
> Four rings of light upon the ceiling overhead,
> An atmosphere of Juliet's tomb.

And, above all, there is no rhetoric, although there is
Elizabethan reading in the background. Were I a French

critic, skilled in their elaborate art of writing books about books, I should probably go to some length discussing Mr. Eliot's two sorts of metaphor: his wholly unrealizable, always apt, half ironic suggestion, and his precise realizable picture.   It would be possible to point out his method of conveying a whole situation and half a character by three words of a quoted phrase; his constant aliveness, his mingling of very subtle observation with the unexpectedness of a backhanded cliché.   It is, however, extremely dangerous to point out such devices.   The method is Mr. Eliot's own, but as soon as one has reduced even a fragment of it to formula, someone else, not Mr. Eliot, someone else wholly lacking in his aptitudes, will at once try to make poetry by mimicking his external procedure.   And this indefinite 'someone' will, needless to say, make a botch of it.

For what the statement is worth, Mr. Eliot's work interests me more than that of any other poet now writing in English.   The most interesting poems in Victorian English are Browning's 'Men and Women', or, if that statement is too absolute, let me contend that the form of these poems is the most vital form of that period of English, and that the poems written in that form are the least like each other in content.   Antiquity gave us Ovid's 'Heroides' and Theocritus' woman using magic.   The form of Browning's 'Men and Women' is more alive than the epistolary form of the 'Heroides'.   Browning included a certain amount of ratiocination and of purely intellectual comment, and in just that proportion he lost intensity.   Since Browning there have been very few good poems of this sort.   Mr. Eliot has made two notable additions to the list.   And he has placed his people in contemporary settings, which is much more difficult than to render them with medieval romantic trappings.   If it is permitted to make comparison with a different art, let me say that he has used contemporary detail very much as Velasquez used contemporary detail in 'Las Meninas'; the cold gray-green tones of the Spanish painter have, it seems to me, an emotional value not unlike the emotional value of Mr. Eliot's rhythms, and of his vocabulary.

James Joyce has written the best novel of my decade, and perhaps the best criticism of it has come from a Belgian who said, 'All this is as true of my country as of Ireland'.   Eliot has a like ubiquity of application.   Art does not avoid universals, it strikes at them all the harder in that it strikes through particulars.   Eliot's work rests apart from that of the many new writers who have used the present freedoms to no advantage, who have gained no new precisions of language, and no variety in their cadence.   His men in shirt-sleeves, and his society ladies, are not a local manifestation; they are the stuff

of our modern world, and true of more countries than one.
I would praise the work for its fine tone, its humanity,
and its realism; for all good art is realism of one sort
or another.

It is complained that Eliot is lacking in emotion.
'La Figlia Che Piange' is sufficient confutation to that
rubbish.

If the reader wishes mastery of 'regular form', the
'Conversation Galante' is sufficient to show that sym-
metrical form is within Mr. Eliot's grasp. You will
hardly find such neatness save in France; such modern
neatness, save in Laforgue.

De Gourmont's phrase to the contrary notwithstanding,
the supreme test of a book is that we should feel some
unusual intelligence working behind the words. By this
test various other new books, that I have, or might have,
beside me, go to pieces. The barrels of sham poetry that
every decade and school and fashion produce, go to pieces.
It is sometimes extremely difficult to find any other
particular reason for their being so unsatisfactory. I
have expressly written here not 'intellect' but 'intelligence.' There is no intelligence without emotion. The
emotion may be anterior or concurrent. There may be emotion without much intelligence, but that does not concern
us.

Versification:

A conviction as to the rightness or wrongness of *vers
libre* is no guarantee of a poet. I doubt if there is
much use trying to classify the various kinds of *vers
libre*, but there is an anarchy which may be vastly over-
done; and there is a monotony of bad usage as tiresome as
any typical eighteenth or nineteenth century flatness.

In a recent article Mr. Eliot contended, or seemed to
contend, that good *vers libre* was little more than a skilful evasion of the better known English metres. His
article was defective in that he omitted all consideration
of metres depending on quantity, alliteration, etc.; in
fact he wrote as if metres were measured by accent. This
may have been tactful on his part, it may have brought his
article nearer to the comprehension of his readers (that
is, those of the 'New Statesman', in which the article
appeared, people who are chiefly concerned with sociology
of the 'button' and 'unit' variety). But he came nearer
the fact when he wrote elsewhere: 'No *vers* is *libre* for
the man who wants to do a good job.'

Alexandrine and other grammarians have made cubby-holes

for various groupings of syllables; they have put names
upon them, and have given various labels to 'metres' con-
sisting of combinations of these different groups. Thus it
would be hard to escape contact with some group or other;
only an encyclopedist could ever be half sure he had done
so. The know categories would allow a fair liberty to the
most conscientious traditionalist. The most fanatical
vers-librist will escape them with difficulty. However,
I do not think there is any crying need for verse with
absolutely no rhythmical basis.

On the other hand, I do not believe that Chopin wrote
to a metronome. There is undoubtedly a sense of music that
takes count of the 'shape' of the rhythm in a melody rather
than of bar divisions, which came rather late in the history of written music and were certainly not the first or
most important thing that musicians tried to record. The
creation of such shapes is part of thematic invention.
Some musicians have the faculty of invention, rhythmic,
melodic. Likewise some poets.

Treatises full of musical notes and of long and short
marks have never been convincingly useful. Find a man
with thematic invention and all he can say is that he gets
what the Celts call a 'chune' in his head, and that the
words 'go into it,' or when they don't 'go into it' they
'stick out and worry him.'

You can not force a person to play a musical masterpiece correctly, even by having the notes correctly printed
on the paper before him; neither can you force a person to
feel the movement of poetry, be the metre 'regular' or
'irregular.' I have heard Mr. Yeats trying to read Burns,
struggling in vain to fit the 'Birks o' Aberfeldy' and
'Bonnie Alexander' into the mournful keen of the 'Wind
among the Reeds'. Even in regular metres there are incompatible systems of music.

I have heard the best orchestral conductor in England
read poems in free verse, poems in which the rhythm was so
faint as to be almost imperceptible. He read them with the
author's cadence, with flawless correctness. A distinguished statesman read from the same book, with the intona-
tions of a legal document, paying no attention to the movement inherent in the words before him. I have heard a
celebrated Dante scholar and medieval enthusiast read the
sonnets of the 'Vita Nuova' as if they were not only prose,
but the ignominious prose of a man devoid of emotions: an
utter castration.

The leader of orchestra said to me, 'There is more for a
musician in a few lines with something rough or uneven,
such as Byron's

> There be none of Beauty's daughters
>   With a magic like thee;

than in whole pages of regular poetry.'
  Unless a man can put some thematic invention into *vers
libre*, he would perhaps do well to stick to 'regular'
metres, which have certain chances of being musical from
their form, and certain other chances of being musical
through his failure in fitting the form. In *vers libre* his
sole musical chance lies in invention.
  Mr. Eliot is one of the very few who have brought in a
personal rhythm, an identifiable quality of sound as well
as of style. And at any rate, his book is the best thing
in poetry since ... (for the sake of peace I will leave
that date to the imagination). I have read most of the
poems many times; I last read the whole book at breakfast
time and from flimsy and grimy proof-sheets: I believe
these are 'test conditions.' Confound it, the fellow can
write – we may as well sit up and take notice.

Note

1 The real books are those where a writer talks of himself in talking about the customs of his contemporaries
   – their dreams, their vanities, their loves, and their
   follies.

7. CONRAD AIKEN, DIVERS REALISTS, 'DIAL'

8 November 1917, vol. lxiii, 454–5

Aiken (1889–1973), a contemporary of Eliot's at Harvard,
was an American poet, novelist and critic. His reminiscences of Eliot's earlier years are to be found in an
essay, King Bolo and Others, in 'T.S. Eliot: A Symposium',
edited by R. March and Tambimuttu (London, 1947), pp. 20–3,
and in 'Ushant, an Essay' (New York, 1952). 'Selected
Letters of Conrad Aiken', edited by Joseph Killorin (New
Haven, Conn. 1978), contains letters to Eliot and discusses
him and his work with other correspondents.
  This is an extract from a longer review, dealing with
current poetry, which was reprinted complete in 'Scepti-
cisms' (New York, 1919), pp. 203–5.

Mr. T.S. Eliot, whose book 'Prufrock and Other Observations' is really hardly more than a pamphlet, is also a realist, but of a different sort. Like Mr. Gibson, Mr. Eliot is a psychologist; but his intuitions are keener; his technique subtler. For the two semi-narrative psychological portraits which form the greater and better part of his book, 'The Love Song of J. Alfred Prufrock' and the 'Portrait of a Lady,' one can have little but praise. This is psychological realism, but in a highly subjective or introspective vein; whereas Mr. Gibson, for example, gives us, in the third person, the reactions of an individual to a situation which is largely external (an accident, let us say), Mr. Eliot gives us, in the first person, the reactions of an individual to a situation for which to a large extent his own character is responsible. Such work is more purely autobiographic than the other - the field is narrowed, and the terms are idiosyncratic (sometimes almost blindly so). The dangers of such work are obvious: one must be certain that one's mental character and idiom are sufficiently close to the norm to be comprehensible or significant. In this respect, Mr. Eliot is near the border-line. His temperament is peculiar, it is sometimes, as remarked heretofore, almost bafflingly peculiar, but on the whole it is the average hyper-aesthetic one with a good deal of introspective curiosity; it will puzzle many, it will delight a few. Mr. Eliot writes pungently and sharply, with an eye for unexpected and vivid details, and, particularly in the two longer poems and in the 'Rhapsody on a Windy Night,' he shows himself to be an exceptionally acute technician. Such free rhyme as this, with irregular line lengths, is difficult to write well, and Mr. Eliot does it well enough to make one wonder whether such a form is not what the adorers of free verse will eventually have to come to. In the rest of Mr. Eliot's volume one finds the piquant and the trivial in about equal proportions.

8. EZRA POUND, A LETTER FROM REMY DE GOURMONT, 'LITTLE REVIEW'

December 1917, vol. ix, 6-7

This is an extract from a longer article, in which Pound compares the attitude of de Gourmont towards art and literature with that of the English intellectuals of the day.

G.W. Prothero (1848-1922), a distinguished historian, was editor of the 'Quarterly Review'.

If only my great correspondent could have seen letters I received about this time from English alleged intellec- tuals!!!!!!! The incredible stupidity, the ingrained refusal of thought!!!!! Of which more anon, if I can bring myself to it. Or let it pass? Let us say simply that De Gourmont's words form an interesting contrast with the methods employed by the British literary episcopacy to keep one from writing what one thinks, or to punish one (financially) for having done so.

Perhaps as a warning to young writers who can not afford the loss, one would be justified in printing the following:

                              50a. Albemarle Street, London W.
22 October, '14
                    Dear Mr. Pound:
                              Many thanks for your
                    letter of the other day. I am afraid I
                    must say frankly that I do not think I
                    can open the columns of the Q.R. -
                    at any rate at present - to anyone asso-
                    ciated publicly with such a publication
                    as 'Blast'. It stamps a man too disad-
                    vantageously.

                              Yours truly,
                                   G.W. Prothero.

                    Of course, having accepted your
                    paper on the *Noh*, I could not refrain
                    from publishing it. But other things
                    would be in a different category.

I need scarcely say that the 'Quarterly Review' is one of the most profitable periodicals in England, and one of one's best 'connections', or sources of income. It has, of course, a tradition.

                    It is not that Mr. Keats (if that be his real name,
          for we almost doubt that any man in his senses would
          put his real name to such a rhapsody) -

wrote their Gifford of Keats' 'Endymion'. My only comment is that the 'Quarterly' has done it again. Their Mr. A. Waugh is a lineal descendent of Gifford, by way of

mentality. A century has not taught them manners. In the
eighteen forties they were still defending the review of
Keats. And more recently Waugh has lifted up his senile
slobber against Mr. Eliot. It is indeed time that the
functions of both English and American literature were
taken over by younger and better men.

As for their laying the birch on my pocket. I compute
that my support of Lewis and Brzeska has cost me at the
lowest estimate about £20 per year, from one source alone
since that regrettable occurrence, since I dared to discern a great sculptor and a great painter in the midst of
England's artistic desolation. ('European and Asiatic
papers please copy'.)

Young men, desirous of finding before all things smooth
berths and elderly consolations, are cautioned to behave
more circumspectly.

9. MAY SINCLAIR, 'PRUFROCK AND OTHER OBSERVATIONS':
A CRITICISM, 'LITTLE REVIEW'

December 1917, vol. iv, 8-14.

Sinclair (1870-1946) was an English novelist. She was
sympathetic to the new poetry, as is shown by this review
and by her short piece on Imagism in the 'Egoist' (1 June
1915).

So far I have seen two and only two reviews of Mr. Eliot's
poems: one by Ezra Pound in the 'Egoist', one by an anonymous writer in the 'New Statesman'. I learn from Mr.
Pound's review that there is a third, by Mr. Arthur Waugh,
in the 'Quarterly'.

To Mr. Ezra Pound Mr. Eliot is a poet with genius as in-
contestable as the genius of Browning. To the anonymous
one he is an insignificant phenomenon that may be approp-
riately disposed of among the Shorter Notices. To Mr.
Waugh, quoted by Mr. Pound, he is a 'drunken Helot'. I do
not know what Mr. Pound would say to the anonymous one,
but I can imagine. Anyhow, to him the 'Quarterly' reviewer is 'the silly old Waugh'. And that is enough for
Mr. Pound.

It ought to be enough for me. Of course I know that

genius does inevitably provoke these outbursts of silli-
ness. I know that Mr. Waugh is simply keeping up the good
old manly traditions of the 'Quarterly', 'so savage and
tartarly,' with its war-cry: 'Ere's a stranger, let's
'eave 'arf a brick at 'im!' And though the behaviour of
the 'New Statesman' puzzles me, since it has an editor
who sometimes knows better, and really ought to have known
better this time, still the 'New Statesman' also can plead
precedent. But when Mr. Waugh calls Mr. Eliot 'a drunken
Helot,' it is clear that he thinks he is on the track of a
tendency and is making a public example of Mr. Eliot. And
when the anonymous one with every appearance of delibera-
tion picks out his 'Boston Evening Transcript', the one
insignificant, the one negligible and trivial thing in a
very serious volume, and assures us that it represents Mr.
Eliot at his finest and his best, it is equally clear that
we have to do with something more than mere journalistic
misadventure. And I think it is something more than Mr.
Eliot's genius that has terrified the 'Quarterly' into
exposing him in the full glare of publicity and the 'New
Statesman' into shoving him and his masterpieces away out
of the public sight.

For 'The Love-Song of J. Alfred Prufrock', and the
'Portrait of a Lady' are masterpieces in the same sense
and in the same degree as Browning's 'Romances' and 'Men
and Women'; the 'Preludes' and 'Rhapsody on a Windy Night'
are masterpieces in a profounder sense and a greater
degree than Henley's 'London Voluntaries'; 'La Figlia Che
Piange' is a masterpiece in its own sense and in its own
degree. It is a unique masterpiece.

But Mr. Eliot is dangerous. Mr. Eliot is associated
with an unpopular movement and with unpopular people. His
'Preludes' and his 'Rhapsody' appeared in 'Blast.' They
stood out from the experimental violences of 'Blast' with
an air of tranquil and triumphant achievement; but, no
matter; it was in 'Blast' that they appeared. That circumstance alone was disturbing to the comfortable respectability of Mr. Waugh and the 'New Statesman'.

And apart from this purely extraneous happening, Mr.
Eliot's genius is in itself disturbing. It is elusive;
it is difficult; it demands a distinct effort of attention. Comfortable and respectable people could see, in
the first moment after dinner, what Mr. Henley and Mr.
Robert Louis Stevenson and Mr. Rudyard Kipling would be
at; for the genius of these three travelled, comfortably
and fairly respectably, along the great high roads. They
could even, with a little boosting, follow Francis Thompson's flight in mid-air, partly because it was signalled
to them by the sound and shining of his wings,

partly because Thompson had hitched himself securely
to some well-known starry team. He was in the poetic
tradition all right. People knew where they were with
him, just as they know now where they are with Mr. Davies
and his fields and flowers and birds.

But Mr. Eliot is not in any tradition at all, not even
in Browning's and Henley's tradition. His resemblances to
Browning and Henley are superficial. His difference is
twofold; a difference of method and technique; a difference of sight and aim. He does not see anything between
him and reality, and he makes straight for the reality he
sees; he cuts all his corners and his curves; and this
directness of method is startling and upsetting to comfortable, respectable people accustomed to going superfluously
in and out of corners and carefully round curves. Unless
you are prepared to follow with the same nimbleness and
straightness you will never arrive with Mr. Eliot at his
meaning. Therefore the only comfortable thing is to sit
down and pretend, either that Mr. Eliot is a 'Helot' too
drunk to have any meaning, or that his 'Boston Evening
Transcript' which you do understand is greater than his
'Love Song of Prufrock' which you do not understand. In
both instances you have successfully obscured the issue.

Again, the comfortable and respectable mind loves conventional beauty, and some of the realities that Mr. Eliot
sees are not beautiful. He insists on your seeing very
vividly, as he sees them, the streets of his 'Preludes' and
and 'Rhapsody'. He insists on your smelling them.

[Quotes 'Rhapsody on a Windy Night', CPP, p. 24, 'Regard
that woman' to 'rancid butter'.]

He is

>   aware of the damp souls of housemaids
> Sprouting despondently at area gates.

And these things are ugly. The comfortable mind turns
away from them in disgust. It identifies Mr. Eliot with a
modern tendency; it labels him securely 'Stark Realist',
so that lovers of 'true poetry' may beware.

It is nothing to the comfortable mind that Mr. Eliot is

> ...moved by fancies that are curled
> Around these images, and cling:
> The motion of some infinitely gentle
> Infinitely suffering thing.

It is nothing to it that the emotion he disengages
from his ugliest image is unbearably poignant. His poignancy is as unpleasant as his ugliness, disturbing to
comfort.

We are to observe that Mr. Eliot's 'Observations' are
ugly and unpleasant and obscure.

Now there is no earthly reason why Mr. Eliot should not
be ugly and unpleasant if he pleases, no reason why he
should not do in words what Hogarth did in painting, provided he does it well enough. Only, the comfortable mind
that prefers So and So and So and So to Mr. Eliot ought to
prefer Hogarth's 'Paul Before Felix' to his 'Harlot's
Progress'. Obscurity, if he were really obscure, would be
another matter. But there was a time when the transparent
Tennyson was judged obscure; when people wondered what
under heaven the young man was after; they couldn't tell
for the life of them whether it was his 'dreary gleams' or
his 'curlews' that were flying over Locksley Hall.
Obscurity may come from defective syntax, from a bad style,
from confusion of ideas, from involved thinking, from
irrelevant association, from sheer piling on of ornament.
Mr. Eliot is not obscure in any of these senses.

There is also an obscurity of remote or unusual objects,
or of familiar objects moving very rapidly. And Mr.
Eliot's trick of cutting his corners and his curves makes
him seem obscure where he is clear as daylight. His
thoughts move very rapidly and by astounding cuts. They
move not by logical stages and majestic roundings of the
full literary curve, but as live thoughts move in live
brains. Thus 'La Figlia Che Piange':

[Quotes 'La Figlia Che Piange', CPP, p. 34.]

I suppose there are minds so comfortable that they
would rather not be disturbed by new beauty and by new
magic like this. I do not know how much Mr. Eliot's
beauty and magic is due to sheer imagination, how much to
dexterity of technique, how much to stern and sacred
attention to reality; but I do know that without such
technique and such attention the finest imagination is
futile, and that if Mr. Eliot had written nothing but that
one poem he would rank as a poet by right of its perfection.

But Mr. Eliot is not a poet of one poem; and if there
is anything more astounding and more assured than his performance it is his promise. He knows what he is after.
Reality, stripped naked of all rhetoric, of all ornament,
of all confusing and obscuring association, is what he is
after. His reality may be a modern street or a modern

drawing-room; it may be an ordinary human mind suddenly
and fatally aware of what is happening to it; Mr. Eliot
is careful to present his street and his drawing-room as
they are, and Prufrock's thoughts as they are: live
thoughts, kicking, running about and jumping, nervily, in
a live brain.

Prufrock, stung by a longing for reality, escapes from
respectability into the street and the October fog.

[Quotes 'Prufrock', CPP, p. 13, 'The yellow fog' to 'fell
asleep'.]

Prufrock has conceived the desperate idea of disturbing
the universe. He wonders

[Quotes 'Do I dare' to 'how should I presume?']

Prufrock realises that it is too late. He is middle-
aged. The horrible drawing-room life he has entered has
got him.

[Quotes CPP p. 15, 'And the afternoon' to 'I was afraid'.]

His soul can only assert itself in protests and memories.
He would have had more chance in the primeval slime.

I should have been a pair of ragged claws
Scuttling across the floors of silent seas.

As he goes downstairs he is aware of his futility,
aware that the noticeable thing about him is the 'bald
spot in the middle of my hair'. He has an idea; an idea
that he can put into action: -

I shall wear the bottoms of my trousers rolled.

He is incapable, he knows that he is incapable of any
action more momentous, more disturbing.

And yet - and yet -

I have heard the mermaids singing, each to each.

I have seen them riding seaward on the waves
Combing the white hair of the waves blown back
When the wind blows the water white and black.

We have lingered in the chambers of the sea
By sea-girls wreathed with seaweed red and brown
Till human voices wake us, and we drown.

Observe the method. Instead of writing round and round
about Prufrock, explaining that his tragedy is the tragedy
of submerged passion, Mr. Eliot simply removes the covering from Prufrock's mind: Prufrock's mind, jumping quickly
from actuality to memory and back again, like an animal,
hunted, tormented, terribly and poignantly alive. The
Love-Song of Prufrock is a song that Balzac might have
sung if he had been as great a poet as he was a novelist.

It is nothing to the 'Quarterly' and to the 'New Statesman' that Mr. Eliot should have done this thing. But it
is a great deal to the few people who care for poetry and
insist that it should concern itself with reality. With
ideas, if you like, but ideas that are realities and not
abstractions.

10. BABETTE DEUTSCH, ANOTHER IMPRESSIONIST, 'NEW REPUBLIC'

16 February 1918, vol. xiv, 89

Deutsch (b. 1895) is an American poet and critic. She
gave a general appraisal of Eliot in Heirs of the Symbolists, 'This Modern Poetry' (New York, 1935), pp. 117-32.

A slim little book, bound in pale yellow wrapping-paper,
'Prufrock' invites inspection, as much by the novelty of its
appearance as the queer syllables of its title. The
individual note which these suggest is even more emphatically pronounced in the poems between its covers.

The initial one, which gives its name to the volume, is
'The Love Song of J. Alfred Prufrock.' Mr. Prufrock, as
he explains in his amorous discursions, is no longer
young; his hair has perceptibly thinned, his figure has
lost what Apollonian contours it may have possessed. He
is self-conscious, introspective, timid. In a-metrical
but fluent lines, embroidered with unique metaphor, he
draws himself; his desires, his memories, his fears. 'Do
I dare,' he asks,

Disturb the universe?
In a minute there is time
For decisions and revisions which a minute will reverse.

> For I have known them all already, known them all –
> Known the evenings, mornings, afternoons,
> I have measured out my life with coffee-spoons ...

In the end, he does not presume.

The method used in this poem is typical of Mr. Eliot's work. Impressions are strung along on a tenuous thread of sense. A familiar situation: the hesitating amours of the middle-aged, the failure of a certain man to establish the expected relation with a certain woman, is given in poetic monologue. The language has the extraordinary quality of common words uncommonly used. Less formal than prose, more nervous than metrical verse, the rhythms are suggestive of program music of an intimate sort. This effect is emphasized by the use of rhyme. It recurs, often internally, with an echoing charm that is heightened by its irregularity. But Mr. Eliot, like M. Géraldy, of whom he is vaguely reminiscent, is so clever a technician that the rhymes are subordinated to afford an unconsidered pleasure.

In these 'observations' there is a glimpse of many slight but memorable things: of dirty London streets, crowded with laborers, dilettantes, prostitutes; of polite stupidities in country houses; of satiric fencings; of the stale aroma of familiar things. Mostly they are impressions of a weary mind, looking out upon a crowded personal experience with impartial irony. They have the hall-marks of impressionism: remoteness from vulgar ethics and aesthetics, indifference to the strife of nations and classes, an esoteric humor thrown out in peculiar phrases. Something of Eliot's quality may be got from 'The Boston Evening Transcript,' whimsically suggestive of that fragment of Sappho's: 'Evening, thou that bringest all that bright morning scattered; thou bringest the sheep, the goat, the child back to her mother.'

[Quotes 'The Boston Evening Transcript', CPP, p. 28.]

11. MARIANNE MOORE, A NOTE ON T.S. ELIOT'S BOOK, 'POETRY'

April 1918, vol. xii, 36-7

Moore (1887–1972) was the author of several collections of poetry, and her 'Selected Poems' appeared in 1935 with an

introduction by Eliot. She was editor of the 'Dial' from
1925 to 1929.

It might be advisable for Mr. Eliot to publish a fangless
edition of 'Prufrock and Other Observations' for the
gentle reader who likes his literature, like breakfast
coffee or grapefruit, sweetened. A mere change in the
arrangement of the poems would help a little. It might
begin with 'La Figlia Che Piange', followed perhaps by the
'Portrait of a Lady'; for the gentle reader, in his eagerness for the customary bit of sweets, can be trusted to
overlook the ungallantry, the youthful cruelty, of the
substance of the 'Portrait'. It may as well be admitted
that this hardened reviewer cursed the poet in his mind
for this cruelty while reading the poem; and just when he
was ready to find extenuating circumstances - the usual
excuses about realism - out came this 'drunken helot' (one
can hardly blame the good English reviewer whom Ezra Pound
quotes!) with that ending. It is hard to get over this
ending with a few moments of thought; it wrenches a piece
of life at the roots.
    As for the gentle reader, this poem could be followed by
the lighter ironies of 'Aunt Nancy', (1) the 'Boston Evening
Transcript', etc. One would hardly know what to do with
the two London pieces. Whistler in his post-impressionistic
English studies - and these poems are not entirely unlike
Whistler's studies - had the advantage of his more static
medium, of a somewhat more romantic temperament, and of the
fact that the objects he painted half-hid their ugliness
under shadows and the haze of distance. But Eliot deals
with life, with beings and things who live and move almost
nakedly before his individual mind's eye - in the darkness,
in the early sunlight, and in the fog. Whatever one may
feel about sweetness in literature, there is also the word
honesty, and this man is a faithful friend of the objects
he portrays; altogether unlike the sentimentalist who
really stabs them treacherously in the back while pretending affection.

Note

1 So in original.

12. EDGAR JEPSON, RECENT UNITED STATES POETRY, 'ENGLISH
REVIEW'

May 1918, vol. xxvi, 426-8

Jepson (1863-1938) was a well-known novelist, critic and
translator.
     This is an extract from a longer essay. A reply from
William Carlos Williams is the next item.

But the queer and delightful thing is that in the scores
of yards of pleasant verse and wamblings and yawpings
which have been recently published in the Great Pure Republic I have found a poet, a real poet, who possesses in the
highest degree the qualities the new school demands.
Western-born of Eastern stock, Mr. T.S. Eliot is United
States of the United States; and his poetry is securely as
autochthonic as Theocritus. It is new in form, as all
genuine poetry is new in form; it is musical with a new
music, and that without any straining after newness. The
form and music are a natural, integral part of the poet's
amazingly fine presentation of his vision of the world.
     Could anything be more United States, more of the soul
of that modern land, than 'The Love Song of J. Alfred
Prufrock'? It is the very wailing testament of that soul
with its cruel clarity of sophisticated vision, its thin,
sophisticated emotions, its sophisticated appreciation of
a beauty, and its sophisticated yearning for a beauty it
cannot dare to make its own and so, at last, live.
     This is in very truth the lover of the real, up-to-date
United States:

     In the room the women come and go,
     Talking of Michelangelo.

     And indeed there will be time
     To wonder, 'Do I dare?' and, 'Do I dare?'
     Time to turn back and descend the stair,
     With a bald spot in the middle of my hair -

     Do I dare
     Disturb the universe?
     In a minute there is time
     For decisions and revisions which a minute will reverse.

For I have known them all already, known them all -
Have known the evenings, mornings, afternoons,
I have measured out my life with coffee spoons;
I know the voices dying with a dying fall
Beneath the music from a farther room.
        So how should I presume?

And then the end:

I have heard mermaids singing, each to each.

I do not think that they will sing to me.

I have seen them riding seaward on the waves
Combing the white hair of the waves blown back
When the wind blows the water white and black.

We have lingered in the chambers of the sea
By sea-girls wreathed with seaweed red and brown
Till human voices wake us, and we drown.

Never has the shrinking of the modern spirit from life
been expressed so exquisitely and with such truth.
    Consider, again, that lovely poem, 'La Figlia Che
Piange':

[Quotes 'La Figlia Che Piange', CPP, p. 34.]

How delicate and beautiful in the emotion! How exquisite and beautiful the music! This is the very fine
flower of the finest spirit of the United States. It
would be the last absurdity for such a poet to go West
and write for that plopp-eyed bungaroo, the Great-Hearted
Young Westerner on the make. It seems incredible that
this lovely poem should have been published in 'Poetry' in
the year in which the school awarded the prize to that
lumbering fakement, 'All Life in a Life.'

13. WILLIAM CARLOS WILLIAMS, PROLOGUE, 'LITTLE REVIEW'

May 1919, vol. vi, 76-8

Williams (1883-1963), American poet, was a contemporary of
Ezra Pound at the University of Pennsylvania. They met
during the academic year 1902-3 when Williams was a student

of dentistry, though subsequently he changed to medicine
which he was to practise in Rutherford, New Jersey.
Williams had a life-long antipathy towards Eliot's poetry,
a feeling intensified by 'The Waste Land', his reaction to
which he described in his 'Autobiography' (1951). In 'I
Wanted to Write a Poem' (1958) Williams recalled that he
read 'Prufrock' during the composition of 'Kora in Hell'
(1920). This review was incorporated into the Prologue to
that work.

A somewhat petulant English college friend of my brother's
once remarked that Britons make the best policemen the
world has ever seen. I agree with him. It is silly to go
into a puckersnatch because some brass-button-minded nin-
compoop in Kensington flies off the handle and speaks
openly about our United States prize poems. This Mr.
Jepson - 'Anyone who has heard Mr. J. read Homer and discourse on Catullus would recognize his fitness as a judge
and respecter of poetry' - this is Ezra! - this champion
of the right is not half a fool. His epithets and phrases
- slipshod, rank bad workmanship of a man who has shirked
his job, lumbering fakement, cumbrous artificiality,
maundering dribble, rancid as Ben Hur - are in the main
well-merited. And besides he comes out with one fairly
lipped cornet blast: the only distinctive U.S. contributions to the arts have been ragtime and buck-dancing.
   Nothing is good save the new. If a thing have novelty
it stands intrinsically beside every other work of artistic excellence. If it have not that, no loveliness or
heroic proportion or grand manner will save it. It will
not be saved above all by an attentuated intellectuality.
   Our prize poems have been mostly junk - though there is
a certain candid indecency of form about Lindsay's work
that is attractive. But these poems are especially to be
damned not because of superficial bad workmanship but as
Mr. J. again correctly adjudges, because they are rehash,
repetition - just as Eliot's more exquisite work is
rehash, repetition in another way of Verlaine, Baudelaire, Maeterlinck, - conscious or unconscious: - just as
there are Pound's early paraphrases from Yeats and his
constant later cribbing from the renaissance, Provence and
the modern French: men content with the connotations of
their masters.
   But all U.S. verse is not bad according to Mr. J: there
is 'The Love Song of J. Alfred Prufrock.'
   It is convenient to have fixed standards of comparison:
all antiquity! And there is always some everlasting

Polonius of Kensington forever to rate highly his eternal
Eliot. It is because Eliot is a subtle conformist. It
tickles the palate of this archbishop of procurers to a
lecherous antiquity to hold up Prufrock as a New World
type. Prufrock the nibbler at sophistication, endemic in
every capital, the not quite (because he refuses to turn
his back) is 'the soul of that modern land' the United
States!

> Blue undershirts,
> Upon a line,
> It is not necessary to say to you
> Anything about it -

I cannot question Eliot's observation. 'Prufrock' is a
masterly portrait of the man just below the summit but the
type is universal, the model in this case might be Mr. J.
No. The New World is Montezuma or, since he was stoned
to death in a parley, Guatemozin who had the city of
Mexico leveled over him before he was taken:
For the rest, there is no man even though he dare who
can make beauty his own and 'so at last live,' at least
there is no man better situated for that achievement than
another. As Prufrock longed for his silly lady so Kensington longs for its Hardanger dairymaid. By a mere twist
of the imagination, if Prufrock only knew it, the whole
world can be inverted (why else are there wars?) and the
mermaids be set warbling to whoever will listen to them.
Seesaw and blind-man's-buff converted into a sort of foot-
ball.
But the summit of United States achievement, according
to Mr. J. - who can discourse on Catullus - is that very
beautiful poem of Eliot's 'La Figlia Che Piange': just the
right amount of everything drained through, etc., etc.,
etc., etc., the rhythm delicately studied out and - IT
CONFORMS! ergo here we have 'the very fine flower of the
finest spirit of the United States.'
Examined closely this poem reveals a highly refined
distillation. Added to the already 'faithless' formula of
yesterday we have a conscious simplicity:

> Simple and faithless as a smile and shake of the hand.

The perfection of that line is beyond cavil. Yet, in
the last stanza, this paradigm, this very fine flower of
U.S. art is warped out of alignment, obscured in meaning
even to the point of an absolute unintelligibility by the
inevitable straining after a rhyme! - the very cleverness
with which this straining is covered being a sinister
token in itself.

And I wonder how they should have been together!

So we have no choice but to accept the work of this fumbling conjurer.

Upon the Jepson filet Eliot balances his mushroom. It is the latest touch from the literary cuisine, it adds to the pleasant outlook from the club window. If to do this, if to be a Whistler at best, in the art of poetry, is to reach the height of poetic expression, then Ezra and Eliot have approached it and *tant pis* for the rest of us.

The Adobe Indian hag sings her lullaby:

The beetle is blind
The beetle is blind
The beetle is blind
The beetle is blind, etc., etc.,

and Kandinsky in his 'Über das Geistige in der Kunst' sets down the following axioms for the artist:

Every artist has to express himself
Every artist has to express his epoch.
Every artist has to express the pure and eternal
    qualities of the art of all men.

So we have the fish and the bait but the last rule holds three hooks at once – not for the fish however.

I do not overlook De Gourmont's plea for a meeting of the nations but I do believe that when they meet Paris will be more than slightly abashed to find parodies of the middle ages, Dante and Langue D'Oc foisted upon it as the best in United States poetry. Even Eliot who is too fine an artist to allow himself to be exploited by a blockhead grammaticaster turns recently toward 'one definite false note' in his quatrains, which more nearly approach America than ever 'La Figlia Che Piange' did. Ezra Pound is a Boscan who has met his Navagiero.

'Poems'

London, May 1919

14. UNSIGNED REVIEW, NOT HERE, O APOLLO, 'TIMES LITERARY
SUPPLEMENT'

12 June 1919, no. 908, 322

The other work under review was 'The Critic in Judgment'
by John Middleton Murry, published, like Eliot's 'Poems',
by the Hogarth Press.

In spite of the interest now taken in poetry, and the
diverse and interesting experiments made in writing it, it
still suffers from two defects which troubled it in the
Victorian age, namely, that it contains either too little
of the content of the writer's mind or much that is not
the real content of his mind. Either the poets have a
great difficulty in saying anything at all or else they
say anything too easily. Mr. Murry, in his 'Critic in
Judgment,' says so much, and so easily, that we find it
hard to discover what he is writing about. His metre,
blank verse, sways him with its memories of past masters -
Shakespeare, Milton, Browning, Tennyson. They seem almost
to dictate to him what he is to say, so that, as we read,
we fade out of one poet into another, aware only of
changes of manner, the matter itself escaping us. The
Critic, whose purpose and character are always vague,
begins in the style of Browning and then passes into
Tennyson. It is Browning who says:-

> Let him put up that scribble on the wall
> To worry old Belshazzar, till he tired

            With all the tiredness of a lesser man...
            And you, eternal Toby, bark outside
            Weary beside a lamp-post, while the shadows
            Torment me for the thousand millionth time
            There on the wall.

It is Tennyson who follows, soon, with this:-

                        In them do I believe.
            Nay, you but mock me. How could they believe
            Who felt no doubt? How can I not believe,
            Flung up upon the stage by unseen hands
            To unheard music, speaking lines unknown
            Into a void of darkness?

Then there are echoes of Swinburne:-

            Not thus may mine eyes sleep, not thus mine arms
            Slacken, nor thus my broken lips receive
            The kiss of mortal death desirable.

Then beginnings of Miltonic periods:-

                        Thou art not he
            Foretold, that should speak comfortable words -
            Sweetest most bitter thine, and tongued with fire.

Then early Shakespeare or Marlowe:-

            My name is Helen and my spirit is love,
            By fame once Menelaus' bride ravished
            By bowman Paris across the Aegean sea
            To be the doom of ships and many men
            Imbattled on the plains of Ilium.

Then this passage fades again into Milton. As for the
lyrics, they too turn from style into style. One begins
pure Swinburne:-

            Life holds not any higher thing than love
             Nor shall men find another rose than this
            And be immortal, not in the heights above
             Nor in the deeps, save only where love is.

But the next four lines are like an Elizabethan song:-

            For him who seeks believing
            Love hath no weary days,
            Love hath no thorny ways
            But joys beyond receiving.

It is a very curious case of writing made almost automatic by unconscious influences; or are they conscious?
Does Mr. Murry mean all these imitations? We do not know,
and we are still uncertain of the aim of his poem. But we
do know that the fading of influence into influence makes
it very hard to read. The very fluency lulls the mind to
sleep; and at the end we are left only with the impression
that the writer has read many poets, and that they will
not let him reach what he has to say. It is like those
dreams in which one is continually prevented from packing
up and catching a train. These ghosts from the past make
Mr. Murry speak with alien jaws, distract him from his
purpose, whatever it may be. His task is to forget them.

Mr. Eliot's case is the opposite. We may guess that he
is fastidiously on his guard against echoes. There shall
not be a cadence in his few verses that will remind anyone
of anything. His composition is an incessant process of
refusing all that offers itself, for fear that it should
not be his own. The consequence is that his verse, novel
and ingenious, original as it is, is fatally impoverished
of subject matter. For he is as fastidious of emotions as
of cadences. He seems to have a 'phobia' of sentimental-
ity, like a small schoolboy who would die rather than kiss
his sister in public. Still, since he is writing verses
he must say something, and his remarkable talent exercises
itself in saying always, from line to line and word to
word, what no one would expect. Each epithet, even, must
be a surprise, each verb must shock the reader with unexpected associations; and the result is this:-

    Polyphiloprogenitive
    The sapient sutlers of the Lord
    Drift across the window-panes.
    In the beginning was the Word.

    In the beginning was the Word.
    Superfetation of τὸ ἕν,
    And at the mensual turn of time
    Produced enervate Origen.

Mr. Eliot, like Browning, likes to display out-of-the-way
learning, he likes to surprise you by every trick he can
think of. He has forgotten his emotions, his values, his
sense of beauty, even his common-sense, in that one desire
to surprise, to get farther away from the obvious than any
writer on record, be he Donne or Browning, or Benlowes
even. We say he has forgotten all these things, because
there is no doubt of his talents. They are evident in
'The Hippopotamus,' and even in 'Sweeney Among the

Nightingales,' where he carries the game of perversity as
far at least as anyone has ever carried it. But poetry is
a serious art, too serious for this game. Mr. Eliot is
fatally handicapping himself with his own inhibitions; he
is in danger of becoming silly; and what will he do then?
Or else he is in danger of writing nothing at all, but
merely thinking of all the poems he has refused to write;
a state which would be for a poet, if not hell, at least
limbo. He is probably reacting against poetry like that
of Mr. Murry. But you cannot live on reactions; you must
forget them and all the errors which past writers have
committed; you must be brave enough to risk some positive
follies of your own. Otherwise you will fall more and
more into negative follies; you will bury your talent in
a napkin and became an artist who never does anything but
giggle faintly. The final effect of these two little
books is to leave us all the more melancholy because of
their authors' cleverness. If they were nothing, it would
not matter; but they are something, and they are very
laboriously writing nothing.

15. FROM AN UNSIGNED REVIEW, IS THIS POETRY?, 'ATHENAEUM'

20 June 1919, 491

'The Critic in Judgment' was again the other work under
review.

The 'ordinary man,' the ghostly master or terror of most
writers, would certainly ask the same question about Mr.
Eliot, and answer it with a decided negative.

    Polyphiloprogenitive
    The sapient sutlers of the Lord
    Drift across the window-panes.
    In the beginning was the Word.

Thus begins one of Mr. Eliot's poems, provocative of the
question and of the jeering laugh which is the easy reaction to anything strange, whether it be a 'damned
foreigner' or a Post-Impressionist picture. Mr. Eliot is
certainly damned by his newness and strangeness; but those

two qualities, which in most art are completely unimportant, because ephemeral, in him claim the attention of even
the serious critic. For they are part of the fabric of
his poetry. Mr. Eliot is always quite consciously 'trying
for' something, and something which has grown out of and
developed beyond all the poems of all the dead poets.
Poetry to him seems to be not so much an art as a science,
a vast and noble and amusing body of communal feeling upon
which the contemporary poet must take a firm stand and
then launch himself into the unknown in search of new discoveries. That is the attitude not of the conventional
poet, but of the scientist who with the help of working
hypotheses hopes to add something, a theory perhaps or a
new microbe, to the corpus of human knowledge. If we
accept, provisionally, Mr. Eliot's attitude, we must admit
that he comes well equipped to his task. The poetry of
the dead is in his bones and at the tips of his fingers:
he has the rare gift of being able to weave, delicately
and delightfully, an echo or even a line of the past into
the pattern of his own poem. And at the same time he is
always trying for something new, something which has
evolved - one drops instinctively into the scientific
terminology - out of the echo or the line, out of the last
poem of the last dead poet, something subtly intellectual
and spiritual, produced by the careful juxtaposition of
words and the even more careful juxtaposition of ideas.
The cautious critic, warned by the lamentable record of
his tribe, might avoid answering the question: 'And is
this poetry?' by asking to see a little more of Mr. Eliot
than is shown in these seven short poems and even
'Prufrock.' But, to tell the truth, seven poems reveal a
great deal of any poet. There is poetry in Mr. Eliot,
as, for instance, in the stanzas:

        The host with someone indistinct
        Converses at the door apart,
        The nightingales are singing near
        The Convent of the Sacred Heart,

        And sang within the bloody wood
        When Agamemnon cried aloud,
        And let their liquid siftings fall
        To stain the stiff dishonoured shroud.

Yet the poetry often seems to come in precisely at the
moment when the scientist and the science, the method and
the newness, go out. A poem like 'The Hippopotamus,' for
all its charm and cleverness and artistry, is perilously
near the pit of the jeu d'esprit. And so scientific and

scholarly a writer as Mr. Eliot might with advantage consider whether his method was not the method of that
'terrible warning,' P. Papinius Statius. We hope that Mr.
Eliot will quickly give us more and remove our melancholy
suspicion that is the product of a Silver Age.

'Ara Vos Prec'

London, February 1920

16. JOHN MIDDLETON MURRY, THE ETERNAL FOOTMAN, 'ATHENAEUM'

20 February 1920, 239

Murry (1889-1957), critic, biographer, novelist and editor,
worked for the 'Westminster Gazette', 'Nation' and the
'Times Literary Supplement'. He married Katherine Mansfield in 1913. During 'the brief and brilliant life'
(Eliot's words) of the 'Athenaeum' under his editorship he
published important early essays by Eliot, who acknowledged his debt to Murry in the Preface to the 1928 edition
of 'The Sacred Wood'. Eliot also contributed a foreword
to 'Katherine Mansfield and Other Essays' (1959), while
Murry wrote on Eliot's drama in 'Unprofessional Essays',
published in 1956.

Here is Mr. T.S. Eliot, and here once again is the question: What are we to make of him? It is not a question
that even the most assiduous (assiduity is demanded) and
interested (interest is inevitable) of his readers would
care to answer with any accent of finality. For Mr. Eliot,
who is a connoisseur in discrepancy between intention and
achievement, is likely to be himself an example of it.
Nothing so sharpens one's sensitiveness to false notes in
life at large as experience of them in oneself; so that
there is more than a remote chance that even in regard to
'Ara Vos Prec' and while we hold it in our hands Mr. Eliot
may whisper deprecatingly:

> That is not it at all,
> That is not what I meant, at all.

Yes, it seems to us sometimes that the inmost vital
core of Mr. Eliot's poetry, the paradoxical impulse of
his expression, is his determination to be free to whisper
that refrain in our ear; it seems that he is like the
chameleon who changes colour infinitely, and every change
is protective. True, the range of variation is not truly
infinite; there are colours which the chameleon cannot
compass. But the chameleon, if he were an artist, would
make it an essential of his art not to be lured against a
background which he could not imitate.

The question for the critic is to determine whether Mr.
Eliot - a conscious artist if ever there was one - has at
any moment allowed himself to stray beyond his functional
limit. That limit is. set in the case of Mr. Eliot at the
point where discrepancy ceases between intention and
achievement, between soul and body, man and the Universe.
At a crucial moment in his beautiful - we insist, precisely beautiful - 'Love Song of J. Alfred Prufrock,'

> The Eternal Footman snickers.

Since that day Mr. Eliot has fallen deeper and deeper into
the clutches of the Footman, who has come to preside over
his goings out and his comings in. The Footman has grown
into a monstrous Moloch. All that Mr. Eliot most deeply
feels is cast into his burning belly - or almost all.

Yet consider the case of men, and of their more perfect
exemplars who are poets. It is only when the Eternal
footman has given notive, when no longer

> Human voices wake us and we drown,

when we pass out of the limbo of discordant futility, that
there comes to us all the crash, the collapse, the
ecstasy, the peace of surrender. Mr. Eliot is like us,
terribly like us, for all that he is much more clever;
the difference is that the Footman clings to his service
longer. With the truly aristocratic, as we know, the
Footman will stay for fifteen shillings when he would
leave Mr. Bleistein and fifteen guineas; and we admit the
implication that Mr. Eliot is truly distinguished.
Another implication is that it is difficult for Mr. Eliot
to talk to us, and difficult (as the present essay proves)
for us to talk to him.

The further question arises - we continue to speak in
parables on a matter hardly susceptible of discussion

otherwise - whether we are to accept that Footman or not.
Is it polite of us, have we a right, to seek an interview
with Mr. Eliot when the Footman is not there?   The rightness of an action is fortunately not measured by its ease
of execution, but neither can we accept the dogma that the
difficult is necessarily the virtuous path.   Have we a
right to say in our turn: 'It was not that at all,' to
insist that the Footman in the long run makes everything
impossible for us also, to gather up tell tale accents
that have escaped, bubble-clear and bubble-frail, from
under the Footman's all-regarding eye?   May we, for instance, perpend

> The notion of some infinitely gentle
>   Infinitely suffering thing.

and seek in it a solvent to the icy brilliance of an all
but inexpugnable society manner?   May we proceed thence,
following a tenuous and evanescent clue, and ask not
whether 'Gerontion' is solidly and definitely anything,
but what it was that brought him to his premature old age?
Is there anything other than that which we found (if indeed we found it) cowering beneath the strange notion,
which would be apt

> To lose beauty in terror, terror in inquisition?

The Footman snickers audibly.   But do we care?   Rather,
do we care now?   We, who have lost with the capability the
desire to be respectable, can stop our ears to him when
there is a chance of hearing something that is all important for us to know, whose sub-terrene tremor is not
wholly lost.

> Think at last
> I have not made this show purposelessly
> And it is not by any concitation
> Of the backward devils.
> I would meet you upon this honestly.
> I that was near your heart was removed therefrom
> To lose beauty in terror, terror in inquisition...

Assuredly we are not tempted to think it was purposelessly
made.   The conviction of purpose remains whether we accept
the Footman or reject him.   True, we should prefer that he
were dismissed, partly because his going (or our sense
that he is gone) makes elucidation (or what we think elucidation) easier, but also in part because he can never be
wholly abolished.   The sense of the Footman belongs to a

generation; he is our *datum*, our constant. But by an
effort of imaginative will he can be compressed within the
circle of our vision to less than a bogey-size. Mr. Eliot,
more ably than ourselves, can stand apart from the Footman
and his victim both. Is it necessary that he should turn
himself into a bigger Footman still, and yet a bigger
when that one too has been compressed, and a bigger *ad
infinitum*?

Nowadays it is consciousness that makes cowards of us
all. The complexity of our enemy is indicated by the fact
of Mr. Eliot's determination that it shall make a brave
man of him. But is it possible really? At least, Mr.
Eliot would admit that it is a super-cowardice; he would
claim that, indeed, as his exact intention. To make virtues of our vices is a good way of disarming them; but is
it the best? Surely it cannot be unless with it is preserved the instinct that it must be abandoned when it begins to prey upon the vitals. *Impavidum ferient ruinae*.
We do not doubt it for one moment with Mr. Eliot; but
we have a motion that in the last resort the ruins will
count for more than the impavidity that marks his unflinching diagnosis.

[Quotes 'Gerontion', CPP, p. 38, 'After such knowledge' to
'our impudent crimes'.]

17. UNSIGNED REVIEW, A NEW BYRONISM, 'TIMES LITERARY
SUPPLEMENT'

18 March 1920, no. 948, 184

The death of Swinburne marked the end of an age in English
poetry, the age which began with Blake. It was impossible
for any poet after Swinburne to continue the romantic tradition; he carried his own kind of versification and the
romantic attitude as far as they could be carried, and
both died with him. Now our poets have to make another
beginning, to find a method of expression suited to their
different attitude; and of this fact they are almost over-
conscious. They have indeed often been led into an
obvious error by that over-consciousness; because they
must find new ways of expression and because they react
differently to the great facts of life, some of them
appear to think that the very subject-matter of their

verse must be different. This was the error of the eighteenth century; it sought for a new subject-matter and
chose one more suitable for prose than poetry, with the
result that it developed a style suited for neither, the
style which ended in invocations like - 'Innoculation,
heavenly maid, descend -' and was parodied in the Loves
of the Triangles.

The romantic movement itself was at first a return to
the proper subject-matter of poetry and to a poetical
technique. In its decline it narrowed the subject-matter
of poetry to themes which seemed obviously and easily
poetical, and its technique also became obviously and too
easily poetical. So the young poets of to-day are apt to
insist that they will make poetry of what they choose; but
their choice is not always so free as they think. It is
conditioned by reaction, disgust, *ennui*; they want no more
of La belle dame sans merci, or of King Arthur or Pan or
Proserpine, just as they want no more of rhythms such as

By the tideless, dolorous, midland sea -

so they choose themes and rhythms the very opposite of
these. Often they seem in their poetry to be telling us
merely how they refuse to write poems and not how they
wish to write them. It is like the bridge-movement of the
Choral symphony; a continual rejection of themes and
rhythms, but without anything positive to follow.

Mr. Eliot is an extreme example of this process. His
cleverness, which is also extreme, expresses itself almost
entirely in rejections; his verse is full of derisive
reminiscences of poets who have wearied him. As for
subject-matter, that also is all refusal; it can be expressed in one phrase; again and again he tells us that he
is 'fed-up' with art, with life, with people, with things.
Everyone for him seems to be a parody of exhausted and out-
of-date emotions. To read his verse is to be thrown
deliberately into that mood which sometimes overcomes one
in the streets of a crowded town when one is tired and
bewildered, the mood in which all passers-by look like
over-expressive marionettes pretending to be alive and all
the more mechanical for their pretence. In such a mood
one is morbidly aware of town squalor; everything seems to
have been used and re-used again and again; the symbol of
all life is cigarette ends and stale cigarette smoke; the
very conversation is like that, it has been said a thousand times and is repeated mechanically; in fact all
things are done from habit, which has mastered life and
turned it into an endlessly recurring squalor.

[Quotes 'Portrait of a Lady', CPP, p. 20, 'You will see me' to 'ideas right or wrong?']

'Recalling things that other people have desired' - Mr. Eliot's verse is always doing that; and, like jesting Pilate, he will not wait for an answer to his own question - 'Are these ideas right or wrong?' He asks it and goes on to something else with a hope, that is too like despair, that something may come of it. But nothing does come -

> And I must borrow every changing shape
> To fing expression ... dance, dance,
> Like a dancing bear,
> Cry like a parrot, chatter like an ape.
> Let us take the air, in a tobacco trance -

That may be satire on some one else, but it does exactly express the effect of his own verse, not once or twice but all the time. The habit of those whom he describes has got into his own technique, into his very way of experiencing; he, like the lesser romantics, has found too easy a way of functioning, and he functions and functions just as narrowly as if he were still writing about the Holy Grail:-

[Quotes 'Preludes', CPP, p. 22, Part II.]

This might be a prelude to something, some passion or reality that would suddenly spring out of it; but with Mr. Eliot it is not. Near the end, after an enumeration of all the squalors he can think of, he says:-

> I am moved by fancies that are curled
> Around these images and cling:
> The motion of some infinitely gentle
> Infinitely suffering thing.

That being so, why does he not tell us about it? It might be interesting; but no. After this momentary relenting, this flicker of natural feeling, he ends:-

> Wipe your hand across your mouth, and laugh;
> The worlds revolve like ancient women
> Gathering fuel in vacant lots.

But if that is so, why write verse about it; why not commit suicide? Art presumes that life is worth living, and must not, except dramatically or in a moment of exasperation or irony, say that it isn't. But Mr. Eliot writes only to say that it isn't; and he does not do it so well

as the author of Ecclesiastes, who at least keeps the
momentum and gusto of all the experiences he pretends to
have exhausted.   For Mr. Eliot -

> Midnight shakes the memory
> As a madman shakes a dead geranium.

There we are reminded a little of his countryman Poe,
and 'The Love Song of J. Alfred Prufrock' is like Poe even
in its curious and over-conscious metrical effects.   They
seem to be, as so often in Poe, independent of the poem
itself, as if the writer could not attain to a congruity
between the tune beating in his head and any subject-
matter.   In this poem he is really, with the poet part of
him, questing for beauty, but the other part refuses it
with a kind of nausea:-

[Quotes 'Prufrock', CPP, pp. 16-17, 'Shall I part my hair'
to end.]

So it ends.   Human voices for Mr. Eliot drown everything;
he cannot get away from his disgust of them; he is 'fed
up' with them, with their volubility and lack of meaning.
'Words, words, words' might be his motto; for in his
verse he seems to hate them and to be always expressing
his hatred of them, in words.   If he could he would write
songs without words; blindly he seeks for a medium free of
associations, not only for a tune but also for notes that
no one has sung before.   But all this is mere habit; art
means the acceptance of a medium as of life; and Mr.
Eliot does not convince us that his weariness is anything
but a habit, an anti-romantic reaction, a new Byronism
which he must throw off if he is not to become a recurring
decimal in his fear of being a mere vulgar fraction.

18. ROBERT NICHOLS, AN IRONIST, 'OBSERVER'

18 April 1920, 7

Nichols (1893-1944) was a minor Georgian poet.

Mr. Eliot is known to the world at large through the

columns of the 'Athenaeum' as a widely erudite critic
possessed of a natural distinction in style and such a
mordant perspicacity as is hardly to be matched in British
or North American letters to-day. To some few else he is
known also as the poet of 'Prufrock.' The Ovid Press has
now gathered up 'Prufrock' and the later 'Poems,' and displays them to the world in one of the most beautiful productions of the modern press. The paper and printing
(with initials and colophon by Mr. E.A. Wadsworth) are
superb.

Let me say it at once: Mr. Eliot is, more especially in
his later work, emphatically not an 'easy' poet. Nor is
the reason far to seek. Mr. Eliot mostly does not deal
with what are popularly considered the main streams of
emotion. Not for him the generalised joys or sorrows of a
Whitman or a Shelley, nor such rhythms as roll the con-
senting reader he scarcely knows whither upon the bosom of
the flood. No; Mr. Eliot is not going to appear to lose
his head or suffer the reader to lose his. Mr. Eliot,
like the poet in 'Candida,' muses to himself and the world
overhears him; but not before he wishes it to; no, not by
a long chalk. For, you see, the stuff of his musings is
complicated, and Mr. Eliot does not pretend it is easy.
'The primrose by the river's brim' is for Mr. Eliot most
emphatically neither a simple primrose nor a possible in-
gredient in a Disraelian salad. It is primarily something
that someone else has written about, and which has thus
become invested with such associations as can but destroy
the innocence of Mr. Eliot's eye and apprehension. The
pity is, he seems to hint, that there have been so many
poems and, yes, it must be confessed, so few really satisfactory salads:-

[Quotes 'Prufrock', CPP, pp. 14-15, 'And I have known the
eyes' to 'how should I begin?']

It is, perhaps, this sense of everything having happened a trifle earlier in the day that gives me an impression of there being a preponderance of afternoons in Mr.
Eliot's poetry: -

[Quotes 'Portrait of a Lady', CPP, p. 18, 'Among the
smoke' to 'left unsaid'.]

Or, if not of afternoons, of early evenings:-

Let us go then, you and I,
When the evening is spread out against the sky
Like a patient etherized upon a table.

Ah, that patient etherized upon the table! It is not the
evening only lying there in such lassitude; it is Mr.
Eliot's perpetual spectator; it is the wistful and ironic
evocation of all super-sophisticated persons; it is, alas!
our cultured selves at this late and almost, it would
sometimes seem, deliquescent stage of civilisation.
Under the spell of Mr. Eliot's gentle and wavering
rhythms we become slightly etherized, and when the spell
has sufficiently o'ercrowed our animal spirits we proceed, at once investigator and investigated, to inspect
our emotions 'as if a magic lantern threw the nerves in
patterns on a screen'; a doleful piece of introspective
dissection, a lamentable appraisement. Our scientific
precision but informs us the nature of our trouble:-

> You will see me any morning in the park
> Reading the comics and the sporting page.
> Particularly I remark
> An English countess goes upon the stage.
>
> I keep my countenance,
> I remain self-possessed
> Except when a street piano, mechanical and tired
> Reiterates some worn-out common song
> With the smell of hyacinths across the garden
> Recalling things that other people have desired.

And when the scientist has done the artist steps in with
his comedian melancholy to draw this conclusion:-

> Though I have seen my head (grown slightly bald)
>   brought in upon a platter,
> I am no prophet - and here's no great matter;
> I have seen the moment of my greatness flicker,
> And I have seen the eternal Footman hold my coat, and
>   snicker,
> And in short, I was afraid.

The irony of things-as-they-are haunts the poet as it
haunted his forerunner Laforgue and levies board-wages
upon all his emotions. Yet the poet has his moments:-

> I am moved by fancies that are curled
> Around these images and cling:
> The notion of some infinitely gentle
> Infinitely suffering thing.

The moment, however, will not last, and I cannot but
puzzle whether it is not that capacity for enjoying the

quintessential emotions precipitated from the still of
literature which Mr. Eliot so superabundantly possesses
and cultivates, that has vitiated his taste for those
distractingly heterogeneous emotions which are the
material offered him as an artist by Life itself. Irony
is a good servant, but a bad master; the Footman, however
eternal, should be kept in his place even if one is only
the perennially passing visitor to the earthly mansion.
Mr. Eliot has a taste for the more terrible realities - if
he would only indulge it. He has the power of evoking
'the still, sad music of humanity' from the most quotid-
ian, sordid, and apparently unpromising of materials.
Here is an interior - as unqualified in statement as a
Sickert, but in addition informed with something of the
understanding and compassion of a Rembrandt:-

[Quotes 'Preludes', CPP, pp. 22-3, Part III.]

    It is a pity, I feel, that Mr. Eliot seems in his later
poems to have acquired a habit of sheering away from so
immediate and poignant a reality in order to make remote
and somewhat generalised fun about 'The Boston Evening
Transcript,' the visit of a Cambridge intellectual to New
England, the editor of the 'Spectator,' and the Established Church.

19. DESMOND MacCARTHY, NEW POETS, T.S. ELIOT, 'NEW STATESMAN'

8 January 1921, vol. xvi, 418-20

Sir Desmond MacCarthy (1877-1952) was educated at Eton and
Trinity College, Cambridge, where he became a friend of
G.E. Moore, Bertrand Russell, Lytton Strachey, Leonard
Woolf and others. He was a distinguished literary and
drama critic. He edited 'Life and Letters' and contributed regularly to the 'New Statesman', of which he was
literary editor in the 1920s.

When two people are discussing modern poetry together the
name of T.S. Eliot is sure to crop up. If one of them is
old-fashioned, and refuses to see merit in the young poets
who attempt to do more than retail 'the ancient divinations

of the Muse,' the other is sure to say sooner or later:
'But what about Eliot? You may dislike *vers libre* (I
admit it is easy to write it badly) and attempts to mani-
pulate in verse the emotional coefficients of modern
experience, still what do you think of Eliot? You cannot
dismiss him.' And the other (I do not think I am attribut-
ing to him an unusual amount of sensibility or judgment)
will reply: 'Well ... yes ... Eliot ... I grant you there
seems to be something in him.' I wish to try to find out
here what that 'something' is which recommends the poems
of Mr. Eliot, if not to the taste, at least to the literary judgment of even those who think the young poets are,
for the most part, on the wrong path.

Mr. Eliot, like Mr. Ezra Pound, is an American. This
is not a very important fact about him, still it has its
importance. Both poets resemble each other in two
respects, one of which I will deal with at once, in connection with their nationality. When either of them
publishes a book, they publish at the same time that they
are scholars, who have at least five languages at command,
and considerable out-of-the-way erudition. The allusions
in their poems are learned, oblique, and obscure; the
mottoes they choose for their poems are polyglot, the
names that occur to them as symbolic of this or that are
known only to book-minded people. In short, they both
share the national love of bric-à-brac. A half-forgotten
name, an echo from a totally forgotten author, a mossy
scrap of old philosophy exercise over their imaginations
the charm that the patina of time upon a warming-pan or
piece of worm-eaten furniture does upon their more frivo-
lous compatriots. Both poets are illegitimate descend-
ants of the poet Browning, in whom the instinct of the
collector was equally strong - with a difference I shall
presently mark. Both share with Browning a passion for
adapting the vivid colloquialism of contemporary speech to
poetic purposes. It has not been grasped so far as I
know by critics, that linguistically Browning stands in
the same relation to Victorian poets as Wordsworth *thought*
he himself did as a poet, and in a measure truly, to the
poets of the eighteenth century. Mr. Eliot has woven a
very remarkable literary style, composed in almost equal
parts of literary and erudite allusions and crisp collo-
quialisms, in which to clothe the emotions he wishes to
express. Let me make here at once the most adverse comment I have to make on his work, namely, that he is always
in danger of becoming a pedant, a pedant being one who
assumes that his own reading, wide or narrow, is common
property or ought to be, so that any reference he makes
is of general validity and bound to wake the same echoes

in his reader's mind as it does in his own. Collector of
bric-à-brac, mystificator, mandarin, loving to exclude as
well as to touch intimately and quickly his readers, he
would be lost as a poet were it not for his cautious and
very remarkable sincerity. When a reader seizes an
obscure reference he is flattered; it gives him a little
thrill. But though this thrill may seal him one of the
poet's admirers, it is not an aesthetic thrill. In the
same way even the verbal obscurity of a poet may tell in
his favour, once he has convinced us that his meaning is
worth grasping; in the effort to get at his meaning we
may actually get his phrases by heart, and the phrase
which sticks always acquires merit in our eyes. I do not
say that Mr. Eliot's reputation owes much to these causes,
but that they have helped it in some quarters I believe.
Certainly he is a poet whom to admire at all fervently
marks one down as among those who are certainly not a prey
to the obvious.

FitzGerald did not like Browning (partly because he knew
Tennyson very well perhaps), and in one of his letters he
throws out a phrase about 'that old Jew's curiosity shop.'
Now Browning's curiosity shop is a huge rambling place,
cobwebby, crammed, Rembrandtesque, while Mr. Eliot's
reminds one rather of those modern curiosity shops in
which a few choice objects, a white Chinese rhinoceros,
a pair of Queen Anne candlesticks, an enamelled box, a
Renaissance trinket or two, a small ebony idol are set out
at carefully calculated distances on a neat cloth in the
window (one sees at a glance they are very expensive -
no bargains here); but there is behind no vast limbo of
armour, cabinets, costumes, death-masks, sword-sticks,
elephants' tusks, dusty folios, gigantic cracked old
mirrors, sedan chairs, wigs, spinets, and boxes, containing pell-mell, watch-keys, miniatures, lockets, snuffers,
and tongue-scrapers. The man who keeps the shop is not a
creature with a Rabelaisian gusto for acquisition, whose
hand shakes with excitement as he holds up the candle,
expatiating volubly, but a sedate, slightly quizzical,
aloof individual - a selector, perhaps, rather than a collector to whose maw the most indigestible treasures are
delicious nutriment. Such is the difference between
Browning's and Mr. Eliot's attitude towards the harvest of
erudition.

I have compared them so far only to differentiate them,
moreover Mr. Eliot's subject is always the ingredients of
the modern mind and never, as was often the case with
Browning, of the minds and souls of men and women who
lived long ago. But it is instructive to compare them
also at points in which they resemble each other, always

remembering that the temperament of the elder poet is hot,
responsive, ebullient, and simple, while that of the
younger is subtle, tender, disillusioned, complicated and
cool. Both are possessed by the passion of curiosity to a
greater degree than is common with poets; in both the analytical interest is extremely strong. Consequently, Mr.
Eliot, too, loves to exploit that borderland between prose
and poetry which yields as much delight to the intellect
as to the emotions - if not more. Most of his work is
done in that region, and the most obvious thing to say
about it as a whole is that even when it is not poetry it
is always good literature. Reread 'The Love Song of J.
Alfred Prufrock' or 'Portrait of a Lady'; it will be
obvious that he not only owes much to the diction and
rhythm of Browning, but that he is doing the same thing as
Browning for a more queasy, uneasy, diffident, complex
generation. Here is the opening of the 'Portrait':

[Quotes CPP, p. 18, 'Among the smoke' to 'hair and finger-
tips'.]

'The latest Pole transmit the Preludes, and through his
hair and finger-tips' - is not that pure Browning? Like
Browning, too, Mr. Eliot's favourite form is a soliloquy
of the spirit or monologue. Many of his poems thus fall
between the lyrical and the dramatic form; they are little
mental monodramas, broken now and then after the manner of
Browning by a line or two of dialogue or by exclamations
such as are common in Browning's poems ('Here comes my
husband from his whist'), or by asides to the reader; but
these asides never have the argumentative, buttonholing
quality of Browning's. There is nothing of the impassioned advocate, so characteristic in Browning, in Mr.
Eliot. He is rather a scrupulous, cool analyst of
extremely personal and elusive modes of feeling, and his
method (this is his most distinctive characteristic as a
writer) is to convey an elusive shade of feeling, or a
curious, and usually languid, drift of emotion, by means
of the rapid evocation of vivid objects and scenes. He
does not care whether or not there is a logical or even a
casual association between these objects he presents to us
one after the other. He is like a dumb man who is trying
to explain to us what he is feeling by taking up one
object after another and showing it to us, not intending
that we should infer that the object is the subject of his
thoughts, but that we should feel the particular emotion
appropriate to it. This makes his poems hard even when
they are not (and they often are) too obscure. The reader
is always liable to dwell too long on these scenes or

objects which he evokes so skilfully, instead of just
skimming swiftly off them, as it were, an emotion they
suggest, and then passing on to the next. A poet who
thinks in pictures and allusions, and expects us to understand his mood and thought by catching one after the other
the gleams of light flashed off by his phrases must often
be obscure, because compact phrases (Mr. Eliot's are
extraordinarily compact) are apt to scatter refracted
gleams which point in different directions. Indeed, we
are often expected to catch not one of these flashes but
several. First, however, let me give an example of his
method of thinking in pictures or symbols. Take one of
his later poems, 'Gerontion.' The whole poem is a description at once of an old man's mind, and of a mood which recurs often in Mr. Eliot's poems, namely, that of one to
whom life is largely a process of being stifled, slowly
hemmed in and confused; to whom experience, truthfully
apprehended, gives only tantalisingly rare excuses for
the exercise of the lyrical faculty of joy within him.
His (Mr. Eliot's) problem as a poet is the problem of the
adjustment of his sense of beauty to these sorry facts.
His weakness as a poet is that he seems rather to have
felt the glory of life through literature; while his reflection of all that contrasts with it has the exciting
precision of direct apprehension. 'The contemplation of
the horrid or sordid by the artist,' he says in one of his
criticisms, 'is the necessary and negative aspect of the
impulse towards beauty.' In him this impulse in a negative direction is far the strongest of the two.

[Quotes 'Gerontion', CPP, p. 37, 'Here I am' to 'windy
spaces'.]

   Now, in the first verse of what proves later a dark
intricate poem the symbolism is obvious; yet it is an
example of the characteristics which make Mr. Eliot
obscure. When the old man says he has not fought in the
salt marshes, etc., we know that he means that he has not
tasted the violent romance of life. We must not dwell too
literally on the phrases by which he builds up the impression of sinister dilapidation and decay - 'Blistered in
Brussels, patched and peeled in London,' etc. In reading
Mr. Eliot an undue literalness must at all costs be
avoided.

   I that was near your heart was removed therefrom
   To lose beauty in terror, terror in inquisition.
   I have lost my passion: why should I need to keep it
   Since what is kept must be adulterated?

These lines, which occur in the same poem, are perhaps
the most personal he has published. Mr. Eliot has something of the self-protective pride, reserve and sensibility of the dandy - like Laforgue. His impulse is not to
express himself in poetry, but to express some mood, some
aspect of life which needs expression. He sets about it
coolly, like a man making up a prescription, taking down
now this bottle, now that from the shelf, adding an acid
from one and a glowing tincture from another. He belongs
to that class of poets whose interest is in making a work
of art, not in expressing themselves; and the fact that
his subject-matter, on the other hand, is psychological
and intimate, makes the result particularly piquant. But
even the works of the most detached poet, if he is not
imitating old poems, have an affinity to each other which
has its roots in temperament. The temperament, as in
Laforgue's work, which shows itself in Mr. Eliot's is that
of the ironic sentimentalist.

> But where is the penny world I bought
> To eat with Pipit behind the screen?

he asks, after concluding that he will not want Pipit in
Heaven.

> Where are the eagles and the trumpets?

> Buried beneath some snow-deep Alps.
> Over buttered scones and crumpets
>   Weeping, weeping multitudes
> Droop in a hundred A.B.C.'s.

The contrast between peeps into glory and the sordidness
of life is never far from his mind. (It is in literature
that he himself has seen the eagles and heard the trumpets - not in life.) His style has two other marked
characteristics. His phrases are frequently echoes, yet
he is the reverse of an imitative poet. They are echoes
tuned to a new context which changes their subtlety. He
does not steal phrases; he borrows their aroma.

> Defunctive music under sea
>   Passed seaward with the passing bell
> Slowly: the God Hercules
>   Had left him, that had loved him well.

> The horses, under the axletree
>   Beat up the dawn from Istria
> With even feet. Her shuttered barge
>   Burned on the water all the day.

Just as 'weeping, weeping multitudes' in the other poem
quoted above, is an echo from Blake, so 'Defunctive music'
comes from 'The Phoenix and the Turtle' and 'Her barge
burned on the water' of course from 'Antony and Cleopatra.'
But the point is that the poet means to draw a subtle
whiff of Cleopatra and poetic passion across our minds, in
order that we may feel a peculiar emotion towards the sordid little siren in the poem itself, just as he also uses
later a broken phrase or two from 'The Merchant of Venice'
for the sake of reminding us of Shakespeare's Jew, compared with the 'Bleistein' of the poem. His other characteristic is the poetic one of intensity; it is the exciting concision of his phrasing which appeals especially to
his contemporaries:

> I should have been a pair of ragged claws
> Scuttling across the floors of silent seas

> ...the smoke that rises from the pipes
> Of lonely men in shirt sleeves, leaning out of windows.

He is master of the witty phrase, too,

> My smile falls heavily among the bric-à-brac,

and is, to my mind, the most interesting of 'the new
poets.'

20. CLIVE BELL, PLUS DE JAZZ, 'NEW REPUBLIC'

21 September 1921, vol. xxviii, 94

Bell (1881-1964) was an English art critic and journalist.
In 1906 he married Vanessa, the sister of Virginia Woolf.
An important member of the Bloomsbury Group, his central
ideas were set out in 'Art' (1914) and 'Civilization'
(1928).
    This is an extract from a very much longer essay on
jazz and its influence on modern art.

Similarly, it may claim Mr. T.S. Eliot - a poet of uncommon merit and unmistakably in the great line - whose

agonizing labors seem to have been eased somewhat by the comfortable ministrations of a black and grinning muse. Midwifery, to be sure, seems an odd occupation for a lady whom one pictures rather in the rôle of a flapper: but a midwife was what the poet needed and in that capacity she has served him.   Apparently it is only by adopting a demurely irreverent attitude, by being primly insolent, and by playing the devil with the instrument of Shakespeare and Milton, that Mr. Eliot is able occasionally to deliver himself of one of those complicated and remarkable imaginings of his: apparently it is only in language, of an exquisite purity so far as material goes, but twisted and ragged out of easy recognition that these nurslings can be swathed.   As for surprise, that, presumably, is an emotion which the author of 'Ara Vos Prec' is not unwilling to provoke.   Be that as it may, Mr. Eliot is about the best of our living poets, and, like Stravinsky, he is as much a product of the Jazz movement as so good an artist can be of any.

'Poems'

New York, February 1920
(the American edition of 'Ara Vos Prec')

21. MARION STROBEL, PERILOUS LEAPING, 'POETRY'

June 1920, vol. xvi, 157–9

Marion Strobel (1895–1966), an American novelist, poet
and critic, was associate editor of 'Poetry' from 1919 to
1924, and co-editor from 1943 to 1949.

Mr. Eliot evidently believes that a view from a mountain
cannot be appreciated unless the ascent is a perilous
leaping from crag to crag. At least the first pages of
his latest book (an American reprint, with a few additions, of 'Prufrock and Other Observations,' published in
1917 by the London 'Egoist') are filled with intellectual
curios – curios that form a prodigious array of hazards
leading up to the big poems. Lovers of exercise will find
their minds flexed, if not inert, after following the
allusions and ellipses of 'Gerontion.' It is as though,
in this initial poem, Mr. Eliot went through his morning
callisthenics saying: 'This, my good people is a small part
of what I do to give you a poem;' or more accurately perhaps: 'Come – work with me – show you deserve true
beauty.' And with a 'Whoop-la' – for he is in beautiful
condition – he swings from romance to realism, to religion, to history, to philosophy, to science, while you and
I climb pantingly, wearily, after him, clinging to a few
familiar words, and looking from time to time at sign-
posts along the way to reassure ourselves of the fact that
this does lead us to true beauty.
   The poems guaranteed-to-produce-white-blood-corpuscles-

in-any-brain come before page 37 (a specific hint for the
faint-hearted). Fortified by a dictionary, an encyclo-
pedia, an imagination, and a martyr's spirit, even these
may be enjoyed. They are certainly remarkable for their
mystifying titles, their coy complexities of content, and
their line-consuming words. What, for instance, could be
more naive than the introduction to Sweeney in 'Sweeney
Erect':

> Paint me a cavernous waste shore
>   Cast in the unstilled Cyclades,
> Paint me the bold anfractuous rocks
>   Faced by the snarled and yelping seas.
>
> Display me Aeolus above
>   Reviewing the insurgent gales
> Which tangle Ariadne's hair
>   And swell with haste the perjured sails.
>
> Morning stirs the feet and hands
>   (Nausicaa and Polypheme).
> Gesture of orang-outang
>   Rises from the sheets in steam....
>
> Sweeney addressed full length to shave....

However, in among these stepping-stones to the poems
that are worth a great deal of trouble to get - though one
resents being reminded of the fact by Mr. Eliot himself -
are one or two resting-places, such as the whimsical
pathos of 'A Cooking Egg,' the gentle crudity of 'Sweeney
Among the Nightingales,' and the sophisticated humor of
'The Hippopotamus.' And I must further acknowledge that
Mr. Eliot's humor is the cultivated progeny of a teasing
spirit of fun and a keen audacity - the mixture of the Zoo
and the True Church in 'The Hippopotamus' will tickle the
palate of the most blasé epicurean.
    And now, feeling that the ascent has been long and
hard, we reach the summit, and are repaid by reading 'The
Love Song of J. Alfred Prufrock' and 'Portrait of a Lady.'
These two poems are so far superior to the gymnastics that
precede, and to the interesting versatilities that follow
them, that they must be classed alone.
    'Prufrock,' which was first published by 'Poetry' in
1915, is a psychological study of that rather piteous
figure, the faded philandering middle-aged cosmopolite; a
scrupulous psychological study, for the pervasive beauty
of the imagery, the rhythms used, and the nice repetitions, all emphasize the sympathetic accuracy of the context. For instance the three lines:

I grow old.... I grow....
I shall wear the bottoms of my trousers rolled.

Shall I part my hair behind? Do I dare to eat a peach?

In 'Portrait of a Lady' we find a like startling acuteness for details, with a dramatic ending which is a fitting
example for the definition, 'L'art est un étonnement
heureux.'
And possibly - possibly - it is wise to work up to
'J. Alfred Prufrock' and 'Portrait of a Lady,' and to
slide pleasantly down again on the humor and ironies of
the poems following; for we might become dizzy if we found
ourselves on a mountain without the customary foundations.

22. E.E. CUMMINGS, T.S. ELIOT, 'DIAL'

June 1920, vol. lxviii, 781-4

Edward Estlin Cummings (1894-1962) emerged as a leading
poet of the American avant-garde during the 1920s. His
'Selected Poems, 1923-1958' was published by Faber & Faber
in 1960. Eliot gave his opinion of Cummings in a letter
to Charles Norman dated 13 September 1957: 'I have a very
high opinion of Mr Cummings as a poet, in spite of my dislike of his typography' (cited by Charles Norman in
'E.E. Cummings: The Magic-Maker' (New York, 1964),
p. 120). Norman also reports some remarks of Malcolm
Cowley's, dealing with Cummings's view of 'The Waste Land':
'E.E. Cummings asked me why Eliot couldn't write his own
lines instead of borrowing from dead poets. In his
remarks I sensed a feeling almost of betrayal.'
Reprinted in 'A Miscellany', edited by George J. Firmage and published in 1958 as a privately printed edition.
The essay may be found in the edition of 1966, published
in London by Peter Owen, on pp. 25-9.

The somewhat recently published 'Poems' is an accurate and
uncorpulent collection of instupidities. Between the
negative and flabby and ponderous and little bellowings of
those multitudinous contemporaries who are obstinately
always 'unconventional' or else 'modern' at the expense of

being (what is most difficult) alive, Mr. T.S. Eliot
inserts the positive and deep beauty of his skilful and
immediate violins ... the result is at least thrilling.
     He has done the trick for us before. In one of the was
it two 'Blasts' skilfully occurred, more than successfully framed by much soundness noise, the 'Rhapsody' and
'Preludes.' In one of the God knows nobody knows how many
there will be 'Others', startlingly enshrined in a good deal
of noiseless sound 'Prufrock' and 'Portrait of a Lady'
carefully happened. But 'this slim little volume' as a
reviewer might say achieves a far more forceful presentation, since it competes with and defeats not mere blas-
ters and differentists but τὸ 'ἐν-s and origens and all
that is Windily and Otherwise enervate and talkative.
     Some Notes on the Blank Verse of Christopher Marlowe
are, to a student of Mr. T.S., unnecessarily illuminating:

     ...this style which secures its emphasis by always
     hesitating on the end of caricature at the right
     moment...
     ...this intense and serious and indubitably great
     poetry, which, like some great painting and sculpture,
     attains its effects by something not unlike caricature.

Even without this somewhat mighty hint, this something
which for all its slipperyness is after all a door-knob to
be grasped by anyone who wishes to enter the 'some great'
Art-Parlours, ourselves might have constructed a possibly
logical development from 'Preludes' and 'Rhapsody on a
Windy Night' along 'J. Alfred' and 'Portrait' up the two
Sweeneys to let us say 'The Hippopotamus.' We might have
been disgracefully inspired to the extent of projecting as
arithmetical, not to say dull, a classification of Eliot
as that of Picasso by the author of certain rudimentary
and not even ecclesiastical nonsense entitled 'The
Caliph's Design.' But (it is an enormous but) our so
doing necessarily would have proved worthless, precisely
for the reason that before an Eliot we become alive or
intense as we become intense or alive before a Cézanne or
a Lachaise: or since, as always in the case of superficial
because vertical analysis, to attempt the boxing and
labeling of genius is to involve in something inescapably
rectilinear - a formula, for example - not the artist but
the 'critic.'
     However, we have a better reason. The last word on
caricature was spoken as far back as 1913. 'My dear it's
all so perfectly ridiculous' remarked to an elderly Boston
woman an elderly woman of Boston, as the twain made their
noticeably irrevocable exeunt from that most colossal of

all circusses, the (then in Boston) International. (1)
'My dear if some of the pictures didn't look like something it wouldn't be so amusing' observed, on the threshold, the e.B.w., adding 'I should hate to have my portrait painted by any of those "artists"!' 'They'll never
make a statue of *me*' stated with polyphiloprogenitive conviction the e.w.o.B.

Sway in the wind like a field of ripe corn.

Says Mr. Eliot.
   In the case of 'Poems,' to state frankly and briefly
what we like may be as good a way as another of exhibiting
our numerous 'critical' incapacities. We like first, to
speak from an altogether personal standpoint, that any and
all attempts to lassoo Mr. Eliot with the Vorticist
emblem have signally failed. That Mr. E. Pound (with
whose Caesarlike refusal of the kingly crown we are
entirely familiar) may not have coiled the rope whose
fatal noose has, over a few unfortunate Britons, exclud-
ingly rather than includingly settled, makes little or no
difference since the hand which threw the lariat and the
bronc' which threw the steers alike belong to him. Be it
said of this peppy gentleman that, insofar as he is responsible for possibly one-half of the most alive poetry
and probably all of the least intense prose committed,
during the last few years, in the American and English
languages, he merits something beyond the incoherent
abuse and inchoate adoration which have become his daily
breakfast-food - merits in fact the doffing of many
kelleys; that insofar as he is one of history's greatest
advertisers he is an extraordinarily useful bore, much
like a rivetter which whatever you may say asserts the
progress of a skyscraper; whereas that insofar as he is
responsible for the overpasting of an at least attractive
manifesto, 'Ezra Pound,' with an at least pedantic war-
cry, 'Vorticism,' he deserves to be drawn and quartered by
the incomparably trite brush of the great and the only and
the Wyndham and the Lewis - if only as an adjectival gar-
nish to that nounlike effigy of our hero by his friend
The Hieratic Buster. Let us therefore mention the fact,
for it seems to us worthy of notice - that at no moment
do T.S. Eliot and E.P. propaganda simultaneously inhabit
our consciousness.
   Second, we like that not any of 'Poems'' fifty-one
pages fails to impress us with an overwhelming sense of
technique. By technique we do not mean a great many
things, including: anything static, a school, a noun, a
slogan, a formula, These Three For Instant Beauty, Ars Est

Celare, Hasn't Scratched Yet, Professor Woodberry, Grape
Nuts. By technique we do mean one thing: the alert hatred
of normality which, through the lips of a tactile and co-
hesive adventure, asserts that nobody in general and some
one in particular is incorrigibly and actually alive.
This some one is, it would seem, the extremely great
artist: or, he who prefers above everything and within
everything the unique dimension of intensity, which it
amuses him to substitute in us for the comforting and comfortable furniture of reality. If we examine the means
through which this substitution is allowed by Mr. Eliot to
happen in his reader, we find that they include: a vocabulary almost brutally tuned to attain distinctness; an
extraordinarily tight orchestration of the shapes of
sound; the delicate and careful murderings – almost invari-
ably interpreted, internally as well as terminally, through
near-rhyme and rhyme – of established tempos by oral
rhythms. Here is an example of Eliot's tuning:

> Apeneck Sweeney spreads his knees
> Letting his arms hang down to laugh,
> The zebra stripes along his jaw
> Swelling to maculate giraffe.

Here is a specimen of his compact orchestration:

> I have seen them riding seaward on the waves
> Combing the white hair of the waves blown back
> When the wind blows the water white and black.
>
> We have lingered in the chambers of the sea
> By sea-girls wreathed with seaweed red and brown
> Till human voices wake us, and we drown.

Here is Eliot himself directing the exquisitely and
thoroughly built thing:

> His laughter was submarine and profound
> Like the old man of the sea's
> Hidden under coral islands
> Where worried bodies of drowned men drift down in
>   the green silence,
> Dropping from fingers of surf.

To come to our final like, which it must be admitted is
also our largest – we like that no however cautiously
attempted dissection of Mr T.S.'s sensitivity begins to
touch a few certain lines whereby become big and blundering
and totally unskilful our altogether unnecessary fingers:

[Quotes 'Rhapsody on a Windy Night', CPP, p. 25, 'The
lamp hummed' to 'a paper rose'.]

At the risk of being jeered for an 'uncritical' remark we
mention that this is one of the few huge fragilities before which comment is disgusting.

Note

1 The International Exposition of Modern Art, better
   known as the Armory Show, was held in the 69th Regiment
   Armory in New York City from 15 February to 15 March
   1913. A portion of the exhibition later travelled to
   Chicago and Boston. The show was highly controversial
   and of major importance in awakening Americans to the
   new art of modernism.

23. MARK VAN DOREN, ANGLO-SAXON ADVENTURES IN VERSE,
'NATION' (NEW YORK)

26 June 1920, vol. cx, 856a

Mark Van Doren (1894-1972), an American critic and poet,
was literary editor of the 'Nation' from 1924 to 1928.
His 'Collected Poems' was published in 1939.
    This is an extract from a longer review which surveyed
current productions in poetry.

But the most amazing man is T.S. Eliot, whose first for-
mally collected volume, long awaited by those who think
they recognize downright, diabolical genius when they see
it, is distinctly and preciously an event. It is not
known how long the author of 'The Hippopotamus,' 'Sweeney
Among the Nightingales,' 'The Love Song of J. Alfred Prufrock,' 'Rhapsody on a Windy Night,' and 'The Boston
Evening Transcript' will remain in England, whither he
went two years ago to set up as a critic. Whatever
happens, it is hoped that he keeps somehow to poetry.
For he is the most proficient satirist now writing in
verse, the uncanniest clown, the devoutest monkey, the
most picturesque ironist; and aesthetically considered, he

is one of the profoundest symbolists. His sympathy and
his vision travel together, striking like bitter lightning
here, flowering damply and suddenly like mushrooms there.
Three extracts from the twenty-four poems are not enough,
but must do:

[Quotes 'Prufrock', CPP, p. 13, 'The yellow fog' to 'fell
asleep'; 'Rhapsody on a Windy Night', CPP, p. 25, 'Half-
past two' to 'I held him'; 'Morning at the Window', CPP,
p. 27.]

Mr. Eliot will never be popular at this rate. But when
will he not have readers?

24. LOUIS UNTERMEYER, IRONY DE LUXE, 'FREEMAN'

30 June 1920, vol. i, 381-2

Untermeyer (1885-1977), an American poet and critic, gave
a general account of Eliot's work up to and including
'Murder in the Cathedral' in 'Modern American Poetry' (New
York, 1942), pp. 420-4.

For two or three years the poetry of T.S. Eliot has been
championed warmly by a few protagonists and condemned even
more heatedly by many who suspected the young author of
all things from charlatanry to literary anarchism. Those
who have read it have talked of this product, not as
poetry, but as a precipitant, a touchstone; they pronounced 'Eliot' as though the name were either a shibbo-
leth or a red flag. Controversy was difficult. For, with
the exception of two longish poems and half a dozen
scattered verses, this native of St. Louis continued to
publish his occasional pieces in England and threatened at
the age of thirty-one to take on the proportions of a
myth. This volume then, is doubly welcome, for it enables
one not only to estimate Eliot's actual achievement but to
appraise his influence.
    This influence, although exceedingly limited, is indis-
putable. And it is even more remarkable when one perceives that the present volume, including all of Eliot's
poetical works, contains just twenty-four examples, five

of them being in French. In these two dozen pieces there
can be heard, beneath muffled brilliancies, two distinct
and distinctive idioms. The first embodies the larger
curve, the more flexible music; in it are held the shifting delicacies and strange nuances of 'The Love Song of
J. Alfred Prufrock' and the sensitized 'Portrait of a
Lady.' It is the idiom which Conrad Aiken has exploited
(and amplified) in 'The Jig of Forslin,' 'Senlin,' and
'Nocturne of Remembered Spring.' The second accent is
sharper, swifter, more obviously sparkling. A far more
definite tone of voice, it lends itself so easily to
imitation that it has quickly captivated most of the
younger British insurgents. Osbert Sitwell, whose anti-
war verses are still remembered, frankly models his new
quatrains on the plan of 'Sweeney Among the Nightingales'
and gives us (in part) such experiments in satiric futur-
ism as:

> The dusky king of Malabar
> Is chief of Eastern potentates;
> Yet he wears no clothes, except
> The jewels that decency dictates....
>
> But Mrs. Freudenthal, in furs,
> From Brioche dreams to mild surprise
> Awakes; the music throbs and purrs.
> The 'cellist with albino eyes
>
> Rivets attention; is, in fact,
> The very climax; pink eyes flash
> Whenever, nervous and pain-racked,
> He hears the drums and cymbals clash.

Herbert Read, another of the younger poets, echoes the
strain with slight variations in his recent 'Huskisson
Sacred and Profane.' Even Robert Nichols, turning from
his precise Shakespearian sonnets, his academic nymphs
and correctly English fauns, indites 'The Spring Son,' the
quatrains of which run like:

> Sinclair has bought a new top hat,
>   A jetty coat and honey gloves,
> A cane topped by a glass-eyed cat,
>   And Sinclair goes to meet his loves.
>
> Sinclair would make his muslin choice, -
>   Spring and his father say he must;
> Corah has ankles and a voice,
>   Nancy has French and a neat bust.

It is but a step to the more acerb original.   Here are
two illustrative segments from Eliot himself:

Apeneck Sweeney spreads his knees
Letting his arms hang down to laugh,
The zebra stripes along his jaw
Swelling to maculate giraffe ...

Grishkin is nice: her Russian eye
Is underlined for emphasis;
Uncorseted, her friendly bust
Gives promise of pneumatic bliss.

It is this vein that tempts him most - and is his un-
doing.   For irony, no matter how agile and erudite -
and Eliot's is both - must contain heat if it is to
burn.   And heat is one of the few things that can not
be juggled by this acrobatic satirist.   With amazing
virtuosity, he balances and tosses fragments of philosophy, history, science, tea-table gossip, carelessly
screened velleities.   There are times when he discards
his flashing properties, changes his vocabulary of
rare words for a more direct irony which is not only
amusing but incisive.   'The Hippopotamus,' that audacious whimsicality, is an example, with its:

[Quotes CPP, p. 49, stanzas 1, 2, 3 and 6.]

But at least two-thirds of Eliot's sixty-three
pages attain no higher eminence than extraordinarily
clever - and eminently uncomfortable - verse.   The
exaltation which is the very breath of poetry - that
combination of tenderness and toughness - is scarcely
ever present in Eliot's lines.   Scarcely ever, I re-
iterate, for a certain perverse exultation takes its
place; an unearthly light without warmth which has the
sparkle if not the strength of fire.   It flickers
mockingly through certain of the unrhymed pictures and
shines with a bright pallor out of the two major poems.
These two are the book's main exhibit, its jewelled
medallion.   Medallion, too, in the sense that both of
them complement each other, obverse and reverse.   The
'Portrait of a Lady,' the franker and more easily com-
municable, is a half-sympathetic, half-scornful study
in the impressionist manner of the feminine dilettante,
the slightly-faded *précieuse* hovering tremulously on
the verge of an abortive 'affair.'

[Quotes 'Portrait of a Lady', CPP, p. 18, 'Among the
smoke' to 'the conversation slips'.]

'The Love Song of J. Alfred Prufrock' is even more
adroit though less outspoken. Sensitive to the pitch of
concealment, this is an analysis of the lady's sexual
opposite - an inhibited, young-old philanderer, tired of
talk and the eternal tea-tables; a prey to boredom that
breeds its own revulsion, a victim too sunk in himself to
escape it. For him, eternally, it seems that

> In the room the women come and go
> Talking of Michelangelo.

Prufrock would shatter the small talk, pierce the
whispered inanities, cry out!
But he can neither discharge his protest nor find words
for it. He listens politely; he accepts the proffered
cup; he chatters on aimlessly. It is the quiet tragedy of
frustration, the *revolté* buried in the gentleman.

[Quotes CPP, p. 16, 'No! I am not' to 'trousers rolled'.]

Yet Prufrock is not all psychology. Eliot can be
delicately fantastic and purely pictorial when the mood is
on him. He can speak of early morning with

> ...the damp souls of housemaids
> Sprouting despondently at area gates.

He hears the laughter of Mr. Apollinax (who sounds suspi-
ciously like Bertrand Russell) 'tinkling among the tea-
cups' and he thinks of

> ...Priapus in the shrubbery
> Gaping at the lady in the swing.

He watches the fog rubbing its back upon the window-
panes.

[Quotes CPP, p. 13, 'The yellow smoke' to 'fell asleep'.]

But these are the exceptional moments. For the most
part, Eliot cares less for his art than he does for his
attitudes. Disdaining the usual poetic cant, he falls
into another tradition; he leans towards a kind of versi-
fying which, masquerading under the title of 'occasional'
or 'social' verse may be found in many a *Lyra Eleganti-
arum*. Pliny had in mind this type when he wrote: 'These
pieces commonly go under the title of poetical amusements;
but these amusements have sometimes gained as much reputation to their authors as works of a far more serious

nature.' And some two thousand years later, Locker-
Lampson described their qualities again: 'The tone should
not be pitched too high; it should be terse and rather in
the conversational key; the rhythm should be crisp and
sparkling, the rhyme frequent and never forced...' Both
Pliny and Locker-Lampson might have been reviewing Eliot's
conversational ironies. For Eliot's gift is seldom the
poet's. His contribution is related to poetry only at
rare intervals. His lines, for the most part, are written
in a new *genre* or, to be more accurate, in a modernization
of a surprisingly old one. They are, primarily, a species
of mordant light verse; complex and disillusioned *vers de
société*.

25. RAYMOND WEAVER, WHAT AILS PEGASUS?, 'BOOKMAN'
(NEW YORK)

September 1920, vol. lii, 59

Weaver (1888–1948), an American critic, is known particularly for his study of Melville, first published in 1921.
  This passage is taken from a longer review of contemporary poetry.

The 'Poems' – ironically so-called – of T.S. Eliot, if not
heavy and pedantic parodies of the 'new poetry', are
documents that would find sympathetic readers in the
waiting-room of a private sanatorium. Clinically analyzed
they suggest in conclusion one of Mr. Eliot's lines: 'After
such knowledge, what forgiveness?' As a parodist, Mr.
Eliot is lacking in good taste, invention, and wit. Compared with Rudyard Kipling, Thackeray, and Phoebe Cary
(among the most accomplished parodists in the language)
Mr. Eliot is prodigiously labored and dull. General incomprehensibility and sordidness of detail (defects not
difficult to imitate, but excessively difficult to parody)
are Mr. Eliot's distinguishing traits. He is usually
intelligible only when he is nasty. His similes are without humor and without point:

He laughed like an impossible [sic] foetus.

Midnight shakes the memory
As a madman shakes a dead geranium.

The world revolves like ancient women
Gathering fuel in vacant lots.

Mr. Eliot may cynically have perpetrated this slim volume
in order to glean from the tributes of his admirers
material for a new 'Dunciad'.

26. PADRAIC COLUM, STUDIES IN THE SOPHISTICATED, 'NEW
REPUBLIC'

8 December 1920, vol. xxv, 54

Colum (1881-1973) was a playwright for the Abbey Theatre
in Dublin, who spent much of his life in the United States.
    The review from which this extract is taken opened with
a consideration of Pound's 'Instigations' (1920), which
reprinted Pound's 'Poetry' (August 1917) review of 'Prufrock and Other Observations' (No. 6).

To give prose the precedence of verse in a review that
deals with both is possibly wrong, but there is an excuse
for it in the present case. The 'Instigations' of Ezra
Pound deal in many places with the poems of T.S. Eliot.
Some of these passages make the best introduction that
could be written for the poems. They are eulogistic, and
at least in one passage, possibly extravagantly eulogistic. Mr. Eliot's form is compared to Ovid's form in the
'Heroides,' and to Browning's form in 'Men and Women.'
'The form of "Men and Women" is more alive than the epistolary form of the "Heroides,"' Mr. Pound says, and then he
goes on to suggest that the present-day poet has made a
certain advance on Browning's form - 'Browning included a
certain amount of ratiocination and of purely intellectual
comment, and in just that proportion he lost intensity.'
Mr. Eliot has stripped away the ratiocination and the
intellectual comment.
    His first volume has been published in the present year
- a small collection of twenty-four pieces, four being in
French. Had Mr. Eliot excluded such pieces as 'The Boston

Evening Transcript,' 'Hysteria,' 'Cousin Nancy,' one would
be able to judge his poetry without making a reference to
The Smart Set. That he has included these is evidence that
he is not amongst the super-sophisticated.

I do not know if these poems mark the beginning of a
cycle in poetry, but I am sure that they mark the end of
one. Twenty years ago Mr. Yeats published 'The Wind Among
the Reeds.' He brought a new set of symbols into poetry.
He heard 'the Shadowy Horses, their long manes a-shake,
their hoofs heavy with tumult.' Today Mr. Eliot sees that
'The red-eyed scavengers are creeping from Kentish Town and
Golder's Green.' The cycle is complete: the vague and
visionary territory has become defined as points on a subway, and municipal employees have taken the place of creatures out of a myth.

And the truth is that our imaginations are put at no
loss by the change in symbols. Mr. Eliot, like the Mr.
Yeats of 'The Wind Amongst the Reeds,' is a symbolist.
He, too, has his Aedh, his Hanrahan, his Michael Robartes.
But he calls them Sweeney, J. Alfred Prufrock, Mr. Apollinax. The Hippopotamus of the Zoo takes the place of the
boar with bristles and the deer with no horns. The change,
of course, would not be real if there were no poetry transmitted through the symbols. Poetry is transmitted. In
such poems as 'Gerontion,' 'The Love Song of J. Alfred
Prufrock,' 'Portrait of a Lady,' 'Cooking Egg,' we get a
glimpse of the visions and tragedies that are in the soul -
it does not matter that the soul in these situations has to
look out on restaurants instead of on temples, and on
'rocks, moss, stonecrop, iron, merds,' instead of on the
mountains and the sea.

Mr. Eliot has learned from Jules Laforgue how to make
modern settings as well as how to parade a mockery of the
literary allusion. This by itself would serve to put him
with the modernists. But he is modern in a way that is
more significant. He has the modern approach to the soul,
or, let us say, to the psyche - to the soul that is not an
entity but a collection of complexes - the soul that is at
once positive and reticent, obscured and clairvoyant. The
poet is well aware of the tragedy that is marked by a
yawn, and the dreadful dismissal that is in a cliché repeated. His art is indeed achieved when he can give us
such revelations in the medium of verse.

For a generation there have been attempts to do this
kind of thing in English, and verse in which ennui turns
upon disillusion has gone the rounds. But now that Mr.
Eliot has published we see that in this verse there were
only approaches. Mr. Eliot's work is complete; he has
adapted a modern technique, and his personae are stabilized

into types. The group in the workshop were aware that he
was completing a tendency, and for that reason they were
speaking of him with Ovid and Browning before he had published a book. I have said that if he does not mark the
beginning of a cycle he certainly marks the end of one.
This poetry of his will act in the body literary like those
tremendous fellows, the corpuscles in the blood that seize
upon and devour the de-vitalized corpuscles. **Romantic**
poetry, in its spent stages, will encounter Sweeney and
Prufrock and will not know what has happened to it. But
that comparison is wrong: the poetry of Mr. Eliot, in spite
of its being so well exercised and so well disinfected,
belongs after all to Byzantium; the shadows of a long decay
are upon it all.

'The Waste Land'

'Criterion', London, October 1922, vol. i, 50-64;
'Dial', New York, November 1922, vol. lxxiii, 473-85;
first edition, New York, 15 December 1922

27. UNSIGNED NOTICE OF THE FIRST ISSUE OF THE 'CRITERION' AND REVIEW OF 'THE WASTE LAND', 'TIMES LITERARY SUPPLEMENT'

26 October 1922, no. 1084, 690

If we are to judge by its first number, the 'Criterion' is not only that rare thing amongst English periodicals, a purely literary review, but it is of a quality not inferior to that of any review published either here or abroad. Of the seven items which make up this number there are at least five that we should like to see preserved in a 'permanent' form. And of these five there are two, the long poem by Mr. T.S. Eliot called 'The Waste Land' and Dostoevski's 'Plan of a Novel,' now first translated into English, that are of exceptional importance. We cannot imagine a more untidy plan for a novel or anything else than this one by Dostoevski, and yet, even on a first reading, one has a confused impression of having passed through an exciting and significant experience. To the student of Dostoevski this so-called 'plan' will reveal much; it is full of hints of spiritual discoveries which, we may be confident, Dostoevski would have fully revealed. And it is very interesting to see how entirely the *points d'appui* of a Dostoevski novel consist of such flashes. Of orderly planning in the ordinary or even in the Jamesian sense there is no trace. He must have found composition extremely difficult. There is no machinery of which the momentum carries him on. He had to create every page.

Mr. Eliot's poem is also a collection of flashes, but there is no effect of heterogeneity, since all these flashes are relevant to the same thing and together give what seems to be a complete expression of this poet's

vision of modern life. We have here range, depth, and
beautiful expression. What more is necessary to a great
poem? This vision is singularly complex and in all its
labyrinths utterly sincere. It is the mystery of life
that it shows two faces, and we know of no other modern
poet who can more adequately and movingly reveal to us the
inextricable tangle of the sordid and the beautiful that
make up life. Life is neither hellish nor heavenly; it
has a purgatorial quality. And since it is purgatory,
deliverance is possible. Students of Mr. Eliot's work
will find a new note, and a profoundly interesting one, in
the latter part of this poem.

Of the other items in this number we may single out an
excellent short story by May Sinclair, an interesting
literary study by Sturge Moore, and a maliciously urbane
and delightful article on 'Dullness,' by George Saintsbury. What literary school, then, does this new quarterly
represent? It is a school which includes Saintsbury,
Sturge Moore, and T.S. Eliot. There is no such school,
obviously. It becomes apparent that the only school
represented is the school of those who are genuinely
interested in good literature.

28. UNSIGNED COMMENT ON THE 'DIAL' AWARD OF $2,000 TO
'THE WASTE LAND', 'NEW YORK TIMES BOOK REVIEW'

26 November 1922, 12

Note the mistake over Eliot's middle name.

The annual award of the 'Dial,' amounting to $2,000, has
been given this year to T.S. Eliot, the American poet
living in England. This award, which is not presented as
a prize, but in recognition of able work, was given last
year to Sherwood Anderson, the novelist. Thomas Seymour
Eliot, to give him his full name, is a Harvard graduate
and a writer who may be regarded as the poetical leader
of the Younger Generation. His volume, 'Poems,' containing such unusual efforts as 'The Love Song of J. Alfred
Prufrock' and the 'Portrait of a Lady,' appeared several
seasons ago. A new volume from his pen, 'The Waste Land,'
a single poem of some length, is shortly to be published

by Boni & Liveright. Mr. Eliot's work is marked by an
intense cerebral quality and a compact music that has
practically established a movement among the younger men.

29. UNSIGNED ACCOUNT OF WHY ELIOT WAS AWARDED THE 'DIAL'S'
PRIZE, 'DIAL'

December 1922, vol. lxxiii, 685-7

The next item (No. 30) is Edmund Wilson's essay on 'The
Waste Land'. This is the discussion that appeared elsewhere in the same issue of the 'Dial'.

The editors have the pleasure of announcing that for the
year 1922 the 'Dial's' award goes to Mr T.S. Eliot.

Mr Eliot has himself done so much to make clear the
relation of critic to creative artist that we hope not to
be asked whether it is his criticism or his poetry which
constitutes that service to letters which the award is
intended to acknowledge. Indeed it is our fancy that
those who know one or the other will recognize the propriety of the occasion; those who know both will recognize further in Mr Eliot an exceedingly active influence
on contemporary letters.
Influence in itself, however, is no service, and what
makes Mr Eliot a significant artist is that his work, of
whatever nature, is an indication of how ineffective the
temptation to do bad work can, for at least once, become.
Few American writers have published so little, and fewer
have published so much which was worth publication. We
do not for a moment suspect Mr Eliot of unheard-of capaci-
ties; it is possible that he neither has been pressed to
nor can write a popular novel. But the temptation not to
arrive at excellence is very great, and he is one of the
rare artists who has resisted it. A service to letters
peculiarly acceptable now is the proof that one can arrive
at eminence with the help of nothing except genius.
Elsewhere in this issue will be found a discussion of
Mr Eliot's poetry, with special reference to his long
work, 'The Waste Land,' which appeared in the 'Dial' of a
month ago; in reviewing 'The Sacred Wood,' and elsewhere,

we have had much to say of his critical work, and may have
more. At this moment it pleases us to remember how much
at variance Mr Eliot is with those writers who having
themselves sacrificed all interest in letters, are calling
upon criticism to do likewise in the name of the particular science which they fancy can redeem the world from
every ill but themselves. As a critic of letters Mr Eliot
has always had preeminently one of the qualifications which
he requires of the good critic: 'a creative interest, a
focus upon the immediate future. The important critic is
the person who is absorbed in the present problems of art,
and who wishes to bring the forces of the past to bear upon
the solution of these problems.' This is precisely what Mr
Eliot has wished, and accomplished, in his function as
critic of criticism. It is impossible to read the opening
essays of 'The Sacred Wood' without recognizing that it is
from these pages that the attack upon perverted criticism
is rising. The journalists who wish critics to be for ever
concerned with social laws, economic fundamentals, and the
science of psychoanalysis, and never by any chance with the
erection into laws of those personal impressions which are
the great pleasure of appreciation, would do well to destroy Mr Eliot first; for it is from him that new critics
are learning 'that the "historical" and the "philosophical"
critics had better be called historians and philosophers
quite simply' and that criticism has other functions, and
other pleasures to give.

There is another, quite different sense, in which Mr
Eliot's work is of exceptional service to American letters.
He is one of a small number of Americans who can be judged
by the standards of the past - including therein the body
of Occidental literature. It is a superficial indication
of this that Mr Eliot is almost the only young American
critic who is neither ignorant of nor terrified by the
classics, that he knows them (one includes Massinger as
well as Euripides) and understands their relation to the
work which went before and came after them. There are in
his poems certain characters, certain scenes, and even
certain attitudes of mind, which one recognizes as
peculiarly American; yet there is nowhere in his work that
'localism' which at once takes so much of American writing
out of the field of comparison with European letters and
(it is often beneficial to their reputations) requires for
American writers a special standard of judgement. We feel
nothing aggressive and nothing apologetic in his writing;
there is the assumption in it that the civilized American
no less than the civilized German can count Shakespeare and
even Poe as part of his inheritance.

When 'Prufrock' in paper covers first appeared, to become

immediately one of the rarest of rare books (somebody
stole our as early as 1919) Mr Eliot was already redoubt-
able. Since then, poet with true invention, whom lassitude has not led to repeat himself, critic again with
invention and with enough metaphysics to draw the line at
the metaphysical, his legend has increased. We do not
fancy that we are putting a last touch to this climax; we
express gratitude for pleasure received and assured. If
pleasure is not sufficiently high-toned a word, you may,
in the preceding paragraphs, take your pick.

    Mr Eliot's command of publicity is not exceptional, and
we feel it necessary to put down, for those who care for
information, these hardily gleaned facts of his biography.
In 1888 he was born in St. Louis; in 1909 and 1910 he received, respectively, the degrees of Bachelor and of Master
of Arts at Harvard; subsequently he studied at the Sorbonne, the Harvard Graduate School, and Merton College,
Oxford. He has been a lecturer under both the Oxford and
the London University Extension Systems, and from 1917 to
1919 he was assistant editor of the 'Egoist.' We have
heard it rumoured that he is still 'À Londres, un peu
banquier'; those who can persuade themselves that facts
are facts will find much more of importance in the 'Mélange
Adultère de Tout,' from which the quotation comes; as that
poem was written several years ago it omits the names of
Mr Eliot's books: 'The Sacred Wood,' 'Poems,' and 'The
Waste Land' (not to speak of the several volumes later
incorporated in 'Poems') and omits also the fact that Mr
Eliot is now editor of the 'Criterion,' a quarterly which
we (as it were *en passant*) hereby make welcome. The most
active and, we are told, the most influential editor-
critic in London found nothing to say of one of the contributions to the first number except that it was 'an
obscure, but amusing poem' by the editor. We should hate
to feel that our readers can judge of the state of criticism in England by turning to the first page of our '
November issue and reading the same poem there.

30. EDMUND WILSON, THE POETRY OF DROUTH, 'DIAL'

December 1922, vol. lxxiii, 611-16

Wilson (1895-1972), an important American critic, wrote
extensively on Eliot, including T.S. Eliot, 'New Republic'

(13 November 1929), lx, 341-9, a fuller version of which
appeared in 'Axel's Castle' (1931). He wrote on Eliot as
poet and public figure in 'The Bit Between My Teeth'
(1966), and on 'The Waste Land' drafts in 'The Devils and
Canon Barham' (1973).

Mr T.S. Eliot's first meagre volume of twenty-four poems
was dropped into the waters of contemporary verse without
stirring more than a few ripples. But when two or three
years had passed, it was found to stain the whole sea.
Or, to change the metaphor a little, it became evident
that Mr Eliot had fished a murex up. His productions,
which had originally been received as a sort of glorified
vers de société, turned out to be unforgettable poems,
which everyone was trying to rewrite. There might not be
very much of him, but what there was had come somehow to
seem precious and now the publication of his long poem,
'The Waste Land,' confirms the opinion which we had begun
gradually to cherish, that Mr Eliot, with all his limitations, is one of our only authentic poets. For this new
poem – which presents itself as so far his most considerable claim to eminence – not only recapitulates all his
earlier and already familiar motifs, but it sounds for the
first time in all their intensity, untempered by irony or
disguise, the hunger for beauty and the anguish at living
which lie at the bottom of all his work.
     Perhaps the best point of departure for a discussion of
'The Waste Land' is an explanation of its title. Mr Eliot
asserts that he derived this title, as well as the plan of
the poem 'and much of the incidental symbolism,' from a
book by Miss Jessie L. Weston called 'From Ritual to
Romance.' 'The Waste Land ' it appears, is one of the
many mysterious elements which have made of the Holy Grail
legend a perennial puzzle of folk-lore; it is a desolate
and sterile country, ruled over by an impotent king, in
which not only have the crops ceased to grow and the ani-
mals to reproduce their kind, but the very human inhabi-
tants have become unable to bear children. The renewal of
the Waste Land and the healing of the 'Fisher King's'
wound depend somehow upon the success of the Knight who
has come to find the Holy Grail.
     Miss Weston, who has spent her whole life in the study
of the Arthurian legends, has at last propounded a new
solution for the problems presented by this strange tale.
Stimulated by Frazer's 'Golden Bough' – of which this
extraordinarily interesting book is a sort of offshoot –
she has attempted to explain the Fisher King as a

primitive vegetable god – one of those creatures who, like
Attis and Adonis, is identified with Nature herself and in
the temporary loss of whose virility the drouth or inclem-
ency of the season is symbolized; and whose mock burial is
a sort of earnest of his coming to life again. Such a
cult, Miss Weston contends, became attached to the popular
Persian religion of Mithraism and was brought north to
Gaul and Britain by the Roman legionaries. When Christianity finally prevailed, Attis was driven underground and
survived only as a secret cult, like the Venus of the
Venusberg. The Grail legend, according to Miss Weston,
had its origin in such a cult; the Lance and Grail are the
sexual symbols appropriate to a fertility rite and the
eerie adventure of the Chapel Perilous is the description
of an initiation.
    Now Mr Eliot uses the Waste Land as the concrete image
of a spiritual drouth. His poem takes place half in the
real world – the world of contemporary London, and half in
a haunted wilderness – the Waste Land of the mediaeval
legend; but the Waste Land is only the hero's arid soul
and the intolerable world about him. The water which he
longs for in the twilit desert is to quench the thirst
which torments him in the London dusk. – And he exists not
only upon these two planes, but as if throughout the whole
of human history. Miss Weston's interpretation of the
Grail legend lent itself with peculiar aptness to Mr
Eliot's extraordinarily complex mind (which always finds
itself looking out upon the present with the prouder eyes
of the past and which loves to make its oracles as deep
as the experience of the race itself by piling up stratum
upon stratum of reference, as the Italian painters used to
paint over one another); because she took pains to trace
the Buried God not only to Attis and Adonis, but further
back to the recently revealed Tammuz of the Sumerian-
Babylonian civilization and to the god invited to loosen
the waters in the abysmally ancient Vedic Hymns. So Mr
Eliot hears in his own parched cry the voices of all the
thirsty men of the past – of the author of Ecclesiastes
in majestic bitterness at life's futility, of the Children
of Israel weeping for Zion by the unrefreshing rivers of
Babylon, of the disciples after the Crucifixion meeting
the phantom of Christ on their journey; of Buddha's renunciation of life and Dante's astonishment at the weary
hordes of Hell, and of the sinister dirge with which
Webster blessed the 'friendless bodies of unburied men.'
In the centre of his poem he places the weary figure of
the blind immortal prophet Tiresias, who, having been
woman as well as man, has exhausted all human experience
and, having 'sat by Thebes below the wall and walked among

the lowest of the dead,' knows exactly what will happen
in the London flat between the typist and the house-
agent's clerk; and at its beginning the almost identical
figure of the Cumaean Sibyl mentioned in Petronius, who -
gifted also with extreme longevity and preserved as a sort
of living mummy - when asked by little boys what she
wanted, replied only 'I want to die.' Not only is life
sterile and futile, but men have tasted its sterility and
futility a thousand times before. T.S. Eliot, walking the
desert of London, feels profoundly that the desert has
always been there. Like Tiresias, he has sat below the
wall of Thebes; like Buddha, he has seen the world as an
arid conflagration; like the Sibyl, he has known everything and known everything vain.

Yet something else, too, reaches him from the past: as
he wanders among the vulgarities which surround him, his
soul is haunted by heroic strains of an unfading music.
Sometimes it turns suddenly and shockingly into the jazz
of the music-halls, sometimes it breaks in the middle of a
bar and leaves its hearer with dry ears again, but still
it sounds like the divine rumour of some high destiny from
which he has fallen, like indestructible pride in the
citizenship of some world which he never can reach. In a
London boudoir, where the air is stifling with a dust of
futility, he hears, as he approaches his hostess, an echo
of Anthony and Cleopatra and of Aeneas coming to the house
of Dido - and a painted panel above the mantel gives his
mind a moment's swift release by reminding him of Milton's
Paradise and of the nightingale that sang there. - Yet
though it is most often things from books which refresh
him, he has also a slight spring of memory. He remembers
someone who came to him with wet hair and with hyacinths
in her arms, and before her he was stricken senseless and
dumb - 'looking into the heart of light, the silence.'
There were rain and flowers growing then. Nothing ever
grows during the action of the poem and no rain ever falls.
The thunder of the final vision is 'dry sterile thunder
without rain.' But as Gerontion in his dry rented house
thinks wistfully of the young men who fought in the rain,
as Prufrock longs to ride green waves and linger in the
chambers of the sea, as Mr Apollinax is imagined drawing
strength from the deep sea-caves of coral islands, so in
this new poem Mr Eliot identifies water with all freedom
and illumination of the soul. He drinks the rain that
once fell on his youth as - to use an analogy in Mr
Eliot's own manner - Dante drank at the river of Eunoë
that the old joys he had known might be remembered. But -
to note also the tragic discrepancy, as Mr Eliot always
does - the draught, so far from renewing his soul and

leaving him pure to rise to the stars, is only a drop
absorbed in the desert; to think of it is to register its
death. The memory is the dead god whom – as Hyacinth – he
buries at the beginning of the poem and which – unlike his
ancient prototype – is never to come to life again.
Hereafter, fertility will fail; we shall see women deliberately making themselves sterile; we shall find that love
has lost its life-giving power and can bring nothing but
an asceticism of disgust. He is travelling in a country
cracked by drouth in which he can only dream feverishly of
drowning or of hearing the song of the hermit-thrush which
has at least the music of water. The only reappearance of
the god is as a phantom which walks beside him, the delir-
ious hallucination of a man who is dying of thirst. In
the end the dry-rotted world is crumbling about him – his
own soul is falling apart. There is nothing left to prop
it up but some dry stoic Sanskrit maxims and the broken
sighs from the past, of singers exiled or oppressed. Like
de Nerval, he is disinherited; like the poet of the
'Pervigilium Veneris,' he is dumb; like Arnaut Daniel in
Purgatory, he begs the world to raise a prayer for his
torment, as he disappears in the fire.

It will be seen from this brief description that the
poem is complicated; and it is actually even more complicated than I have made it appear. It is sure to be
objected that Mr Eliot has written a puzzle rather than a
poem and that his work can possess no higher interest than
a full-rigged ship built in a bottle. It will be said
that he depends too much upon books and borrows too much
from other men and that there can be no room for original
quality in a poem of little more than four hundred lines
which contains allusions to, parodies of, or quotations
from, the Vedic Hymns, Buddha, the Psalms, Ezekiel,
Ecclesiastes, Luke, Sappho, Virgil, Ovid, Petronius, the
'Pervigilium Veneris,' St Augustine, Dante, the Grail
Legends, early English poetry, Kyd, Spenser, Shakespeare,
John Day, Webster, Middleton, Milton, Goldsmith, Gérard de
Nerval, Froude, Baudelaire, Verlaine, Swinburne, Wagner,
'The Golden Bough,' Miss Weston's book, various popular
ballads, and the author's own earlier poems. It has
already been charged against Mr Eliot that he does not
feel enough to be a poet and that the emotions of longing
and disgust which he does have belong essentially to a
delayed adolescence. It has already been suggested that
his distaste for the celebrated Sweeney shows a superficial mind and that if he only looked more closely into
poor Sweeney he would find Eugene O'Neill's Hairy Ape; and
I suppose it will be felt in connexion with this new poem
that if his vulgar London girls had only been studied by

Sherwood Anderson they would have presented a very different appearance. At bottom, it is sure to be said, Mr
Eliot is timid and prosaic like Mr Prufrock; he has no
capacity for life, and nothing which happens to Mr Prufrock can be important.

Well: all these objections are founded on realities,
but they are outweighed by one major fact - the fact that
Mr Eliot is a poet. It is true his poems seem the products
of a constricted emotional experience and that he appears
to have drawn rather heavily on books for the heat he could
not derive from life. There is a certain grudging margin,
to be sure, about all that Mr Eliot writes - as if he were
compensating himself for his limitations by a peevish
assumption of superiority. But it is the very acuteness of
his suffering from this starvation which gives such poignancy to his art. And, as I say, Mr Eliot is a poet - that
is, he feels intensely and with distinction and speaks
naturally in beautiful verse - so that, no matter within
what walls he lives, he belongs to the divine company.
His verse is sometimes much too scrappy - he does not dwell
long enough upon one idea to give it its proportionate
value before passing on to the next - but these drops,
though they be wrung from flint, are none the less authentic crystals. They are broken and sometimes infinitely
tiny, but they are worth all the rhinestones on the mar-
ket. I doubt whether there is a single other poem of equal
length by a contemporary American which displays so high
and so varied a mastery of English verse. The poem is - in
spite of its lack of structural unity - simply one triumph
after another - from the white April light of the opening
and the sweet wistfulness of the nightingale passage - one
of the only successful pieces of contemporary blank verse -
to the shabby sadness of the Thames Maidens, the cruel
irony of Tiresias' vision, and the dry grim stony style of
the descriptions of the Waste Land itself.

That is why Mr Eliot's trivialities are more valuable
than other people's epics - why Mr Eliot's detestation of
Sweeney is more precious that Mr Sandburg's sympathy for
him, and Mr Prufrock's tea-table tragedy more important
than all the passions of the New Adam - sincere and carefully expressed as these latter emotions indubitably are.
That is also why, for all its complicated correspondences
and its recondite references and quotations, 'The Waste
Land' is intelligible at first reading. It is not necessary to know anything about the Grail Legend or any but
the most obvious of Mr Eliot's allusions to feel the force
of the intense emotion which the poem is intended to convey - as one cannot do, for example, with the extremely
ill-focussed Eight Cantos of his imitator Mr Ezra Pound,

who presents only a bewildering mosaic with no central
emotion to provide a key. In Eliot the very images and
the sound of the words - even when we do not know precisely why he has chosen them - are charged with a strange
poignancy which seems to bring us into the heart of the
singer. And sometimes we feel that he is speaking not
only for a personal distress, but for the starvation of a
whole civilization - for people grinding at barren office-
routine in the cells of gigantic cities, drying up their
souls in eternal toil whose products never bring them profit, where their pleasures are so vulgar and so feeble
that they are almost sadder than their pains. It is our
whole world of strained nerves and shattered institutions,
in which 'some infinitely gentle, infinitely suffering
thing' is somehow being done to death - in which the
maiden Philomel 'by the barbarous king so rudely forced'
can no longer even fill the desert 'with inviolable
voice.' It is the world in which the pursuit of grace
and beauty is something which is felt to be obsolete - the
reflections which reach us from the past cannot illumine
so dingy a scene; that heroic prelude has ironic echoes
among the streets and the drawing-rooms where we live.
Yet the race of the poets - though grown rarer - is not
yet quite dead: there is at least one who, as Mr Pound
says, has brought a new personal rhythm into the language
and who has lent even to the words of his great predecessors a new music and a new meaning.

31. GILBERT SELDES, T.S. ELIOT, 'NATION' (NEW YORK)

6 December 1922, vol. cxv, 614-16

Seldes (1893-1970), an American critic, was managing editor of the 'Dial' from 1920 to 1923. For an account of
the part he played in publishing 'The Waste Land', see
Noel Stock, 'The Life of Ezra Pound' (London, 1974),
pp. 313-15. See also the Introduction to T.S. Eliot,
'The Waste Land: A Facsimile and Transcript of the Original Drafts', edited by Valerie Eliot (London, 1971).

The poems and critical essays of T.S. Eliot have been
known to a number of readers for six or seven years; small

presses in England have issued one or two pamphlet-like
books of poetry; in America the 'Little Review' and the
'Dial' have published both prose and verse. In 1920 he
issued his collected 'Poems,' a volume of some sixty
pages, through Knopf, and the following year the same
publisher put forth 'The Sacred Wood,' a collection of
fourteen essays devoted to two subjects, criticism and
poetry. This year a volume no larger than the first, containing one long poem, is issued. The position, approaching eminence, which Mr. Eliot holds is obviously not to be
explained in terms of bulk.

It is peculiarly difficult to write even the necessary
journalism about Mr. Eliot. From its baser manifestation
he is fortunately immune and his qualities do not lend
themselves to trickery. The secret of his power (I will
not say influence) as a critic is that he is interested in
criticism and in the object of criticism, as a poet that
he understands and practices the art of poetry. In the
first of these he is exceptional, almost alone; in both,
his work lies in the living tradition and outside the wil-
fulness of the moment. We are so far gone in the new
movement that even to say that he practices aesthetic
criticism and impersonal poetry will be confusing. I can
only explain by distinguishing his work from others.

At the present moment criticism of literature is almost
entirely criticism of the ideas expressed in literature; it
is interested chiefly in morals, economics, sociology, or
science. We can imagine a critic *circa* 1840 declaring
that 'Othello' is a bad play because men should not kill
their wives; and the progress is not very great to 1922
when we are as likely as not to hear that it is a bad play
because Desdemona is an outmoded kind of woman. To be
sure the economic, sociological, and psychoanalytical
interest has largely displaced the moral one, and critics
(whether they say a book is good or bad) are inclined to
judge the importance of a writer of fiction by the accuracy of his dream-interpretations or the soundness of his
economic fundamentals. Their creative interest is in
something apart from the art they are discussing; and what
Mr. Eliot has done, with an attractive air of finality, is
to indicate how irrelevant that interest is to the art of
letters. He respects these imperfect critics in so far as
they are good philosophers, moralists, or scientists; but
he knows that in connection with letters they are the victims of impure desires (the poet *manqué* as critic) or of
impure interests (the fanatical Single-taxer (1) as critic).
'But Aristotle,' he says, 'had none of these impure desires to satisfy; in whatever sphere of interest, he
looked solely and steadfastly at the object; in his short

and broken treatise he provides an eternal example - not
of laws, or even of method, for there is no method except
to be very intelligent, but of intelligence itself swiftly
operating the analysis of sensation to the point of principle and definition.' Again, more specifically, 'The
important critic is the person who is absorbed in the present problems of art, and who wishes to bring the forces
of the past to bear upon the solution of these problems.
If the critic considers Congreve, for instance, he will
always have at the back of his mind the question: What has
Congreve got that is pertinent to our dramatic art? Even
if he is solely engaged in trying to understand Congreve,
this will make all the difference: inasmuch as to understand anything is to understand from a point of view.'
Criticism, for Mr. Eliot, is the statement of the structures in which our perceptions, when we face a work of art,
form themselves. He quotes Remy de Gourmont: 'To erect his
personal impressions into laws is the great effort of man
if he is sincere.'

The good critic, as I understand Mr. Eliot, will be concerned with the aesthetic problem of any given work of art;
he will (I should add) not despise ideas, but if he is intelligent he will recognize their place in a work of art
and he will certainly not dismiss as paradoxical nonsense
Mr. Eliot's contention that his baffling escape from ideas
made Henry James the most intelligent man of his time. It
is not an easy task to discover in each case what the aesthetic problem is; but that is the task, precisely, which
every good critic of painting, let us say, is always compelled to attempt and which no critic of letters need
attempt because he can always talk (profoundly, with the
appearance of relevance, endlessly) about ideas. Mr.
Eliot has accomplished the task several times, notably in
his essay on 'Hamlet,' about which essay a small literature has already been produced. I have not space here to
condense the substance of that or of the other critical
essays - they are remarkably concise as they are - nor to
do more than say that they are written with an extraordinary distinction in which clarity, precision, and
nobility almost always escaping magniloquence, are the
elements.

In turning to Mr. Eliot as poet I do not leave the
critic behind since it is from his critical utterances
that we derive the clue to his poetry. He says that the
historical sense is indispensable to anyone who would continue to be a poet after the age of twenty-five, and
follows this with a statement which cannot be too closely
pondered by those who misunderstand tradition and by those
who imagine that American letters stand outside of

European letters and are to be judged by other standards:

> The historical sense compels a man to write not
> merely with his own generation in his bones, but with a
> feeling that the whole of the literature of Europe from
> Homer and within it the whole of the literature of his
> own country has a simultaneous existence and composes a
> simultaneous order.

This is only the beginning of 'depersonalization.' It
continues:

> What happens is a continual surrender of himself
> (the poet) as he is at the moment to something which is
> more valuable. The progress of an artist is a continual
> self-sacrifice, a continual extinction of personality
> ... the more perfect the artist, the more completely
> separate in him will be the man who suffers and the
> mind which creates; the more perfectly will the mind
> digest and transmute the passions which are its
> material.... The intensity of the poetry is something
> quite different from whatever intensity in the supposed
> experience it may give the impression of.... Impres-
> sions and experiences which are important for the man
> may take no place in the poetry, and those which become
> important in the poetry may play quite a negligible
> part in the man, the personality....

And finally:

> It is not in his personal emotions, the emotions
> provoked by particular events in his life, that the
> poet is in any way remarkable or interesting. His
> particular emotions may be simple, or crude, or flat.
> The emotion in his poetry will be a very complex thing,
> but not with the complexity of the emotions of people
> who have very complex or unusual emotions in life....
> The business of the poet is not to find new emotions,
> but to use the ordinary ones and, in working them up
> into poetry, to express feelings which are not in
> actual emotions at all.... Poetry is not a turning
> loose of emotion, but an escape from emotion; it is not
> the expression of a personality, but an escape from
> personality. But, of course, only those who have per-
> sonality and emotions know what it means to want to
> escape from these things.

The significant emotion has its life in the poem and
not in the history of the poet; and recognition of this,

Mr. Eliot indicates, is the true appreciation of poetry.
Fortunately for the critic he has written one poem, 'The
Waste Land,' to which one can apply his own standards. It
develops, carries to conclusions, many things in his remarkable earlier work, in method and in thought. I have
not that familiarity with the intricacies of French verse
which could make it possible for me to affirm or deny the
statement that technically he derives much from Jules
Laforgue; if Remy de Gourmont's estimate of the latter be
correct one can see definite points of similarity in the
minds of the two poets:

> His natural genius was made up of sensibility,
> irony, imagination, and clairvoyance; he chose to
> nourish it with positive knowledge (*connaisances posi-*
> *tives*), with all philosophies and all literatures, with
> all the images of nature and of art; even the latest
> views of science seem to have been known to him....
> It is literature entirely made new and unforeseen, dis-
> concerting and giving the curious and rare sensation
> that one has never read anything like it before.

A series of sardonic portraits - of people, places,
things - each the distillation of a refined emotion, make
up Mr. Eliot's 'Poems.' The deceptive simplicity of these
poems in form and in style is exactly at the opposite extreme from false naivete; they are unpretentiously sophisticated, wicked, malicious, humorous, and with the distillation of emotion has gone a condensation of expression.
In 'The Waste Land' the seriousness of the theme is
matched with an intensity of expression in which all the
earlier qualities are sublimated.

In essence 'The Waste Land' says something which is not
new: that life has become barren and sterile, that man is
withering, impotent, and without assurance that the waters
which made the land fruitful will ever rise again. (I
need not say that 'thoughtful' as the poem is, it does not
'express an idea'; it deals with emotions, and ends precisely in that significant emotion, inherent in the poem,
which Mr. Eliot has described.) The title, the plan, and
much of the symbolism of the poem, the author tells us in
his 'Notes,' were suggested by Miss Weston's remarkable
book on the Grail legend, 'From Ritual to Romance'; it is
only indispensable to know that there exists the legend of
a king rendered impotent, and his country sterile, both
awaiting deliverance by a knight on his way to seek the
Grail; it is interesting to know further that this is part
of the Life or Fertility mysteries; but the poem is self-
contained. It seems at first sight remarkably disconnected,

confused, the emotion seems to disengage itself in spite
of the objects and events chosen by the poet as their
vehicle. The poem begins with a memory of summer
showers, gaiety, joyful and perilous escapades; a moment
later someone else is saying 'I will show you fear in a
handful of dust,' and this is followed by the first lines
of 'Tristan und Isolde,' and then again by a fleeting recollection of loveliness. The symbolism of the poem is
introduced by means of the Tarot pack of cards; quotations,
precise or dislocated, occur; gradually one discovers a
rhythm of alternation between the visionary (so to name
the memories of the past) and the actual, between the spoken and the unspoken thought. There are scraps, fragments; then sustained episodes; the poem culminates with
the juxtaposition of the highest types of Eastern and
Western asceticism, by means of allusions to St. Augustine and Buddha; and ends with a sour commentary on the
injunctions 'Give, sympathize, control' of the Upanishads,
a commentary which reaches its conclusion in a pastiche
recalling all that is despairing and disinherited in the
memory of man.

A closer view of the poem does more than illuminate the
difficulties; it reveals the hidden form of the work, indicates how each thing falls into place, and to the reader's surprise shows that the emotion which at first
seemed to come in spite of the framework and the detail
could not otherwise have been communicated. For the
theme is not a distaste for life, nor is it a disillusion,
a romantic pessimism of any kind. It is specifically concerned with the idea of the Waste Land - that the land
was fruitful and now is not, that life had been rich,
beautiful, assured, organized, lofty, and now is dragging
itself out in a poverty-stricken, and disrupted and ugly
tedium, without health, and with no consolation in
morality; there may remain for the poet the labor of
poetry, but in the poem there remain only 'these fragments I have shored against my ruins' - the broken
glimpses of what was. The poem is not an argument and I
can only add, to be fair, that it contains no romantic
idealization of the past; one feels simply that even in
the cruelty and madness which have left their record in
history and in art, there was an intensity of life, a
germination and fruitfulness, which are now gone, and that
even the creative imagination, even hallucination and
vision have atrophied, so that water shall never again be
struck from a rock in the desert. Mr. Bertrand Russell
has recently said that since the Renaissance the clock of
Europe has been running down; without the feeling that it
was once wound up, without the contrasting emotions as one

looks at the past and at the present, 'The Waste Land'
would be a different poem, and the problem of the poem
would have been solved in another way.

The present solution is in part by juxtaposition of
opposites. We have a passage seemingly spoken by a slut,
ending

> Goonight Bill.   Goonight Lou.   Goonight May.
>   Goonight.
> Ta ta. Goonight. Goonight.

and then the ineffable

> Good night, ladies, good night, sweet ladies, good
>   night, good night.

Conversely the turn is accomplished from nobility or
beauty of utterance to

> The sounds of horns and motors, which shall bring
> Sweeney to Mrs. Porter in the spring.

And in the long passage where Tiresias, the central
character of the poem, appears the method is at its
height, for here is the coldest and unhappiest revelation
of the assault of lust made in the terms of beauty:

[Quotes 'The Waste Land', CPP, pp. 68-9, 'At the violet
hour' to 'the stairs unlit'.]

It will be interesting for those who have knowledge of
another great work of our time, Mr. Joyce's 'Ulysses,' to
think of the two together. That 'The Waste Land' is, in a
sense, the inversion and the complement of 'Ulysses' is at
least tenable. We have in 'Ulysses' the poet defeated,
turning outward, savoring the ugliness which is no longer
transmutable into beauty, and, in the end, homeless. We
have in 'The Waste Land' some indication of the inner life
of such a poet. The contrast between the forms of these
two works is not expressed in the recognition that one is
among the longest and one among the shortest of works in
its genre; the important thing is that in each the theme,
once it is comprehended, is seen to have dictated the
form. More important still, I fancy, is that each has
expressed something of supreme relevance to our present
life in the everlasting terms of art.

Note

1 Single Tax: a reform proposed by the American economist
   Henry George in his book 'Progress and Poverty' (1879).
   George's proposal was 'to abolish all taxation save
   that upon land values'.

32. LOUIS UNTERMEYER, DISILLUSION VS. DOGMA, 'FREEMAN'

17 January 1923, vol. vi, 453

The 'Dial's' award to Mr. T.S. Eliot and the subsequent
book-publication of his 'The Waste Land' have occasioned a
display of some of the most enthusiastically naive super-
latives that have ever issued from publicly sophisticated
iconoclasts. A group, in attempting to do for Mr. Eliot
what 'Ulysses' did for Mr. Joyce, has, through its emphatic reiterations, driven more than one reader to a study
rather than a celebration of the qualities that character-
ize Mr. Eliot's work and endear him to the younger cere-
bralists. These qualities, apparent even in his earlier
verses, are an elaborate irony, a twitching disillusion,
a persistent though muffled hyperaesthesia. In 'The Love
Song of J. Alfred Prufrock' and the extraordinarily sensitized 'Portrait of a Lady,' Mr. Eliot fused these qualities in a flexible music, in the shifting nuances of a
speech that wavered dexterously between poetic colour and
casual conversation. In the greater part of 'Poems,'
however, Mr. Eliot employed a harder and more crackling
tone of voice; he delighted in virtuosity for its own
sake, in epigrammatic velleities, in an incongruously
mordant and disillusioned *vers de société*.
   In 'The Waste Land,' Mr. Eliot has attempted to combine
these two contradictory idioms with a new complexity.
The result - although, as I am aware, this conclusion is
completely at variance with the judgment of its frenetic
admirers - is a pompous parade of erudition, a lengthy extension of the earlier disillusion, a kaleidoscopic movement in which the bright-coloured pieces fail to atone for
the absence of an integrated design. As an echo of contemporary despair, as a picture of dissolution of the
breaking-down of the very structures on which life has
modelled itself, 'The Waste Land' has a definite authen-
ticity. But an artist is, by the very nature of creation,

pledged to give form to formlessness; even the process of
disintegration must be held within a pattern. This pattern is distorted and broken by Mr. Eliot's jumble of narratives, nursery-rhymes, criticism, jazz-rhythms,
'Dictionary of Favourite Phrases' and a few lyrical
moments. Possibly the disruption of our ideals may be
reproduced through such a *mélange*, but it is doubtful
whether it is crystallized or even clarified by a series
of severed narratives – tales from which the connecting
tissue has been carefully cut – and familiar quotations
with their necks twisted, all imbedded in that formless
plasma which Mr. Ezra Pound likes to call a Sordello-form.
Some of the intrusions are more irritating than incomprehensible. The unseen sailor in the first act of 'Tristan und Isolde' is dragged in (without point or preparation) to repeat his 'Frisch weht der Wind'; in the midst
of a metaphysical dialogue, we are assured

> O O O O that Shakespeherian Rag –
> It's so elegant
> So intelligent.

Falling back on his earlier *métier*, a species of sardonic
light verse, Mr. Eliot does not disdain to sink to doggerel that would be refused admission to the cheapest of
daily columns:

> When lovely woman stoops to folly and
> Paces about her room again, alone,
> She smoothes her hair with automatic hand,
> And puts a record on the gramophone.

Elsewhere, the juxtaposition of Andrew Marvell, Paul
Dresser and others equally incongruous is more cryptic
in intention and even more dismal in effect:

> But at my back from time to time I hear
> The sound of horns and motors, which shall bring
> Sweeney to Mrs. Porter in the spring.
> O the moon shone bright on Mrs. Porter
> And on her daughter
> They wash their feet in soda water
> *Et O ces voix d'enfants, chantant dans la coupole!*

It is difficult to understand the presence of such
cheap tricks in what Mr. Burton Rascoe has publicly informed us is 'the finest poem of this generation.' The
mingling of wilful obscurity and weak vaudeville compels
us to believe that the pleasure which many admirers derive

from 'The Waste Land' is the same sort of gratification
attained through having solved a puzzle, a form of self-
congratulation. The absence of any verbal acrobatics from
Mr. Eliot's prose, a prose that represents not the slightest departure from a sort of intensive academicism, makes
one suspect that, were it not for the Laforgue mechanism,
Mr. Eliot's poetic variations on the theme of a super-
refined futility would be increasingly thin and incredibly
second rate.

As an analyst of desiccated sensations, as a recorder
of the nostalgia of this age, Mr. Eliot has created something whose value is, at least, documentary. Yet, grant-
ing even its occasional felicities, 'The Waste Land' is a
misleading document. The world distrusts the illusions
which the last few years have destroyed. One grants this
latter-day truism. But it is groping among new ones: the
power of the unconscious, an astringent scepticism, a mystical renaissance - these are some of the current illusions to which the Western World is turning for assurance
of their, and its, reality. Man may be desperately in-
secure, but he has not yet lost the greatest of his emotional needs, the need to believe in something - even in
his disbelief. For an ideal-demanding race there is
always one more God - and Mr. Eliot is not his prophet.

33. ELINOR WYLIE, MR. ELIOT'S SLUG-HORN, 'NEW YORK
EVENING POST LITERARY REVIEW'

20 January 1923, 396

Elinor Wylie (1885-1928), married to William Rose Benét,
was a poet and novelist. Her 'Collected Poems' appeared
in 1932.

The reviewer who must essay, within the limits of a few
hundred temperate and well-chosen words, to lead even a
willing reader into the ensorcelled mazes of Mr. T.S.
Eliot's 'Waste Land' perceives, as the public prints have
it, no easy task before him. He will appear to the mental
traveller as dubious a guide as Childe Roland's hoary
cripple with malicious eye; he lies in every word, unless
by some stroke of luck, some lightning flash of

revelation, he succeeds in showing forth the tragic sincerity and true power of that mysterious and moving spectacle, 'The Waste Land,' the mind of Mr. Eliot, the
reflected and refracted mind of a good - or rather a bad -
quarter of the present generation.

Amazing comparisons have been drawn between Mr. Eliot
and certain celebrated poets; his admirers do not couple
him with Pound nor his detractors with Dante, and both are
justified in any annoyance which they may feel when others
do so. His detractors say that he is obscure; his friends
reply that he is no more cryptic than Donne and Yeats; his
detractors shift their ground and point out with perfect
truth that he has not the one's incomparable wit nor the
other's incomparable magic; his friends, if they are wise,
acquiesce. It is stated that he is not so universal a
genius as Joyce; the proposition appears self-evident to
any one who believes with the present reviewer, that Joyce
is the sea from whose profundity Eliot has fished up that
very Tyrian murex with which Mr. Wilson rightly credits
him. Some comparisons, indeed, suggest the lunatic asy-
lums where gentlemen imagine themselves to be the authors
of Caesar's Commentaries and the Code Napoléon.

But when we begin to inquire what Mr. Eliot is, instead
of what he is not - then if we fail to respond to his
accusing cry of 'Mon semblable - mon frère!' I am inclined
to think that we are really either hypocrite readers or
stubborn ones closing deliberate eyes against beauty and
passion still pitifully alive in the midst of horror. I
confess that once upon a time I believed Mr. Eliot to be a
brutal person: this was when I first read the 'Portrait of
a Lady.' I now recognize my error, but my sense of the
hopeless sadness and humiliation of the poor lady was perfectly sound. I felt that Mr. Eliot had torn the shrinking creature's clothes from her back and pulled the
drawing-room curtains aside with a click to admit a flood
of shameful sunlight, and I hated him for his cruelty.
Only now that I know he is Tiresias have I lost my desire
to strike him blind as Peeping Tom.

This power of suggesting intolerable tragedy at the
heart of the trivial or the sordid is used with a skill
little less than miraculous in 'The Waste Land,' and the
power is the more moving because of the attendant conviction, that this terrible resembling contrast between
nobility and baseness is an agony in the mind of Mr. Eliot
of which only a portion is transferred to that of the
reader. He is a cadaver, dissecting himself in our sight;
he is the god Atthis who was buried in Stetson's garden
and who now arises to give us the benefit of an anatomy
lesson. Of course it hurts him more than it does us, and

yet it hurts some of us a great deal at that. If this is
a trick, it is an inspired one. I do not believe that it
is a trick; I think that Mr. Eliot conceived 'The Waste
Land' out of an extremity of tragic emotion and expressed
it in his own voice and in the voices of other unhappy men
not carefully and elaborately trained in close harmony,
but coming as a confused and frightening and beautiful
murmur out of the bowels of the earth. 'I did not know
death had undone so many.' If it were merely a piece of
virtuosity it would remain astonishing; it would be a work
of art like a fine choir of various singers or a rose
window executed in bright fragments of glass. But it is
far more than this; it is infused with spirit and passion
and despair, and it shoots up into stars of brilliance or
flows down dying falls of music which nothing can obscure
or silence. These things, rather than other men's out-
cries, are shored against any ruin which may overtake Mr.
Eliot at the hands of Fate or the critics. As for the
frequently reiterated statement that Mr. Eliot is a dry
intellectual, without depth or sincerity of feeling, it is
difficult for me to refute an idea which I am totally at a
loss to understand; to me he seems almost inexcusably
sensitive and sympathetic and quite inexcusably poignant,
since he forces me to employ this horrid word to describe
certain qualities which perhaps deserve a nobler tag in
mingling pity with terror. That he expresses the emotion
of an intellectual is perfectly true, but of the intensity
of that emotion there is, to my mind, no question, nor do
I recognize any reason for such a question. A very
simple mind expresses emotion by action: a kiss or a
murder will not make a song until they have passed through
the mind of a poet, and a subtile mind may make a simple
song about a murder because the murder was a simple one.
But the simplicity of the song will be most apparent to
the subtlest minds; it will be like a queer masquerading
as a dairy maid. But as for Mr. Eliot, he has discarded
all disguises; nothing could be more personal and direct
than his method of presenting his weariness and despair by
means of a stream of memories and images the like of which,
a little dulled and narrowed, runs through the brain of
any educated and imaginative man whose thoughts are
sharpened by suffering. I should perhaps have doubted the
suitability of such a stream as material for poetry, just
as I do now very much doubt the suitability of Sanskrit
amens and abracadabras, but these dubieties are matters of
personal taste and comparatively unimportant beside the
fact that, though Mr. Eliot may speak with the seven
tongues of men and of angels, he has not become as sounding brass and tinkling cymbal. His gifts, whatever they

are, profit him much; his charity, like Tiresias, has
suffered and foresuffered all. If he is intellectually
arrogant and detached – and I cannot for the life of me
believe that he is – he is not spiritually either the one
or the other; I could sooner accuse him of being sentimental. Indeed, in his tortured pity for ugly and ignoble
things he sometimes comes near to losing his hardness of
outline along with his hardness of heart; his is not a
kindly tolerance for weakness and misery, but an obsessed
and agonized sense of kinship with it which occasionally
leads him into excesses of speech, ejaculations whose
flippancy is the expression of profound despair.

Were I unable to feel this passion shaking the dry
bones of 'The Waste Land' like a great wind I would not
give a penny for all the thoughts and riddles of the poem;
the fact that Mr. Eliot has failed to convince many readers that he has a soul must be laid as a black mark
against him. Either you see him as a parlor prestidigita-
tor, a character in which I am personally unable to visual-
ize him, or else you see him as a disenchanted wizard,
a disinherited prince. When he says *Shantih* three times
as he emerges from 'The Waste Land' you may not think he
means it: my own impulse to write *Amen* at the end of a
poem has been too often and too hardly curbed to leave any
doubt in my mind as to Mr. Eliot's absorbed seriousness;
he is fanatically in earnest. His 'Waste Land' is Childe
Roland's evil ground, the names of all the lost adventur-
ers his peers toll in his mind increasing like a bell.
He has set the slug-horn to his lips and blown it once
and twice: the squat, round tower, blind as the fool's
heart, is watching him, but he will blow the horn again.

34. CONRAD AIKEN, AN ANATOMY OF MELANCHOLY, 'NEW REPUBLIC'

7 February 1923, vol. xxxiii, 294-5

Mr. T.S. Eliot is one of the most individual of contemporary poets, and at the same time, anomalously, one of the
most 'traditional.' By individual I mean that he can be,
and often is (distressingly, to some) aware in his own
way; as when he observes of a woman (in 'Rhapsody on a
Windy Night') that the door 'opens on her like a grin' and
that the corner of her eye 'Twists like a crooked pin.'
Everywhere, in the very small body of his work, is similar

evidence of a delicate sensibility, somewhat shrinking,
somewhat injured, and always sharply itself. But also,
with this capacity or necessity for being aware in his
own way, Mr. Eliot has a haunting, a tyrannous awareness
that there have been many other awarenesses before; and
that the extent of his own awareness, and perhaps even the
nature of it, is a consequence of these. He is, more than
most poets, conscious of his roots. If this consciousness
had not become acute in 'Prufrock' or the 'Portrait of a
Lady,' it was nevertheless probably there: and the roots
were quite conspicuously French, and dated, say, 1870-
1900. A little later, as if his sense of the past had
become more pressing, it seemed that he was positively
redirecting his roots - urging them to draw a morbid
dramatic sharpness from Webster and Donne, a faded dry
gilt of cynicism and formality from the Restoration. This
search of the tomb produced 'Sweeney' and 'Whispers of
Immortality.' And finally, in 'The Waste Land,' Mr.
Eliot's sense of the literary past has become so over-
mastering as almost to constitute the motive of the work.
It is as if, in conjunction with the Mr. Pound of the
'Cantos,' he wanted to make a 'literature of literature' -
a poetry not more actuated by life itself than by poetry;
as if he had concluded that the characteristic awareness
of a poet of the 20th century must inevitably, or ideally,
be a very complex and very literary awareness able to
speak only, or best, in terms of the literary past, the
terms which had moulded its tongue. This involves a kind
of idolatry of literature with which it is a little difficult to sympathize. In positing, as it seems to, that
there is nothing left for literature to do but become a
kind of parasitic growth on literature, a sort of mistle-
toe, it involves, I think, a definite astigmatism - a
distortion. But the theory is interesting if only because
it has colored an important and brilliant piece of work.

'The Waste Land' is unquestionably important, unquestionably brilliant. It is important partly because its
433 lines summarize Mr. Eliot, for the moment, and demonstrate that he is an even better poet than most had
thought; and partly because it embodies the theory just
touched upon, the theory of the 'allusive' method in
poetry. 'The Waste Land' is, indeed, a poem of allusion
all compact. It purports to be symbolical; most of its
symbols are drawn from literature or legend; and Mr. Eliot
has thought it necessary to supply, in notes, a list of
the many quotations, references, and translations with
which it bristles. He observes candidly that the poem
presents 'difficulties,' and requires 'elucidation.'
This serves to raise at once, the question whether these

difficulties, in which perhaps Mr. Eliot takes a little pride, are so much the result of complexity, a fine elaborateness, as of confusion. The poem has been compared, by one reviewer, to a 'full-rigged ship built in a bottle,' the suggestion being that it is a perfect piece of construction. But *is* it a perfect piece of construction? Is the complex material mastered, and made coherent? Or, if the poem is not successful in that way, in what way *is* it successful? Has it the formal and intellectual complex unity of a microscopic 'Divine Comedy'; or is its unity - supposing it to have one - of another sort?

If we leave aside for the moment all other considerations, and read the poem solely with the intention of understanding, with the aid of the notes, the symbolism, of making out what it is that is symbolized, and how these symbolized feelings are brought into relation with each other and with the other matters in the poem; I think we must, with reservations, and with no invidiousness, conclude that the poem is not, in any formal sense, coherent. We cannot feel that all the symbolisms belong quite inevitably where they have been put; that the order of the parts is an inevitable order; that there is anything more than a rudimentary progress from one theme to another; nor that the relation between the more symbolic parts and the less is always as definite as it should be. What we feel is that Mr. Eliot has not wholly annealed the allusive matter, has left it unabsorbed, lodged in gleaming fragments amid material alien to it. Again, there is a distinct weakness consequent on the use of allusions which may have both intellectual and emotional value for Mr. Eliot, but (even with the notes) none for us. The 'Waste Land,' of the Grail Legend, might be a good symbol, if it were something with which we were sufficiently familiar. But it can never, even when explained, be a good symbol, simply because it has no immediate associations for us. It might, of course, be a good *theme*. In that case it would be *given* us. But Mr. Eliot uses it for purposes of overtone; he refers to it; and as overtone it quite clearly fails. He gives us, superbly, a waste land - not *the* Waste Land. Why, then, refer to the latter at all - if he is not, in the poem, really going to use it? Hyacinth fails in the same way. So does the Fisher King. So does the Hanged Man, which Mr. Eliot tells us he associates with Frazer's Hanged God - we take his word for it. But if the precise association is worth anything, it is worth *putting into the poem*; otherwise there can be no purpose in mentioning it. Why, again, Datta, Dayadhvam, Damyata? Or Shantih. Do they not say a good deal less

for us than 'Give: sympathize: control' or 'Peace'? Of
course; but Mr. Eliot replies that he wants them not
merely to mean those particular things, but also to mean
them in a particular way - that is, to be remembered in
connection with a Upanishad. Unfortunately, we have none
of us this memory, nor can he give it to us; and in the
upshot he gives us only a series of agreeable sounds which
might as well have been nonsense. What we get at, and I
think it is important, is that in none of these particular
cases does the reference, the allusion, justify itself intrinsically, make itself felt. When we are aware of these
references at all (sometimes they are unidentifiable) we
are aware of them simply as something unintelligible but
suggestive. When they have been explained, we are aware
of the material referred to, the fact, (for instance, a
vegetation ceremony,) as something useless for our enjoyment or understanding of the poem, something distinctly
'dragged in,' and only, perhaps, of interest as having
suggested a pleasantly ambiguous line. For unless an
allusion is made to live identifiably, to flower, where
transplanted, it is otiose. We admit the beauty of the
implicational or allusive method; but the key to an implication should be in the implication itself, not outside of
it. We admit the value of esoteric pattern: but the pattern should itself disclose its secret, should not be
dependent on a cypher. Mr. Eliot assumes for his allusions, and for the fact that they actually allude to something, an importance which the allusions themselves do
not, as expressed, aesthetically command, nor, as
explained, logically command; which is pretentious. He is
a little pretentious, too, in his 'plan,' - 'qui pourtant
n'existe pas.' If it is a plan, then its principle is
oddly akin to planlessness. Here and there, in the wilderness, a broken finger-post.
    I enumerate these objections not, I must emphasize, in
derogation of the poem, but to dispel, if possible, an
illusion as to its nature. It is perhaps important to
note that Mr. Eliot, with his comment on the 'plan,' and
several critics, with their admiration of the poem's woven
complexity, minister to the idea that 'The Waste Land' is,
precisely, a kind of epic in a walnut shell: elaborate,
ordered, unfolded with a logic at every joint discernible;
but it is also important to note that this idea is false.
With or without the notes the poem belongs rather to that
symbolical order in which one may justly say that the
'meaning' is not explicitly, or exactly, worked out. Mr.
Eliot's net is wide, its meshes are small; and he catches
a good deal more - thank heaven - than he pretends to. If
space permitted one could pick out many lines and passages

and parodies and quotations which do not demonstrably, in
any 'logical' sense, carry forward the theme, passages
which unjustifiably, but happily, 'expand' beyond its purpose. Thus the poem has an emotional value far clearer and
and richer than its arbitrary and rather unworkable logical value. One might assume that it originally consisted
of a number of separate poems which have been telescoped –
given a kind of forced unity. The Waste Land conception
offered itself as a generous net which would, if not
unify, at any rate contain these varied elements. We are
aware of a superficial 'binding' – we observe the antici-
pation and repetition of themes, motifs; 'Fear death by
water' anticipates the episode of Phlebas, the cry of the
nightingale is repeated, but these are pretty flimsy links,
and do not genuinely bind because they do not reappear
naturally, but arbitrarily. This suggests, indeed, that
Mr. Eliot is perhaps attempting a kind of program music in
words, endeavoring to rule out 'emotional accidents' by
supplying his readers, in notes, with only those associations which are correct. He himself hints at the musical
analogy when he observes that 'In the first part of Part V
three themes are employed.'
    I think, therefore, that the poem must be taken, – most
invitingly offers itself, – as a brilliant and kaleidoscopic confusion; as a series of sharp, discrete, slightly
related perceptions and feelings, dramatically and lyric-
ally presented, and violently juxtaposed, (for effect of
dissonance) so as to give us an impression of an intensely
modern, intensely literary consciousness which perceives
itself to be not a unit but a chance correlation or con-
glomerate of mutually discolorative fragments. We are invited into a mind, a world, which is a 'broken bundle of
mirrors'; a 'heap of broken images,' Isn't it that Mr.
Eliot, finding it 'impossible to say just what he means,'
– to recapitulate, to enumerate all the events and discoveries and memories that make a consciousness, – has
emulated the 'magic lantern' that throws 'the nerves in
patterns on a screen'? If we perceive the poem in this
light, as a series of brilliant, brief, unrelated or dimly
related pictures by which a consciousness empties itself
of its characteristic contents, then we also perceive
that, anomalously, though the dropping out of any one picture would not in the least affect the logic or 'meaning'
of the whole, it would seriously detract from the value of
the portrait. The 'plan' of the poem would not greatly
suffer, one makes bold to assert, by the elimination of
'April is the cruellest month,' or Phlebas, or the Thames
daughters, or Sosostris or 'You gave me hyacinths' or 'A
woman drew her long black hair out tight'; nor would it

matter if it did. These things are not important parts of
an important or careful intellectual pattern; but they are
important parts of an important emotional ensemble. The
relations between Tiresias (who is said to unify the poem,
in a sense, as spectator) and the Waste Land, or Mr.
Eugenides, or Hyacinth, or any other fragment, is a dim
and tonal one, not exact. It will not bear analysis, it
is not always operating, nor can one with assurance, at
any given point, say how much it is operating. In this
sense 'The Waste Land' is a series of separate poems or
passages, not perhaps all written at one time or with one
aim, to which a spurious but happy sequence has been
given. This spurious sequence has a value - it creates
the necessary superficial formal unity; but it need not be
stressed, as the Notes stress it. Could one not wholly
rely for one's unity, - as Mr. Eliot *has* largely relied -
simply on the dim unity of 'personality' which would
underlie the retailed contents of a single consciousness?
Unless one is going to carry unification very far, weave
and interweave very closely, it would perhaps be as well
not to unify at all; to dispense, for example, with arbitrary repetitions.

We reach thus the conclusion that the poem succeeds -
as it brilliantly does - by virtue of its incoherence, not
of its plan; by virtue of its ambiguities, not of its
explanations. Its incoherence is a virtue because its
'donnée' is incoherent. Its rich, vivid, crowded use of
implication is a virtue, as implication is *always* a
virtue; - it shimmers, it suggests, it gives the desired
strangeness. But when, as often, Mr. Eliot uses an
implication beautifully - conveys by means of a picture-
symbol or action-symbol a feeling - we do not require to
be told that he had in mind a passage in the Encyclo-
pedia, or the color of his nursery wall; the information
is disquieting, has a sour air of pedantry. We 'accept'
the poem as we would accept a powerful, melancholy tone-
poem. We do not want to be told what occurs; nor is it
more than mildly amusing to know what passages are, in
the Straussian manner, echoes or parodies. We cannot
believe that every syllable has an algebraic inevitabil-
ity, nor would we wish it so. We could dispense with the
French, Italian, Latin and Hindu phrases - they are
irritating. But when our reservations have all been
made, we accept 'The Waste Land' as one of the most
moving and original poems of our time. It captures us.
And we sigh, with a dubious eye on the 'notes' and
'plan,' our bewilderment that after so fine a performance
Mr. Eliot should have thought it an occasion for calling
'Tullia's ape a marmosyte.' Tullia's ape is good enough.

35. HAROLD MONRO, NOTES FOR A STUDY OF 'THE WASTE LAND':
AN IMAGINARY DIALOGUE WITH T.S. ELIOT, 'CHAPBOOK'

February 1923, no. 34, 20-4

Monro (1879-1932), English poet and editor, founded the
'Poetry Review' in 1912, and edited 'Poetry and Drama'
(1914). He opened the Poetry Bookshop, and was the publisher of the five volumes of 'Georgian Poetry'. His
'Collected Poems' (1933) contained a biographical sketch
by F.S. Flint and a critical note by Eliot. An obituary
by Pound appeared in the 'Criterion' in July 1932.

I.
An Imaginary Dialogue with T.S. Eliot (*Mr. Eliot's
answers are in Italics*).

I have just read your poem 'The Waste Land' five or six
times. I don't suppose you consider me capable of understanding it? - *Well?* - I was much interested in your new
periodical the 'Criterion,' in which it appeared, and I
also saw it in the American 'Dial.' - *Well?* - I observed
that in England it was treated chiefly with indignation or
contempt, but that the 'Dial' awarded you its annual prize
of two thousand dollars. - *Well?*
    I suppose it is not very easy for those who have not
read your book 'The Sacred Wood' to understand your poetry.
Some insight into your mind is advisable. - *Possibly.* -
An article appeared in a recent number of the 'Dial' pur-
porting to elucidate your poem. Do you think that Mr.
Edmund Wilson, Jr., the writer of that article, was justified in stating that (though it consists of little more
than four hundred lines) it 'contains allusions to, parodies of, or quotations from' (here he enumerates thirty-
three sources)? - *Possibly.* - I can only recognize a dozen
or so. This may be because my reading is not sufficiently
wide. - *Possibly.* - *Well?*
    I have heard it suggested that you write for one hypo-
thetical intelligent reader. - *Well?* - Do you think such a
reader at present exists? - *I'm not sure.* - Do you think
perhaps that he is yet to be born? - *That depends.*
    I think you do your public an injustice. Presumably
the Editors who awarded you that prize may be gifted with
some intelligence? - *I am not prepared to judge.* - And Mr.
Edmund Wilson, Jr., makes the assertion that your

'trivialities are more valuable than other peoples'
epics.' He at any rate has an instinct for appreciation.
- *I am not prepared to judge.* - Myself, I am inclined to
think that some of your favourable critics, however un-
willingly, do as much damage to your repu - *That doesn't
matter anyway.*

Did you submit your poem to the 'London Mercury'? - *No.*
- If you had, do you think the 'L.M.' would have accepted
it? - *No.* - But if some friend of yours had submitted it
for you, and if it had been accepted, would you have
minded? - *Yes.* - Why? - *I don't know. It doesn't concern
me.*

Let me see: where are we now? I was saying - *I haven't
heard you say anything much yet.* - Very well: I was about
to say that 'The Waste Land' seems to me as near to Poetry
as our generation is at present capable of reaching. But,
thinking about it the other evening, I suddenly remembered
a sentence from 'The Sacred Wood': 'the moment an idea has
been transferred from its pure state in order that it may
become comprehensible to the inferior intelligence it has
lost contact with art.' And then, another: 'It is not in
his personal emotions, the emotions provoked by particular
events in his life, that the poet is in any way remarkable
or interesting.' These and other similar passages almost
make one feel that one ought not to be appreciative, as if,
indeed, it were low and vulgar to enjoy a work of literature for its own sake. *That depends upon the condition of
your mind, and the kind of enjoyment you feel.* - You, no
doubt, felt nothing personal in writing 'The Waste Land'?
- *No doubt.* - But, Mr. Eliot, surely your disgust for the
society that constitutes the world of to-day may be described as a personal emotion? - *If you refer to 'The
Sacred Wood' again you will find this sentence: 'Honest
criticism and sensitive appreciation is directed not upon
the poet but upon the poetry.'*

I am completely in agreement with it.

May I direct some criticism upon your poem? But first
I should mention that I know it was not written for me.
You never thought of me as among your potential appreciative audience. You thought of nobody, and you were true
to yourself. Yet, in a sense, you did think of me. You
wanted to irritate me, because I belong to the beastly
age in which you are doomed to live. But, in another
sense, your poem seems calculated more to annoy Mr. Gosse,
or Mr. Squire, than me. I imagine them exclaiming: 'The
fellow *can* write; but he *won't*.' That would be because
just when you seem to be amusing yourself by composing
what they might call *poetry*, at that moment you generally
break off with a sneer. And, of course, they can't

realise that your faults are as virtuous as their virtues
are wicked, nor that your style is, as it were, a mirror
that distorts the perfections they admire, which are in
truth only imitations of perfections. Your truest passages seem to them like imitations of imperfections. I
am not indulging in personalities, but only using those
gentlemen as symbols. - *Well, direct your criticisms anywhere you like. You are becoming slightly amusing, but
not yet worth answering....*

2.

Most poems of any significance leave one definite impression on the mind. This poem makes a variety of impressions, many of them so contradictory that a large
majority of minds will never be able to reconcile them,
or conceive of it as an entity. Those minds will not go
beyond wondering why it so often breaks itself up violently, changes its tone and apparently its subject. It
will remain for them a *pot-pourri* of descriptions and episodes, and while deprecating the lack of *style*, those
people will console themselves with soft laughter. That
influential London Editor-critic who dismissed it as 'an
obscure but amusing poem' is an instance.
  Obscure it is, and amusing it can be too; but neither
quite in the way he seems to have meant. They who have
only one definition for the word poem may gnash their
teeth, or smile. One definition will not be applicable
to 'The Waste Land.' Of course, most poets write of
dreaming, and use the expression that they *dream* in its
conventional rhetorical sense, but this poem actually is a
dream presented without any poetic boast, bluff or pad-
ing; and it lingers in the mind more like a dream than a
poem, which is one of the reasons why it is both obscure
and amusing. It is not possible to see it whole except in
the manner that one may watch a cloud which, though
remaining the same cloud, changes its form repeatedly as
one looks. Or to others it may appear like a drawing that
is so crowded with apparently unrelated details that the
design or meaning (if there be one) cannot be grasped
until those details have been absorbed into the mind, and
assembled and related to each other.

3.

A friend came to me with the discovery that he and I
could not hope to understand Mr. Eliot's poems; we had not

the necessary culture: impossible for us to recognise the allusions. I asked him whether the culture could be grown in a bottle or under a frame, or in the open. Mr. Edmund Wilson, Jr., tells us, on the other hand, that 'it is not necessary to know ... any but the most obvious of Mr. Eliot's allusions to feel the force of the intense emotion which the poem is intended to convey.' I was inclined to side with Mr. Wilson, so we confined ourselves to discussing the permissibility of introducing, as Mr. Eliot does, into the body of a poem, wholly or partly, or in a distorted form, quotations from other poems. 'In the absence of inverted commas,' said my friend, 'the ignorant, when they are French quotations (seeing that Mr. Eliot has written several French poems) or German even, might mistake them for lines belonging to the poem itself. It is simple cribbing. The distortions are more serious still. For instance

> When lovely woman stoops to folly and
> Paces about the room again, alone,
> She smooths her hair with automatic hand,
> And puts a record on the gramophone.

is an outrage, and a joke worthier of 'Punch' than of a serious poet. Also I much prefer the Bible, Spenser, Shakespeare, Marvell and Byron to Eliot. Marvell wrote:

> But at my back I always hear
> Time's wingèd chariot hurrying near.

Eliot writes:

> But at my back in a cold blast I hear
> The rattle of the bones, and chuckle spread from ear
>   to ear.

Well, that is simply a meretricious travesty of one of the most beautiful couplets in English poetry. It is wicked.'
I answered: 'It is only a natural jeer following upon an exposure of emotion. A schoolboy is hardly as nervous of showing his feelings. The matter cannot be judged in your manner. What we have to find out is whether T.S. Eliot is a sufficiently constructive or imaginative, or ingenious poet to justify this freedom that he exercises.'
He answered: 'Yes, but...

> But at my back I always hear
> Eliot's intellectual sneer.

- Now I'm doing it myself.'

4.

This poem is at the same time a representation, a criticism, and the disgusted outcry of a heart turned cynical.
It is calm, fierce, and horrible: the poetry of despair
itself become desperate. Those poor little people who
string their disjointed ejaculations into prosaic sem-
blances of verse - they pale as one reads 'The Waste
Land.' They have no relation to it: yet, through it, we
realise what they were trying, but have failed, to represent. Our epoch sprawls, a desert, between an unrealised
past and an unimaginable future. The Waste Land is one
metaphor with a multiplicity of interpretations.

5.

These are the opening lines:

April is the cruellest month, breeding
Lilacs out of the dead land, mixing
Memory and desire, stirring
Dull roots with spring rain.
Winter kept us warm, covering
Earth in forgetful snow, feeding
A little life with dried tubers.

36. HARRIET MONROE, A CONTRAST, 'POETRY'

March 1923, vol. xxi, 325-30

Harriet Monroe (1860-1936), a minor American poet, was the
founder and editor of 'Poetry: A Magazine of Verse'.
Pound, as foreign editor, sent her a copy of 'The Love
Song of J. Alfred Prufrock' in October 1914. In spite of
her considerable opposition, Pound was able to persuade
her to publish the poem, and it finally appeared in June
1915.
     This review contrasts 'The Waste Land' with 'The Box of
God' by Lew Sarett, to the advantage of the latter.
Sarett (1888-1954) was a minor American poet.

It happens that I have read these two books - but neither
for the first time - under the same lightly veiled sun-
shine of this mild winter afternoon; and the contrasts between them are so complete and so suggestive that I am
tempted toward the incongruity of reviewing them together.

In the important title-poems of the two we have an
adequate modern presentation of two immemorial human
types. One might call these types briefly the indoor and
the outdoor man, but that would be incomplete; they are
also the man who affirms and the man who denies; the
simple-hearted and the sophisticated man; the doer, the
believer, and the observant and intellectual questioner.
These two types have faced each other since time began
and they will accuse each other till quarrels are no more.
Both, in their highest development, are dreamers, men
commanded by imagination; seers who are aware of their
age, who know their world. Yet always they are led by
separating paths to opposite instincts and conclusions.

Mr. Eliot's poem - kaleidoscopic, profuse, a rattle and
rain of colors that fall somehow into place - gives us the
malaise of our time, its agony, its conviction of futility, its wild dance on an ash-heap before a clouded and
distorted mirror.

I will show you fear in a handful of dust,

he cries, and he shows us confusion and dismay and disintegration, the world crumbling to pieces before our eyes
and patching itself with desperate gayety into new and
strangely irregular forms. He gives us, with consummate
distinction, what many an indoor thinker thinks about life
today, what whole groups of impassioned intellectuals are
saying to each other as the great ball spins.

Yet all the time there are large areas of mankind to
whom this thinking does not apply; large groups of another
kind of intellectuals whose faith is as vital and constructive as ever was the faith of their crusading forefathers.
To the men of science, the inventors, the engineers, who
are performing today's miracles, the miasma which afflicts
Mr. Eliot is as remote a speculative conceit, as futile a
fritter of mental confectionery, as Lyly's euphemism must
have been to Elizabethan sailors. And these men are
thinkers too, dreamers of larger dreams than any group of
city-closeted artists may evoke out of the circling pipe-
smoke of their scented talk. These men are creating that
modern world which the half-aware and over-informed poets
of London and Montmartre so darkly doom.

It is their spiritual attitude which Mr Sarett's poem
presents - not statedly and consciously, but by a larger

and more absolute implication than he may be aware of.
'The Box of God' is an outdoor man's poem of faith - the
creed of the pioneer, of the explorer, the discoverer,
the inventor in whatever field; of the man who sees
something beckoning ahead, and who must follow it, where-
ever it leads; of the hero who has the future in his
keeping, who, though called by different names in different ages, is always the same type. Mr. Sarett makes an
Indian guide his spokesman - an Indian guide who rebels
against confinement in that ritualistic 'box of God', the
little Catholic church in the mountains in which his 'conversion' has been registered.

> Somebody's dere.... He's walk-um in dose cloud....
> You see-um? Look! He's mak'-um for hees woman
> De w'ile she sleep, dose t'ing she want-um most -
> Blue dress for dancing. You see, my frien'?... ain't?
> He's t'rowing on de blanket of dose sky
> Dose plenty-plenty handfuls of white stars;
> He's sewing on dose plenty teet' of elk,
> Dose shiny looking-glass and plenty beads.
> Somebody's dere ... somet'ing he's in dere ...
>
> Sh-sh-sh-sh! Somet'ing's dere!.... You hear-um?
>   ain't?
> Somebody - somebody's dere, calling ... calling ...
> I go ... I go ... me! ... me ... I go....

In primitive times the bard was aware of this man - he
sang his deeds in heroic song. If the modern bard is not
aware of him, the lack is due, not to superior intellectual sublety, but to myopic vision, narrow experience and
closely imprisoned thought. Mr. Eliot lives with spe-
cialists - poets of idle hands and legs and supersensi-
tized brains; varied by a bank clerk routine with second-
rate minds. One can not imagine him consorting with
heroes or highwaymen, or getting on intimate terms with
Thomas A. Edison if he were granted a confidental hour;
and it is hopeless to expect an all-round great poem of
our time from a man who could not thrill at such a
contact.
    Mr. Sarett's poem is not about Thomas A. Edison either;
but the spirit of such men is in it, and something of the
force of the world-builder, wherever he is found. We live
in a period of swift and tremendous change: if Mr. Eliot
feels it as chaos and disintegration, and a kind of wild
impudent dance-of-death joy, Mr. Sarett feels it as a new
and larger summons to faith in life and art. This poet
has lived with guides and Indians; last summer, while

taking his vacation as a forest ranger of the government,
he chased a pair of bandits through Glacier Park for
forty-eight hours alone, and single-handed brought them
back to camp for trial. He could talk with Thomas A.
Edison, or perhaps with a sequoia or a skyscraper. He has
the experience and character-equipment to write poems
expressive of the particular kind of heroic spirit which
is building the future while nations are painfully digging
their way out of the past. 'The Box of God' is one such
poem; and in it his art, while less fluid and fluent and
iridescent than Mr. Eliot's, is of a rich and nobly beautiful pattern and texture which suggests that he may prove
adequate to the task. One feels that he is merely at the
beginning, that he is just getting into his stride.

But I would not be understood as belittling the importance of Mr. Eliot's glistening, swiftly flowing poem
of human and personal agony because it does not say the
whole thing about the age we live in. Mr. Eliot would be
the first to disclaim such an intention - he would probably say that 'The Waste Land' is the reaction of a suffering valetudinarian to the present after-the-war chaos in
Europe, with its tumbling-down of old customs and sancti-
ties. It is a condition, not a theory, which confronts
him; and he meets the condition with an artist's invocation of beauty. One would expect a certain deliberateness
in Mr. Eliot's art, but this poem surprises with an effect
of unstudied spontaneity. While stating nothing, it suggests everything that is in his rapidly moving mind, in a
series of shifting scenes which fade in and out of each
other like the cinema. The form, with its play of many-
colored lights on words that flash from everywhere in the
poet's dream, is a perfect expression of the shifting
scenes which fade in and out of each other like the
cinema. The form, with its play of many-colored lights on
words that flash from everywhere in the poet's dream, is a
perfect expression of the shifting tortures in his soul.
If one calls 'The Waste Land' a masterpiece of decadent
art, the word must be taken as praise, for decadent art,
while always incomplete, only half-interpretive, is pitifully beautiful and tragically sincere. The agony and
bitter splendor of modern life are in this poem, of that
part of it which dies of despair while the world is building its next age.

If Mr. Eliot's subject is essentially a phantasmagoric
fade-out of God, Mr. Sarett's is the search for God, for a
larger god than men have ever entrapped in the churchly
boxes they have made for him. Both poems are, in a sense,
the poet's meditations, interrupted by the intrusion of
remembered words once uttered by others: in Sarett's case

by the long-dead Indian guide, in Eliot's by Lil's husband, by Mrs. Porter, by Shakespeare, Spenser, Dante,
Baudelaire, and many other poets of many languages. And
both poems have a certain largeness and finality: they do
excellent-well what they set out to do, and they suggest
more than they say - they invite to thought and dreams.

37. J.M., REVIEW, 'DOUBLE DEALER'

May 1923, vol. v, 173-4

Burton Rascoe's review appeared in the 'New York Tribune',
5 November 1922, section 5, 8.

                    Here, said she,
    Is your card, the drowned Phoenician Sailor.

'The Waste Land' is, it seems to me, the agonized outcry
of a sensitive romanticist drowning in a sea of jazz.
When Mr. Burton Rascoe calls it 'perhaps the finest poem
of this generation,' one is compelled to challenge the
verdict because comparisons in the arts are unjust in the
first place and 'The Waste Land' is not as a whole superb.
But one would be very foolish indeed who would deny that
it contains magnificent elements and supremely beautiful
lines.
    This medley of catch-phrases, allusions, innuendoes,
paraphrase and quotation gives unmistakable evidence of
rare poetic genius. One is certain that, read by Mr.
Eliot, to whom every allusion is clear, for whom every
catchword has a ghostly portent, for whom every quotation
has an emotional and intellectual connotation of intense
significance, 'The Waste Land' is a great poem. To us who
cannot read with Mr. Eliot's spectacles, colored as they
are by Mr. Eliot's experience, it must remain a hodge-
podge of grandeur and jargon. It cannot, from the standpoint of the average reader or of the average writer of
verse, be appraised as a complete success.
    Mr. Eliot, an immortal by instinct, finds himself sub-
merged - a 'drowned Phoenician Sailor' - in the garish and
to him not charming swirl of animalistic, illiterate human
life, now seething on both sides of the Atlantic. Caught

in this maelstrom, he catches glimpses of the world of drama and romance and stable beauty which he would prefer and which, no question, he has found in books. From that ideal world come floating ghostly cadences, images and reminders. To these straws he clings, as a sort of salvation.

> O swallow swallow
> *Le Prince d'Aquitaine à la tour abolie*
> These fragments I have shored against my ruins

The fragments from the other world which Mr. Eliot clings to in 'The Waste Land,' like the fragments which he quotes in 'The Sacred Wood,' are of the very heart of poetry: 'Those are pearls that were his eyes,' echoes throughout.

Taking the poem as a whole, the average reader will object that many passages, as pure art, are not satisfactory. I venture to repeat that Mr. Eliot's own intellectual or emotional associations give to some of the language used in 'The Waste Land' a significance which it does not and cannot have for another individual. The discords, in Mr. Eliot's opinion and in that of certain readers, no doubt, have their place in the pattern, adding a beauty of contrast, heightening the effect of the harmonies. To me the discords seem unsatisfactory discords. 'The Waste Land' is a poem containing passages of extreme beauty, but I believe there are few persons who can read it all with sustained delight.

It opens:

[Quotes CPP, p. 61, 'April is' to 'shower of rain'.]

A little farther on Mr. Eliot writes:

[Quotes CPP, p. 61, 'What are the roots' to 'sound of water'.]

In 'Death by Water' (Part IV of the poem) one finds:

[Quotes CPP, p. 71.]

In 'A Game of Chess' (Part II) one finds:

> 'Do
> You know nothing? Do you see nothing?
>   Do you remember
> Nothing?'
>   I remember
> Those are pearls that were his eyes.

Many of us have contended for a long time that T.S. Eliot is one of the most exceptional men of letters of his epoch. 'The Waste Land' confirms that belief. How much of it or of his previous work is indelible I would not venture to estimate. That that work reveals a genius and a personality extremely rare, I am certain. And that Mr. Eliot, as poet or as critic or as scholar, eminently deserved such an award as the Dial prize, seems to be incontrovertible.

38. JOHN CROWE RANSOM, WASTE LANDS, 'NEW YORK EVENING POST LITERARY REVIEW'

14 July 1923, vol. iii, 825-6

Ransom (1888-1976) was a distinguished American poet and critic, author of 'The World's Body' (1938) and 'Selected Poems' (1945). He was an influential editor of the 'Kenyon Review'.

This review was reprinted in 'Modern Essays, Second Series', edited by Christopher Morley (New York, 1924), pp. 345-59.

The imagination of a creative artist may play over the surface of things or it may go very deep, depending on the quality and the availability of the artist's mind. Here is fiction, for example, wherein the artist, its author, is going to recite a local body of fact; and this core of fact is not more definitely related to space and time by the illusions of his realism than it already has been related to the whole emotional and philosophical contexts of his life. The thing has been assimilated into his history. It is no longer pure datum, pure spectacle, like a visitation of the angels or like categorical disaster; it does not ravish nor appall him; for it has been thoroughly considered by the artist, through processes both conscious and unconscious, and has been allowed to sink infallibly into its connections.

An appalling thing to Hamlet evidently was death. But Claudius enjoyed the insuperable advantage of being elder to the Prince of Denmark, and therefore could invite him to consider the King's death in the light of authentic evidence of the common mortality of fathers: *sub specie omnium patrum obitorum*. And Horatio, a man of superior practical instincts, to him marvelling how the grave digger could sing at his trade, was enabled to return the inspired answer: 'Custom hath made it in him a property of easiness.'

A property of easiness is what the artist must come to, against even the terrible and the ecstatic moments of history. A great discrimination of nature against America is this requirement, in the field of the comparative literatures; in pioneering America a tribal ethic pronounces that life is real, life is earnest. The property of easiness in the mind is one of the blessings that compensate an old and perfected society for the loss of its youth. And likewise with the individual artist, it comes with experience, and it comes notably with age; though not entirely as reckoned by the Gregorian calendar. The young artist is not to think that his synthesis of experience is worth as much as the old one's. He is not to put an extravagant value on the freshness of his youthful passions, but to make sure that the work of art wants for its material the passion mellowed and toned and understood long after the event: 'recollected in tranquillity,' to use the best of all the literary dogmas. A soul-shaking passion is very good if the artist will wait for it to age; the bigger the passion the deeper it will go in the integrating processes of the mind, and the wider will be the branching associations it will strike out. When it comes forth eventually it will have depth and context, too. It has been fertilized and romanticized. It has been made musical, or symphonic, where, before it gained its subsidiary pieces and was itself subdued to harmony, it was only monotone and meant nothing to delicate ears.

There is a subterranean chamber where the work of artistic gestation takes place. It has always been held that the artist draws for his sources from a depth beyond the fathom of the consciously reasoning mind. An immense literature to this effect - or at least the English fraction of it - has recently been minutely reported by Professor Prescott in 'The Poetic Mind'; and it is an application of the same principle, though quite spontaneous and fresh, which gives the English poet Robert Graves his doctrine of inspiration. We are not to dogmatize about this subliminal consciousness; the psychologists are terribly at sea in defining it; probably it is wrong to refer to it at all as a subconsciousness. Here we inevitably enter the province of pure theory; but critics have to have a revelation of first principles if they are going to speak with any authority about art.

Possibly the following statement of the case might be defended. At one moment we are conscious; but at the next moment we are self-conscious, or interested in the moment that is past, and we attempt to write it down. Science writes it down in one way, by abstracting a feature and trying to forget all the rest. Art writes it down in another way, by giving the feature well enough but by managing also to suggest the infinity of its original context. The excellence of science is its poverty, for it tries to carry only the abstractions into the record, but the excellence of art is its superfluity, since it accompanies these abstractions with much of that tissue of the concrete in which they were discovered. It is as if the thing will not live out of its own habitat, it is dead as soon as science hauls it up and handles it, but art tries to keep it alive by drawing up with it a good deal of its native element.

Today we are superbly in a position to consent to such a doctrine. Since James and Bradley and Bergson, since Kant if we have always had ears to hear, since the Carus Lectures of John Dewey if we only began to listen yesterday, it is borne in upon us that abstract science is incapable of placing the stream of consciousness - the source of all that is - upon the narrow tablets of the record. Art, too, in the last analysis is probably incapable, since at any moment it only complements the record of science and at no moment denies it, so that Coleridge, defining poetry as more than usual emotion, added the remarkable qualification, 'with more than usual order.' But art, if it is not destructive, is at least gently revolutionary. The specific of art which is enough to create its illusion and make it miraculous among the works of the mind is that it fishes out of the stream what would become the dead abstraction of science, but catches it still alive, and can exhibit to us not only its bones and structures but many of the free unaccountable motions of its life. These motions are the contributions that art makes to the record; these free and unpredictable associations discovered for the thing in its stream. They are impertinences to the scientific temper, but delightful to the soul that in the routine of scientific chores is oppressed with the sense of serving a godless and miserly master.

But returning to the level of practice, or the natural history of art. A man repeatedly must come to points where his science fails him, where his boasted intellect throws its little light and still leaves him in darkness; there is then nothing for him to do but to go off and sound the secret cavern for an oracle. That is to say, he abandons his problem to mysterious powers within him which are not the lean and labored processes of his self-conscious reason. And if this abandonment is complete the oracle will speak. After brief silence, after a sleep and a forgetting, but at all events with what must be considered an astonishing celerity, the answer comes out. It is a kind of revelation. He submitted facts, and he receives them related into truths. He deposited a raw realism; he receives it richly romanticized. Evidently the agency which worked for him simply referred his datum to a perfectly organized experience, where no item was missing, and returned it with a context of clinging natural affinities.

But the principle for the artist to proceed upon is that he must *release* his theme to the processes of imagination - a hard principle for the narrow-minded! He must wait like a non-partisan beside his theme, not caring whether it comes forth pro or con; and inevitably, of course, it will be neither. Thr truth that comes by inspiration is not simply the correct conclusion to premises already known; the Pythian never comes down to monosyllables and answers yes and no. The whole matter is worked over freshly by an agent more competent than reason and the conclusion is as unpredictable as the evidence was inaccessible. The man with a cause must abdicate before his genius will work for him. The history of inspiration does not offer cases where passions, even righteous passions, spasms of energy, rages and excitements, and even resolutions that seem likely to remove mountains have enabled artists to call the spirits from the vasty deep. History offers cases like Goethe's, who wrote, recalling certain moments in the composition of *Faust*: 'The difficulty was to obtain, by sheer force of will, what in reality is obtainable only by a spontaneous act of nature.' But this faculty of release is rare, and by the same token the artists are rare. Probably the history of most of the abortive efforts at art is the history of wilful men who could not abandon their cause, but continued to worry it as a dog worries a bone, expecting to perform by fingers and rules what can come by magic only. And release is peculiarly difficult for the hot blood of youth. The young artist stakes everything upon the heat of his passion and the purity of his fact. Very limited is the assistance which he is capable of receiving from his elders in speeding the tedious rites of time; he is convinced that *alla stoccata* will carry it away.

Other formulas would carry such first principles as well as these, and indeed, ideally, every critic could find them for himself. He needs them if he is to speak

with a greater authority than we now hear him speaking.
He needs to have a theory of inspiration in order that he
may trace error back to its course, and show that the
artist must always sin unless his heart is pure. The
field of literature in our day - perhaps beyond all other
days - is an unweeded garden, in which the flowers and
weeds are allowed to grow side by side because the garden-
ers, who are the critics, do not know their botany. The
commonest and fatallest error in the riot of our letters
is the fundamental failure of the creative imagination,
and it ought always to be exposed. Is it held that this
sort of criticism would be too brutal? Is it equivalent
to telling the artist that he is congenitally defective in
the quality fundamental to art? It is not so bad as that;
a part of the total error by which the artist misses his
art may be due to the fact that his gift, which is
genuine, is under the cloud of some inattention or poor
policy, or, above all, immaturity, which is capable of
treatment. But it does not matter; criticism should
attend to its business anyway; criticism should be prepared to make an example of bad artists for the sake of
the good artists and the future of art.

But what a congenial exercise is furnished the critic
by that strange poem, 'The Waste Land.' In the first
place, everybody agrees beforehand that its author is
possessed of uncommon literary powers, and it is certain
that, whatever credit the critic may try to take from him,
a flattering residue will remain. And then his poem has
won a spectacular triumph over a certain public and is
entitled to an extra quantity of review. Best of all, Mr.
Eliot's performance is the apotheosis of modernity, and
seems to bring to a head all the specifically modern
errors, and to cry for critic's ink of a volume quite
disproportionate to its merits as a poem.

The most notable surface fact about 'The Waste Land' is
of course its extreme disconnection. I do not know just
how many parts the poem is supposed to have, but to me
there are something like fifty parts which offer no
bridges the one to the other and which are quite distinct
in time, place, action, persons, tone, and nearly all the
unities to which art is accustomed. This discreteness
reaches also to the inside of the parts, where it is indicated by a frequent want of grammatical joints and marks
of punctuation; as if it were the function of art to break
down the usual singleness of the artistic image, and then
to attack the integrity of the individual fragments. I
presume that poetry has rarely gone further in this direction. It is a species of the same error which modern
writers of fiction practice when they laboriously

disconnect the stream of consciousness and present items
which do not enter into wholes. Evidently they think with
Hume that reality is facts and pluralism, not compounds
and systems. But Mr. Eliot is more enterprising than
they, because almost in so many words he assails the
philosophical or cosmical principles under which we form
the usual images of reality, naming the whole phantasma-
goria Waste Land almost as plainly as if he were naming
cosmos Chaos. His intention is evidently to present a
wilderness in which both he and the reader may be
bewildered, in which one is never to see the wood for the
trees.

Against this philosophy – or negation of philosophy –
the critic must stand fast. It is good for some purposes,
but not for art. The mind of the artist is an integer,
and the imaginative vision is a single act which fuses its
elements. It is to be suspected that the author who holds
his elements apart is not using his imagination, but using
a formula, like a scientist anxious to make out a 'case';
at any rate, for art such a procedure suggests far too
much strain and tension. For imagination things cohere;
pluralism cannot exist when we relax our obsessions and
allow such testimony as is in us to come out. Even the
most refractory elements in experience, like the powerful
opposing wills in a tragedy, arrive automatically at their
'higher synthesis' if the imagination is allowed to treat
them.

There is a reason besides philosophical bias which
makes the disconnection in the poem. The fragments could
not be joined on any principle and remain what they are.
And that is because they are at different stages of fertilization; they are not the children of a single act of
birth. Among their disparities one notes that scraps from
many tongues are juxtaposed; and yet one knows well that
we are in different 'ages of intelligence' when we take
the different languages on our lips; we do not quote Greek
tragedy and modern cockney with the same breath or with
the same kinds of mind. We cannot pass, in 'The Waste
Land,' without a convulsion of the mind from '0 0 0 0 that
Shakespeherian Rag,' to 'Shantih shantih shantih.' And
likewise, the fragments are in many metres, from the comparatively formal metre which we know as the medium of
romantic experiences in the English thesaurus to an extremely free verse which we know as the medium of a half-
hearted and disillusioned art. But, above all, some fragments are emotions recollected in tranquillity and others
are emotions kept raw and bleeding, like sores we continue
to pick. In other words, the fragments vary through
almost every stage, from pure realism to some point just

short of complete fertilization by the romantic imagination, and this is a material which is incapable of synthesis.

A consequence of this inequality of material is a
certain novelty of Mr. Eliot's which is not fundamentally
different from parody. To parody is to borrow a phrase
whose meaning lies on one plane of intelligence and to
insert it into the context of a lower plane; an attempt
to compound two incommensurable imaginative creations. Mr.
Eliot inserts beautiful quotations into ugly contexts.
For example:

> When lovely woman stoops to folly, and
> Paces about her room again, alone,
> She smoothes her hair with automatic hand,
> And puts a record on the gramophone.

A considerable affront against aesthetic sensibilities.
Using these lovely borrowed lines for his own peculiar
purposes, Mr. Eliot debases them every time; there is not,
I believe, a single occasion where his context is as
mature as the quotation which he inserts into it; he does
not invent such phrases for himself, nor, evidently, does
his understanding quite appreciate them, for they require
an organization of experience which is yet beyond him.
The difficulty in which he finds himself is typically an
American one. Our native poets are after novelty; they
believe, as does Mr. Eliot in one of his prose chapters,
that each age must have its own 'form.' The form in
which our traditionary poetry is cast is that of another
generation and therefore No-thoroughfare. What the new
form is to be they have not yet determined. Each of the
new poets must experiment with a few usually, it appears,
conceiving forms rather naïvely, as something which will
give quick effects without the pains and delays of complete fertilization. Mr. Eliot has here tried out such a
form and thereby reverted to the frailties of his nativ-
ity. The English poets, so far as they may be general-
ized, are still content to work under the old forms and,
it must be said in their favor, it is purely an empirical
question whether these are unfit for further use; the
poets need not denounce them on principle. But it may be
put to the credit of Mr. Eliot that he is a man of better
parts generally than most of the new poets, as in the
fact that he certainly bears no animus against the old
poetry except as it is taken for a model by the new poets;
he is sufficiently sensitive to its beauties at least to
have held on with his memory to some of its ripest texts
and to have introduced them rather wistfully into the

forbidding context of his own poems, where they are
thoroughly ill at ease.

The criticism does not complete itself till it has compared 'The Waste Land' with the earlier work of its
author. The volume of 'Poems' which appeared a year previously hardly presaged the disordered work that was to
follow. The discrepancy is astonishing. Sweeney and Prufrock, those heroes who bid so gayly for immortality in
their own right, seem to come out of a fairly mature and
at any rate an equal art. They are elegant and precious
creations rather than substantial, with a very reduced
emotional background, like the art of a man of the world
rather than of a man of frankly poetic susceptibilities;
but the putative author is at least responsible. He has
'arrived'; he has by self-discipline and the unconscious
lessons of experience integrated his mind. The poem
which comes a year later takes a number of years out of
this author's history, restores him intellectually to his
minority. I presume that 'The Waste Land,' with its burden of unregenerate fury, was disheartening to such critics as Mr. Aldington, who had found in the 'Poems' the
voice of a completely articulate soul; I presume that for
these critics the 'Poems' are automatically voided and
recalled by the later testament; they were diabolically
specious, and the true heart of the author was to be revealed by a very different gesture. But I prefer to
think that they were merely precocious. They pretended to
an intellectual synthesis of which the author was only
intellectually aware, but which proved quite too fragile
to contain the ferment of experience. One prefers 'The
Waste Land' after all, for of the two kinds it bears the
better witness to its own sincerity.

'The Waste Land' is one of the most insubordinate poems
in the language, and perhaps it is the most unequal. But
I do not mean in saying this to indicate that it is permanently a part of the language; I do not entertain that
as a probability. The genius of our language is notoriously given to feats of hospitality: but it seems to me
it will be hard pressed to find accommodations at the same
time for two such incompatibles as Mr. Wordsworth and the
present Mr. Eliot; and any realist must admit that what
happens to be the prior tenure of the mansion in this case
is likely to be stubbornly defended.

39. ALLEN TATE, A REPLY TO RANSOM, 'NEW YORK EVENING POST
LITERARY REVIEW'

4 August 1923, vol. iii, 886

Tate (1899-1979), an important American poet and critic,
was associated with Ransom in the Fugitive Group. After
Eliot's death he edited a collection of essays by various
hands which appeared first in the 'Kenyon Review' and was
later published as 'T.S. Eliot: The Man and His Work' (New
York, 1966).
    This item is a letter from Tate to the literary editor
disagreeing with Ransom's earlier review.

SIR: John Crowe Ransom's article, Waste Lands, in the
'Literary Review' of July 14, violates so thoroughly the
principle of free critical inquiry and at the same time
does such scant justice to the school of so-called philosophic criticism, to which one supposes he belongs, that
it may be of interest to your readers to consider the
possible fallacy of his method and a few of the errors
into which it leads him.
    Mr. Ransom begins by building up a rather thorough-
going schematism of the origin and process of artistic
creation, and though he grants that 'other formulas would
carry first principles just as well as these,' he urges
that the critic, 'needs a theory of inspiration, in order
that he may trace error back to its source.' The maker of
these phrases evidently knows nothing of the genetic criticism since the day of Wundt or of the Freudian emphasis
of later days on the psychological origins of art as a
standard of aesthetics; at any rate, he is unaware of the
ultimate futility of this kind of inquiry when its results
are dragged in to serve as critical arbiters. Theories of
inspiration are valuable, though less so than interesting,
but Mr. Ransom, it seems to me, has offered only an
abstract restatement of superannuate theories of consciousness, which do not constitute a theory of inspiration - whatever such a theory may be: all to the end that
a philosophy of discontinuity is not only lamentable but
entirely wrong. What this has to do with aesthetics it is
hard to conceive. But Mr. Ransom rightly says that the
critic 'should be prepared to make an example of the bad
artists for the sake of the good artists'; but this
example cannot be made by exorcising pluralism to the

advantage of a gentler but equally irrelevant ghost: 'For
the imagination things cohere; pluralism cannot exist when
we relax our obsessions and allow such testimony as is in
us to come out.'   In other words, no honest man can be a
pluralist - which is not only palpably untenable but quite
outside the course of his argument.   And if we *have* heeded
too little the Carus lectures of John Dewey or failed to
let the mire of Kantianism cling to our feet, what is Mr.
Ransom going to do about the writings of Remy de Gourmont
and, closer home, certain words uttered as far back as
1896 by Mr. George Santayana?   And isn't it difficult to
see how Professor Prescott and Robert Graves (!) can be
heeded along with Kant and Bradley?

And coming to 'The Waste Land' itself, Mr. Ransom is
quite consistent in so far as he condemns the poem for its
anti-philosophical *mélouge*.   He wonders why T.S. Eliot is
chaotic in his verse and so rigidly coherent in his prose,
and accounts for the discrepancy on the doubtful ground
that T.S. Eliot is determined to exploit pluralism at all
costs, even at the risk of being charged with insincerity.
Doubtless Mr. Ransom knows the difference between the
instrument, Logic, and the material, Reality; but I do not
believe he shows it here.   I take it that Keats wrote
about as incoherent prose as we have, yet in certain odes
he gives us Mr. Ransom's 'higher synthesis': how would
Mr. Ransom explain this?   I suppose Keats was insincere in
his letters because he exposes a multiverse.   Mr. Ransom
asks whether this sort of criticism would be too brutal.
Well not so brutal as irrelevant.

The real trouble with Mr. Ransom's article comes out
when he proceeds to comment on specific aspects of 'The
Waste Land.'   Mr. Eliot is a pluralist; he has not
'achieved' a philosophy; *argal*, he is immature, and his
poem is inconsiderable.   I take it that Anatole France is
immature.   But Mr. Ransom's worry on this point really is
his inability to discover the form of the poem, for, says
he, it presents metres so varied and such lack of grammar
and punctuation and such a bewildering array of discrete
themes, that he is at loss to see the poem as one poem at
all.   Whatever form may be, it is not, I dare say, regularity of metre.   Artistic forms are ultimately attitudes,
and when Mr. Ransom fails to understand Mr. Eliot's purpose in using lines from other poets, like 'When lovely
woman stoops to folly,' calling it parody, we are aware
of a naivete somewhat grosser than that which he ascribes
elsewhere in his essay to modern experimentation generally.   He makes his point by a highly imaginative *petitio
principii*: the fragments are at different stages of
'fertilization' and represent different levels of

intelligence; and then, too, Eliot inserts these quotations into a context never so rich as their proper abode. Is it possible that Mr. Ransom thinks that these beautiful fragments were put into 'The Waste Land' simply to lend it a 'beauty' which its author could not achieve for himself? And is he confusing parody with irony? His definition of parody, without the dogmatic implication that one plane of consciousness is 'higher' than another, is really a definition of irony: the incongruous is not always the deformed or ludicrous. And it is probably true that metres are never more than an organic scaffolding upon which the poet hangs an attitude; the 'form' of 'The Waste Land' is this ironic attitude which Mr. Ransom relegates to the circus of Carolyn Wells. My remarks here are excessive; at this point in Mr. Ransom's argument we suspect that he should not be taken seriously.

It is to be regretted also that T.S. Eliot repudiates his first volume *ipso facto* by writing 'The Waste Land.' The only discoverable difference between 'Poems' and 'The Waste Land' is certainly not one of central attitude. Mr. Eliot, an intellectual romanticist, need not commit himself to the same intuition of the world to-day as yesterday; he must shift all the time, for his motive is curiosity, not prepossession, even though he is driven always by the same thirst. The free intelligence cannot harbor a closed system.

And if tradition means sameness, then Mr. Eliot cannot survive with Wordsworth. But Mr. Ransom doesn't say just where it is that poems survive. However, it is likely that the value of 'The Waste Land' as art is historical rather than intrinsic; but the point of my objection to John Crowe Ransom's essay is that the method he employs is not likely to give T.S. Eliot much concern. And my excuse for this extended objection is that Mr. Ransom is not alone. He is a *genre*.

40. HELEN McAFEE, THE LITERATURE OF DISILLUSION, 'ATLANTIC'

August 1923, vol. cxxxii, 227

Helen McAfee (1884–1956), an American literary critic, was managing editor of the 'Yale Review'.

This is an extract from a longer article concerned with
the general disillusionment of literature after the war.

Under pressure of war emotion we did undoubtedly idealize
one another, - at least, all those on one side, - and we
sometimes forgot to judge men's motives on the basis of
our accumulated knowledge of human nature. The rebound to
self-criticism and cynicism had to come. But another
element has entered in during these last five years.
'Happy is he who suffers and knows why,' says one of
Claudel's dying heroines. With the spectacle of the peace
before them, and its aftermath in Europe, some men no
longer see why they suffered.
     Certainly the most striking dramatization of this depth
of confusion and bitterness is Mr. Eliot's 'The Waste
Land.' As if by flashes of lightning it reveals the wreck
of the storm. For this effect it is clear that the author
has consciously striven - indeed he refers to his work as
'my ruins.' The poem is written in what is called the
Expressionist manner - a manner peculiarly adapted to the
present temper. It does not present the social order in a
series of concentric circles, as in Dante, with the individual passing from one to the other in mathematical succession; or as a wall against which the individual dashes
himself, - usually in vain, - as in Tolstoy or Ibsen. It
rather presents his mind, or his mood, as the centre
around which the world gyrates wildly, and with which it
makes few contacts, and those chiefly enigmatic. To students of psychology the method of procedure in 'The Waste
Land' must be highly significant. Impressions, fragments
of experience, memories of other men's writings, drift
through the author's consciousness at the bidding of the
subconsciousness. There is little attempt at completion of
any one pattern out of the mass of details and allusions,
or at logical climax. But the parts move with a certain
rhythm, - the rhythm of daydreams, - and, dream-fashion,
resolve one into another and so achieve a whole. It is
mood more than idea that gives the poem its unity. And
that mood is black. It is as bitter as gall; not only with
a personal bitterness, but also with the bitterness of a
man facing a world devastated by a war for a peace without
ideals. The humor - for it has humor - is sordid, gro-
tesque. Yet even in the barren ugliness of 'The Waste
Land' there is redeeming grace. After quoting a bit from
that most delightful of all spring poems, the 'Pervigilium
Veneris,' and two other lines equally fine, Mr. Eliot seems
content to rest his case - 'These fragments,' he writes,
'I have shored against my ruins.'

41. EDGELL RICKWORD, UNSIGNED REVIEW, A FRAGMENTARY POEM,
'TIMES LITERARY SUPPLEMENT'

20 September 1923, no. 1131, 616

Rickword (b. 1898), an English poet and critic, was editor
of the 'Calendar of Modern Letters'. His 'Collected Poems'
appeared in 1967.

   This review was reprinted in 'PN Review' (1979), no. 1,
vi, supplement xi-xii. The magazine devoted a special
supplement to Rickword's work. The review also reappeared in Rickword's 'Essays and Opinions 1921-31',
edited by Alan Young (Manchester, 1974), 42-4.

Between the emotion from which a poem rises and the reader
there is always a cultural layer of more or less density
from which the images or characters in which it is expressed may be drawn.   In the ballad 'I wish I were where
Helen lies' this middle ground is but faintly indicated.
The ballad, we say is *simpler* than the 'Ode to the Nightingale'; it evokes very directly an emotional response.   In
the ode the emotion gains resonance from the atmosphere of
legendary association through which it passes before reaching us.   It cannot be called better art, but it is certainly more sophisticated and to some minds less poignant.
From time to time there appear poets and a poetic audience
to whom this refractory haze of allusion must be very
dense; without it the meanings of the words strike them so
rapidly as to be inappreciable, just as, without the air,
we could not detect the vibration of light.   We may remember with what elaboration Addison, among others, was
obliged to undertake the defence of the old ballads before
it was recognized that their bare style might be admired
by gentlemen familiar with the classics.
   The poetic personality of Mr. Eliot is extremely sophisticated.   His emotions hardly ever reach us without
traversing a zig-zag of allusion.   In the course of his
four hundred lines he quotes from a score of authors and
in three foreign languages, though his artistry has
reached that point at which it knows the wisdom of sometimes concealing itself.   There is in general in his work
a disinclination to awake in us a direct emotional response.   It is only, the reader feels, out of regard for
some one else that he has been induced to mount the platform at all.   From there he conducts a magic-lantern show;

but being too reserved to expose in public the impressions
stamped on his own soul by the journey through the Waste
Land, he employs the slides made by others, indicating
with a touch the difference between his reaction and
theirs.   So the familiar stanza of Goldsmith becomes

> When lovely woman stoops to folly and
> Paces about her room again, alone,
> She smoothes her hair with automatic hand,
> And puts a record on the gramophone.

To help us to elucidate the poem Mr. Eliot has provided some notes which will be of more interest to the
pedantic than the poetic critic.   Certainly they warn us
to be prepared to recognize some references to vegetation
ceremonies.   This is the cultural or middle layer, which,
whilst it helps us to perceive the underlying emotion, is
of no poetic value in itself.   We desire to touch the inspiration itself, and if the apparatus of reserve is too
strongly constructed, it will defeat the poet's end.   The
theme is announced frankly enough in the title, 'The Waste
Land'; and in the concluding confession,

> These fragments I have shored against my ruins,

we receive a direct communication which throws light on
much which had preceded it.   From the opening part, 'The
Burial of the Dead,' to the final one we seem to see a
world, or a mind, in disaster and mocking its despair.
We are aware of the toppling of aspirations, the swift
disintegration of accepted stability, the crash of an
ideal.   Set at a distance by a poetic method which is
reticence itself, we can only judge of the strength of the
emotion by the visible violence of the reaction.   Here is
Mr. Eliot, a dandy of the choicest phrase, permitting
himself blatancies like 'the young man carbuncular.'   Here
is a poet capable of a style more refined than that of any
of his generation parodying without taste or skill - and
of this the example from Goldsmith is not the most
astonishing.   Here is a writer to whom originality is
almost an inspiration borrowing the greater number of his
best lines, creating hardly any himself.   It seems to us
as if the 'The Waste Land' exists in the greater part in
the state of notes.   This quotation is a particularly
obvious instance:-

> London Bridge is falling down falling down falling
>   down
> *Poi s'ascose nel foco che gli affina*

>   *Quando fiam ceu chelidon* - O swallow swallow
>   *Le Prince d'Aquitaine à la tour abolie.*

The method has a number of theoretical justifications.
Mr. Eliot has himself employed it discreetly with delicious effect. It suits well the disillusioned smile
which he had in common with Laforgue; but we do sometimes
wish to hear the poet's full voice. Perhaps if the
reader were sufficiently sophisticated he would find
these echoes suggestive hints, as rich in significance as
the sonorous amplifications of the romantic poets. None
the less, we do not derive from this poem as a whole the
satisfaction we ask from poetry. Numerous passages are
finely written; there is an amusing monologue in the vernacular, and the fifth part is nearly wholly admirable.
The section beginning

>   What is that sound high in the air...

has a nervous strength which perfectly suits the theme;
but he declines to a mere notation, the result of an
indolence of the imagination.

Mr. Eliot, always evasive of the grand manner, has
reached a stage at which he can no longer refuse to
recognize the limitations of his medium; he is sometimes
walking very near the limits of coherency. But it is the
finest horses which have the most tender mouths, and some
unsympathetic tug has sent Mr. Eliot's gift awry. When
he recovers control we shall expect his poetry to have
gained in variety and strength from this ambitious
experiment.

42. CLIVE BELL, T.S. ELIOT, 'NATION AND ATHENAEUM'

22 September 1923, vol. xxxiii, 772-3

This review also appeared as The Elusive Art of T.S. Eliot
in 'Vanity Fair', September 1923, 53.

To be amongst the first to think, say, or do anything, is
one of the silliest and most harmless of human ambitions:
I was one of the first in England to sing the praises of

Eliot. I shall not forget going down to a country house for the Easter of 1916 - or was it '17? - with 'Prufrock' in my pocket, and hearing it read aloud to a circle of guests with whose names I am too modest to bribe your good opinion. Only this I will say, no poet could ask for a better send off. 'The Love Song of J. Alfred Prufrock' was read aloud two or three times and discussed at intervals; it was generally admired or, at any rate, allowed to be better than anything of the sort that had been published for some time: and it pleases me to remember that its two most ardent admirers were a distinguished mathematician (not Bertrand Russell) and an exquisite lady of fashion.

To me 'Prufrock' seemed a minor masterpiece which raised immense and permissible hopes: my opinion has not changed, but my hopes have dwindled slightly. For, as yet, Eliot has written nothing better than 'Prufrock,' which seems less surprising when we discover that, in a sense, he has written nothing else; - for the last seven years, I mean, he has been more or less repeating himself. He has lost none of the qualities which made me then describe him as 'about the best of our younger poets'; his intelligence and wit are as sharp as ever, and his phrasing is still superior to that of any of his contemporaries: but he has not improved.

Eliot, it seems to me, has written nothing wittier, more brilliantly evocative of a subtle impression, than 'Mr. Apollinax'; and that, I believe, he wrote before he came to England. It is proper to add that if in this style he has not improved upon himself, neither has anyone, in the interval, improved upon him. As for phrasing - a term which in his case I prefer to 'diction' (musicians will understand why) - it is his great accomplishment; and if you will open 'Prufrock' at the very first page you will come on the following passage:-

> Let us go, through certain half-deserted streets,
> The muttering retreats
> Of restless nights in one-night cheap hotels
> And sawdust restaurants with oyster-shells:
> Streets that follow like a tedious argument
> Of insidious intent
> To lead you to an overwhelming question...

than which, in my opinion, he has done nothing better. Before contradicting me let the reader count at least ten, and give his memory a jog. In Mr. Eliot's later poems he will find, to be sure, better phrases than any of these; but is he sure they are by Mr. Eliot? The poet has a disconcerting habit of omitting inverted commas. 'Defunctive music,' for instance, is from Shakespeare; and not only the Elizabethans are laid under contribution. The other day a rather intemperate admirer quoted at me the line,

'The army of unalterable law,'

and declared that no modern could match it. You know it is by Meredith.

If you will read carefully Eliot's three longer poems – 'Prufrock,' 'Gerontion,' and 'The Waste Land' – I think you will see what I mean – even if you do not agree with me – in saying that he has been more or less repeating himself. And here we come at Eliot's essential defect. He lacks imagination; Dryden would have said 'invention,' and so will I if you think it would sweeten my discourse. Eliot belongs to that anything but contemptible class of artists whose mills are perfect engines in perpetual want of grist. He cannot write in the great manner out of the heart of his subject; his verse cannot gush as a stream from the rock: birdlike he must pile up wisps and straws of recollection round the tenuous twig of a central idea. And for these wisps and straws he must go generally to books. His invention, it would seem, cannot be eked out with experience, because his experience, too, is limited. His is not a receptive nature to experience greatly. Delicate and sensitive admirers have found, I know, the key to a lifelong internal tragedy in those lines with their choice Elizabethan tang:-

I that was near your heart was removed therefrom
To lose beauty in terror, terror in inquisition.
I have lost my passion: why should I need to keep it
Since what is kept must be adulterated?

But for my part, I cannot believe they are wrung from the heart of tragic experience. The despairing tone which pervades Eliot's poetry is not, it seems to me, so much the despair of disillusionment as the morbidity of 'The Yellow Book.'

But how the man can write! And the experience, if it be small, is perfectly digested and assimilated; it has gone into the blood and bones of his work. Admit that the butter is spread unconscionably thin; at least the poet may claim, with the mad hatter, that it was the best butter. By his choice of words, by his forging of phrases, by his twisting, stretching, and snapping of rhythms – manipulations possible only to an artist with

an exact ear - Eliot can make out of his narrow vision and
meagre reaction things of perpetual beauty.

> At the violet hour, the evening hour that strives
> Homeward, and brings the sailor home from sea,
> The typist home at tea time, clears her breakfast,
>   lights
> Her stove, and lays out food in tins.

(Mark the transition - the technical one I mean - the
stress and scarcely adumbrated stress - 'HOMEward, and
brings the sailor *home* from sea, the typist *home* at tea-
time,' so as to run on in a breath ' clears her breakfast.'
A less dexterous artist would have had to break the flow
with a full stop to show that he had changed the subject.)
The line,

> Her drying combinations touched by the sun's last rays,

is a piece of obvious comic-weekly humour, unworthy of so
fastidious a writer. But try a line or two lower down:

> He, the young man carbuncular, arrives,
> A small house-agent's clerk, with one bold stare,
> One of the low on whom assurance sits
> As a silk hat on a Bradford millionaire.

In its own modern way it is as neat as Pope, and one can
almost see Mr. Arnold Bennett going to the races. I
should be surprised if Eliot were ever to write a great
poem; but he might easily write three or four which would
take their places amongst the most perfect in our language.
    Eliot reminds me of Landor: I believe he will not dis-
dain the comparison. Landor wrote half-a-dozen of the
most perfect poems in English, and reams of impeccable
dullness. Like Eliot he had very little imagination or
invention; a narrow vision and, as a rule, tepid reactions; unlike Eliot he was incontinent. Spiritually, he
looked out of the window of a suburban villa on the furniture of a suburban garden: the classical statue he set up
in the middle of the grass plot was more often than not a
cast.   No, it was something more spacious than a villa
garden; but it bore a horrid likeness to a public park.
Yet, on the rare occasions when Landor could apprehend
the hum-drum world he inhabited with something like passion, his art enabled him to create a masterpiece. There
is not much more feeling or understanding of feeling in
'The Maid's Lament' than may be found in a prize copy of
elegiacs by an accomplished sixth-form boy; most of the

sentiments have grown smooth in circulation, and the
images ('the shades of death,' 'this lorn bosom burns,'
'tears that had melted his soft heart,' 'more cold than
daisies in the mould') have been the small change of minor
poetry these three hundred years: yet 'The Maid's Lament'
justly takes its place in 'The Oxford Book of Verse.'

Eliot is said to be obscure; and certainly 'The Waste
Land' does not make easy reading. This I deplore, holding,
with the best of English critics, that 'wit is most to be
admired when a great thought comes dressed in words so
commonly received that it is understood by the meanest
apprehensions.' Only let us not forget that 'Prufrock,'
which at first seemed almost unintelligible, now seems
almost plain sailing, and that 'Sweeney Erect,' which was
described as 'gibberish,' turns out to be a simple and
touching story; so when we cudgel our brains over his
latest work let us hesitate to suppose that we cudgel in
vain. It was decided, remember, that Gray's odes were
quite incomprehensible; so were 'In Memoriam' and 'The
Egoist'; and the instrumentalists - those practical experts
- assured the conductor that no orchestra ever would play
Beethoven's symphonies, for the very simple reason that
they were unplayable. I respect the man who admits that
he finds Eliot's poetry stiff; him who from its obscurity
argues insincerity and mystification I take for an ass.

Turn to Eliot's criticism ('The Sacred Wood') if you
want proof of his sincerity, and of one or two more qualities of his. Here he gives you some of the most interesting criticism and quite the silliest conclusions going.
Here is a highly conscious artist, blessed with an
unusually capable intellect and abnormal honesty, whose
analysis of poetical methods is, therefore, bound to be
masterly; who is never flabby, and who never uses well-
sounding and little-meaning phrases to describe a quality
in a work of art or a state of his own mind. Eliot is an
exceptional critic. Unluckily, he is a cubist. Like the
cubists, he is intent upon certain important and neglected
qualities in art; these he detects unerringly, and he has
no eyes for any others. His vision, you remember, was
said to be narrow. He has an *a priori* theory, which is no
sillier than any other *a priori* theory, and he applies it
unmercifully. It leads him into telling us that 'Corio-
lanus' is better than 'Hamlet' and 'The Faithful Shepherd-
ess' than 'Lycidas' - it leads him into absurdity. His
conclusions are worthless; the argument and analysis by
which he arrives at them are extraordinarily valuable. As
in his poetry, in criticism his powerful but uncapacious
mind can grasp but one thing at a time; that he grasps
firmly. He disentangles with the utmost skill an

important, hardly come at, and too often neglected quality
in poetry; and if it were the only quality in poetry he
would be almost the pontiff his disciples take him for.
Not quite - for no aesthetic theory can explain his in-
discreet boosting of the insignificant Miss Sinclair and
the lamentable Ezra Pound. These predilections can be
explained only by a less intelligent, though still perfectly honourable, misconception.

43. J.C. SQUIRE ON ELIOT'S FAILURE TO COMMUNICATE, 'LONDON
MERCURY'

October 1923, vol. viii, 655-6.

Sir John Squire (1884-1958) was a Georgian poet, parodist
and editor of the 'London Mercury'. He was profoundly
opposed to modernism in all its forms.
    This passage is taken from a longer review. The other
poets considered were Lindsay, Millay and Alice Meynell.

I read Mr. Eliot's poem several times when it first
appeared; I have now read it several times more; I am
still unable to make head or tail of it. Passages might
easily be extracted from it which would make it look like
one of those wantonly affected productions which are written by persons whose one hope of imposing on the credulous
lies in the cultivation of a deliberate singularity. It
is impossible to feel that when one reads the whole thing:
it may bewilder and annoy, but it must leave the impression on any open-minded person that Mr. Eliot does mean
something by it, has been at great pains to express himself, and believes himself to be exploring a new avenue
(though we may think it a dark cul-de-sac) of poetic
treatment. The work is now furnished with an extensive
apparatus of notes. There are references to Ezekiel,
Marvell, 'The Inferno,' Ovid, Wagner, St. Augustine, Sir
James Frazer, and the Grail legend. But though these will
tell those who do not know where Mr. Eliot got his·quota-
tions and symbolism from, they do not explain what these
allusions are here for. The legend about the Cumæan Sibyl,
which Rossetti paraphrased in verse, combined with the
title and one casual reference, suggest that Mr. Eliot

believes the poem to be about the decay of Western civilisation and his own utter sickness with life. But even with this knowledge I confess that I do not see where it comes in. There is a vagrant string of drab pictures which abruptly change, and these are interspersed with memories of literature, lines from old poets, and disconnected ejaculations. This is a fair specimen of the poem's progress:

[Quotes 'What the Thunder said', CPP, pp. 67-8, 'While I was fishing' to 'Tereu'.]

After which we proceed to the Smyrna currant merchant who asked Mr. Eliot (or somebody else perhaps) to tea at the Cannon Street Hotel, and we conclude with 'Shantih shantih shantih,' which, we are told, is 'a formal ending to an Upanishad.' Conceivably, what is attempted here is a faithful transcript, after Mr. Joyce's obscurer manner, of the poet's wandering thoughts when in a state of erudite depression. A grunt would serve equally well; what is language but communication, or art but selection and arrangement? I give it up; but it is a pity that a man who can write as well as Mr. Eliot writes in this poem should be so bored (not passionately disgusted) with existence that he doesn't mind what comes next, or who understands it. If I were to write a similar poem about this poem the first line from another work which would stray into the medley would be Mr. Chesterton's emphatic refrain 'Will someone take me to a pub?' The printing of the book is scarcely worthy of the Hogarth Press.

44. WILLIAM ROSE BENÉT, AMONG THE NEW BOOKS. POETRY AD LIB, 'YALE REVIEW'

October 1923, vol. xiii, 161-2

William Rose Benét (1886-1950), together with his wife, Elinor Wylie, and his brother, Stephen Vincent Benét, were important American critics, especially in New York during the 1930s.
     This is an extract from a longer review.

The books before me are all interesting. The most import-
ant seem to me to be 'The Waste Land,' by T.S. Eliot,
'Introducing Irony' and 'The Sardonic Arm,' by Maxwell
Bodenheim, and 'Roman Bartholow,' by Edwin Arlington
Robinson.

There has been much discussion of Eliot's book already,
and the best and last word upon it - to my mind - was said
by Conrad Aiken in the 'New Republic.' I myself have but
one thing to say about 'The Waste Land' - that I found it
deeply emotional underneath all attitudinizing, that it
moved me (for all its eccentricity), and that its oddity
fascinated.

That is *one* opinion. These feelings of mine about 'The
Waste Land' overcame my irritation at the pedantic 'Notes'
and at certain other posturings. After all, there may be
beauty, pathos, the springs of sincere spiritual agony in

Silk handkerchiefs, cardboard boxes, cigarette ends
Or other testimony of summer nights

- just as beauty and pathos are undeniable in

...Son of man,
You cannot say, or guess, for you know only
A heap of broken images, where the sun beats,
And the dead tree gives no shelter, the cricket no
    relief,
And the dry stone no sound of water.

You ask me just exactly what 'The Waste Land' means in
every line and phrase, and I can give you but a botched
explanation. Go to Mr. Aiken for the best discussion of
its peculiar structure or lack of structure. 'The Waste
Land' means in general no more than Mr. Eliot's earlier
'Gerontion' meant, in 'Ara Vos Prec.' I have always
cared strongly for Mr. Eliot's 'apeneck Sweeney,' whether
among the nightingales or not, and for his apocalyptic
hippopotamus. The jungle of his mind seems to me very
fertile. And he can do remarkably moving things with
reticences and sharply struck discords. For pendants to
Aiken, look up the reviews of 'The Waste Land' by Edmund
Wilson, Jr. and Elinor Wylie: the former having appeared
in the 'Dial,' and latter in the 'Literary Review.' I am
one of those who feel that Mr. Eliot earned his two thousand dollar 'Dial' prize....

45. CHARLES POWELL, REVIEW, 'MANCHESTER GUARDIAN'

31 October 1923, 7

Powell (1878-1951), the son of a Methodist minister, was
appointed to the 'Manchester Guardian' as an editorial
assistant in 1915. His obituary in the 'Guardian' of
19 September 1951 says of him: 'He was in fact an austere
Nonconformist, and his moral attitude would have made him
more at home in the stern Puritan England of the Common-
wealth or in some strict Dissenting sect of the eighteenth
century than in the lax world he knew.' He wrote a book of
parodies with John Drinkwater, 'The Poets in the Nursery'
(1920). At the time of writing this review he was literary
critic for the 'Manchester Guardian'.

This poem of 430 lines, with a page of notes to every three
pages of text, is not for the ordinary reader. He will
make nothing of it. Its five sections, called successively
'The Burial of the Dead,' 'A Game of Chess,' and so on, for
all they will signify to him, might as well be called 'Tom
Thumb at the Giant's Causeway,' or 'The Devil among the
Bailiffs,' and so on. The thing is a mad medley. It has a
plan, because its author says so; and presumably it has
some meaning, because he speaks of its symbolism; but meaning, plan, and intention alike are massed behind a smoke-
screen of anthropological and literary erudition, and only
the pundit, the pedant, or the clairvoyant will be in the
least aware of them. Dr. Frazer and Miss J.L. Weston are
freely and admittedly his creditors, and the bulk of the
poem is under an enormously composite and cosmopolitan
mortgage: to Spenser, Shakespeare, Webster, Kyd, Middleton,
Milton, Marvell, Goldsmith, Ezekiel, Buddha, Virgil, Ovid,
Dante, St. Augustine, Baudelaire, Verlaine, and others.
Lines of German, French, and Italian are thrown in at will
or whim; so, too, are solos from nightingales, cocks,
hermit-thrushes, and Ophelia. When Mr. Eliot speaks in his
own language and his own voice it is like this at one
moment:

[Quotes CPP, p. 61, 'April is' to 'dried tubers'.]

and at another moment like this:

[Quotes CPP, p. 68, 'Unreal City' to 'at the Metropole'.]

For the rest one can only say that if Mr. Eliot had been
pleased to write in demotic English 'The Waste Land' might
not have been, as it just is to all but anthropologists
and *literati*, so much waste paper.

46. F.L. LUCAS, REVIEW, 'NEW STATESMAN'

3 November 1923, vol. xxii, 116-18

Lucas (1894-1967), an English literary critic, was best
known for his work on Greek and Elizabethan drama. A
Fellow of King's College, he taught English at the University of Cambridge.

'Solitudinem faciunt, *poëma* appellant.'

   Among the maggots that breed in the corruption of poetry
one of the commonest is the bookworm. When Athens had de-
cayed and Alexandria sprawled, the new giant-city, across
the Egyptian sands; when the Greek world was filling with
libraries and emptying of poets, growing in erudition as
its genius expired, then first appeared, as pompous as
Herod and as worm-eaten, that *Professorenpoesie* which
finds in literature the inspiration that life gives no
more, which replaces depth by muddiness, beauty by echoes,
passion by necrophily. The fashionable verse of Alexandria grew out of the polite leisure of its librarians, its
Homeric scholars, its literary critics. Indeed, the
learned of that age had solved the economic problem of living by taking in each others' dirty washing, and the
'Alexandra' of Lycophron, which its learned author made so
obscure that other learned authors could make their for-
tunes by explaining what it meant, still survives for the
curious as the first case of this disease and the first
really bad poem in Greek. The malady reappears at Rome in
the work of Catullus' friend Cinna (the same whom with a
justice doubly poetic the crowd in 'Julius Caesar' 'tears
for his bad verses'), and in the gloomy pedantry that mars
so much of Propertius; it has recurred at intervals ever
since. Disconnected and ill-knit, loaded with echo and
allusion, fantastic and crude, obscure and obscurantist -
such is the typical style of Alexandrianism.

Readers of 'The Waste Land' are referred at the outset,
if they wish to understand the poem or even its title, to
a work on the ritual origins of the legends of the Holy
Grail by Miss J.L. Weston, a disciple of Frazer, and to
the 'Golden Bough' itself. Those who conscientiously
plunge into the two hundred pages of the former interesting, though credulous, work, will learn that the basis of
the Grail story is the restoration of the virility of a
Fisher King (who is an incarnation, like so many others in
Frazer, of the Life-spirit), and thereby of the fertility
of a Waste Land, the Lance and the Grail itself being
phallic symbols. While maintaining due caution and remembering how

> Diodorus Siculus
> Made himself ridiculous,
> By thinking thimbles
> Were phallic symbols,

one may admit that Miss Weston makes a very good case.
With that, however, neither she nor Mr. Eliot can rest
content, and they must needs discover an esoteric meaning
under the rags of superstitious Adam. Miss Weston is
clearly a theosophist, and Mr. Eliot's poem might be a
theosophical tract. The sick king and the waste land symbolise, we gather, the sick soul and the desolation of
this material life.

But even when thus instructed and with a feeling of
virtuous research the reader returns to the attack, the
difficulties are but begun. To attempt here an interpretation, even an intelligible summary of the poem, is to
risk making oneself ridiculous; but those who lack the
common modern gift of judging poetry without knowing what
it means, must risk that. 'The Waste Land' is headed by
an allusion from Petronius to the Sibyl at Cumae, shrunk
so small by her incredible age that she was hung up in a
bottle and could only squeak, 'I want to die.' She typi-
fies, I suppose, the timeworn soul's desire to escape from
the 'Wheel' of things. The first of the five sections
opens in spring with one of the snatches of poetry that
occur scattered about the poem:

> April is the cruellest month, breeding
> Lilacs out of the dead land, mixing
> Memory and desire, stirring
> Dull roots with spring rain.

The next moment comes a spasm of futile, society conversation from a Swiss resort, followed by a passionate outburst

at the sterile barrenness of life, though not without hope
of its redemption. This is far the best passage in the
book:

> What are the roots that clutch, what branches grow
> Out of this stony rubbish? Son of man,
> You cannot say, or guess, for you know only
> A heap of broken images where the sun beats,
> And the dead tree gives no shelter, the cricket no
>   relief,
> And the dry stone no sound of water.

Then, suddenly, a verse of 'Tristan und Isolde' and an
echo of Sappho (the vanity of human love?). Next instant
there appears a clairvoyante, and in the mystic 'Tarot'
cards of her fortune-telling are revealed those mysterious
figures that flit through the poem, melting into each
other in a way that recalls Emerson's 'Brahma' - the
Phoenician sailor, who 'is not wholly distinct from Prince
Ferdinand of Naples' and seems to be reincarnate in the
Smyrna currant-merchant; the Fisher King; and the Frazer-
ite Hanged Man or sacrificed priest, who merges later into
the Christ of the walk to Emmaus.
  Then we are thrust into the squalid, 'unreal' Inferno of
London Bridge.
  The second section contains a dialogue between two
jaded lovers in luxury, an interlude about the rape of
Philomela the nightingale (spiritual beauty violated by
the world?), and a pothouse story of a wrangle between two
women about the husband of one of them. In the third part
the Fisher King appears fishing in the first person behind
the gashouse, and there recur the *motifs* of the nightingale and of unreal London, also:

> Mr. Eugenides, the Smyrna merchant
> Unshaven, with a pocket full of currants
> *C.i.f.* London.

But before the reader has time to breathe, 'I, Tiresias,'
is watching the seduction of a tired typist after tea by a
'young man carbuncular' - a typical instance of that
squalor which seems perpetually to obsess Mr. Eliot with
mixed fascination and repulsion. A note explains that
Tiresias, being a person of double sex, unites in some way
all the other persons in the poem. There is more suburban
sordidness, and the section ends gasping half a sentence
from St. Augustine and another half from Buddha.
  In 'IV. - Death by Water' (one of the stock ways, in
Frazer, of killing the vegetation king and ensuring rain

by sympathetic magic) the Phoenician sailor is duly
drowned. Section V., which brings the rain of deliverance
to the Waste Land, is, by the author's account, a mixture
of the Walk to Emmaus, of the approach to the Chapel Perilous in Arthurian Legend (taken by Miss Weston to signify
initiation into the mysteries of physical and spiritual
union), and of the state of Eastern Europe! Deliverance
comes with the magic formula; 'Datta, dayadhvam, damyata -
give, sympathise, control', and the poem ends:

> London Bridge is falling down falling down falling down
> *Poi s'ascose nel foco che gli affina*
> *Quando fiam ceu chelidon* - O swallow, swallow
> *Le Prince d'Aquitaine à la tour abolie*
> These fragments I have shored against my ruins
> Why then Ile fit you. Hieronymo's mad againe.
> Datta. Dayadhvam. Damyata.
>   Shantih shantih shantih

(The punctuation largely disappears in the latter part
of the poem - whether this be subtlety or accident, it is
impossible to say. 'Shantih' is equivalent to the 'Peace
that passeth understanding' - which in this case it certainly does.)

All this is very difficult; as Dr. Johnson said under
similar circumstances, 'I would it were impossible.' But
the gist of the poem is apparently a wild revolt from the
abomination of desolation which is human life, combined
with a belief in salvation by the usual catchwords of
renunciation - this salvation being also the esoteric
significance of the savage fertility-rituals found in the
'Golden Bough,' a watering, as it were, of the desert of
the suffering soul.

About the philosophy of the poem, if such it be, it
would be vain to argue; but it is hard not to regret the
way in which modern writers of real creative power abandon
themselves to the fond illusion that they have philosophic
gifts and a weighty message to deliver to the world, as
well. In all periods creative artists have been apt to
think they could think, though in all periods they have
been frequently harebrained and sometimes mad; just as
great rulers and warriors have cared only to be flattered
for the way they fiddled or their flatulent tragedies.
But now, in particular, we have the spectacle of Mr.
Lawrence, Miss May Sinclair, and Mr. Eliot, all sacrific-
ing their artistic powers on the altar of some fantastic
Mumbo-Jumbo, all trying to get children on mandrake roots
instead of bearing their natural offspring.

Perhaps this unhappy composition should have been left

to sink itself: but it is not easy to dismiss in three
lines what is being written about as a new masterpiece.
For at present it is particularly easy to win the applause
of the blasé and the young, of the coteries and the
eccentricities. The Victorian 'Spasmodics' likewise had
their day. But a poem that has to be explained in notes
is not unlike a picture with 'This is a dog' inscribed beneath. Not, indeed, that Mr. Eliot's notes succeed in
explaining anything, being as muddled as incomplete. What
is the use of explaining 'laquearia' by quoting two lines
of Latin containing the word, which will convey nothing to
those who do not know that language, and nothing new to
those who do? What is the use of giving a quotation from
Ovid which begins in the middle of a sentence, without
either subject or verb, and fails to add even the reference? And when one person hails another on London Bridge
as having been with him 'at Mylae,' how is the non-
classical reader to guess that this is the name of a Punic
sea-fight in which as Phoenician sailor, presumably, the
speaker had taken part? The main function of the notes is,
indeed, to give the references to the innumerable authors
whose lines the poet embodies, like a mediaeval writer
making a life of Christ out of lines of Virgil. But the
borrowed jewels he has set in its head do not make Mr.
Eliot's toad the more prepossessing.

In brief, in 'The Waste Land' Mr. Eliot has shown that
he can at moments write real blank verse; but that is all.
For the rest he has quoted a great deal, he has parodied
and imitated. But the parodies are cheap and the imitations inferior. Among so many other sources Mr. Eliot
may have thought, as he wrote, of Rossetti's 'Card-
Dealer,' of 'Childe Harold to the Dark Tower Came,' of
the 'Vision of Sin' with its same question:

To which an answer peal'd from that high land,
But in a tongue no man could understand.

But the trouble is that for the reader who thinks of them
the comparison is crushing. 'The Waste Land,' adds nothing to a literature which contains things like these. And
in our own day, though Professor Santayana be an inferior
poet, no one has better reaffirmed the everlasting 'No'
of criticism to this recurrent malady of tired ages, 'the
fantastic and lacking in sanity':

Never will they dig deep or build for time
Who of unreason weave a maze of rhyme,
Worship a weakness, nurse a whim, and bind
Wreaths about temples tenantless of mind,
Forsake the path the seeing Muses trod,
And shatter Nature to discover God.

47. HUMBERT WOLFE, WASTE LAND AND WASTE PAPER, 'WEEKLY
WESTMINSTER'

17 November 1923, n.s., vol. i, 94

Wolfe (1885-1940) was an English poet, critic and essayist.
He published his autobiography 'And Now a Stranger' in
1933.
    The other book reviewed was 'The Poetical Works of Gil-
bert Frankau'.

I begin by admitting that I do not understand Mr. Eliot's
poem in the sense that I could not pass an examination
upon it. If, for example, I were set the following three
questions (two compulsory),

    (1) What relation does the expressed desire of the
Cumæan Sibyl to die bear to the poem that it prefaces?
    (2) How far does each part of the poem carry on the
meaning of its predecessor and point on to the conclusion?
    (3) Is it really necessary, in order to understand the
poem, to make a detailed study of the literature of anthro-
pology? Illustrate your reply by reference to Miss Jessie
L. Weston's book 'From Ritual to Romance,' 'Handbook of
Birds of Eastern North America,' and Bradley's 'Appearance
and Reality.'

I should be prepared to give answers, and I am certain
that they would be quite unlike the answers that others
who, equally with me, admire the poem, would give, and,
like all the answers, would be unsatisfactory to Mr. Eliot.
But that doesn't bother me in the least. Part of the
truth about poetry is its beautiful and essential unintelligibility, just as obscurity is its most fatal
defect. Unintelligibility, in my use of the word here,
conveys that rushing sense of suggestion hiding behind
the actual written word that almost stuns the receptive
mind, as might a too bright light projected upon a sensitive eye. All poetry worthy of the name shakes just perceptibly beyond the ordinary power of the mind, but it
shakes in brightness not in darkness. It is not that the
poet can't make himself clear to us, but it is that true
poetry is always reaching out beyond itself to the
thoughts and feelings for which no words have yet been
found. There is about it always an unprospected land,
no-man's because it is trodden, in default of fools, by

angels. From all of which it follows that everybody who
cares for poetry must always fail in an examination of a
strict kind. To confess, therefore, that I don't understand Mr. Eliot's poem seems to me to be no more a criticism of it than to say that (in the same sense) I don't
understand Shakespeare's sonnets. Neither needs in that
sense to be understood.

But that is not to say that I don't get from 'The Waste
Land' just those thrills that I associate with what I believe to be poetry. I do emphatically, and if they come
by unusual channels that after all is the best tribute
that could be paid to any work of art. Let me first show
how indisputably in the recognised fashion Mr. Eliot can
produce his effect:

> ...yet there the nightingale
> Filled all the desert with inviolable voice
> And still she cried, and still the world pursues,
> 'Jug Jug' to dirty ears.
>
> To Carthage then I came
>
> Burning burning burning burning
> O Lord thou pluckest me out
> O Lord thou pluckest
>
> burning
>
> Gentile or Jew
> O you who turn the wheel and look to windward,
> Consider Phlebas, who was once handsome and tall as
> you.

That is the old recognisable way of beauty, and having
shown himself master of it, Mr. Eliot is at liberty to
play any tricks that he chooses. Nobody can accuse him of
writing queerly because he won't compete in the open. The
queer stuff can now be approached with an easier mind.
And what are we to suppose is hidden under these excursions from the Starnbergersee by way of a hyacinth garden
and fortune-telling by cards to 'the brown fog of a winter
dawn' in London? Is it the soul sprawling from mountains
out of spring past a viscous summer into the drabbest of
winters? I don't interpret, because even as I attempt
interpretation Mr. Eliot assaults me with

> You! hypocrite lecteur! - mon semblable, - mon frère!

Well, if I am his brother I shall proceed by saying
that the next movement, 'The Game of Chess,' is the symbol
of nightingale of beauty singing in the ears of all of us,

choked with the dirt of the common burdens of mortality.
Ending how? Why thus:

> Good night, ladies, good night, sweet ladies, good
>   night, good night.

(That line hits me between the eyes. It is (to me)
poetry's closing-time.)
As to the third movement, 'The Fire Sermon,' nightingale sings again:

> Twit twit twit
> Jug jug jug jug jug jug
> So rudely forced.
> Tereu

between the rats in the slime, the wanton typist in her
sodden attic and

>   where the walls
> of Magnus Martyr hold
> Inexplicable splendour of Ionian white and
>   gold.

Rats, lust, inexplicable splendour all in one tumbled
heap:

>   la la
> To Carthage then I came.

So then the fourth movement, 'Death by Water,' and how
things lovely endure by dying before loveliness decays,
and here no nightingale need sing. Fifth movement and
last, 'What the Thunder said.' Here are the 'falling
towers,' the black end when:

> A woman drew her long black hair out tight
> And fiddled whisper music on those strings
> And bats with baby faces in violet light.

Thus we have progressed through every form of ruin and despair over the Waste Land to where:

> London Bridge is falling down falling down falling
>   down.

As I began by saying, I don't pretend to understand,
but end with the sense that the five movements are knit
together by some invulnerable strand. There remains in my

mind a sound of high and desolate music. So poetry should
end.

It is just worth while perhaps mentioning Mr. Frankau's
book at the end of this attempt to understand Mr. Eliot's
poems. Because there is nothing unintelligible about Mr.
Frankau, except in so far as he thinks well to reprint
verse of the Visitors' Book type from some Eton journal
and 'The Wipers Times.' But the intelligibility of Mr.
Frankau is interesting side by side with Mr. Eliot's unintelligibility. It wouldn't be true to say that Mr. Eliot
begins where Mr. Frankau leaves off, because Mr. Frankau
seems never to leave off. But it would be true to say that
by every standard which Mr. Frankau's verse professes Mr.
Eliot is wrong, and that by every true standard he is
right. Mr. Frankau still believes that volubility, hearty
emotionalisms, and a Kipling metre are ingredients of
poetry. Mr. Eliot does not think so. Mr. Frankau likes
length without depth. Mr. Eliot does not. Mr. Frankau
reports what is immediately under his eyes without seeing
it. Mr. Eliot is looking elsewhere.

Finally, under the stress of one emotion, Mr. Frankau
writes a verse like this:

> Whether it last for the Seven Years,
> Or whether it end in a day,
> Peoples of Earth, let us swear an oath,
> 'No truce with the Beasts in Grey.'

Under the stress of another thus:

> Woman o' mine, heart's anodyne
>   Against unkindly fate,
> Love's aureole about my soul,
>   Wife, mistress, comrade, mate.

Mr. Eliot is unlikely to write similar verses.

48. GORHAM B. MUNSON, THE ESOTERICISM OF T.S. ELIOT, '1924'

1 July 1924, no. 1, 3-10.

Gorham Bert Munson (1896-1969), an American critic, was the
founder and editor of 'Secession', a magazine of the avant-

garde. In 1938, he organised the American Social Credit
Movement.

Some expert - my choice would be Mr. Ezra Pound - should
write a moderately long brochure on the versification of
T.S. Eliot. Mr. Eliot wrote such a brochure on the metric
of Pound and it sharpened considerably our insight into
the construction and finesse of his poetry. We need much
more of this precise service. Mr. Pound, for example,
could show us very exactly the crossing of Mr. Eliot's
style by French influences, he could discuss at length
what he has already mentioned; 'Mr. Eliot's two sorts of
metaphor: his wholly unrealizable, always apt, half ironic
suggestion, and his precise realizable picture,' he could
elaborate on Mr. Eliot's thematic invention.
    Surely in reading the 'Poems' and 'The Waste Land' all
serious students of poetry feel what Mr. Pound calls the
sense of an unusual intelligence working behind the words.
I shall make a trial at placing this intelligence in relation to the complicated and confused literary and cultural
currents of our era. We can make a start toward such
placement if we examine closely the peculiar esotericism
of 'The Waste Land.' It is permissible to concentrate
only on 'The Waste Land' because that poem is a summation
of Mr. Eliot's intellectual and emotional attitudes: it
recapitulates almost all the themes which were given
shape in the collected 'Poems.'
    The full purport of esoteric writing is concealed from
the 'average reader.' It requires for comprehension a
more or less stringent initiation in certain ways of feeling, thinking and expressing, which are not common. To
the uninitiated such writing is simply obscure. But esotericism is not properly a term of reproach, for it may be
inescapable.
    One type, that arising from the nature of the subject-
matter, Mr. Pound has admirably explained. 'Obscurities
inherent in the thing occur when the author is piercing,
or trying to pierce into, uncharted regions; when he is
trying to express things not yet current, not yet worn
into phrase; when he is ahead of the emotional, or philosophic sense (as a painter might be ahead of the color-
sense) of his contemporaries.' I think this is true of
certain modern writers, whom I call the higher Romantics.
If they have an intense desire to communicate experience,
they suffer peculiarly, for their desire is constantly
frustrated by the undeveloped emotional or philosophical
sense of their readers.
    Another type arises from obscurities inherent in the

treatment. The author is an experimenter and tries to pierce into uncharted regions of technic and form. He tries to arrange the non-representative properties of literature *in vacuo*, to devise what Mr. Eliot in his essay on Jonson calls a 'creative fiction.' The subject-matter perhaps has little logic of its own, and the author's structural logic is ahead of the contemporary aesthetic sense.

Either type of esotericism is highly commendable. Each represents an advance and each if well done is complete in itself. The demand upon the reader is legitimate, for he has only to find the proper key in his own sensibility or in his own experience, and then turn it with his own intellect. If the reader fails, it is he who is deficient, not the work.

But the esotericism of 'The Waste Land' is different: it is deliberate mystification. For in structure the poem is loose: it is full of interstices. Episode does not inevitably follow episode: transitions do not carry us, willy-nilly, from theme to theme, from movement to movement. Its unity depends upon Mr. Eliot's personality, not upon the poem's functions and their adjustments and relations. The structural effect is very much like that given by a revolving light: a sequence of flashes and blanks without significance until referred to the purpose of the lighthouse and the controlling hand of the keeper. I say this in spite of certain formal achievements within the poem: the firm Virgilian outline of the seduction scene witnessed by Tiresias, the triumphant progression through most utterly banal chatter, speeded up by the bartender's cries, 'HURRY UP PLEASE IT'S TIME,' to the cool and lovely line from 'Hamlet,' 'Good night, ladies, good night, sweet ladies, good night, good night.' Themes are stated, caught up later, recur. There is a general cumulative movement, the poem has a half-visible crescendo. It dies nicely with 'shantih shantih shantih.' But the two planes on which 'The Waste Land' moves - the plane of myth and the plane of present day London - are not strictly related. Passages of fine poetry may be deleted without spoiling one's aesthetic pleasure of the whole, though diminishing the sum total derived from the detail. Symbols, characters, and associations appear quite arbitrarily.

I am compelled to reject the poem as a sustained harmoniously functioning structural unit.

On the other hand, it is amazing how simple is the state of mind which these broken forms convey. The poet is hurt, wistful, melancholy, frail: modern civilization is a waste land, a sterile desert, in which he wanders

forlornly: there is no water to slake his spiritual
drouth. Yet there was water once, there was beauty, and
the poem shifts to the plane of the past, to the plane of
great mythology.

> When lovely woman stoops to folly and
> Paces about her room again, alone,
> She smoothes her hair with automatic hand,
> And puts a record on the gramophone.

The stanza is a minute simulacrum of the central process
of the poem which is to take ancient beauty by the neck
and twist it into modern ugliness. Mr. Eliot is very
fatigued. There can be no question that he suffers, at
moments his cry is as sharp as that of a man mangled by
the speeding wheels of a subway express, it is bitter as
a confession extorted by wheel and rack. We respect that
cry.
   But about the nature of this state of mind there is
nothing occult. It is in fact a very familiar mood. We
have had a great deal of the poetry of melancholy and
drouth in the last half century, most of it inferior to
Mr. Eliot's, but nevertheless it has worn into common
currency its emotions.
   Assuming that Mr. Eliot wished to convey such emotions
to the reader, to make them still more deeply a part of
our general experience, it should not have been difficult
for him to escape opacity. Classical lucidity was entirely possible. How shall we account then for the
obstacles he has placed to the reader's ready comprehension?
   To win a complete understanding of 'The Waste Land,'
the reader must scan eleven pages of notes, he must have a
considerable learning in letters or be willing to look up
references in Milton, Ovid, Middleton, Webster, Spenser,
Verlaine, St. Augustine, etc., etc., in order to associate
them with their first context, he must read Latin, Greek,
French and German, he must know Frazer's 'Golden Bough'
and steep himself in the legend of the Holy Grail, studying in particular Miss Weston's 'From Ritual to Romance.'
The texture of 'The Waste Land' is excessively heavy with
literary allusions which the reader of good will, knowing
that it is not unjust to make severe requisitions upon his
knowledge, will diligently track down. But our reader of
good will is entitled, I think, to turn sour when he discovers that after all his research he has not penetrated
into some strange uncharted region of experience but has
only fathomed the cipher of a quite ordinary and easily
understandable state of mind.

I know that more whole-hearted admirers of the poem
than I are exclaiming at this point: 'But you are missing
the point! Mr. Eliot wished to give a cumulative effect
to his cries of hurt and barrenness. He wished to give a
sense of one long cry of protest throughout history, a
sense of dryness running through the ages, a yearning passed
on from one individual to another until it reaches him in
twentieth-century London.' To that my answer is that the
sense of outcry reinforced by outcry is simply not created
in the text. It is added to the text by deliberate processes of memory and learning by Mr. Eliot. It is added
to the text by equally deliberate processes on the part of
the reader. It is dependent on something too removed from
the actual lines, and so I cannot feel it as integral.

The conclusion must be that the esotericism of 'The
Waste Land' derives neither from abstruseness of subject
nor from abstruseness of technic. It is artificially con-
cocted by omissions, incompletions and unnecessary spe-
cialization in the assembling of those circumstances which
ought to evoke in the reader the whole effect of the given
emotion. Again the question rises, why does Mr. Eliot
tamper with these circumstances so as to make them not
explicable in themselves?

It is a reasonable conjecture to say that Mr. Eliot
does not want to communicate his suffering to the general
reader. To such he desires to be incomprehensible. His
obfuscation of the circumstances which react together as a
formula for his emotion is an example of dandyism. In his
desire to make his suffering inscrutable to all but a
chosen coterie of his similars, he is affecting what is
commonly called a romantic mannerism, a mannerism that
cannot be credited, however, to the great romantics. He
constructs a mask for himself.

Our ideas of aristocracy have become sentimentalized.
In its healthy state, the idea of aristocracy is a union
of some idea of what is best in human nature with the idea
of rule or control. For our purpose I suppose we can
agree that the highest value is intelligence, so I can be
more precise and say that the union of the ideas of intelligence and control constitutes the idea of aristocracy.
In certain epochs the vortices of intelligence and social
power have coincided, and the idea of aristocracy has been
healthy. But in our epoch it is a truism that social
power is vested in men of an inventive acquisitive
narrow nature whose general intelligence is relatively
low, whose care for humane values is slight, whose cunning
is abnormally developed. The men of creative intelligence
are thus forced to work against the grain of a society
ruled by the acquisitive impulse. Many of them have

become depressed at the odds against them and have pinned
the insignia of an aloof defeat upon their work. Depression and even collapse in this state of affairs are certainly marks of a sensitive spirit. But it is a senti-
mentality of which I suspect Mr. Eliot guilty to believe
that depression is a symptom of aristocracy. For the
aristocrat cannot take pride in a dandyism of defeat, he
cannot relinquish the effort to control. With the whole
force of his being he seeks to understand: to understand
the forces in himself, the forces of his age. With the
whole force of his being he seeks to externalize his knowledge of these so lucidly and powerfully that it wins a
place as leaven in the general cultural experience. He
does not accept the crucifixion of his sensibility as a
proof of superiority. He finds his proof in the trans-
cendance of his crucifixions. Joy, serenity, the tokens
of victory are his distinguishing marks. In the surrender
to despair of its creative will the European mind loses
its aristocracy.

Mr. Eliot, we know, has taken great pains to blend with
the European mind. Who will dispute his thorough natural-
ization? But the mind into which he has been assimilated
is in wretched case. Founded upon classicism, it has been
shaken by the tremendous challenges issued to classical
authorities from revolutionary science. It lacks the
vitality to surrender the old and to make adjustment to
the new. The upheavals of war and politics have agonized
it to the last point. It has no hope, no vision. In 'Der
Untergang des Abendlandes' Oswald Spengler crystallizes
its resignation into an attitude. Herr Spengler is a
fatalist. Cultures, he believes, obey definite biological
laws. They are rigidly deterministic. They live out a
birth, growth, brilliant maturity, decay, death, and these
processes cannot be halted. Decay he calls 'civilization':
it is the stage of huge cities and their nomadic life, of
great wars and dictators, of the advent of formless traditionless masses. We are in it: 'We must will the
inevitable or nothing': the inevitable is fellahdom.

It is easy to see that in part 'The Waste Land' is a
poetic equivalent to 'Der Untergang des Abendlandes.' Mr.
Eliot recalls the brilliant apogee of culture, he portrays
in contrast the sterile decay of contemporary 'civilization,' he makes his own positive assertion in the detest-
able apeneck guffawing Sweeney, symbol of the formless and
the traditionless. Before the age, which he has charac-
terized elsewhere as singularly dull, the poet is weary.

The reader has observed that I have been shifting the
interest in 'The Waste Land' from the aesthetic to the
moral and cultural, and that we are now wholly involved in

the poem as a summary of the modern cultural situation.
The possibility not allowed for by the mind of Mr. Eliot
is this: the entrance into consciousness of some new fac-
tor. We can only say, the future will be so and thus,
provided no indeterminable elements of human consciousness, now dormant, commence to function. The fallacy of
rationalism of the determinist type is that it is not
rational enough. It does not question its assumptions.
Trace back far enough and its fundamental entities turn
out to be matter and motion, both as a matter of fact un-
knowns, and defined in terms of each other. This type of
rationalism is not a coordinating part of the complex
vision of the whole human being: it is really uncontrolled
and amok.

We may take heart in surveying 'The Waste Land' and the
defunct state of the European mind if we turn again to
science in the name of which some very leaden messages
have been offered us in the past. I quote from that acute
scientific observer, J.W.N. Sullivan.

'Once a crack has appeared in a closed universe, it
goes on spreading. Since Maxwell's day the cracks have so
multiplied and spread that already nothing remains of the
old Newtonian universe except a few fragments. It has not
even the validity of a first sketch, for the main lines in
a sketch are right. But the modern universe of physics is
essentially different from the universe of the eighteenth
century. All the primary entities are quite different.
The directions in which explanations are sought are quite
different. The relation of man to the universe is quite
different. The universe of modern science has fundamentally nothing in common with the scientific universe on
which rationalism was built. It is not merely that hypotheses have changed. The role of the hypothesis has
changed. The universe, which was to be explained in terms
of little billiard balls and the law of the inverse square
is now a universe where even mystics, to say nothing of
poets and philosophers, have a right to exist. The present scientific picture of the universe, although incomparably more profound than that of the eighteenth century,
allows much more room to possibilities. It allows them,
and is not concerned to conflict with them.

'So that we reach the conclusion that mysticism and
science can quite well live together. Except on the basis
of a rationalism whose foundations have long since
crumbled there is no conflict whatever between mystical
insight and science. And the man who prides himself on
the complete absence of mystery in his view of the world
is not only not representing the scientific outlook but
will speedily become quite unable to understand it.'

Let us not take too seriously the 'scientific' pretensions nor grant too much authority to those who tell us
that in view of our future the arts are twaddle, for the
future belongs to mechanics, technology, economics and
especially politics.

How far the American mind reproduces the vision or
rather the supine attitude of the European mind is a
speculation. I say speculation, because in spite of the
best will to discover it I cannot say that there exists,
in the sense that the European mind exists, an American
mind. There are in my estimation several American writers
who contain the nucleus for a striking and vastly important American mind, but America is not yet an intelligent
community. Europe is: it has a concensus of intelligent
opinion which I have called its mind: I can find no such
concensus in America to compare with it. But although
we cannot make distinctions in thought, we can in those
things that nourish thought. America has a fresh bound-
less energy which Europe has lost. Most of it is quanti-
tative, but the possibility always exists of converting
some of it to qualitative. Energy is the first requisite
to meet the elastic situation of today. America has hope,
whereas Europe moves toward hopelessness and resignation.
Hope is the spur of energy. America has laxer traditions
than Europe. Ordinarily, this is deplorable. But if we
are called upon to put away old traditions and to formu-
late new, it is an advantage. There is less inertia to
overcome. And from the laxness of traditions in America,
it follows that we are by temperament probably romantics.
In chaos, it is generally agreed, the romantic is better
able to find footing than the less flexible classicist.

Consequently, it is not surprising that such a viewpoint as that published by Mr. Eliot does not initiate any
movement in America, does not even secure a general passive acceptance, does not least of all awake anything in
our experience which impulsively corroborates it. Nay, we
are scarcely enough affected to make a serious contradiction. A decade ago, smarting with a sense of inferiority,
blaspheming our environment on which we transferred our
weaknesses, we looked to Europe as the determinator of
values. It was the heyday of the exile and the cosmopolitan mind. Today, our painters, writers and intellectuals
know that they are deeply implicated in the unformed and
unpredictable American destiny. They hibernate in Europe
and rush back as from a feast which has unexpectedly
turned out to be a famine. They are conscious of a great
though unarticulated difference between the activity of
the American scene and that of Europe. They have even met
Europeans who have calmly declared that Europe is dead and

the future belongs to America. They realize that the
power of initiative has crossed the Atlantic.

America has energy and hope. It has weak traditions
and a romantic temperament. It is becoming conscious of
a fundamental difference between it and Europe. In the
words of the Cumaean Sibyl, inscribed at the top of 'The
Waste Land,' Europe 'wants only to die.' America wants
to live.

But America has not realized its responsibility in the
present crisis. It has not realized that its national
destiny is more than a matter of national self-respect.
It has not recognized clearly that the leadership of the
human spirit has been resigned and that it, if anyone,
must assume it. It has the primary qualifications: un-
tapped energetics and spiritual naivete. It has lately
acquired self-reliance. It seems not fanciful to predict
that it will next acquire a sense of international responsibility.

And then perhaps it will at last be ready to receive
Whitman. It will be expectant and humble, waiting for the
Word that will release it, for the Word that will spell a
new slope of human consciousness. Whitman is not the
Word, but he formed syllables of it, immense generative
syllables. America will wait while these do their deep
hidden work, arousing latent power. On the threshold of
creative vision one must wait.

Mr. Eliot lacks those deeper dimensions that the new
slope will utilize. He is almost purely a sensibility
and an intellect: he seems a unified man: at least one
gets no sense of a disastrous internecine conflict in him.
He loves beauty, he is wounded by ugliness: the age is
severe on 'beauty-lovers' who cannot go below the surface.
It lacerates unmercifully those whose intellects work only
at the tips of their sense, who make an ideal of the
senses thinking, of sensuous thought. This formula Mr.
Eliot believes accounts for much of the excellence of
Elizabethan literature.

The formula for literary masterwork in our age will be
more complex, more inclusive, much more difficult than
that. It will involve the correlated functions of the
whole human consciousness and it will demand the utmost
purification of that consciousness. On a tremendous scale
our age duplicates some of the features which introduced
so much zest into Elizabethan life. Our vital source in
antiquity will be, perhaps, the religious and philosophical cultures of the East instead of Graeco-Roman culture.
Our New World will be Higher Space, and our explorers, our
Columbuses and Magellans, will be such scientists as Ein-
stein and Bohr. Our artists will have a wealth of new

materials: our intellectual world expands and fills with
possibilities: it is a time for curiosity and daring.
'The Waste Land' is a funeral keen for the nineteenth
century. In the twentieth it is a subjective aberration
from the facts.

'Poems 1909-1925'

London, 23 November 1925

49. LEONARD WOOLF, 'JUG JUG' TO DIRTY EARS, 'NATION AND ATHENAEUM'

5 December 1925, vol. xxxviii, 354

Woolf (1880-1969), an English literary critic and essayist, married Virginia Woolf in 1912. In 1919 they published Eliot's 'Poems' at the Hogarth Press.

This is from a longer review that considered poetry by Hardy and Blunden as well as Eliot. Eliot's work, however, received the larger part of Woolf's attention.

To the Victorian and to most of his ancestors the poet was a nightingale. The bird and the man did but sing because they must, and, though the song might be sad, it must also be sweet - indeed the sweetest songs are those which tell of saddest thought. We have changed all that: Mr. Eliot, who is a long way the best of the modern poets, makes his nightingales sing

'Jug Jug' to dirty ears,

and tells us how

The nightingales are singing near
The Convent of the Sacred Heart,

And sang within the bloody wood
When Agamemnon cried aloud
And let their liquid siftings fall
To stain the stiff, dishonoured shroud.

The dirty ears and the liquid siftings are now as essential a part of the nightingale's song as the magic case-
ments, the perilous seas, the verdurous glooms, and the
winding mossy ways....

There are many who will welcome this collected edition
of Mr. Eliot's poems. Personally I *like* Mr. Eliot's poems
so much that I am afraid of appearing exaggerated in
criticizing them. When I get a book of his into my hands,
I become fascinated; I simply cannot stop rereading the
poems until something physical from outside forces me to
shut the book. Naturally I think that there is something
rare in the book itself to cause so rare a reaction. In
the first place I believe it to be poetry, for real
poetry is very rare. Mr. Eliot is a real poet. That he
is difficult to understand, I admit; and this difficulty
will cause many people to miss the poetry. But if anyone
will read the opening of 'The Waste Land,' and the whole
of 'Gerontion,' without fussing very much about whether or
not he is understanding exactly what the author means,
he will suddenly be amazed and delighted by the mere
beauty of the poetry:-

[Quotes 'Gerontion', CPP, p. 37, 'Here I am' to 'flies,
fought'.]

Secondly, Mr. Eliot has not only got the poetry, but he
has found the instrument, the tune, the measure, the
method which exactly fit the singing of 'Jug Jug' to
dirty ears. I feel the spirit of 1922 moving in 'The
Waste Land' more violently and potently than in any other
contemporary poem: the spirit of the age is breathed into
it much as the spirit of 1850 was breathed into 'In
Memoriam.'

I have admitted that Mr. Eliot's poetry is difficult to
understand, but I admit it with so many qualifications
that the admission is valueless. I am sure that I understand every poem which Mr. Eliot has written; I could not
tell you exactly what every word and line mean, but that
is not necessary for an understanding and appreciation of
the poems. In fact, the real criticism of Mr. Eliot is
that he is too easy to understand, because he is always
saying the same thing in different ways. His method,
which alone involves obscurity, consists in keeping two
tunes going at the same time, often one against the
other. First, he works persistently through allusions:
in the simplest case four words, lifted from Shakespeare
and inserted in a poem called 'Burbank with a Baedeker:
Bleistein with a Cigar,' evoke the image of Cleopatra and
how her barge burned on the water, an image which is flung

in the face of the Princess Volupine, the 'Chicago Semite Viennese' Bleistein, and Sir Ferdinand Klein.   Secondly, he attempts to communicate rather subtle emotions by the crude and violent juxtaposition of discordant scenes, thoughts, emotions.   My only criticism of him is that the theme which he plays on these subtle strings is always the same and is very old.   The splendour and romance of our desires and imaginations, the sordidness of reality — that is the theme of Prufrock, of Sweeney, of Burbank, of The Waste Land, of the Hollow Men.   The nightingale never sings anything but 'Jug Jug' to dirty ears.   The mind is eternally 'aware of the damp souls of housemaids sprouting despondently at area gates,' while eternally looking for the barge of Cleopatra burning all day upon the water. The end of life is 'an old man driven by the Trades to a sleepy corner,' with 'thoughts of a dry brain in a dry season,' and the world when it ends, will end 'not with a bang but a whimper.'

50. EDGELL RICKWORD, THE MODERN POET, 'CALENDAR OF MODERN LETTERS'

December 1925, vol. ii, 278-81

This review was reprinted in 'Towards Standards of Criticism', edited by F.R. Leavis (London, 1933), pp. 100-6. Rickword was mainly concerned with 'The Waste Land.'   The review was also reprinted in a collection of Rickword's critical writings edited by Alan Young, 'Essays and Opinions 1921-31' (Manchester, 1974), pp. 180-4.

If there were to be held a Congress of the Younger Poets, and it were desired to make some kind of show of recognition to the poet who has most effectively upheld the reality of the art in an age of preposterous poeticising, it is impossible to think of any serious rival to the name of T.S. Eliot.   Yet, to secure the highest degree of unanimity, such a resolution would have to be worded to the exclusion of certain considerations, and it would concentrate attention on the significance of this work to other poets, rather than on its possession of that quality of 'beauty' for which the ordinary reader looks, though we

do not doubt that on this count, too, perhaps the final
one, it will slowly but certainly gain the timid ears
which only time can coax to an appreciation of the unfamiliar.

'That Mr. T.S. Eliot is the poet who has approached
most nearly the solution of those problems which have
stood in the way of our free poetic expression,' and 'that
the contemporary sensibility, which otherwise must have
suffered dumbly, often becomes articulate in his verse,'
are resolutions which express a sort of legal minimum to
which individual judgments must subscribe.

The impression we have always had of Mr. Eliot's work,
reinforced by this commodious collection in one volume,
may be analysed into two coincident but not quite simul-
taneous impressions. The first is the urgency of the
personality, which seems sometimes oppressive, and comes
near to breaking through the so finely-spun aesthetic
fabric; the second is the technique which spins this fabric and to which this slender volume owes its curious
ascendency over the bulky monsters of our time. For it is
by his struggle with technique that Mr. Eliot has been
able to get closer than any other poet to the physiology
of our sensations (a poet does not speak merely for himself) to explore and make palpable the more intimate dis-
ressses of a generation for whom all the romantic escapes
had been blocked. And, though this may seem a heavy burden to lay on the back of technique, we can watch with the
deepening of consciousness, a much finer realisation of
language, reaching its height in passages in 'The Waste
Land' until it sinks under the strain and in 'The Hollow
Men' becomes gnomically disarticulate.

The interval is filled with steady achievement, and
though the seeds of dissolution are apparent rather
early, there is a middle period in which certain things
are done which make it impossible for the poet who has
read them to regard his own particular problems of expression in the same way again; though he may refuse the path
opened, a new field of force has come into being which
exerts an influence, creates a tendency, even in despite
of antipathy. Such a phenomenon is not in itself a measure of poetic achievement; Donne produced it in his
generation; much smaller men, Denham and Waller, in
theirs.

Let us take three main stages in this development of
technique, the three poems which are, in essence, Mr.
Eliot's poem, 'The Love Song of J. Alfred Prufrock,'
'Gerontion' and 'The Waste Land.' (The neo-satiric quatrains do not raise any fundamental queries, they are the
most easily appreciated of Mr. Eliot's poems, after

'La Figlia Che Piange.'   The French poems remind us of
Dryden's prefaces (*vide* Swift), and there are half-a-dozen
other mere *jeux d'esprit*.)

'Gerontion' is much nearer to 'The Waste Land' than
'The Love Song' is to 'Gerontion.'   The exquisite's witty
drawing-room manner and the deliberate sentimental rhythms
give way to more mysterious, further-reaching symbols, and
simpler, not blatantly poetic rhythms.   As an instance, we
have in 'The Love Song':-

> For I have known them all already, known them all –
> Have known the evenings, mornings, afternoons,
> I have measured out my life with coffee spoons.

But in 'The Waste Land':-

> And I Tiresias have foresuffered all
> Enacted on this same divan or bed;
> I who have sat by Thebes below the wall
> And walked among the lowest of the dead.

The relation and the differences of these passages
hardly need stressing, but, though I had not intended to
enter into an examination of the psychological content of
these poems, I find that this subject of fore-knowledge is
cardinal to the matter.   Fore-knowledge is fatal to the
Active man, for whom impulse must not seem alien to the
end, as it is to the vegetative life of the poets, whose
ends are obscured in the means.   The passage in 'Gerontion' beginning: 'After such knowledge, what forgiveness?'
and the remainder of the poem are such profound commentary
on the consequent annihilation of the will and desire that
they must be left to more intimate consideration.   The
passage is a dramatic monologue, an adaptation one might
hazard of the later Elizabethan soliloquy, down even to
the Senecal:-

> Think
> Neither fear nor courage saves us.   Unnatural vices
> Are fathered by our heroism.   Virtues
> Are forced upon us by our impudent crimes.

'Gerontion' is a poem which runs pretty close to 'The
Waste Land,' and it is free from the more mechanical
devices of the later poem, but lacks its fine original
verse-movements.   In the Sweeney quatrains, especially
in the last stanzas of 'Among the Nightingales,' the noble
and the base, the foul and fine, are brought together with

a shock; the form has little elasticity, and tends to become, like the couplet, stereotyped antithesis. In the
fluid medium of 'The Waste Land' the contrast may be
brought about just as violently, or it may be diffused.
This contrast is not, of course, the whole content of the
poem, but Mr. Eliot has most singularly solved by its
means the problem of revoking that differentiation between
poetic and real values which has so sterilised our recent
poetry. His success is intermittent; after a short passage of exquisite verse he may bilk us with a foreign quotation, an anthropological ghost, or a mutilated quotation. We may appreciate his intention in these matters,
the contrast, the parody, enriches the emotional aura
surrounding an original passage, but each instance must
be judged on its own merits; whether the parody, for instance, is apposite. On this score Mr. Eliot cannot be
acquitted of an occasional cheapness, nor of a somewhat
complacent pedantry, and since we cannot believe that
these deviations are intrinsic to the poetic mind, we must
look for their explanation elsewhere. We find it in the
intermittent working of Mr. Eliot's verbal imagination.
He has the art of words, the skill which springs from
sensitiveness, and an unmatched literary apprehension
which enables him to create exquisite passages largely at
second-hand (lines 60-77). It is when this faculty fails
of imaginative support, as it must at times, that certain
devices are called in; the intellect is asked to fill in
gaps (possibly by reference to the notes, when they are,
as they rarely are, helpful) which previous poets have
filled in with rhetoric, perhaps, but at any rate by a
verbal creation which stimulates the sensibility. The
object of this verbal effort is not merely to stimulate
the sensibility, since disjunctive syllables can do that,
but to limit, control, and direct it towards a more intense apprehension of the whole poem. That is where a
failure in verbal inventiveness is a definite poetic
lapse. In a traditional poet it would result in a patch
of dull verse, in Mr. Eliot's technique we get something
like this:-

To Carthage then I came

Burning burning burning burning
O Lord thou pluckest me out
O Lord thou pluckest

burning.

Whether this is better or worse than dull verse I need
not decide; that it is a failure, or the aesthetic scheme

which would justify it is wrong, can I think be fairly
upheld.

Though we may grasp the references to Buddah's Fire
Sermon and Augustine's 'Confessions,' and though Mr. Eliot
may tell us that 'the collocation of these two representa-
tives of eastern and western asceticism, as the culmina-
tion of this part of the poem, is not an accident,' we
find it difficult to be impressed. It is the danger of
the aesthetic of 'The Waste Land' that it tempts the poet
to think the undeveloped theme a positive triumph and
obscurity more precious than commonplace. The collocation of Buddah and Augustine is interesting enough, when
known, but it is not poetically effective because the
range of their association is only limited by widely dispersed elements in the poem, and the essential of poetry
is the presence of concepts in mutual irritation.

This criticism might be extended to the general consideration of the technique of construction used in 'The
Waste Land'; it is still exploited as a method, rather
than mastered. The apparently free, or subconsciously
motivated, association of the elements of the poem allows
that complexity of reaction which is essential to the poet
now, when a stable emotional attitude seems a memory of
historical grandeur. The freedom from metrical conformity,
though not essential as 'Don Juan' shows, is yet an added
and important emancipation, when the regular metres lan-
guish with hardly an exception in the hands of mechani-
cians who are competent enough, but have no means of
making their consciousness speak through and by the
rhythm. Mr. Eliot's sense of rhythm will, perhaps, in the
end, be found his most lasting innovation, as it is the
quality which strikes from the reader the most immediate
response.

51. LOUISE MORGAN, THE POETRY OF MR. ELIOT, 'OUTLOOK'
(LONDON)

20 February 1926, vol. lvii, 135-6

Louise Morgan, an English critic, published a study of
writers contemporary with Eliot, entitled 'Writers at
Work', in 1931. The book by Untermeyer referred to is
'American Poetry since 1900' (New York, 1923).

No poet of the present generation has been more violently
attacked or more passionately admired, and more perfectly
misunderstood than Mr. T.S. Eliot. Over and over again
the critics, some of them poets, 'new poets,' themselves,
have repeated that he is merely clever, very very clever,
that he is an erudite charlatan, often incomprehensible
and obscure, that he has a brain and no heart. Since the
publication of his collected poems the same criticisms
have reappeared in the reviews; once more we are told that
he is a cerebralist only, and a disillusioned one besides.
Indeed, a facile but grotesquely irrelevant analogy which
originated two years ago with Mr. Louis Untermeyer, in his
book on 'American Poetry,' is employed again in the current quarterlies by two critics, both poets - the comparison of 'The Waste Land' to a cross-word puzzle.

Incredible that any reader sensitive to poetry should
not be aware of the profound emotional quality in Mr.
Eliot's work. To have emerged untouched from 'Preludes,'
or 'Rhapsody on a Windy Night,' or 'Morning at the Window,'
or 'The Love Song of J. Alfred Prufrock,' or 'The Waste
Land,' is a feat comparable with strolling in full evening
dress through a tropical tornado or an arctic blizzard un-
scathed. There are various reasons for this strange in-
sensibility. One is the popular fallacy that feeling and
thought are incompatible, that when a man begins to use
his brain he must cease to feel. As if, when the blood
goes racing to the brain, the heart is not obliged to beat
faster! The peculiar emotional force in Mr. Eliot's
poetry is mainly due to the mental control he constantly
exercises over his feelings, giving the effect so to
speak of the hounds of feeling straining at the taut leash
of the mind. Or to vary the figure, the source of his
poetry is deep in his heart as the source of the spring
is deep in the bowels of the mountain, but as it issues
it is filtered and purified by the active sunlight of his
brain. Another current fallacy allied to the one just
mentioned is that poetry does not flourish on disillusion.
But what did 'Hamlet', which is stuffed full of the world's
finest poetry, spring from! The chiefest reason, however,
is that this poet is as uncompromisingly and as self-
awarely new as were Wordsworth and Coleridge in the last
decade of the eighteenth century.

In Mr. Eliot we have evidence of one of those renewals
of poetry which happen roughly once in a century, and
which spring from direct and deliberately made contact
with the common life and speech of the moment. That
actual life and speech which gives poetry a fresh vitality
becomes in its turn literesque and sterile, until another
contact creates another renewal. The test of Mr. Eliot's

power is that he gives the sense of his own time in no
local or provincial way, but as a part of all the time
that has gone before it, implying inevitably the timeless
in time. With a kind of dramatic tenderness he isolates
the essential human thing from all its infinite varieties
of manifestations. Actaeon and Diana are but different
symbols for Sweeney and Mrs. Porter. The poor little
typist, torpidly seduced by the carbuncular clerk, is
lovely woman that stoops to folly. It is as if he had
opened all the tight little bundles into which we parcel
up our consciousness - parchment and seals for our knowledge of history, white tissue and ribbon for our aesthetic functions, brown paper and string with double knots
for our physiological - had opened them and strewn their
contents flat under the midday sun, Leicester's velvet
cloak near the typist's drying combinations, the singing
mermaids from the chambers of the sea next to Prufrock's
trousers with the bottoms rolled. An important peculiarity of his method in procuring this effect of the life
of all time expressing itself in the particular disguise
of the moment, is the use of literary quotations. He is
the first poet to set echoing in his lines the overtones
of an experience which is often richer and sharper than
our direct encounter with life and nature - our experience with literature.

    We have alluded to his dramatic quality; no other poet
since Shakespeare has put dauntlessly cheek by jowl the
sublime and the commonplace. In a minor way, and necessarily much more condensed form, the same intensely dramatic effect of reality is achieved by the setting together
in Prufrock's mind of his white flannel trousers and the
siren beauty of the sea, as by the juxtaposition of the
drunken porter and Macbeth's terrible ecstasy. It is
by his daring to make use of this dualism which is so
integral a part of all life but which has only rarely
before been considered the proper material for poetry,
that Mr. Eliot secures his most deeply moving effects,
sincere and simple effects which because they do not
understand them are labelled 'obscure' and 'merely clever'
by the worldly-wise critics. His instrumentation, to
mention only one other detail of his technique, is constantly varied, as often as not from line to line;
apparently wilful, it is carefully and subtly calculated.
He rhymes or does not rhyme, uses assonance, repetition,
the latter with singular beauty, or ignores all the
accepted mechanical means of conjuring up the poetic mood,
entirely to suit his own turn. He contrives to cap a tragic stanza powerfully with the doggerel rhyme of 'visit'
with 'is it?'; he succeeds with such novel experiments as

making rhymes out of a grammatical ending, as in the opening lines of 'The Waste Land'; he employs the refrain to
help achieve a deeply exciting sound pattern in Lil's
friend's monologue in the same poem. The following passage will serve as an indication of his tonal quality in
which there is a magic rarely heard since 'Kubla Khan'
and 'Christabel':-

[Quotes CPP, p. 73, 'A woman drew' to 'exhausted wells'.]

   Without doubt for many and lamentable decades still we
shall have variations on the familiar themes, on sentimental old, unhappy, far off things and romantic peaks in
Darien, just as couplets in the prescribed eighteenth
century manner persisted far down into the nineteenth.
But in the meantime the generation of 1925 has as clear
and deliberate a statement of a new order of poetic values
in the 'Poems' of Mr. T.S. Eliot as had the generation of
1798 when Wordsworth and Coleridge challenged the old
order of that day with the 'Lyrical Ballads.'

52. JOHN MIDDLETON MURRY ON ELIOT AND THE 'CLASSICAL'
REVIVAL, 'ADELPHI'

February-March 1926, vol. iii, 585-95, 648-53

This article, spread over two issues, attempts to place
Eliot in relation to his contemporaries. It is interesting also to note Murry's response to 'The Hollow Men',
which he read in the course of composing this piece.

                              I.

One reads not seldom nowadays of a 'classical' revival in
modern literature. There is a certain justification for
the term. A fairly definite tendency can be observed
among modern writers since the publication of Mr. Lytton
Strachey's 'Eminent Victorians.' In biography the line
of descent passes from Mr. Strachey through Mr. Geoffrey
Scott with his 'Portrait of Zélide' to Mr. Bonamy Dobrée
with his 'Essays in Biography' - subjects, standards, and
methods all taken from the eighteenth century; in fiction

we have the amusing exercises of Mr. David Garnett in imitation of Defoe. These are all in their way good books;
Mr. Strachey's two - 'Eminent Victorians' and 'Queen Vic-
toria' - are more than good books: I should understand
anyone who called them perfect ones. In the theatre, too,
on the more popular levels, there has been the remarkable
success of 'The Beggar's Opera' at the Hammersmith and
the present revival of Dibdin: on the more esoteric, the
persistent revival of Restoration plays, sometimes in
public, as 'The Way of the World,' more often by the
efforts of the new play-producing societies.

There is no reason why this large and general movement
of the public taste should not be called a 'classical'
revival, save that the phrase suggests much more than the
reality. It suggests, moreover, that the new wave of
classicism succeeds a previous romanticism. Actually this
is not the case. What went before the new classical movement was not anything that could be usefully called romanticism: but rather a literature of social optimism and
religious nullity. (a) Mr. Wells, Mr. Bennett, Mr. Shaw,
Mr. Galsworthy, all represent an extreme phase of confidence in modern society. They are, of course, social
reformers: they do not believe the social machine is perfect - far from it - but they do believe the machine can
be perfected, and that, when it is perfected, all will go
well.

That was the last phase of the pre-war mentality. The
classical revival belongs to the after-war period. It is
an expression of a universal scepticism. In so conscious
a practitioner as Mr. Strachey it is the manifestation of
a certain amused contempt for the Victorian equivocations; and the reason why his remarkable books have had a
vogue beyond all expectation for writings of their kind
is that people in general share this contempt. On the
still more popular levels - represented by 'The Beggar's
Opera' - there is a corresponding weariness of social
problems and seriousness, and an inarticulate conviction
that idealism and high-falutin' did not save us from disaster, but rather took us into it. The universal desire
is to be amused without *arrière-pensée*. The 'classical'
revival is an expression or a satisfaction of this universal desire.

Therefore it is far better to call it an Augustan than
a 'classical' revival, since classicism stands for a good
deal more than scepticism and amusement. The Augustan
revival represents the reaction from a collapsed, and
consequently a false, idealism; and probably the impulse
would, in times of greater energy, have produced a movement of realism. But precisely at this moment the chaos

of consciousness is so extreme that the effort necessary
to deal with modern life realistically would be prodigious; on the other hand, the general lassitude among men
of ability is such that even a moderate effort of the kind
would be refused. More than this, the scepticism of the
intelligentsia is so complete that it involves the art of
literature itself. Why make an effort? What is the
point? Why not remain content with amusing ourselves
and giving amusement to others? Why take literature
seriously? Isn't that a part of the old Victorian humbug?

So the scepticism, because it is complete, naturally
takes the line of least resistance. Idealism, even the
writer's idealism for his craft, in other than a superficial sense, is the enemy. It is not to be required of
literature that it should aim at discerning and expressing
some beauty which is the truth in the welter of contemporary life. Hence the vogue of the eighteenth century,
wherein human beings can be contemplated, as it were, in
a condition of paradisal ignorance of the complexities
which now assail them: and, to correspond with this, in
the writers who affect to give some picture of contemporary life, a complete cynicism and detachment. The
human beings they depict are mere talking machines:
intellectual marionettes. They are not given, and they
are not intended to have, any creative truth: their purpose is not to reveal, but to amuse.

Such a scepticism is a very complete thing: it is
really impervious to criticism, for any criticism directed
against it must proceed from some sort of idealism, which
a complete scepticism rejects out of hand. So long as its
practitioners do not tire of it themselves, so long as the
mood of the *intelligentsia* is such that it is amused by it
- so long the Augustan revival will endure; and that may
be a very long time. For a change from an absolute
scepticism must, by the nature of the case, be a profound
change indeed - of the same order as a revivalist conversion. At the mere mention of such a possibility the
Augustans would - on their own principles very legitimately - burst, not into Homeric laughter (for that is
scarcely in their line), but into a discreet and annihi-
lating smile.

Probably it will never happen to them; but it may one
day happen to the public which reads them: for its time
is not so fully taken up as theirs. Whereas they have the
occupation of doing what they do so well, their readers
have not. They read in a day what costs a year to write.
There are not, or are not yet, 365 Augustans to succeed
each other throughout the revolving year; and even with
the liberal supply of plays and dances there may be a few

blank days. The blank day is the devil, and the devil's
chosen moment. Blank days are not so harmless as blank
cartridges: one of them may easily blow the 'classical'
revival sky-high in the souls of its devotees. Then they
would change into *dévots*: and the last state would be
worse than the first. Which God forbid.

The 'classical' revival, in so far as it is homogeneous, is based upon an absolute scepticism, and is,
like the hedonistic philosophy with which it is allied,
impervious to criticism. Criticism of its postulates can
be rejected as a begging of the question; while its actual
literary achievements seldom fall conspicuously short of
the circumscribed perfection which is their aim.

But the 'classical' movement is not really homogeneous,
not wholly Augustan. It has a 'serious' wing. The cynical and the serious classicists are lumped together by a
perfunctory criticism. Nothing is more remarkable in the
utterances of journalists who affect the classical revival
than an indiscriminate juxtaposition of the names of Mr.
Lytton Strachey, Mrs. Virginia Woolf, Mr. Aldous Huxley,
Mr. David Garnett, and Mr. T.S. Eliot. Mr. Strachey, Mr.
Garnett, and Mr. Huxley do indeed belong together, though
there are signs of incipient *malaise* in Mr. Huxley: but
Mrs. Virginia Woolf and Mr. Eliot are of another kind.
They are serious, while the others are cynical, 'classi-
cists.'

We shall have later most sharply to distinguish between
Mrs. Woolf and Mr. Eliot, for their seriousness has important points of difference. Mrs. Woolf, being a woman, is
serious as Falstaff was a coward, on instinct: Mr. Eliot
rather by premeditation. But a similar seriousness finds
a similar manifestation in both of them: each desires to
be loyal to what we can only call the modern consciousness - a complex state of mind, a spiritual 'atmosphere'
which exists now, and has never existed before. Each en-
deavours to create something adequate to the welter of
dissatisfactions and desires which has invaded the sensitive mind during and since the war. Mrs. Woolf's 'Jacob's
Room' and Mr. Eliot's 'The Waste Land' belong essentially
to the same order. Both are failures; though 'The Waste
Land' is the more impressive, because the more complete
and conscious failure. One might almost say that Mr.
Eliot's poem is permeated (and made remarkable) by a sense
that the mere writing of it was a blasphemy.

But, not to indulge in subtleties of criticism, the
immediate effect of these two works is the same: the exercise of a prodigious intellectual subtlety to produce the
effect of a final futility. The word is just, however
harsh it may appear to those who are aware of the gifts of

the authors. Both are unusually fine critics; both are
tormented by the longing to create. But their creations,
despite the approval of the *quidnuncs* and the *claqueurs*,
are futile. Fifty, ten years hence no one will take the
trouble (no small one) to read either of these works, unless there should be some revolutionary happening in their
authors - some liberation into a real spontaneity - which
will cause these records of their former struggle in the
wilderness to be studied with the sympathy and curiosity
which a contemporary now bestows upon them.

These two writers are indeed interesting. The contradiction between so much serious intention, so much proved
ability, and so paradoxical an outcome - *parturiunt mon-
tes; nascetur ridiculus mus* - is at first sight scarcely
less than portentous; so is the contrast between the failure, intrinsic and external, of these serious classicists
and the twofold success of the cynical classicists with
whom they are so undiscriminatingly confused.

Yet the contradiction and the contrast are easy to explain. It is precisely because Mrs. Woolf and Mr. Eliot
are more serious than their fellow-classicists (b) that
they fail. For to be serious is not to be cynical; and
not to be cynical is to be lacking in the attitude which
gives the possibility of perfection to contemporary
classicism. The attitude must be congruous with the
method. In the cynical classicists it is: a technique of
detachment for an attitude of detachment. With the
complexities and heart-searchings of modern life they are
ostentatiously unconcerned; they turn their backs upon it
and seek their relaxation in the trim parterres of the
Augustans. By these same complexities and heart-
searchings the serious classicists are deeply perturbed.
Life attracts them in their own despite, they cannot
ignore it.

They cannot but remember these things are
And they are precious to them.

They strive to grapple with the modern consciousness:
they become experimental, alembicated, obscure. They
achieve nothing.

Yet why not? The question is not answered. The case
is not simply that they use an inappropriate technique for
their subject-matter; indeed, that is not the case at all.
For neither the method of Mrs. Woolf in 'Jacob's Room' nor
that of Mr. Eliot in 'The Waste Land' is classical in any
known sense of the word. Nor can it be supposed that they
believe it is. The classicism, if classicism there is, is
of some novel and esoteric kind, and a classicism which is

227 T.S. Eliot: The Critical Heritage

at once novel and esoteric would be a very queer classicism indeed.

Actually the reason of their failure is simple. Their
works are over-intellectualized; they lack spontaneity;
they are overladen with calculated subtleties (which are
quite different from the instinctive subtleties of the
writer who is master of his purpose, his instrument and
himself); and they fail to produce any unity of impression. The reader is compelled, in the mere effort to
understand, to adopt an attitude of intellectual suspicion, which makes impossible the communication of feeling.
The works offend against the most elementary canon of
good writing: that the immediate effect should be unambiguous.

But why, being classicists, should they offend in this
most unclassical way? The answer to that is that they are
not classicists. As critical intelligences, they have,
and have given utterance to, pro-classical velleities -
for order and clarity and decorum; as creative writers
they are, in spite of all the restraint they impose upon
themselves, disordered, obscure, indecorous. It is not
their fault, they are children of the age against which
they rebel. Above all, they are serious. They wish to
express their real experience. And it happens that their
real experience is such that it gives rise to classical
velleities and defies classical expression.

For there is no *order* in modern experience, because
there is no accepted principle of order. The obvious
paradox of Mr. Eliot the classicist writing 'The Waste
Land' is a mere trifle compared to the inward contradiction between the profession of classical principles such
as his and the *content* of that poem. (c) The poem expresses a self-torturing and utter nihilism: there is
nothing, nothing: nothing to say, nothing to do, nothing
to believe, save to wait without belief for the miracle.
Once its armour of incomprehensibility is penetrated
the poem is found to be a cry of grinding and empty desolation. Nothing could conceivably be more remote from
the complacent scepticism of the cynical Augustans. This
is a voice from the Dark Night of the Soul of a St. John
of the Cross - the barren and dry land where no water is.

To order such an experience on classical principles is
almost beyond human powers. It might conceivably be done,
by an act of violence, by joining the Catholic Church.
St. John of the Cross *was* a Catholic. But the stupendous
difference is that St. John of the Cross was born a Catholic, who thought and felt instinctively in the categories
of the Church. Mr. Eliot was not; he was born into the
same tormenting fluidity as the rest of us. And it is not

likely that he will sell his equivocal birthright; like
the rest of us, sooner or later he will be forced to
crystallize his miracle out of himself. (d)

But what in the name of all incomprehensibles has such
a man, in such a condition, to do with classicism? What
can classicism mean for him? A spiritual technique he
envies and cannot use; a certainty he longs for and cannot embrace - it could mean either of these things. But
to envy classicism is not to be a classicist; it is to
be, most unenviably, a romantic: a romantic who is conscious of sin in being what he is, and cannot take the
plunge into the unknown; whose being knows that there is
but one way, but whose mind, fascinated by ancient certi-
tudes, can discern only nothingness along the only way.

'The Waste Land,' with a vengeance: but surely Mr.
Eliot must know that no classicist ever got there. That
is a station on the mystic path. The only classicism
that knows anything about it is the classicism of the
Catholic Church: and its knowledge derives from the fact
that it has managed to include most romanticisms. If he
requires a nearer precedent it is to the romantics that
he must go.

This profound and absolute contradiction lies beneath
all Mr. Eliot's professions of classicism. He is, essentially, an unregenerate and incomplete romantic; and he
must remain unregenerate and incomplete so long as he
professes classicism: for so long will his professions
and his reality remain utterly divorced.

The overcoming of this divorce between his understanding and his being is precisely the miracle he asks for
in 'The Waste Land.' It will not happen: such miracles
never do happen. (e) A man has to create his own
miracles, by paying for them, outwardly in the eyes of
men and inwardly in his own soul's eye. The outward
price Mr. Eliot is called upon to pay is a public recantation of his 'classicism.' It is unfortunate for him
that his recantation must be public; but, since his profession was public, it is inevitable.

We have pressed home the analysis of Mr. Eliot's condition because he is the most striking example of the
self-stultification involved in the profession of a serious classicism to-day. 'Classicism' is all very well;
but to be coherent, to be viable, it must not be serious.
A serious classicism is a contradiction in terms for a
modern mind; and since, when one is serious, errors of
thought have their direct consequences upon the whole of
the inward man, no criticism of Mr. Eliot can be serious
unless it follows home the visible contradiction of his
professions and his practice to their source in an

internecine conflict between his understanding and his
being. That conflict will never be resolved, can never be
resolved, save at the cost of a sacrifice. There is a
moment, in life and in letters, when a man must lose his
life to save it.

II.

Humpty-Dumpty sat on a wall;
Humpty-Dumpty had a great fall.
And all the King's horses and all the King's men
Couldn't put Humpty together again.

We have tried to show in the particular case of Mr. T.S.
Eliot that a serious classicism at the present time is
self-contradictory and sterile. The objection may, however, be urged that the inward contradiction which is so
palpable and distressing to a serious reader of Mr.
Eliot's work is not a *necessary* contradiction: that the
striking discrepancy between his critical professions
and his creative practice is peculiar to himself.
   It is true, Mr. Eliot is a peculiar case; but his
peculiarity lies simply in the fact that he is the only
classicist among us who is not superficial. Hence his
importance. How far one may regard him as typical of
'the modern mind' is, of course, a matter of opinion.
Mr. Eliot is not superficial, while 'the modern mind,'
regarded as general average, certainly is. Nevertheless,
Mr. Eliot, in the most significant part of him, is typical of 'the modern mind.' He *is* completely sceptical and
antinomian. He differs from the Augustans because his
sceptical and antinomian condition is a torment to him:
he cannot acquiesce in it.
   The disposition is admirable; the results unsatisfactory. He proceeds to proclaim principles that he finds it
impossible to obey. The intellectual part of him desider-
ates an ordered universe, an ordered experience, and an
ordered society; the living, emotional, creative part of
him goes its own disordered way. And the spectacle is
disturbing because he thus lowers himself to the level of
those 'aesthetic' converts who are received into the
Catholic Church, but whose lives are no more edifying
afterwards than before. For if Mr. Eliot really *believed*
in his classical principles he must surely have refrained
from publishing his recent poems, with their confession
of the utter absence of that conviction on which a solid
classicism must be based. He might not be able to refrain from writing them: after all, a man creates as he

can, not as he wills. But to publish them shows that Mr.
Eliot is unwilling to submit himself to the discipline he
professes as an ideal. Therefore he makes the impression
of one who loves the prestige and refuses the obligations
of classicism.

In a simpler man this would be hypocrisy. But Mr.
Eliot has brought the separation of his intellect and his
being to a fine art. Often it gives him pain: but we
fancy he sometimes finds an exquisite pleasure in living
the double life - to have classicism for his wife and
romanticism for his mistress - ô les oaristys! - to walk
with Mr. Charles Whibley on his one arm and Miss Gertrude
Stein on the other. As a feat of good-fellowship it is
considerable; as a contribution to modern thought it is
impressive chiefly by an unconscious cynicism. For
classicism, of the fundamental kind which Mr. Eliot professes, imposes moral obligations. It is not something
to which one can give intellectual assent and ethical
repudiation.

Mr. Eliot might say he can, because he does. So doubtless a priest can ingeminate austerity on Sundays and
disport himself in night-clubs in between. When he is
found out, however, men cease to listen to his preaching,
and his ecclesiastical superior takes disciplinary action.

There's the rub. Mr. Eliot has no spiritual superior.
The apostle of authority has no authority to submit to.
He has to find out what is right and what is wrong for
himself. Excellent, but not very classical: yet not so
excellent when one reflects he has not yet got so far on
his voyage of spiritual discovery as to know that in an
apostle a total divorce between one's principles and one's
practice is a cardinal sin.

How is Humpty-Dumpty to be mended? There seem to be
but two ways. The one more obviously indicated is that he
should make a blind act of faith and join the Catholic
Church: there he will find an authority and a tradition.
The other is that he should make a different act of faith,
trust himself, and see what happens: a principle of
authority may come to birth.

In short, Humpty-Dumpty must choose. Since all the
king's horses and all the king's men have failed he must
try Catholicism or - but what is the name for the alternative? Let us not call it Romanticism. There are many
romanticisms, as there are many classicisms. And most of
them have the same relation to true Romanticism as Augustanism holds to a true Classicism. It is the way (in
literature) of Shakespeare, the way of Keats, the way of
all men who have had to face the universe alone, and win
their way from unbelief to belief, the way of which this

magazine is the small and solitary voice in this country. Along this way a tradition, and a great tradition, may be found - as great, though not so outwardly impressive, as the great Catholic tradition; but one far more truly congenial to the English genius.

England rejected Catholicism four centuries ago. And with the rejection of Catholicism English literature began. It was the expression of the free and freely inquiring spirit of man. For Catholicism was rejected, not because it was essentially false in its view of man's nature, but because it would not allow men to find out things for themselves. Under this star English literature was born: it is, through and through, an individualistic literature. Twice in its progress it has come near to accepting an ordered system for human experience, in the eighteenth century, when it believed that the mysteries of life could be solved by the light of reason and that man was a mechanism; and in the Victorian age, when it believed that the individual and society automatically achieved a mysterious something called progress. Neither of these systems (if the second can be called a system at all) is anything but superficial compared to the Catholic. They are based either on a violence done to man's nature, or to the world he experienced, or to both. But the system of the eighteenth century was at least coherent; it had a philosophy - sensationalism - and an ethic - that nothing was wrong except a crime.

This was called the 'classical' period of English literature: in a sense legitimately, for it was the only period when an ordered and uniform theory of experience was generally accepted by educated men. But the system was too narrow and too unnatural to endure. It broke down eventually because men insisted on believing that they were not machines, but organisms, and that the most vital part of man lay beyond the scope of reason. Nevertheless, this is the only period of English literature that can, not altogether stupidly, be called classical. On its own ground and principles it achieved much, and much that was perfect. If ever men come to believe in that system again, they must return to the Augustan period for their models in life and in letters.

This the Augustans of to-day actually do, and they are right. They return to the Augustan period not because they want to be 'classical' - no man in his senses *wants* to be either classical or romantic for their own sakes, he wants only to function freely - but because the Augustan period suits them: its philosophy, its behaviour, its ideals are congruous with their own. But that Augustan attitude, which was serious enough in its own day, is no longer serious in ours; we know that real experience cannot be confined within the limits of this system. Therefore the serious modern classicist must, by reason of his seriousness, seek his affinities elsewhere than in the Augustan period. But where?

He *might* go to Milton - to the Puritan tradition. Milton has generally been the refuge of English writers who have felt the need of a concrete and palpable tradition. Keats stretched out to Milton when he shrank from the chaos of self-annihilation; Gray and Collins before him had done the same. The Poet Laureate to-day is an avowed disciple of Milton. But Mr. Eliot is a Puritan by descent, and it is precisely against Puritanism that he has been struggling all his life. The classicism he desires is more august and more flexible - it is a Catholic classicism.

There is no such classicism in English literature; there cannot be. You cannot found an English classicism on Chaucer, for all that he was the most truly classical writer we have ever had; because the spiritual certainty which Chaucer possessed and which gave him the freedom to see life steadily and see it whole has disappeared for ever. Chaucer's work, as surely as Dante's, was made possible by the theology of mediaeval Catholicism. These men, because they were bound, were free: they had a theory of the universe in which they believed. Dante could trust his own intellectualism because he believed in that supra-intellectual reality which he used it to articulate. His theology was, so to speak, a metaphysic *of which he was certain.*

Enviable, thrice enviable! But it belongs to the past. That glorious aptitude of the human mind has been lost. The modern trouble is not to accept (or to invent) a theology, but to believe in God. Without that belief theology is vain. Mr. Eliot, as his poems amply reveal, is in a Godless condition. So are thousands of others to-day. They do not care; Mr. Eliot does. To be without a knowledge of God is an agony to him. Wherever 'The Waste Land' is, it is not situated in Bloomsbury. It is a place where a lonely and tormented soul awaits the coming of the living water.

It will not come, it cannot come, because Mr. Eliot will dictate the way it must come. His intellect must be satisfied; he must know all about it; it must come to him by the aqueduct he has elaborately prepared. But there is a gap between the end of his aqueduct and the river of life. That flows in one dimension; he builds in another.

It is not possible for a man so sensitive and so scrupulous as Mr. Eliot to reach a belief in God by the grand old ways. Those grand old ways were not built from man to God, but from God to man. The belief was there, the intellectual explication of it came afterwards. It is easy for a man who inherits a faith to be classical; it is impossible for a man without one to achieve a faith through classicism. Yet classicism without belief in God is Augustanism - or nothingness. In Mr. Eliot it is nothingness; but not so absolute a nothingness that the rebirth of the Phoenix may not be delayed for many years.

P.S. - Throughout this essay I have used the phrase 'belief in God' as the most convenient shorthand for the certainty of a supra-intellectual reality, which cannot, in the ordinary sense of the word, be *known*, but only experienced. That this experiencing is, indeed, the highest form of man's knowing is my conviction; but since it is an *operative* knowledge (*i.e.*, one that reconciles, and is born of the reconciliation of, instinct and intellect), and thus involves a change in kind, it is perhaps better not to call it knowledge.

Notes

a I am not unmindful of the fact that critics of repute - Babbitt, Seillière, Lasserre - French, or of French inspiration, maintain that precisely this *is* 'romanticism.' But romanticism and religious nullity are, in my judgment, mutually exclusive. Whatever we may think of Rousseau, it is foolish to deny the reality of his religious consciousness. To *blame* him for the democratic optimism of the nineteenth century is uncritical; almost as uncritical as it would to blame Jesus because his disciples quarrelled about their places in the Kingdom of Heaven. Similarly, I refuse the name of 'classical' to a movement based on a religious nullity. Ultimately, I hold that classicism assumes the existence of God, and strives to understand Him; in other words, it keeps firmly before it the problem of good and evil and seeks demonstrably to justify the ways of God to men, as in classical Greek drama and Dante: whereas romanticism seeks to discover the existence of God, and is content ineffably to know Him, and in the act of knowledge transcends the distinction between good and evil, as in the high drama of Shakespeare - 'Lear' and 'Antony.' For a true classicism the existence of God is a real intellectual postulate; for a true romanticism a real spiritual experience.
b There is no reason to suppose that Mrs. Woolf or

Mr. Eliot themselves accept inclusion among the
Augustans. The grouping is not mine, and, as I hope
to show, it is utterly uncritical.

c I do not imply that Mr. Eliot is himself unconscious
of the contradiction. That is hardly possible. His
is not the first case of *Video meliora proboque;
Deteriora sequor*. But whether a critic ought at one
and the same time to proclaim classical principles and
publish poetry that defies them is a point in ethics
I cannot decide. My opinion is, pretty emphatically,
in the negative.

d Of course, not out of himself *alone*: the miracle –
regeneration – is precisely the knowledge that he is
not alone.

e Even as I write these words a new complete edition of
Mr. Eliot's poems comes to my hand (Faber & Gwyer,
7s. 6d. net). It contains one poem written later than
'The Waste Land': 'The Hollow Men' (1925). Nothing
could more painfully confirm my statement that the
miracle will not happen. This is a more absolutely
barren poem than 'The Waste Land.' The utterance is
more naked, as though Mr. Eliot had no longer the
energy to cover himself.

> Between the desire
> And the spasm
> Between the potency
> And the existence
> Between the essence
> And the descent
> Falls the shadow

53. I.A. RICHARDS, MR. ELIOT'S POEMS, 'NEW STATESMAN'

20 February 1926, vol. xxvi, 584–5

Richards (1893–1979), one of the seminal figures of
modern literary criticism, was an influential teacher in
the Cambridge of the 1920s. His more important works of
that time include 'Principles of Literary Criticism'
(1924), 'Science and Poetry' (1926) and 'Practical Criticism' (1929). He was one of the founders of Basic
English.
   This review was reprinted in 'Living Age' on 10 April

1926. It also appeared as an appendix in 'Principles of
Literary Criticism', reissued that same year.

We too readily forget that, unless something is very
wrong with our civilisation, we should be producing three
equal poets at least for every poet of high rank in our
great-great-grand-fathers' day. Something must indeed be
wrong; and since Mr. Eliot is one of the very few poets
that current conditions have not overcome, the difficulties which he has faced and the cognate difficulties which
his readers encounter, repay study.

Mr. Eliot's poetry has occasioned an unusual amount of
irritated or enthusiastic bewilderment. The bewilderment
has several sources. The most formidable is the unobtru-
siveness, in some cases the absence, of any coherent
intellectual thread upon which the items of the poem are
strung. A reader of 'Gerontion,' of 'Preludes' or of 'The
Waste Land' may, if he will, after repeated readings,
introduce such a thread. Another reader after much effort
may fail to contrive one. But in either case energy will
have been misapplied. For the items are united by the
accord, contrast, and interaction of their emotional
effects, not by an intellectual scheme that analysis must
work out. The only intellectual activity required takes
place in the realisation of the separate items. We can,
of course, make a 'rationalisation' of the whole experience, as we can of any experience. If we do we are adding
something which does not belong to the poem. Such a logical scheme is, at best, a scaffolding which vanishes when
the poem is constructed. But we have so built into our
nervous systems a demand for intellectual coherence, even
in poetry, that we find a difficulty in doing without it.

This point may be misunderstood, for the charge most
unusually brought against Mr. Eliot's poetry is that it
is over-intellectualised. One reason for this is his use
of allusion. A reader who in one short poem picks up
allusions to: 'The Aspern Papers,' 'Othello,' 'A Toccata
of Galuppi's,' Marston, 'The Phoenix and the Turtle,'
'Antony and Cleopatra' (twice), 'The Extasie,' 'Macbeth,'
'The Merchant of Venice' and Ruskin feels that his wits
are being unusually well exercised. He may easily leap
to the conclusion that the basis of the poem is in wit
also. But this would be a mistake. These things come
in, not that the reader may be ingenious or admire the
writer's erudition (this last accusation has tempted
several critics to disgrace themselves) but for the sake
of the emotional aura which they bring. Allusion in

Mr. Eliot's hands is a technical device for compression.
'The Waste Land' is the equivalent in content to an epic.
Without this device twelve books would have been needed.
But these allusions and the notes in which some of them
are elucidated have made many a petulant reader turn down
his thumb at once.

This objection is connected with another, that of
obscurity. To quote a recent pronouncement upon 'The
Waste Land' from Mr. Middleton Murry: 'The reader is compelled, in the mere effort to understand, to adopt an
attitude of intellectual suspicion, which makes impossible the communication of feeling. The work offends
against the most elementary canon of good writing: that
the immediate effect should be unambiguous.' Consider
first this 'canon.' What would happen, if we pressed it,
to Shakespeare's greatest Sonnets or to 'Hamlet'? The
truth is that very much of the best poetry is necessarily
ambiguous in its immediate effect. Even the most careful
and responsive reader must re-read and do hard work before
the poem forms itself clearly and unambiguously in his
mind. An original poem, as much as a new branch of
mathematics, compels the mind which receives it to grow,
and this takes time. Any one who upon reflection asserts
the contrary for his own case must be either a demi-god
or dishonest; probably Mr. Murry was in haste. His
remarks show that he has failed in his attempt to read the
poem, and they reveal, in part, the reason for his failure, namely, his own over-intellectual approach. To read
it successfully he would have to discontinue his present
self-mystifications.

The critical question in all cases is whether the poem
is worth the trouble it entails. For 'The Waste Land'
this is considerable. There is Miss Weston's 'From
Ritual to Romance' to read, and its 'astral' trimmings
to be discarded - they have nothing to do with Mr. Eliot's
poem. There is Canto XXVI of the 'Purgatorio' to be
studied - the relevance of the close of that Canto to the
whole of Mr. Eliot's work must be insisted upon. It
illuminates his persistent concern with sex, the problem
of our generation as religion was the problem of the
last. There is the central position of Tiresias in the
poem to be puzzled out - the cryptic form of the note
which Mr. Eliot writes on this point is just a little
tiresome. It is a way of underlining the fact that the
poem is concerned with many aspects of the one fact of
sex, a hint that is perhaps neither indispensable nor
entirely successful.

When all this has been done by the reader, when the
materials with which the words are to clothe themselves

have been collected, the poem still remains to be read.
And it is easy to fail in this undertaking. An 'attitude
of intellectual suspicion' must certainly be abandoned.
But this is not difficult to those who still know how to
give their feelings precedence to their thoughts, who can
accept and unify an experience without trying to catch it
in an intellectual net or to squeeze out a doctrine. One
form of this attempt must be mentioned. Some, misled no
doubt by its origin in a Mystery, have endeavoured to give
the poem a symbolical reading. But its symbols are not
mystical but emotional. They stand, that is, not for
ineffable objects but for normal human experience. The
poem, in fact, is radically naturalistic; only its compression makes it appear otherwise. And in this it probably comes nearer to the original Mystery which it per-
petuates than transcendentalism does.

If it were desired to label in three words the most
characteristic feature of Mr. Eliot's technique this might
be done by calling his poetry a 'music of ideas.' The
ideas are of all kinds, abstract and concrete, general and
particular, and, like the musician's phrases, they are
arranged, not that they may tell us something but that
their effects in us may combine into a coherent whole of
feeling and produce a peculiar liberation of the will.
They are there to be responded to, not to be pondered or
worked out. This is, of course, a method used inter-
mittently in very much poetry, and only an accentuation
and isolation of one of its normal resources. The peculiarity of Mr. Eliot's later, more puzzling, work is his
deliberate and almost exclusive employment of it. In the
earlier poems this logical freedom only appears occasionally. In 'The Love Song of J. Alfred Prufrock,' for
example, there is a patch at the beginning and another at
the end, but the rest of the poem is quite straightfor-
ward. In 'Gerontion,' the first long poem in this manner,
the air of monologue, of a stream of associations, is a
kind of disguise and the last two lines:

> Tenants of the house,
> Thoughts of a dry brain in a dry season,

are almost an excuse. The close of 'A Cooking Egg' is
perhaps the passage in which the technique shows itself
most clearly. The reader who appreciates the emotional
relevance of the title has the key to the later poems in
his hand. 'The Waste Land' and 'The Hollow Men' (the most
beautiful of Mr. Eliot's poems, if we reserve a doubt as
to the last section, astonishing though it is) are purely
a 'music of ideas,' and the pretence of a continuous

thread of associations is dropped.

How this technique lends itself to misunderstandings we have seen. But many readers who have failed in the end to escape bewilderment have begun by finding on almost every line that Mr. Eliot has written (if we except certain youthful poems on American topics) that personal stamp which is the hardest thing for the craftsman to imitate and perhaps the most certain sign that the experience, good or bad, rendered in the poem is authentic. Only those unfortunate persons who are incapable of reading poetry can resist Mr. Eliot's rhythms. The poem as a whole may elude us while every fragment, as a fragment, comes victoriously home. It is difficult to believe that this is Mr. Eliot's fault rather than his reader's, because a parallel case of a poet who so constantly achieves the hardest part of his task and yet fails in the easier is not to be found. It is much more likely that we have been trying to put the fragments together on a wrong principle.

Another doubt has been expressed. Mr. Eliot repeats himself in two ways. The nightingale, Cleopatra's barge, the rats and the smoky candle-end recur and recur. Is this a sign of a poverty of inspiration? A more plausible explanation is that this repetition is in part a consequence of the technique above described, and in part something which many writers who are not accused of poverty also show. Shelley, with his rivers, towers and stars, Conrad, Hardy, Walt Whitman and Dostoevsky spring to mind. When a writer has found a theme or image which fixes a point of relative stability in the drift of experience, it is not to be expected that he will avoid it. Such themes are a means of orientation. And it is quite true that the central process in all Mr. Eliot's best poems is the same: the conjunction of feelings which, though superficially opposed - as squalor, for example, is opposed to grandeur - yet tend as they develop to change places and even to unite. If they do not develop far enough the intention of the poem is missed. Mr. Eliot is neither sighing after vanished glories nor holding contemporary experience up to scorn. Both bitterness and desolation are superficial aspects of his poetry. There are those who think that he merely takes his readers into the Waste Land and leaves them there, that in his last poem he confesses his impotence to release the healing waters. The reply is that some readers find in his poetry not only a clearer, fuller realisation of their plight, the plight of a whole generation, than they find elsewhere, but also through the very energies set free in that realisation a return of the saving passion.

54. EDMUND WILSON, STRAVINSKY AND OTHERS, 'NEW REPUBLIC'

10 March 1926, vol. xlvi, 73-4

These comments come at the end of a consideration of
Stravinsky's ballet, 'Les Noces', which communicates 'an
exhilaration as impossible to the jazz orchestra as to the
accomplished modern composer of disintegration and defeat'.

This is perhaps not an inappropriate place to speak of the
collected edition of T.S. Eliot's poems which has just
been published in England. This volume contains nothing
new except a set of poems called 'The Hollow Men,' which
represents an even more advanced stage of the condition
of demoralization already given expression in 'The Waste
Land': the last of these poems - the disconnected thoughts
of a man lying awake at night - consists merely of the
barest statement of a melancholy self-analysis mixed with
a fragment of the Lord's Prayer and a morose parody of
'Here We Go Round the Mulberry Bush.' 'This is the way
the world ends,' the poet concludes, 'Not with a bang,
but a whimper.'
    No artist has felt more keenly than Mr. Eliot the
desperate condition of Europe since the War nor written
about it more poignantly. Yet, as we find this mood of
hopelessness and impotence eating into his poetry so
deeply, we begin to wonder whether it is really the problems of European civilization which are keeping him
awake nights. Mr. Eliot has lived abroad so long that we
rarely think of him as an American and he is never written
about from the point of view of his relation to other
American authors. Yet one suspects that his real significance is less that of a prophet of European disintegration
than of a poet of the American Puritan temperament. Compare him with Hawthorne, Henry James, E.A. Robinson and
Edith Wharton: all these writers have their Waste Land,
which is the aesthetic and emotional waste land of the
Puritan character and their chief force lies in the intensity with which they communicate emotions of deprivation
and chagrin. The young men of Eliot's earlier poems, with
their prudence and their inability to let themselves go,
are like the young men of Henry James's early novels and
like the Hawthorne of the Note-Books; and the later creations of Eliot, with their regrets for having dared too
little, correspond exactly to the middle-aged men of the

later Henry James, of 'The Ambassadors' and 'The Beast in
the Jungle.' What is most important about Mr. Eliot, however, is that even in his deepest dejections and tending,
as he seems to do here, to give his emotions a false significance, he remains a poet of the first order. One is
struck, in going through this new edition, by the fact
that he survives rereading better than almost any of his
contemporaries, American or English.

55. J.C. SQUIRE ON ELIOT'S MEANINGLESSNESS, 'LONDON
MERCURY'

March 1926, vol. xiii, 547-8

This is from a review not only of Eliot's 'Poems' but also
of Blunden's 'English Poems'. The contrast, obviously
enough, works in Blunden's favour.

Mr. Eliot's work is mainly an elaborate expression of disgust. He ends his volume with these lines:

> This is the way the world ends
> This is the way the world ends
> This is the way the world ends
> Not with a bang but a whimper.

and he calls his longest poem 'The Waste Land,' its
apparent object being to reflect in a vagrant and
fatigued sequence of images the exhaustion of our civilisation. The mood is familiar enough: it is what thirty
years ago they used to call 'fin-de-siècle': Baudelaire
without his guts. It is a dyspeptic mood, the mood of a
man of low vitality, a man feeling 'below par.' The
diagnosis on which it is nominally founded seems to me
unsound. Our civilisation appears at least as vigorous
as it was a century ago, and the urban ugliness and the
emptiness of the lives of many people, rich and poor, is
no new thing - neither is the exaggeration of it from
outside. And what new complexion has recently come over
our situation versus the universe I do not make out.
Nevertheless a poet must be granted his opinions and his
mood, though an obstinate pessimism or fierce despair is

more likely to produce moving literature than the muted
dejection which appears habitual with Mr. Eliot, who seems
unable to love anything or, by the same token, to hate.
In the last resort we have to ask ourselves what are the
qualities of his work and what pleasure does it give us.
    Certain powers of intellect and craftsmanship he obvi-
ously possesses. There is an acute, if perverse, mind in
these poems, and a faculty, too seldom employed, for a
faint individual music: Mr. Eliot observes closely, and
he has a vocabulary which will do anything he wants, a
voacbulary which, perhaps, might be richer if it were
poorer, for it is stuffed with terms drawn from obscure
penetralia of learning which are no assistance to his
toiling reader. Unhappily Mr. Eliot has very little regard for his reader. In one of the poems of his earliest
period, when his poems were weary, and comparatively
lucid, reveries over the vacuity of daily life in general
and cultivated tea parties in particular, he depicted himself as mounting his aunt's doorstep and

                                        turning
    Wearily, as one would turn to nod good-bye to
      Rochefoucauld
    If the street were time and he at the end of the
      street.

The lucidity, of late, has vanished, but whenever there is
an opening in the mists which surround the later Mr. Eliot,
he is still to be observed nodding good-bye to Rouche-
foucauld - who stands at the end of a street sparsely
populated with pale typists, cats, barrel-organs, and
footmen going out for a drink. It is not a very infec-
tious attitude; nor does it generate the simple, sensuous,
and passionate. In the later poems Mr. Eliot has reinforced his detachment by a further detachment of speech.
Now and again he is comprehensible and strong (as in the
stanzas about Webster and Donne) or comprehensible and
melodious (as in the first lines of 'The Waste Land' and
the last stanza of 'Sweeney Among the Nightingales'):
usually he is obscure, so inconsequent, that the kindest
thing one can suppose is that he is experimenting with
automatic writing. Why on earth he bothers to write at
all is difficult to conceive: why, since he must write,
he writes page after page from which no human being could
derive any more meaning (much less edification or pleasure) than if they were written in Double-Dutch (which
parts of them possibly are) is to me beyond conjecture.
Why to the Waste Land add a Valley of peculiarly Dry
Bones?

56. ALLEN TATE, A POETRY OF IDEAS, 'NEW REPUBLIC'

30 June 1926, vol. xlvii, 172-3

The article by Edwin Muir to which Tate refers was
published in 'Nation' (New York) (5 August 1925), cxxi,
162-4.

'Poems: 1909-1925' by Mr. T.S. Eliot is a spiritual epilogue to 'The Education of Henry Adams.' It represents
a return of the Anglo-French colonial idea to its home.
A pervasive sense of public duty led Adams into morally
and politically active life, but it was not strong enough
to submerge the 'finer grain,' with which his hereditary
European culture had endowed him. The conflict was disastrous; he repudiated the American adventure too late.
But in Mr. Eliot puritan obligation withdraws into private conscience; a system of conduct becomes a pattern
of sensibility; his meagre romanticism, like the artificially constructed ruin of the eighteenth century, is
strictly an affair of the past, it has nothing whatever
in common with a creed of practical romanticism like that
of William James. Going home to Europe, Mr. Eliot has
had to understand Europe; he could not quite sufficiently
be the European simply to feel that he was there; he has
been forced to envisage it with a reminiscent philosophy.
And it is not insignificant that the quarterly of which
he is the editor is the first British journal which has
attempted to relate the British mind to the total European mind; that has attempted a rational synthesis of the
traditions of Roman culture; that has, in a word, contemplated order. Mr. Eliot's position in this scheme of
recapitulation, of arranging the past when the future
seems to him only vaguely to exist, is in some respects
particularly fortunate. It has enabled him to bring to
England, in his poetry, the sense of a contemporary
spiritual crisis, which shell-shock had already rendered
acute, but of which the English Channel had perhaps kept
out the verbally conscious signification. The essays of
Maurras, Valéry, Massis, the philosophy of Spengler, all
may variously attest to the reality of European disorder.
It is nevertheless the special poetical creation of Mr.
Eliot's cultural disinheritance and gloom.
    It has not, I believe, been pointed out that Mr.
Eliot's poetry is principally a poetry of ideas, that

these ideas have steadily anticipated the attitude of a
later essay on the Function of Criticism. 'The Sacred
Wood' was written in the years of this anticipatory verse,
but this volume is singularly devoid of its chief issues.
For the early essays presuppose a static society and the
orderly procession of letters: Tradition and the Individual Talent presupposes a continuity of traditional
culture as literature. The baroque agony of the poetry
in the corresponding period was preoccupied, however, with
the anarchy which he has subsequently rationalized and for
which he has proposed as remedy the régime of a critical
dictatorship, in The Function of Criticism.

The critical idea of disorder began, in the poetry, as
the desperate atmosphere of isolation. It was obviously
conviction prior to reflection, but to one in Mr. Eliot's
spiritual unrest it speedily becomes a protective idea; it
ceases to be emotion, personal attitude; one ceases reiterating it as such. This rationalization of attitude
puts in a new light the progressive sterilization of his
poetry, It partly explains the slenderness of his production: a poetry with the tendency to ideas betrays itself
into criticism, as it did in Arnold, when it becomes too
explicit, too full. His collected poems is the preparation for a critical philosophy of the present state of
European literature. As this criticism becomes articulate, the poetry becomes incoherent. The intellectual
conception is now so complete that he suddenly finds there
is no symbolism, no expressive correspondence, no poetry,
for it. An emotional poetry uncensored by reason would be
intolerable to his neo-classical predilections. For Mr.
Eliot apprehends his reality with the intellect, and the
reality does not yield a coherent theme. This is evidently the formula of 'The Waste Land' (1922), where the
traditional mythologies are no longer forms of expression,
but quite simply an inexplicable burden the meaning of
which the vulgar brutality of modern life will not permit
the poem to remember. The mythologies disappear altogether in 'The Hollow Men' (1925), for this series of
lyrics stands at the end of his work as the inevitable
reduction to chaos of a poetry of the idea of chaos:

Here we go round the prickly pear....
This is the way the world ends
Not with a bang but a whimper.

The series is substantially an essay on contemporary
Europe.

Throughout Mr. Eliot's poetry two principal devices
advance the presentation of spiritual disorder. They were

previously exploited, the one by Guillaume Apollinaire not
later than 1913, the other by André Salmon in 1910. Very
little of Mr. Eliot's poetry was written before the latter
year. The first is the device of shifted movement, or of
logically irrelevant but emotionally significant conclusion, used with typical success at the end of the 'Preludes'; I quote from Mr. Malcolm Cowley's unpublished
translation of Apollinaire's 'Marizibill':

> Through the Hochstrasse of Cologne
> Evenings she used to come and pass
> Offering herself to who would own
> Then tired of walking streets she drank
> All night in evil bars alone....
>
> People I've seen of every sort
> They do not fit their destiny
> Aimless mechanical as wires
> Their hearts yawn open like their doors
> Their eyes are half-extinguished fires.

For the second device, that of projecting simultaneously
events which are separated in time, destroying the commonplace categorical perception of time and space and erect-
ing the illusion of chaos - a device of tremendous effect
in the Tiresias passage and the Sweeney poems - I quote
stanzas from Salmon's 'Les Veufs de Rose':

> La duègne a secoué ses jupons
> (Chargez le ciel! - Le herse flambe.)
> Le rat de Hamlet, ce bouffon,
> Vient de passer entre ses jambes.
>
> Chassez le rat, chassez les veufs,
> La vieille fermera la porte,
> Rose enfile le maillot neuf
> D'une soeur rivale enfin morte.

Here is the rhythm of Sweeney, Grishkin, Burbank; also
a system of imagery too specific in its properties to have
been learned directly from Laforgue, supposedly Mr. Eliot's
chief French influence.
    While he has all along been under the influence of La-
forgue and Corbière, it has not given him his two major
effects. From these poets he has borrowed, not tricks of
construction so much as attitudes and particular lines;
for example, Mr. Eliot's beautiful line

> Simple and faithless as a smile or shake of the hand -

is a paraphrase, in which the metaphor is made a definite image, of

Simple et sans foi comme un bonjour.

The line was Laforgue's, but now because Eliot has improved it, it is his. And the Elizabethan element is impure. Webster's varied complexity of pattern, its fusion of heterogeneous sensations, breaks down under Mr. Eliot's treatment. It has undoubtedly served him as a model of diction, but the physical presentation of psychological terror and the sense of formal beauty, fused in Webster, are in Eliot, as Mr. Edwin Muir has pointed out, simply mixed, alternately recurring. His Elizabethanism has indubitably been too ingenuously appraised by some critics, and it has thus been objected that such a formula is inadequate to contemporary 'problems'; but even were the formula of most of Eliot's poetry what these critics suppose it to be, criticism might as well assert that Dryden was not the poet of his age because he did not permit the lately 'discovered' law of gravitation to alter the quality of sensitivity in his verse. Mr. Eliot's poetry has attempted with considerable success to bring back the total sensibility as a constantly available material, deeper and richer in connotations than any substance yielded by the main course of English poetry since the seventeenth century.

He has borrowed intelligently from a great many sources; it is only because of an interested romantic criticism that the privilege has fallen into dishonor. Those aspects of recent French poetry which reappear in Eliot have been impugned as echo and faddism; it is forgotten that some of Massinger's best lines are revisions of Tourneur, are unoriginal. And it is not merely as a skilful borrower that Mr. Eliot is the most traditional poet of the age. For him and for all sound criticism down to Pater the body of literature in the Graeco-Roman culture lives as an organism; he has deliberately employed such of its properties as extend, living, into the creative impulse of his age. His attention in both criticism and poetry has been to the poetry, not to the poet; to the essence and not to the momentary vicar of the essence. The attitude is self-contained, impersonal, classical, and the critics of opportunity and private obsession have regretted the lack of personal exploitation; his unfamiliar system of metaphor has offered a great deal for a vulgar age to misunderstand. His conviction that the traditional inspiration, in immediately inherited forms, is exhausted produced the transition

poem, 'The Waste Land': it exhibits this inspiration as it
now exists in decay, and it looks by implication toward a
new world-order the framework of which Mr. Eliot lacked
the excessive divination to supply. He is traditional,
but in defining tradition as life, as a living cultural
memory, instead of a classical dictionary stocked with
literary dei ex machina, he is also the type of contemporary poet.

Mr. Eliot's is a scrupulous, economical mind. It is
possible that he has nothing more to say in poetry. 'The
Hollow Men' ends at least a phase. Whether the difficulty
is the personal quality of his puritan culture, as Mr.
Edmund Wilson seems to believe, or lies in the tangle of
contemporary spiritual forces, it would be hazardous just
now to say. But it is evident that he for some reason –
like Gray who also lived in a critical transition – cannot
'speak out.' Arnold's remarks on Gray in this connection
are of considerable contemporary interest:

> It [the poetry of his age] was intellectual, argu-
> mentative, ingenious ... not interpretative. Main-
> taining and fortifying [his mind] with lofty studies,
> he could not fully educe and enjoy them; the want of
> a genial atmosphere, the failure of sympathy in his
> contemporaries, were too great.... A man born in 1608
> [Milton] could profit by the larger and more poetic
> scope of the English spirit in the Elizabethan age....
> Neither Butler nor Gray could flower. They *never spoke
> out*.

57. CONRAD AIKEN, FROM THE POETIC DILEMMA, 'DIAL'

May 1927, vol. lxxxii, 420-2

It has been often enough, perhaps too often said, of late,
that the almost fatal difficulty which confronts the poet
nowadays is the difficulty of finding a theme which might
be worth his power. If he be potentially a 'major' poet,
this difficulty is thought to be particularly formidable,
if not actually crippling; but for even the 'minor' poet
(to use minor in no pejorative sense) it is considered
serious. Mr T.S. Eliot, whose 'Poems' have been reprinted
by Mr Knopf, has himself contributed something to this
theory. In his admirable note on Blake, in 'The Sacred

Wood,' he suggests that Blake was potentially a major poet
who was robbed of his birthright by the mere accident of
there not being, at the moment, a prepared or traditional
cosmology or mythology of sufficient wealth to engage, or
disengage, his great imaginative power. He was compelled,
in the absence of such a frame, to invent a frame for
himself; and in this was, perhaps inevitably, doomed to
failure. Had he been born to a belief as rich and profound as that which Dante inherited, might he not have
been as great a poet?...

This is an ingenious idea; but it is possible to take
it too seriously. It is obvious enough that some sort of
tradition is a very great help to a poet - it floats him
and sustains him, it carries him more swiftly and easily
than he could carry himself, and it indicates a direction
for him. But a fact too often lost sight of, at the present time, is that the great poet may be, precisely, one
who has a capacity to find, at *any* given moment, a theme
sufficient for the proper exercise of his strength. There
were contemporaries of Dante who were excellent poets, but
for whom the cosmology which enchanted Dante was not evocative. If Blake scanned his horizon in vain for 'huge
cloudy symbols,' Goethe, scanning the same horizon, was
not so unsuccessful. It is true enough that, with the
decay of religion as a force in human life, poetry must be
robbed of that particular *kind* of conviction, as has been
noted by Mr I.A. Richards; but to assume from this that
the poetry of the future must inevitably be a poetry of
scepticism or negation is perhaps to oversimplify the
issue. Poetry has always shown itself able to keep step
easily and naturally with the utmost that man can do in
extending his knowledge, no matter how destructive of
existing beliefs that knowledge can be. Each accretion of
knowledge becomes, by degrees, a part of man's emotional
attitude to the world, takes on affective values or overtones, and is then ready for use in poetry. The universe
does not become each year simpler or less disturbing: nor
is there any reason to suppose that it ever will. The
individual who is born into it will continue to be surprised and delighted by it, or surprised and injured; and
in direct ratio with this surprise and delight or surprise
and injury, he will continue to be a poet.

The wail of contemporary criticism, therefore, to the
effect that poetry can find nothing to cling to, leaves
one a little sceptical: though it is easy enough to sympathize with the individual poets who, suffering from that
delusion, have for the moment lost themselves in self-
distrust. Mr Pound and Mr Eliot are perhaps very typical
victims of this kind. But whereas Mr Pound has evaded

the issue, seeking asylum in a sense of the past (rather
half-heartedly held) Mr Eliot has made a poetry of the
predicament itself. His poetry has been from the outset
a poetry of self-consciousness; of instinct at war with
doubt, and sensibility at odds with reason; an air of
precocious cynicism has hung over it; and his development
as a poet has not been so much a widening of his field –
though at first sight 'The Waste Land' might suggest this
– as a deepening of his awareness of it. Prufrock, who
antedated by a decade the later poem, could not give himself to his emotions or his instincts because he could not
bring himself, *sub specie aeternitatis*, quite to believe
in them: he was inhibited, and preferred to remain a despairing spectator: but at the same time he wished that he
might have been a simpler organism, 'a pair of ragged
claws.' The theme of 'Gerontion,' a good many years
later, is the same: it is again the paralysing effect of
consciousness, the 'after such knowledge, what forgiveness?' And 'The Waste Land' is again a recapitulation,
reaching once more the same point of acute agony of doubt,
the same distrust of decision or action, with its 'awful
daring of a moment's surrender, which an age of prudence
can never retract.'
    The reissue of 'Poems' is not the occasion for a de-
tailed review of Mr Eliot's early work, however; for our
present purpose it is sufficient to note that Mr Eliot
has conspicuously shared the contemporary feeling that
there are no 'large' themes for the poet, and that he has
had the courage and the perspicacity to take as his theme
precisely his themelessness. Why not – he says in effect
– make a bitter sort of joke of one's nihilism and impotence? And in making his bitter joke, he has written some
of the most searchingly unhappy and vivid and individual
of contemporary poetry. One feels that his future is
secure, by virtue of his honesty quite as much as by virtue of his genius....

'Ash-Wednesday'

London and New York, 24 April 1930

58. GERALD HEARD, T.S. ELIOT, 'WEEK-END REVIEW'

3 May 1930, vol. i, 268-9

Heard (1889-1972) was an English historian and writer,
whose publications include 'Science in the Making' (1935)
and 'The Third Morality' (1937).

Mr. Eliot is so serious a poet that he deserves, like all
who have escaped from the idle singing through an empty
day, to be noted, not for the way he says things, but for
the things themselves. His style is that most living
style, a language distinctive because it is fitted so
closely to a personal thought. It is a symptom and can
only be justly criticised if an attempt is made to judge
the thought from which it springs. So his poetry, though
highly stylised, may be appreciated by the ordinary thinking man. Mr. Eliot's poems are not written as exercises
in prosody or illustrations of new sound-patterns; they
are his philosophy. What he says, he says because not
otherwise could he give expression to his strong conviction. 'The Waste Land' could only be understood if it was
realised how deeply the poet had suffered because of the
war's desolation.

The clue to these six poems called 'Ash-Wednesday'
seems to be that the poet has entered on a new stage of
his life. *Adhesit pavimento* might still be written over
them, but also *De profundis*, for the strongest feeling
that they give is of a spirit's communing. They do not
seem addressed to any public, still less to appreciators
of verse.

This, of course, is not to say that they will not interest poetry lovers; but certainly such will be distracted from their love of pure expression by the way that philosophy will keep breaking in. Indeed, it does not seem that it is possible to appreciate this verse unless one can first discover to which of the traditions of English religious verse Mr. Eliot really belongs. On the one side we have the broad organ notes of the main tradition, the expression of a people whose main characteristic is that they have cared for the word rather than the rite, for statement rather than for symbol. It is the tradition which gave the Authorised Version and which speaks through Milton, and through Dryden, though a Catholic. Religion to it is not so much a mystery to be shown forth by symbols and ritual, but is rather 'sanctified common-sense' to be set forth in the most stately language. On the other side is what may be called the iconographic tradition, the tradition which uses words, not for argument or for rhetoric, but to raise visual images, to create hard clear symbols, for it believes the infinite can only so be approached and words may only so be used to shadow it forth.

In English poetry, this tradition runs alongside our main canon. We can trace it back from Hopkins and Thompson, to Crashaw and Donne, back even to the author of the 'Pearl.' Now to which of these two does Mr. Eliot belong? For some time he seemed to be attached to the visual school, but it is only possible to be a true visualiser if the main current is given a wide berth. In English it flows so strongly that for a poet to approach it is to be drawn into its tideway. Francis Thompson realised that. It seems to have been a deliberate attempt to free himself of the associative sound tradition that made him take for his greatest expression of the search for the strayed soul by the divine lover, not the perfect simile of the Good Shepherd, which has followed man for a hundred generations, but the violent, contradictory simile of the dog hunting down its prey.

It is therefore very remarkable that through these verses of Mr. Eliot the Authorised Version breaks out on every hand. 'And God said, "Shall these bones live?"' 'The burden of the grasshopper.' 'Redeem the time.' 'The Word within the world ... The Light in darkness.' 'O, my people, what have I done unto thee!' 'And let my cry come unto Thee.' Who can say how these rhythms would sound to ears which have never echoed to the lectionary's cadences, and who can say that a poet who takes into his verse such phrases entire is not already passing into the main English tradition?

Such a symptom compels speculation as to the poet's spiritual bourne. The process of those who move in the direction of system and meaning is too often assumed to be Anglican, High Anglican, Roman, and probably the chances are in favour of such a solution for those who think visually and not orally. But it is really an accident that poets should so think - and even then the end is not certain. William Morris, a poet of the eye and not the ear, who called Milton a damned rhetorician, and a furious romantic to boot, did not charge into Catholicism from his unhistorical notion of the middle ages, but into Socialism. Taken as a whole, poets should be primarily artists of the ear, and if so they will tend to find their meaning and system in utterance rather than in rite, in prophecy rather than in symbol. Protestantism, because it suspects plastic art, must express its supreme feeling and intuition in poetry. In the richness of Arabic, Mohammedanism found an art medium which compensated it for its plastic art-denying ordinance. The nations to whom a rite and a sacrament are the supreme manifestations of reality must take to plastic expression to symbolise their religious feeling. The major poets must be poets of the ear, and they will always be prophetic, not priestly. That is why England is the home of Protestantism, supreme poetry, and of only a secondary sculpture and painting.

The future of Mr. Eliot's muse is therefore of interest to philosophy as well as to poetry. Will the main English tradition reassert itself with this returned New Englander? It seems to be doing so. If it does, when it wins him his allegiance will mean more than a turn in poetic fashion.

59. FRANCIS BIRRELL, MR. T.S. ELIOT, 'NATION AND ATHENAEUM'

31 May 1930, vol. xlvii, 292-3

Francis Birrell (b. 1889) is a British critic, translator and biographer. He wrote an essay on Diderot for the 'Criterion' (July 1933), xii, 632-41.

When Mr. T.S. Eliot started out on a poetical career which was to astonish many and ravish some, he was primarily a

satirist and a 'wit,' not merely in choice of subject, as
in 'Mr. Apollinax,' but in the definite sardonic quality
with which, by the arts of juxtaposition or abnormal
stressing, he invested words that had not yet had such a
significance:-

> Princess Volupine extends
>   A meagre, blue-nailed, phthisic hand
> To climb the waterstair. Lights, lights,
>   She entertains Sir Ferdinand
>
> Klein.

The sombre melody is intentionally out of key with the
poet's ironic intention. This satire, though less marked
in 'The Waste Land,' still informs some of the more sumptuous passages:-

> On the divan are piled (at night her bed)
> Stockings, slippers, camisoles, and stays.
> I Tiresias, old man with wrinkled dugs
> Perceived the scene, and foretold the rest -
> I too awaited the expected guest.

But in 'Ash-Wednesday' - the ironic intent has completely
vanished from the poems of Mr. Eliot, and with it perhaps
the superficial qualities that made him appeal to the
younger generation. He is now out for what is known as
'beauty,' and 'beauty' is less in request than wit. The
six short poems that make up 'Ash-Wednesday' are an
elaborate study in pure form; and to my mind contain
many passages of great loveliness:-

> At the first turning of the second stair
> I turned and saw below
> The same shape twisted on the banister
> Under the vapour in the fetid air
> Struggling with the devil of the stairs who wears
> The deceitful face of hope and of despair,

or again:-

> Who walked between the violet and the violet
> Who walked between
> The various ranks of varied green
> Going in white and blue, in Mary's colour,
> Talking of trivial things.

The main difficulty I have in facing this remarkable poem
is that I do not understand what it is all about. What are
the 'three white leopards ... under a juniper tree,' what

exactly are the three staircases, and the veiled sisters?
Are they mystical or liturgical images with which I ought
to be acquainted, or are they merely private associations
in the sensibility of Mr. Eliot? On the second assumption, are they permissible? And on the first, how much
information is an author justified in assuming his reader
to possess? Does not such a great poet as Donne positively suffer in the extravagance of his sensibility?
Though to be sure, Mr. Eliot would answer this last question with a violent negative. Then perhaps the difficulties will clear themselves up. When I first read 'The Waste
Land' or even 'Prufrock,' I could hardly make head or tail
of them, yet they now present no particular difficulty.
     A short poem like 'Ash-Wednesday' can only be appreci-
ated by being read all through, and read more than once.
Only thus will the reader be able to absorb the complexity
of its texture, the elaboration of its prosody, the richness and violence of its internal rhymes, its liturgical
sombreness (for I suppose the liturgies of the Church dictate the form as well as the inspiration of the poem).
     Mr. Eliot, very early in his career, developed a
vocabulary. There was about his works, almost from the
start, that authentic smell which enables one to tell them
almost from a distance. No poet has 'arrived' till he has
developed his vocabulary, and some poets have not done so
till late in life. But with the success comes the danger.
The poet may rest content with his vocabulary and develop
a manner and a mannerism. He becomes repetitive. Mr.
Eliot is too inquisitive, emotionally as well as linguistically, for this to be a danger. On the other hand his
temptation is to be too constantly on the move and keep
the reader continually guessing. It is the best danger
for a poet.

60. EDA LOU WALTON, T.S. ELIOT TURNS TO RELIGIOUS VERSE,
'NEW YORK TIMES BOOK REVIEW'

20 July 1930, 9

Walton (1896-1962), American literary critic and poet, was
educated at the University of California, Berkeley. She
taught at New York University from 1924 to 1960.
     It is worth comparing this review with her comments on
Pound's 'A Draft of XXX Cantos' in the 'New York Times

Book Review' (2 April 1933), sect. v, 2, and reprinted in
'Ezra Pound: The Critical Heritage', ed. Eric Homberger
(London, 1972), pp. 256-9. Homberger writes: 'this review
indicates Eliot's authority in New York in 1933. He has
become (though oversimplified) a weapon to be used against
Pound'.

The later manner of T.S. Eliot is actually a direct out-
growth of his earlier poetic manner as seen in 'The Waste
Land.' When Eliot defined his three creeds as Royalism
in politics, Classicism in art, and Anglo-Catholicism in
religion, he did not in truth step out of his position as
'the greatest poet of non-belief,' for the simple reason
that he never actually held that position or aspired to
it. Any one who cares to analyze 'The Waste Land' will
find in it the seeds of the religious poetry to which
Eliot has of late given himself. For 'The Waste Land,' with
its devastating picture of modern life without beauty and
without faith, with its statement of hopeless inability
to grasp values in modern civilization, with its renunciation of the present, was actually the beginning of the
search Eliot was soon to make after God. There were only
two possibilities for this poet from the very start,
either a reiteration - to which there would have been
little point - of the imputed sordidness of our day, or a
search for something more fundamental in the way of an old
or a new faith. To be sure, Eliot might have developed,
as some expected him to do, a new creed based on an
affirmation of a modern intellectual and scientific outlook. That he would do this was, however, never very
likely, since his cry was for romance, beauty and a golden
past. That he did finally accept one of the oldest religions (we should not be surprised to hear that he had
become Roman Catholic) is in accord with his reverence for
the past. The only difficulty lies in understanding how
so analytical an intellect came to acceptance of unques-
tioning faith. And there seems some reason for believing
that Eliot remains as frustrated and as sad in his later
religious poems as he seemed in 'The Waste Land.' For in
these too the theme of death is everywhere and the desire
toward oblivion as strong as ever and stronger. No one
of these poems but states some feeling of incompetence to
accept life, some yearning after nothingness. All that
has been lost from Eliot's poetry is the intensity of
pain which was expressed in 'The Waste Land,' and which,
in these later poems, is muted into a desire-to-believe.

'Ash-Wednesday' is, as its title indicates, a poem of
repentance and renunciation. Its various sections are a
ritualistic chanting working through the personal desire

for oblivion toward some universal statement of the meaning of death in life, and life in death. The poem never
achieves ecstasy of that type of mysticism which frees one,
momentarily, from the awareness of anything else but the
Vision. The poem is pitched low; the tone is one of grief
rather than of wild sorrow, and faith is arrived at only
by acceptance of the Word. 'Ash-Wednesday' is a difficult
poem, much more difficult, although simply enough written,
than is the type of mystic poetry sometimes called 'verbal
mysticism,' which achieves its effects by the projection of
the mind through space by means of a rapidly evolving
series of images. Its difficulty is due to the fact that
the poet asks one to understand not only Catholic symbolism
and medieval literary expression, but a personal symbolism
also. To say, therefore, just what the leopards, the Lady,
the rocks, &c., may mean is almost impossible. One can
merely surmise. But the emotion of the poem is obvious.
    It opens with the poet's renunciation of life; it rises
through the rising desire toward Faith. There is always
the undercurrent of the wish for oblivion. There is birth
moving toward death and death moving toward spiritual
birth. Will the Church forgive the children who walk in
darkness? With this question unanswered, the poet closes
on a prayer for himself that he need not care for life
sufficiently to cling to it, and yet may care enough to
live it and be at peace in God's will.

    And let my cry come unto Thee

    The whole poem is remote and sad. It has, of course,
Eliot's beauty of rhythm and sound. It is not the poem of
a religious teacher, but of an intellectual man who would
wish to renounce any intellectual conception of life and
finds the task very difficult.

61. ORGILL McKENZIE, REVIEW, 'NEW ADELPHI'

June-August 1930, n.s., vol. iii, 336-8

Mrs Orgill McKenzie, British poet and story writer,
published the bulk of her work during the 1930s.

It is a pity that the publishers of 'Ash-Wednesday' have
been so prodigal of paper, for when the reader, having
patiently turned seven all-but-virgin pages, arrives at
the opening line, he is in a mood to purloin for his own
irreverent ends its 'Because I do not hope to turn again.'
But there the frisking ends. Beauty calls us to heel and
keeps us there, except when, in resentment almost, we
deliberately hold back. Mr. Eliot is a poet who has at
times bidden us go study tomes if we want to understand
him. Not that he does that here, but he is here still the
poet who has done it.

It is just that a poet should have the patience and
humility of the reader. It is good that the first shock
of the words be only a surface beauty - the smooth flat
beauty of the thing heard, but good only if the patience
and humility of the reader are at last rewarded; if the
words that were smooth like waters suddenly sharpen like
barbs, and strike the beauty home so that the thing heard
becomes the thing perceived. Enlightenment may come in
needle-pricks or in whole arrow-heads till the poem is
lodged entire in the reader. And then he feels as happy
as in mediaeval paintings the pincushion looks. The disciple experiences something of the pain-edged joy of the
creator. He too has had a kind of travail. The poem he
receives cannot be quite the poet's poem, certainly not
in degree, and probably not altogether in kind; for each
individual has a different set of ideas that rush to
answer the same summoning bell. But the important thing
is that the mob of released ideas should come to satisfying unity in the dispersed air and to a graspable com-
pleteness in infinite space, and not be lured to charge
up a blind alley and be discomfited by a blank wall
which the poet has cleared on the borrowed wings of erudition. If that happens the reader feels he has been
cheated. He will come to heel again when beauty whistles,
but warily this time, like a dog mindful of bygone kicks
that seemed to him unreasonable. A poet's symbolism if it
is self-contained may justly be obscure. There is no
sense of frustration in that soft dusk. Where the reader
needs wings and lacks them, the poet cannot provide ridiculous and necessarily inadequate step-ladders. But where
a poet by intellectual steps reaches a height we cannot in
one bound come by, we feel that he has kicked away the
scaffolding. That is why, when I come to an obscure place
in Mr. Eliot's poems, I remember that formidable list of
annotations and references in a previous volume and ask
myself: 'Am I to go on? Is it worth while going on, or
has he kicked away the scaffolding?'

Through 'Ash-Wednesday' ranges the ghost of

Ecclesiastes, a ghost of such sturdy stuff that at times it
becomes wide alive; and then 'Ash-Wednesday' is the ghost
ranging through Ecclesiastes. The ear feels balked when
it has been made hungry for the older beauty, and waits
for the words of that translator who must have written
wrapped about with fire.

Biblical phrases come twisted a little - the burden of
the grasshopper becomes apparently the *bourdon* of the
grasshopper. The thought is tweaked a little. The dry
bones that in Ezekiel's valley lived clothed again with
sinew here live

> Forgetting themselves and each other, united
> In the quiet of the desert.

'Prophesy to the wind' is not that thereby the slain may
live, but 'for only the wind will listen.'

The preacher says: 'That which now is, in the days to
come shall all be forgotten.' And Mr. Eliot:

> Because I know that time is always time
> And place is always and only place
> And what is actual is actual only for one time
> And only for one place.

Both poets concentrate on the Now which is the only actuality. The past has an existence only in so far as it is
synthesised in the present. The twist is in the conclusion:

'Therefore I hated life' and 'I rejoice that things are
as they are.' Yet it is only a little twist, for Ecclesiastes cannot remain negative: 'a man should rejoice in his
own works for that is his portion.'

Everything in life has its counterpart. If the powers
grow single towards one aim, the opposite weighs down the
balance. Youth is the positive time when one thing is
hotly pursued. Disillusionment comes when the debit
column is first seen to be as positive as what youth
thought alone positive. 'La Peau de Chagrin' grants fulfilment of a wish, but the skin is shrunken thereby, and
the realisation of the shrinking is set over against the
joy of satisfied desire.

'To everything there is a season and a time to every
purpose.' Ecclesiastes sums up the opposites. There is
the balance. God has set one thing over against the
other. 'Whoso removeth a stone shall be hurt thereby.'
And Mr. Eliot prays for 'those who are torn on the horn
between season and season, time and time.' The silent
Word is the centre about which whirls the restlessness of
opposites.

Both poets concentrate on the norm that is the only
peace. 'Be not righteous overmuch, neither make thyself
over-wise. Why shouldest thou destroy thyself?' 'Teach
us to care and not to care. Teach us to sit still.' But
even sitting still is positive and has its positive debit.
   Both poets know the uselessness of that search. 'And I
gave my heart to seek and search out by wisdom concerning
all things ... and behold all is vanity and vexation of
spirit.'

And I pray that I may forget
Those matters that with myself I too much discuss.

But both know that they must go on seeking, not only in
the future, but in the past.

From the window towards the granite shore
The white sails still fly seaward, seaward flying
Unbroken wings.

And the lost heart stiffens and rejoices
In the lost lilac and the lost sea voices.

There *is* no discharge in that war.
   But the search is not the search for life. It is life,
the justification of life and its redemption from vanity.
   Mr. Eliot finds something beyond the first stair of
youth. Beyond it, beyond the second stair of darkness
and disillusion are vision and strength, and something
waited for in the

Lord I am not worthy
but speak the word only.

Even if the poet were to stop at 'all is vanity,' yet,
by the mere beauty of his saying, somehow we could know,
however blindly, that all is *not* vanity. The keenness
of that joy-pain which, while it comes from the hurling of
our slipping selves into the fiery proclamation of a truth
that was dim-lit in us, is (though it cannot be proof)
conviction that here is life with opposites so sharply
mixed that there is something that looks like stasis, but
nothing that is vanity.
   There are many lovely things in these six poems that
are in mood and thought one poem. One of the loveliest is
a stanza in the fourth beginning: 'Here are the years that
walk between.' It flows exquisitely down to the weighted
slowness of the last line: 'While jewelled unicorns draw
by the gilded hearse.'

We may not be able to find out with our feet all the
ways of Mr. Eliot's garden, but even if we were beggars
obliged to sit, because of our intellectual poverty,
without the gate, we could yet fill our eyes with beauty
from peering through the cold twistings of the iron gate.
For Mr. Eliot's poetry is greater than his cleverness.

62. EDMUND WILSON, REVIEW, 'NEW REPUBLIC'

20 August 1930, vol. lxiv, 24-5

The three short and pious poems which T.S. Eliot has
brought out as Christmas cards, since 'The Hollow Men'
announced the nadir of the phase of despair and desolation
given such effective expression in 'The Waste Land,'
seemed comparatively uninspired and mild - far below his
earlier level. One felt that the humility of his new
religious phase was having the effect of enfeebling his
poetry. But his new poem, or group of poems, 'Ash-
Wednesday,' which follows a scheme somewhat similar to
that of 'The Waste Land' and makes a sort of sequel to it,
is a not unworthy successor.
  The poet begins with the confession of the bankruptcy
of his former hopes and ambitions:

[Quotes 'Ash-Wednesday', I, CPP, p. 89, 'Because I do not'
to 'usual reign?', and p. 90, 'Because these wings' to 'of
our death'.]

There follow passages in which the prayer is apparently
being answered: the poet's humility and pious resignation
are rewarded by a series of visions which first console,
then lighten his heart. We find an imagery new for Eliot,
a symbolism semi-ecclesiastical and not without a Pre-
Raphaelite flavor: white leopards, a Lady gowned in white,
junipers and yews, 'The Rose' and 'The Garden,' and
jewelled unicorns drawing a gilded hearse: these are
varied by an interlude which returns to the imagery and
mood of 'The Waste Land':

[Quotes 'Ash-Wednesday', III, CPP, p. 93, 'At the first
turning' to 'and of despair'.]

and a swirling, churning, anguished passage which suggests

certain things of Gertrude Stein's:

[Quotes 'Ash-Wednesday', V, CPP, p. 96, 'If the lost word
is lost' to 'the Silent Word'.]

    At last the themes of the first section recur: the
impotent wings of the agèd eagle seem to revive, as,

[Quotes 'Ash-Wednesday', VI, CPP, p. 98, 'From the wide
window' to 'the sandy earth'.]

The broken prayer, at once childlike and mystically subtle,
with which the poem ends seems to imply that the poet has
come closer to the strength and revelation he craves.
Grace is about to descend.

[Quotes, 'Ash-Wednesday', VI, CPP, pp. 98-9, 'Blessèd
sister' to 'come unto Thee'.]

    The literary and conventional imagery upon which 'Ash-
Wednesday' so largely relies and which is less vivid,
because more artificial, than that of Eliot's earlier
poems, seems to be a definite feature of inferiority: the
'devil of the stairs' and the 'shape twisted on the banis-
ter,' which are in Eliot's familiar and unmistakable personal vein, somehow come off better than the jewelled
unicorn, which incongruously suggests Yeats. And I am
made a little tired by hearing Eliot, only in his early
forties, present himself as an 'agèd eagle' who asks why
he should make the effort to stretch his wings. Yet 'Ash-
Wednesday,' though less brilliant and intense than Eliot
at his very best, is distinguished by most of the qualities which made his other poems remarkable: the exquisite
phrasing in which we feel that every word is in its place
and that there is not a word too much; the metrical mastery which catches so naturally, yet with so true a modu-
lation, the faltering accounts of the supplicant, blending
the cadences of the liturgy with those of perplexed brood-
ing thought; and, above all, that 'peculiar honesty' in
'exhibiting the essential sickness or strength of the
human soul' of which Eliot has written in connection with
Blake and which, in his own case, even at the moment when
his psychological plight seems most depressing and his
ways of rescuing himself from it least sympathetic, still
gives him a place among those upon whose words we reflect
with most interest and whose tones we remember longest.

63. MORTON D. ZABEL, T.S. ELIOT IN MID-CAREER, 'POETRY'

September 1930, vol. xxxvi, 330-7

Zabel (1901-64) was Professor of English at Chicago and
editor of 'Poetry'.

Other works considered, apart from 'Ash-Wednesday',
were 'Journey of the Magi' (1927), 'A Song for Simeon'
(1928), 'Animula' (1929) and 'Dante' (1929).

If only because the history of Mr. Eliot's mind was for
over a decade regarded as typical of the ordeal of the
Twentieth Century intelligence progressing down the *via
obscura* of the modern world, his latest encounters must
command the attention of every contemporary. The hand
that produced 'Sweeney,' 'Prufrock,' and 'The Waste Land'
unquestionably left its thumb-print on the thought and art
of a generation. However little Eliot's former disciples
may be able to follow the recent submissions of the poet
from whom they learned the final accents of disillusionment, his experience remains one of the few authentic
records of intellectual recovery in our time. For five
years, that is, since his last appearance as a poet, he
has perplexed his readers by a slow reversion (announced
as fully achieved in the preface of 'For Launcelot
Andrewes') to the moral absolutism of which 'The Hippopotamus' was an inverted parody, the 'Sunday Morning
Service' a social indictment, 'Gerontion' a broken and
pathetic echo, and the chorus of 'The Hollow Men' a derisive denial. What had long been implicit in his work was
at length fully disclosed: Eliot had never succeeded in
cutting the roots of native puritanism which bound him to
the soil of Christianity. His nostalgia for the heroic
and sanctified glories of the past, when man's rôle in
the universe was less equivocal and his destiny mystically
shrouded by the doctrine of redemption, had finally led
him not to suicide but to the affirmations of faith. His
explorations had never been conducted as far afield as
those of a self-deluded des Esseintes or of Verlaine.
His realism, though crossed with the subtle lineage of
Donne, was in the more immediate line of Arnold, of the
author of 'The City of Dreadful Night,' of Housman and
Hardy. Yet his return to faith might have been forecast
by the courageous a dozen years ago. His early poems
implicitly forecast a conversion as imminent as the

deathbed avowals of those *fin-de-siècle* apostates who
ended by espousing the creeds whereof they had made at
worst a travesty, at best a rich and sensuous symbolism
for their emotional adventures. In their luxuriating
intoxications Eliot took no share. If anything made his
reaction surprising it was the clear-eyed confrontation of
reality in 'The Waste Land,' or the withering and totally
unflattering self-portraiture, singularly unlike the
elaborate conceit of the 'esthete,' in 'Prufrock.' But
the element of self-pity was not lacking, and with it went
an assumption of premature senility, a Byronesque mockery
of conventions, and the extraordinary imaginative audacity
which are unmistakable vestiges of a romanticism always
mistrusted and finally rejected by Eliot in his literary
philosophy. The finality of his despairing self-scrutiny
implied a reserve of idealism to which, escaping suicide,
he must some day fly for recourse. 'The eagles and the
trumpets' might be 'buried beneath some snow-deep Alps,'
but the possibility of digging them out remained. 'The
old man in a dry month, being read to by a boy, waiting
for rain' did not release his last hope of a reviving
shower, even where, across the parched acres of the waste
land, it failed to fall. The straw-stuffed men in their
idiotic dance around the prickly pear, waiting for the
world to end 'not with a bang but a whimper,' could not
forget the phrases of a liturgy promising the resurrection
and the life.
    This poem, 'The Hollow Men' of 1925, serves as a link
between the earlier poems and 'Ash-Wednesday.' In its
complete form it not only provides an endpiece to the age
of desolation and emptiness, but contrives a plea for con-
ciliation.

[Quotes 'The Hollow Men', CPP, p. 84, 'This is the dead
land' to 'a fading star'.]

Reality had claimed of its victim his last desire, but
hope sent a persistent echo through his brain.

[Quotes CPP, p. 85, 'Sightless, unless' to 'empty men'.]

And

[Quotes CPP, p. 85, 'Between the desire' to 'Thine is the
Kingdom'.]

    Here were probably the final lines of Mr. Eliot's
'Inferno.' His present volume, along with the three pamphlet poems lately published, may be considered the

opening cantos of his 'Purgatorio.' These terms are not
applied fortuitously. They are suggested both by Mr.
Eliot's long and penetrating study of Dante, whereof his
recent essay is a record, and by a symbolism which com-
bines liturgical allusion with the properties of the
'Commedia': the 'multifoliate rose,' the turning staircases, the 'blue of Mary's color' which suffuses the
prospects of the future. From Dante Mr. Eliot has en-
deavored to derive the profound and salient simplicity
which, in his own early poems, baffled so many readers by
its resemblance to the ineluctable precision of Laforgue
and Corbière; he has likewise seen in Dante the triumph of
the visual imagination upon which the poet must rely for
his direct, unequivocal, and *symbolical* approach to truth:
a method natural to Mr. Eliot's creative temperament and
wholly at variance with the discursive expositions of neo-
classicism. 'Gerontion,' 'Sweeney Among the Nightingales,' and 'Burbank' employed that method on a miniature
but precise scale, and 'The Waste Land' cut cleanest
to the core of its inner meaning when it found symbolical
instruments of unqualified accuracy (for instance, the
first twenty lines; 11. 77-110; 257-265; and the first
half of part V). In Mr. Eliot's mind Dante's stylistic
splendor is indissoluble from his mediaeval inheritance,
the condition and certitude of his religious avowals, and
the immediate veracity of his imagery. Dante has provided
not only a tutelage for Mr. Eliot's literary concepts, but
a guide toward the conversion which has now capped his
career.

It was likely that Mr. Eliot should find this guide,
not among the exigencies of material life or through flay-
ing his conscience with the rods of logic and dialectic,
but in a great poem. One is not debating his sincerity
when one recalls that his former despairs were tutored by
tragic and decadent poets, whose thoughts and feelings
were imposed on his mind as ineffaceably as their phrases
were imposed on his poems. From the desolation into which
Webster, Donne, de Nerval, and Baudelaire led him, Dante
(not to mention the Bishops Bramhall and Andrewes) stood
ready to conduct him back to safety. The cure was apparently as ready at hand as the torture. It remains to be
seen if it was adopted out of as extreme and inevitable a
necessity, and if it has yielded a poetry as distinguished
by passion and clairvoyance, by discipline in phrase and
outline, by those qualities of 'equipoise, balance and
proportion of tones' which in the 'Homage to John Dryden'
won for Marvell Mr. Eliot's incisive praise.

Mr. Eliot's approach to the doctrine of the Incarnation
is presented in 'Journey of the Magi;' his persistent

weariness in the face of the world's burden - a weariness
and a failure in moral courage hitherto counterbalanced
by the rigorous integrity of his craftmanship - reappears
in 'A Song for Simeon,' where, with his 'eighty years and
no tomorrow,' the tyranny of age and rationality still
oppresses him.   In 'Ash-Wednesday' the torment of confusion and of exhausting intellectual scruples alike begin
to disappear.

[Quotes 'Ash-Wednesday', I, CPP, p. 89, 'Because I do not
hope' to 'usual reign?', and pp. 89-90, 'Consequently I rejoice' to 'words answer'.]

The poem, which is in six brief parts, is constructed
around a paradoxical petition:

    Teach us to care and not to care.

Thus, by several allegorical devices the rejection of
material concerns is described.   The bones of mortal
curiosity, 'scattered and shining,' sing 'We are glad to
be scattered, we did little good to each other.'   The
spirit, climbing three staircases to the cadence of 'Lord,
I am not worthy, but speak the word only,' leaves behind
the deceitful demons of hope and despair.   'Mary's color'
becomes the signal of promise as the poet reproaches himself with the memory of his gospel of desolation: 'O my
people, what have I done unto thee.'

[Quotes 'Ash-Wednesday', V, CPP, p. 97, 'Will the veiled
sister' to 'withered apple-seed'.]

    The final phrases, rejecting again the desperate real-
ism of disillusionment, almost capture peace, the Shantih
of 'The Waste Land,' in an evening of beatitude, charity,
and exaltation, with 'Let my cry come unto Thee' on the
poet's lips.
    Mr. Eliot's religious experience has not thus far im-
pressed one as conceived in intellectual necessity, or as
imposed through other than esthetic forces on a crowded
and exhausted mind.   He will never be capable of forming
a slovenly concept or judgment: his present essay and
poems are distinguished by lucid statement and well-
reasoned concision.   They contain passages of subtle
beauty.   But of the impact of profound conviction and the
absolute creative certitude of which the early poems partook and which still remains for Mr. Eliot's study in 'The
Extasie,' 'The Coy Mistress,' in Baudelaire's 'La Mort,'
or even in the mathematical complexities of 'Charmes,' one

finds little here. The facility of design that made 'The Hollow Men' a flagging and dispirited declamation, devoid of organic fusion, has led to a desultory kind of allegory, subtle enough in itself, but unsharpened by wit or emotional intensity, undistinguished by the complete formal synthesis which Aquinas advocated as a moral property and Dante exemplified in his slightest allusion. As a consequence, the contour of the design, as well as the clean accuracy of reference and the pure aphoristic subtlety, which alone would sustain the key of exaltation demanded by this quest for illusion and transfiguration, is lacking. Eliot spoke with complete authority in his first phase. In his second he displays a conciliatory attitude which may persuade few of his contemporaries but which, as a worse consequence, deprives his art of its once incomparable distinction in style and tone. These brief poems, however, find their place in a remarkable personal document which already contains some of the finest poetry and some of the most significant entries in modern literature.

64. THOMAS MOULT, FROM CONTRASTS IN CURRENT POETRY, 'BOOKMAN' (LONDON)

September 1930, vol. lxxviii, 354-5

Moult (1885-1974), a British critic and novelist, was best known for his poetry compilations, though in none of these did he include work by Eliot.
    The review includes a discussion of 'Anabasis', translated by Eliot from the French of St-John Perse, and published in London on 22 May 1930. The other poets reviewed were E.A. Robinson and Richard Aldington.

Critics of Mr. Aldington will say that he is indebted to Mr. T.S. Eliot for his manner. He was once, but now no longer. Mr. Eliot has influenced more than one writer of to-day's poetry, but he cannot really be imitated. This we may perceive in two remaining books on our list - a collection of six poems entitled (enigmatically) 'Ash-Wednesday,' and a translation of a poem from the French which he considers 'one of the most remarkable poems of this generation.' About 'Ash-Wednesday' we need say little except that those who seek to find plain meanings

in it do so at their peril. Mr. Eliot has not published
the book for the plain man. It is for those who are
willing to follow the drift of a cultured, uncommonly
sensitive philosopher's thoughts in poetry. A scientist's
thoughts too; for poetry is not so much an art to him as
an expression of communal interest in verse:

> Because these wings are no longer wings to fly
> But merely vans to beat the air
> The air which is now thoroughly small and dry
> Smaller and dryer than the will
> Teach us to care and not to care
> Teach us to sit still.

Mr. Eliot has returned from his quest of new discoveries to reflect in his subtly intellectual and spiritual
fashion on the need of faith in human existence – and it
must be faith dressed in austere colours, as the fourth of
his six poems intimates quite plainly.

It is foolish to speculate, but we cannot help feeling
that the parched, tropical colouring of 'Anabasis' was one
of the chief factors in its attraction for Mr. Eliot, and
a stimulus to his desire to translate it. No description
of St.-J. Perse's oratorical poem would be valid, any more
than a description of the 'Song of Solomon' has ever been
valid. All that may usefully be said is that it reads
like an Old Testament book, sublime and arid, lofty and
harsh:

> Men, creatures of dust and folk or divers devices,
> people of business and of leisure, folk of the fron-
> tiers and foreign men, O men of little weight in the
> memory of these lands; people from the valleys and the
> uplands and the highest slopes of this world to the
> shore's end; Seers of signs and seeds, and confessors
> of the western winds, trackers of beasts and of sea-
> sons, breakers of camp in the little dawn wind, seekers
> of water-courses over the wrinkled rind of the world,
> O seekers, O finders of seasons to be up and be gone....

The best way to approach this remarkably well translated piece of 'script' (which the publishers took care to
have remarkably well produced), is to wipe away in our
thought as many centuries as divide civilised man from the
rude crude life of limitless and timeless deserts of
scalding heats and unspeakable cruelties which have never
yet been absorbed and lost in the utilitarian activities
of the modern world. Then in a gold-hot flash we know at
once what the poet means when he writes: 'I have seen the

earth parcelled out in vast spaces, and my thought is not
estranged from the navigator.' He is at one with Eternity
yawning on the sands.

65. WILLIAM ROSE BENÉT, FROM ROUND ABOUT PARNASSUS,
'SATURDAY REVIEW'

18 October 1930, vol. vii, 249

The most distinguished volume of poetry that has come to
us recently is T.S. Eliot's 'Ash-Wednesday,' though it is
a very brief series of flights. The second movement
appeared originally in the 'Saturday Review of Literature.' (1) 'Ash-Wednesday' is another distillation of
Eliot's despair mixed with a rather hopeless appeal for
aid from the Christian religion. 'Teach us to sit still,'
he reiterates. Let us give up, let us sit still. If that
is the most modern and refined interpretation of how we
should feel since once God so loved the world, we can only
say that we violently disagree with it. In fact, even a
superficial perusal of the New Testament will reveal a
Christ who was ever a source of action. This other attitude smacks of a new Pharisaism. The Church, indeed, as
it has developed, is not exempt from snobbery, a spiritual
snobbery that we particularly detest. That the religion
of Jesus Christ should ever be even faintly associated
with this or with a dead-end philosophy is inconceivable.
But the ascetics have always entirely misinterpreted him.
Eliot is a modern anchorite. Also he strives with none,
for none is worth his strife, partaking of Landor's high
conceit of himself. But our old conception of a prophet
from the desert was that the locusts and wild honey had
played the office of a burning coal of fire upon the
tongue. Revelation was spoken upon the prophets' return.
There was no injunction to sit still. Quite the opposite.
There was a wrathful summons to get up and do something.
    Of course, Mr. Eliot and ourself differ so fundamen-
tally in our attitude toward life, especially in our
approach to the mystic, that, though we may deeply admire
the strange, moving music and majestic sombreness of some
of Mr. Eliot's verse, we cannot share at all his continuous vast disillusionment that approaches apathy. When we
are feeling a particularly good health we feel like praising God, and usually do so. Also, we have encountered no

little stark tragedy in the course of our life, but it has
not led us to ask to be allowed to sit still. At that, we
are not known as being notably active. No, as Mr. Dudley
Fitts says, in a recent 'Hound and Horn,' 'What "metaphysical measure" can relate ... Eliot and W.R. Benét' (among
others included in Miss Taggard's 'Circumference:
Varieties of Metaphysical Verse') - and incidentally we had
supposed that Miss Taggard's subtitle was intended to
point out that fact that within *was* variety. The answer
is, quite aside from other considerations, None at All.
Which makes more remarkable the strong impress that the
writing of T.S. Eliot leaves on our mind. We are leagues
removed from his disciples, as we are from all the snob-
bish modern literary cliques, including the Proustian. We
regard it as so-easy-that-it-is-not-worth-doing to write a
parody of Eliot. But not one of the busy little boys who
have gone around copying him has come anywhere near to him.
For a man's soul, whatever it is worth, is his own single
possession. It is one thing that no one else, save perhaps the Devil, can steal from him. What is left out of
the imitations of Eliot is merely everything, because what
is necessarily omitted is the evidence of the soul. He is
one of few modern poets who truly present it.

Note

1   10 December 1927, iv, 429.

66. E.G. TWITCHETT, REVIEW, 'LONDON MERCURY'

October 1930, vol. xxii, 557

Twitchett (b. 1896), an English critic and historian, is
best known for his study of Frances Brett Young, published
in 1936.
    This is taken from a longer review.

The solution of Mr. Eliot's verse demands persistence,
some intellectual spade-work, and, occasionally, prayer.
A mood of irritable unhappiness, a questing intellectual
misery, rewards these exertions; but it must be granted

that an interesting tune often beguiles and encourages
them. Workers on 'The Waste Land' toil to some taking
jazz, and students of the Sweeney poems are at times
arrested by snatches of rich melody rising from the general
grotesqueness with an effect as much of oddity as of
beauty, as if saxophones were suddenly soaring in ecstasy.
Mr. Eliot's new sequence, 'Ash-Wednesday', contains some
gratifying Swinburnian passages, but chiefly agitates to a
new and original music, composed out of erudite little
rhythmical tricks. Phrases are hovered over, snatches of
them are repeated, extended, abbreviated, turned inside
out, and then all goes forward with a burst:

[Quotes 'Ash-Wednesday', I, CPP, p. 89, 'Because I know'
to 'rejoice'.]

That passage, which is typical, is not without a meandering charm, and communicates very well the ineffable sadness which looks back, with a doubtful regret, to the
certainties of youth, and forward, with a faint stirring,
to the consolations of religion. It seems fair to say,
however, that there is too much ineffability about it, as
about the whole sequence. Practically everything that Mr.
Eliot sets down offers a choice of meanings, and it is
clear from his withholding punctuation almost entirely
that he is indifferent which meaning one chooses....

67. BRIAN HOWARD, MR. ELIOT'S POETRY, 'NEW STATESMAN'

8 November 1930, vol. xxxvi, 146

Howard (1905-57) was an English journalist and writer.
Aspects of his life are recorded in 'Brian Howard: Port-
rait of a Failure', edited by Marie-Jacqueline Lancaster
(London, 1968).

It has been the delightful, but exhausting, task of the
writer of this article to collect, during the past year,
an anthology of verse by the younger English poets: one of
the most exhausting things about it has been the number-
less variations, generally in the treble key, upon Mr.
Eliot's renowned poem, 'The Waste Land.' Most of these,

of course, have had to be rejected. It became such a
plague that the moment the eye encountered, in a newly
arrived poem, the words 'stone,' 'dust' or 'dry,' one
reached for the waste-paper basket. But there were a
number of poems that came, showing an equally marked
influence, towards which one felt very differently.
These authors had read their Eliot, but they had profited.
It was not the stones, the dustiness, and the droughts
that affected them so much as the thought that lies behind
this passage from Mr. Eliot's latest poem:

[Quotes 'Ash-Wednesday', I, CPP, p. 89, 'Because I know
that time' to 'which to rejoice'.]

This, perhaps, is the pith, not only of 'Ash-Wednesday,'
but of the whole of Mr. Eliot's poetic message. It is the
fearless, the truly modern, thought behind it that is
influencing many of our better young poets, and influencing them for their good.

It is now some ten years since 'The Waste Land'
appeared, like some austere and unfamiliar flower, in that
blown-up cottage garden which was English poetry immediately after the war. The Georgian poets were busy plant-
ing hardy perennials where hardy perennials grew before.
Not even Mr. Siegfried Sassoon, sedulously slipping weed-
killer into their watering-cans, was successful in deter-
ring their dreary reconstruction. 'Wheels' itself creaked
in vain. (1) The young poets, who, because of their age,
had escaped alive, were dazedly trooping up to help.
Suddenly - 'The Waste Land,' and it may be said, with
small exaggeration, that English poetry of the first half
of the twentieth century began. It is a pity that it was
written by an American, but there you are. We are not
quite so original as we were.

It was Mr. Eliot who suggested to our young poets, more
by his poetry than by his admirable critical work, that
they should begin seriously to think of what poetry really
was. Granted that the guns had stopped, and that it was
possible to hear again the nightingale, and granted that
to 'get into a state' about nightingales is the poet's
function, the time had undoubtedly come to consider the
general nightingale situation, so to speak. Of course,
there is no time at which a poet should not consider it,
but poetry has a way of deciding about the nightingale
situation, and then leaving it. In England, as it happened, it had been decided by the Romantics, and left for
a hundred years. The result was Georgian poetry. The
nightingale had become a mocking-bird. What was to be
done? It was largely Mr. Eliot who supplied the answer.

One must begin again, he suggested, to *think* about the
nightingale. To begin with, what is it? The poet who
asks himself this question at once becomes, unlike Keats,
a metaphysical poet. Keats, you will say, had no need to
ask such a question. Being the particular sort of poet he
was, living at his particular time, and being a genius
into the bargain - you are quite right. But you are quite
wrong if you think that it was not high time for all who
confuse a partiality for bird-songs with an apprehension
of Nature to go into the question of what a nightingale
is.

    In short, at a time when it was long overdue, it was
Mr. Eliot who introduced the present limited, but definite,
metaphysical revival. It was he who reminded our young
poets - taking them, as it were, by the lapel as they were
yawningly replacing the bird baths - that the poetic
transcription of natural history is all the better,
occasionally, for a thought or two about the nature of
reality.

    This newest among Mr. Eliot's longer poems has, it must
be admitted, a certain flamelessness. It rarely transports. But the level kept is a high one, and if one seldom crosses a peak, it is a mountain road. As a technician, no one to-day excels its author in the writing of
free verse. The rhythms are held and broken with the control of a master, and the interior rhyming is as refreshing as it is beautiful. As an illustration of this, the
following is perhaps the best example from 'Ash-Wednesday':

[Quotes 'Ash-Wednesday', V, CPP, p. 96, 'Where shall the
word be found' to 'deny the voice'.]

    The comparative absence of adjectives in the foregoing,
and the inclination towards one-syllable words are both
things to be noted. It is like seeing - feeling - one
sound stone being placed exactly, firmly, and permanently
upon another, and there are many of us who believe that it
is with such stones as these that the seriously damaged
temple of English poetry must be repaired.

    Woven into the text are several liturgical fragments.
The Hail Mary,

    Pray for us now and at the hour of our death.

The priest's preparation for Holy Communion,

    Lord, I am not worthy.

Then from the Bible, Ezekiel,

>   And God said,
>   Shall these bones live?

St. Paul,

>   Redeem the time.

No charge of plagiarism, however, could be brought
against Mr. Eliot any more than it could against Gray.
Mr. Eliot fulfils the one condition upon which the incor-
poration by a poet of the work of others is allowed.   The
total result is entirely his own.
We will not end without saying that 'Ash-Wednesday' is,
in the sum, an important and beautiful poem.   That it is
grave, that it is what is termed 'intellectual,' is true.
But it is this very quietness, this very severity, which
imparts to it that particular quality of beauty so grate-
fully devoured by the sensitive modern mind.   The courage
for fine frenzies is already, let us hope, returning.   It
is being given to us, a trifle savagely, by Mr. Roy Camp-
bell.   But it is Mr. Eliot - and you may see how in the
first quotation in this article - who will have made
these future frenzies possible and valuable again, if
valuable they prove to be.   Because, upon reflection, it
was not the guns that had silenced the nightingale.   It
was the mocking-bird.

Note

1   'Wheels': an anthology of verse edited by Edith Sitwell
    (Oxford, 1916-21) in 6 vols.

68. ALLEN TATE, IRONY AND HUMILITY, 'HOUND AND HORN'

January-March 1931, vol. iv, 290-7

This essay is reprinted in many books, including 'Reac-
tionary Essays' (1936), 'The Limits of Poetry' (1948),
'Collected Essays' (1960), 'T.S. Eliot: Twentieth Century
Views', edited by Hugh Kenner (1962), and Unger,
pp. 289-95.

Every age, as it sees itself, is the peculiarly distracted
one: its chroniclers notoriously make too much of the
variety before their own eyes. We are now inclined to see
the variety of the past as mere turbulence within a fixed
unity, and our own surface standardization as the sign of
a profound disunity of impulse. We have discovered that
the chief ideas that men lived by from about the twelfth
to the eighteenth century were absolute and unquestionable, and that the social turmoil of European history was
simply shortsighted disagreement as to the best ways of
making these deep assumptions socially good. The temper
of literary criticism in the past appears to bear out this
belief. Although writers were judged morally, no critic
expected the poet to give him a morality. The standard of
judgment was largely unconscious; a poem was a piece of
free and disinterested enjoyment for minds mature enough
- that is, convinced enough of a satisfactory destiny -
not to demand of every scribbler a way of life. Dante
invented no formula for society to run itself; he only
used a ready-made one. Turn to the American Humanists, and
and you will find that literature is the reflection of a
secular order that must be controlled. But Mr. John Dos
Passos has been far-sighted enough to detect the chief aim
of modern criticism of nearly every school. This is: to
give up the European and 'belle-lettristic' dabbling with
the arts, and all that that involves, and to study the
American environment with a view to making a better adaptation to it.

To discuss the merits of such a critical outlook lies
outside my argument. It would be equally pointless to
attempt an appraisal of any of its more common guides to
salvation, including the uncommon one of the Thirty-nine
Articles, which have been subscribed to by Mr. T.S. Eliot,
whose six poems published under the title 'Ash-Wednesday'
are the occasion of this review. For it is my thesis that,
in a discussion of Mr. Eliot's poetry, his doctrine has
little to command interest in itself. Yet it appears that
the poetry, notwithstanding the amount of space it gets in
the critical journals, receives less discussion each year.
The moral and religious attitude behind it has been related
to the Thirty-nine Articles, to an intellectual position
that Eliot has defended in prose. The poetry and the prose
are taken together as evidence that the author has made a
rather inefficient adaptation to the modern environment;
or at least he doesn't say anything very helpful to the
American critics in their struggles to adapt themselves.
It is an astonishing fact that, in an atmosphere of 'aesthetics,' there is less discussion of poetry in a typical
modern essay on that fine art than there is in Johnson's

essay on Denham. Johnson's judgment is frankly moralistic,
but he seldom capitulates to a moral sentiment because it
flatters his own moral sense. He requires the qualities
of generality, invention, and perspicuity. He hates Milton for a regicide, but his judgment of 'Paradise Lost' is
the most disinterested in English criticism. Mr. Eliot's
critics are a little less able each year to see the poetry
for Westminster Abbey; the wood is all trees.

I do not pretend to judge how far our social and philosophical needs justify this prejudice, which may be put
somewhat summarily as follows: all forms of human action,
economics, politics, even poetry, and certainly industry,
are legitimate modes of salvation, but the more historical
religious mode is illegitimate. It is sufficient here to
point out that the man who expects to find salvation in
the latest lyric or a well-managed factory will not only
not find it there; he is not likely to find it anywhere
else. If a young mind is incapable of moral philosophy, a
mind without moral philosophy is incapable of understanding poetry. For poetry, of all the arts, demands a serenity of view and a settled temper of the mind, and most of
all the power to detach one's own needs from the experience set forth in the poem. A moral sense so organized
sets limits to the human enterprise, and is content to
observe them. But if the reader lack this sense, the poem
will be only a body of abstractions either useful or
irrelevant to that body of abstractions already forming,
but of uncertain direction, in the reader's mind. This
reader will see the poem chiefly as biography, and he will
proceed to deduce from it a history of the poet's case, to
which he will attach himself if his own case resemble it;
if it doesn't, he will reject it. Either way, the quality
of the poem is ignored. But I will return to this in a
moment.

The reasoning that is being brought to bear upon Mr.
Eliot's recent verse is as follows: Anglo-Catholicism
would not at all satisfy me; therefore, his poetry declines under its influence. Moreover, the poetry is not
contemporaneous; it doesn't solve any labor problems; it
is special, personal, and it can do us no good. Now the
poetry *is* special and personal in quality, which is one
of its merits, but what the critics are really saying is
this - that his case-history is not special at all, that
it is a general form of possible conduct that will not do
for them. To accept the poetry seems to amount to accepting an invitation to join the Anglican Church. For the
assumption is that the poetry and the religious position
are identical. If this were so, why should not the excellence of the poetry induce them to join the Church, in the

hope of writing as well, since the irrelevance of the
Church to their own needs makes them reject the poetry?
The answer is, of course, that both parts of this fallacy
are common. There is an aesthetic Catholicism, and there
is a Communist-economic rejection of art because it is
involved with the tabooed mode of salvation.

The belief is that Mr. Eliot's poetry is a simple
record of the relation of his personality to an environment, and it witnesses the powerful modern desire to judge
an art scientifically, practically, industrially, according to how it works. The poetry is viewed as a pragmatic
result, and it has no use. Now a different heredity-
environment combination would give us, of mechanical
necessity, a different result, a different quantity of
power to do a different and perhaps better work. Doubtless this is true. But there is something disconcerting
in this simple solution to the problem when it is looked
at more closely. Two vastly different records or case-
histories might give us, qualitatively speaking, very
similar results: Baudelaire and Eliot have in common many
qualities but *no history*. Their 'results' have at least
the common features of irony, humility, introspection,
reverence - qualities fit only for contemplation and not
for judgment according to their desirability in our own
conduct.

It is in this, the qualitative sense, that Eliot's
poetry has been, I believe, misunderstood. In this sense,
the poetry is special, personal, of no use, and highly
distinguished. But it is held to be a general formula,
not distinct from the general formula that Eliot subscribed to when he went into the Church.

The form of the poems in 'Ash-Wednesday' is lyrical
and solitary, and there is almost none of the elaborate
natural description and allusion which gave 'The Waste
Land' a partly realistic and partly symbolic character.
These six poems are a brief moment of religious experience in an age that believes religion to be a kind of
defeatism and puts its hope for man in finding the right
secular order. The mixed realism and symbolism of 'The
Waste Land' issued in irony. The direct and lyrical
method of the new poems creates the simpler aesthetic
quality of humility. The latter quality comes directly
out of the former, and there is a nice continuity in Mr.
Eliot's work.

In 'The Waste Land' the prestige of our secular faith
gave to the style its peculiar character. This faith was
the hard, coherent medium through which the discredited
forms of the historic religions emerged only to be
stifled; the poem is at once their vindication and defeat.

They are defeated in fact, as a politician may be defeated
by the popular vote, but their vindication consists in the
withering irony that their subordinate position casts upon
the modern world.

The typical scene is the seduction of the typist by the
clerk, in 'The Fire Sermon.' Perhaps Mr. J.W. Krutch has
not discussed this scene, but a whole generation of critics
have, and from a viewpoint that Mr. Krutch has recently
made popular: the seduction betrays the romantic disillusion of the poet. The mechanical, brutal scene shows what
love really is - that is to say, what it is scientifically,
since science is Truth; it is only an act of practical
necessity, for procreation. The telling of the story by
the Greek seer, who is chosen from a past of illusion and
ignorance, permits the scene to become a *satire on the
foolish values of the past*. The values of the past were
absurd and false; the scientific Truth is both true and
bitter. This is the familiar romantic dilemma, and the
critics have read it into the scene from their own romantic despair.

There is none in the scene itself. The critics, who
being in the state of mind I have described are necessarily blind to an effect of irony, have mistaken the symbols of an ironic contrast for the terms of a philosophic
dilemma. Mr. Eliot knows too much about classical irony
to be overwhelmed by a doctrine in literary biology. For
the seduction scene shows, not what man is, but what *for
a moment* he thinks he is; in other words, the clerk
stands for the secularization of the humane and qualitative values in the modern world. And the meaning of the
contrast between Tiresias and the clerk is not disillusion, but irony. The scene is a masterpiece; perhaps the
most profound vision that we have of modern man.

The importance of this scene as a key to the intention
of 'Ash-Wednesday' lies in the moral identity of humility
and irony and in an important difference between them
artistically. Humility is subjective, a quality of the
moral character, an habitual attitude. Irony is the particular and objective instance of humility - that is, it
is an event or situation which induces humility in the
mind of a spectator; it is that arrangement of experience,
either premeditated by art or accidentally appearing in
the affairs of men, which permits to the spectator an insight superior to that of the actor, and shows him that
the practical formula, the special ambition, of the actor
is bound to fail. Humility is thus the self-respect pro-
ceeding from a sense of the folly of men in their desire
to dominate a natural force or situation. The seduction
scene is the picture of the modern and dominating man.

The cleverness and the pride of conquest of the 'small house agent's clerk' are the badge of science, bumptious practicality, overweening secular faith. The very success of his conquest witnesses its aimless character; it succeeds as a wheel succeeds in turning; he can only do it over again.

His own failure to understand his position is irony, and the poet's insight into it is humility. This is essentially the poetic attitude, an attitude that Mr. Eliot has been approaching with increasing purity. It is not that his recent verse is better or more exciting than that of the period ending with 'The Waste Land.' Actually it is less spectacular and less complex in subject-matter; for Eliot less frequently objectifies his leading emotion, humility, into irony. His form is simple, expressive, homogeneous, and direct, and without the usual elements of violent contrast.

There is a single ironic passage in 'Ash-Wednesday,' and significantly enough it is the first stanza of the first poem. This passage presents objectively the poet *as he thinks himself for the moment to be*. It establishes that humility towards his own merit which sets the whole mood of the poems that follow. And the irony has been overlooked by the critics because they take the stanza as a literal exposition of the latest phase of the Eliot 'case-history' - at a time when, in the words of Mr. Edmund Wilson, 'his psychological plight seems most depressing.' Thus, here is the pose of a Titan too young to be weary of strife, but weary of it nevertheless:

[Quotes 'Ash-Wednesday', I, CPP, p. 89, 'Because I do not hope to turn again' to 'usual reign?'.]

If the six poems are taken together as the focus of a specific religious emotion, the opening stanza, instead of being a naïve personal 'confession,' becomes only a modest but highly effective technical performance. This stanza has two features that are necessary to the development of the unique imagery which distinguishes the religious emotion of 'Ash-Wednesday' from any other religious poetry of our time and which, in fact, probably makes it the only valid religious poetry we have. The first feature is the regular yet halting rhythm, the smooth uncertainty of movement which may either proceed to greater regularity or fall away into improvisation. The second feature is the imagery itself. It is trite; it echoes two familiar passages from English poetry. But the quality to be observed is this: it is secular imagery. It sets forth a special ironic emotion, but this emotion is not identified with

any specific experience. The imagery is thus perfectly
suited to the character of the rhythm. The stanza is a
device for getting the poem under way, starting from a
known and general emotion, in a monotonous rhythm, for a
direction which to the reader is unknown. The ease, the
absence of surprise, with which Mr. Eliot brings out the
subject to be 'discussed' is admirable. After some further and ironic deprecation of his wordly powers, he goes
on:

> And pray to God to have mercy upon us
> And I pray that I may forget
> These matters that with myself I too much discuss
> Too much explain

We are being told, of course, that there is to be some
kind of discourse on God, or a meditation; yet the emotion
is still general. The imagery is even flatter than before; it is imagery at all only in that special context;
for it is the diction of prose. And yet, subtly and im-
perceptibly, the rhythm has changed; it is irregular and
labored. We are being prepared for a new and sudden
effect, and it comes in the first lines of the second
poem:

> Lady, three white leopards sat under a juniper-tree
> In the cool of the day, having fed to satiety
> On my legs my heart my liver and that which had been
>   contained
> In the hollow round of my skull. And God said
> Shall these bones live? shall these
> Bones live?

From here on, in all the poems, there is constant and
sudden change of rhythm, and there is a corresponding
alternation of two kinds of imagery - the visual and tactile imagery common to all poetry and without significance in itself for any kind of experience, and the
traditional religious symbols. The two orders are inextricably fused.

It is evident that Mr. Eliot has hit upon the only
method now available of using the conventional religious
image in poetry. He has reduced it to metaphor, to the
plane of sensation. And corresponding to this process,
there are images of his own invention which he almost
pushes over the boundary of sensation into abstractions,
where they have the appearance of conventional symbols.
The passage I have quoted above is an example of this: for
the 'Lady' may be a nun, or even the Virgin, or again she

may be a beautiful woman; but she is presented, through the serious tone of the invocation, with all the solemnity of a religious figure. The fifth poem exhibits the reverse of the process; it begins with a series of plays on the Logos, which is the most rareified of all the Christian abstractions, and succeeds in creating an *illusion of sensation* by means of a broken and distracted rhythm:

> If the lost word is lost, if the spent word is spent
> If the unheard, unspoken
> Word is unspoken, unheard;
> Still is the unspoken word, the Word unheard,
> The Word without a word, the Word within
> The world and for the world....

'Marina'

London, 25 September 1930

69. MARIANNE MOORE, A MACHINERY OF SATISFACTION, 'POETRY'

September 1931, vol. xxxviii, 337-9

> What seas what shores what grey rocks and what islands
> What water lapping the bow
> And scent of pine and the woodthrush singing through
>   the fog
> What images return
> O my daughter.

This inquiry, without question mark, is the setting of
'Marina.' It is a decision that is to animal existence
a query: death is not death. The theme is frustration
and frustration is pain. To the eye of resolution

> Those who sharpen the tooth of the dog, meaning
> Death
> Those who glitter with the glory of the hummingbird,
>   meaning
> Death
> Those who sit in the sty of contentment, meaning
> Death
> Those who suffer the ecstasy of the animals, meaning
> Death
> Are become unsubstantial.

T.S. Eliot is occupied with essence and instrument,
and his choice of imagery has been various. This time it
is the ship, 'granite islands' and 'woodthrush calling
through the fog.' Not sumptuous grossness but a burnished
hedonism is renounced. Those who naively proffer

consolation put the author beyond their reach, in initiate
solitude. Although solitude is to T.S. Eliot, we infer,
not 'a monarchy of death,' each has his private despera-
tions; a poem may mean one thing to the author and another
to the reader. What matters here is that we have, for
both author and reader, a machinery of satisfaction that
is powerfully affecting, intrinsically and by association.
The method is a main part of the pleasure: lean carto-
graphy; reiteration with compactness; emphasis by word
pattern rather than by punctuation; the conjoining of
opposites to produce irony; a counterfeiting verbally of
the systole, diastole, of sensation - of what the eye
sees and the mind feels; the movement within the movement
of differentiated kindred sounds, recalling the transcen-
dent beauty and ability, in 'Ash-Wednesday,' of the lines:

> One who moves in the time between sleep and waking,
>   wearing
> White light folded, sheathed about her, folded.
> The new years walk, restoring
> Through a bright cloud of tears, the years, restoring
> With a new verse the ancient rhyme.

As part of the revising of conventionality in presentment
there is the embedded rhyme, evincing dissatisfaction with
bald rhyme. This hiding, qualifying, and emphasizing of
rhyme to an adjusted tempo is acutely a pleasure besides
being a clue to feeling that is the source, as in 'Ash-
Wednesday,' of harmonic contour like the sailing descent
of the eagle.

'Marina' is not for those who read inquisitively, as a
compliment to the author, or to find material for the
lecture platform. Apocalyptic declaration is uncompliant
to parody. If charged by chameleon logic and unstudious
didactism with creating a vogue for torment, Mr. Eliot can
afford not to be incommoded, knowing that his work is the
testament of one 'having to construct something upon which
to rejoice.'

'Triumphal March'

London, 8 October 1931

70. MORTON D. ZABEL, THE STILL POINT, 'POETRY'

December 1932, vol. xli, 152-8

Zabel also considered 'Difficulties of a Statesman', which
appeared in 'Commerce' (Paris) (Winter 1931/2), xxix,
79-87, with the English text and French translation (by
Georges Limbour) on opposite pages. The English text was
reprinted in 'Hound and Horn' (October-December 1932), vi,
17-19.

The dubiety of Mr. Eliot's friends and the exultation of
his baiters are both reproved by these new poems of the
past year. They reinforce the impression of personal
distinction conveyed by 'Marina' and the finest passages
of 'Ash-Wednesday,' and thus go far to correct the sensations aroused by the three desultory productions which
marked the approach of those poems.
    'Triumphal March' and 'Difficulties of a Statesman'
are two further installments of 'a poem of some length'
whose crisis is barely passed. In his pamphlet, 'Thoughts
after Lambeth' (1931), Mr. Eliot was encouraged by the
confused efforts of a reviewer in the venerable 'Times
Literary Supplement' (of London) to disavow any intention
of acting as the 'voice of his generation,' and to congratulate himself that at last religion had become
officially divorced from literature in England and could
renew affiliations on its own terms. It is unlikely that
these terms will be understood in the next decade, any
more than in the past, except by sensibilities of the most

unflinching sincerity. The reaction of the critics to
'Ash-Wednesday' was an expense of strength which, fortunately for themselves but regrettably for the state of
contemporary poetry, will not often have to be repeated.

The question, not of Eliot's sincerity, but of his
authority to persuade us of it as a poet, is not, however, finally solved. He has exchanged his recent mystical ambition for a deliberate recall of past and exhausted
agony. No one would have objected had several eminent
poets of the past returned to the style of their first
flights: Swinburne, for example, from the bloated verbos-
ity of 'Thalassius' to the limpid enchantment of 'Ata-
lanta,' or Tennyson from the 'Idyls' to 'Ulysses.' A
growth in stylistic means equivalent to one in mature
intellectual certitude is a correspondence which may be
ideally desirable, but despite the logic of rules and
their makers, is not always possible even in a remarkable
poet. Thus 'Marina' achieved its beauty by being an episode of exquisite, but deceptively lucid, elegaic lyricism
in the key of 'La Figlia Che Piange,' while the present
poems aim to rehabilitate the historic complexity and
irony, and the refracted impressionism, in 'Gerontion' and
'The Waste Land.' It will doubtless remain Eliot's tragedy that his sensibility was formed under circumstances
which had inevitably to be outgrown, and that the style
thereby perfected sprang from the center of his personality. The repudiation of its defects entailed the loss of
its strength, in other words of its essential personality.
This loss he has not consented to suffer. The experience
is not novel to distinguished poetry. But it is an admission of moral and creative limitation almost equivalent to
defeat.

Yet the renewed authority behind Eliot's work since
'The Hollow Men' and 'Animula' (both admittedly intervals
of fatigue and painful gestation) has doubtless derived
from what must be the satisfactory sensation of this stylistic self-determination. The structure of association
and correspondence underlying his manner remains one of
the few forms produced by the modern analysis of consciousness. 'Memory and desire' have had scores of exponents
besides Proust and Eliot; it would be difficult to distinguish other masters. (Joyce, Pound, Werfel, and Larbaud,
like Picasso and Stravinsky, belong to a different order
of artist, and convey a different poetic problem.) The
illimitable distension of Proust's memory and its capacity
for oblique inference produced qualities of dubious merit
and certainly of ruinous influence. But they gave him
what is still his private distinction, a form imposed by
and coeval with its materials. Eliot has perhaps never

been a singly sustained *poetic* talent: it is more and more
apparent that his expression is essentially episodic and
fragmentary, and his impulse speculative. The construction of 'The Waste Land' tells as much. The method is too
spasmodic and arbitrary to carry a poem through moments of
vision longer than those of extreme pathos, or through
intervals of lucidity sustained by something more than
rare occasions of association and recollection. Basically
he is prey to fits of pity and anguish, to those 'broken
images,' 'dry thoughts,' and 'memories shored' so frequently mentioned by way of explanatory deference or apology in his earlier works. If Eliot has voiced anything
for 'his generation' it is their voluntary surrender to
a type of sensibility which is fundamentally chaotic and
ruinous. His measure of genius, like Proust's, lies
exactly in his recognition of this danger, in his critical
(although to obvious minds seductive) depiction of it in
his work. 'Triumphal March' and 'Difficulties of a Statesman' are not without organic defect, but they revive the
inherited, multiplied, and brilliantly compacted experience of 'The Waste Land' as only their author could revive it, and having done so, it is to he hoped that they
have brought him past the crisis of indecision and conscientious masochism they record, and thus nearer to the
goal which they, like 'Ash-Wednesday,' seek.

[Quotes 'Triumphal March', CPP, p. 127, 'Stone, bronze'
to 'our sausages' and 'There he is now' to 'perceiving,
indifferent'.]

   It would be a rare mechanism that could convey these
ideas and sensations perfectly, and this one is not perfect. It is not the logic of poetic resolution and decision, but of rearranging a jumbled stage-set for an
agonistic exhibition. The following passage from the
second of these poems is an astonishingly explicit dia-
gram of exactly those components of irony, self-pity, and
enchanted recollection which never appear so specious as
when they thus betray their self-conscious combination:

[Quotes 'Difficulties of a Statesman', CPP, pp. 129-30,
'Meanwhile the guards' to 'among these heads'.]

It is unedifying to find Mr. Eliot encouraging those commentators who have held that his poems are to be taken at
their face-value.
   It is far more than face-value that is discernible in
their finest passages. The pure pathos in 'Marina' is
echoed in their surest lines, and where this pathos

collides with the distorted utterance and jargon of
contemporary civilization - its military inventories,
diplomatic and political phrases, statistical reports,
etc. - the impingement is logical and the effect powerful. They succeed in converting the inbred historical
and literary derivations which have so often threatened
Eliot's art with haemophilia into a synthesis of extraordinary energy. As portions of a consecutive document
they manage to define a decisive stage of their author's
progress, and propel him closer to the central and focal
certitude of whose achievement his poems may still be our
period's most remarkable record. His faith in the existence of that certitude has never been more beautifully
stated:

> O hidden under the dove's wing, hidden in the turtle's
>   breast,
> Under the palmtree at noon, under the running water
> At the still point of the turning world. O hidden.

'Sweeney Agonistes'

London, 1 December 1932

71. D.G. BRIDSON, REVIEW, 'NEW ENGLISH WEEKLY'

12 January 1933, vol. ii, 304

Bridson (b. 1910), an English critic and writer, has
worked for the BBC as a radio producer.

It is difficult to criticise Mr. Eliot. It is difficult,
in fact, to fix him 'pinned and wriggling on the wall.'
His elusiveness, needless to say, is invaluable to him.
No sooner has a critic pronounced his later work a manifestation of his return to the fold, than a true disciple
ups and denies the assertion flatly. The form is more
regular, it seems, yet the implication is more subtle than
ever. So let it be with Sweeney. But when Mr. Eliot
labels his work 'fragments of an Aristophanic melodrama,'
he gives us an axis of reference.

   In the first place, then, we do not readily think of
Mr. Eliot as the modern Aristophanes. Aristophanic his
moods may be, but Aristophanic they have certainly never
appeared. The belly-shaking laughter of many passages in
'Ulysses' are as Aristophanic as we choose to call them.
But an Aristophanic melodrama by Mr. Eliot...! Sooner
a parody of the Sermon on the Mount by St. Thomas
Aquinas! And when a man of high seriousness (such we
esteem Mr. Eliot) turns himself (as Mr. Eliot has done)
to satiric melodrama or farce on the broad scale, we can
hazard a guess at the result. We can remember Flaubert's
dreary 'Candidate.' And we can remember also the tremendous 'Apes of God' which Mr. Lewis gave us in a spell of

disgusted mirth. How will Mr. Eliot's humour compare
with Mr. Lewis's? We know very well (say, we suspect)
that it won't compare at all.

A good deal might be said about the form of the fragments now published, - reprinted, by the way, from the
'Criterion.' In the first place, their nature suggests
that the whole is not conspicuous for (what Frere called)
'the utter impossibility of the story.' They appear to be
rather fragments of a 'melodrama' in which 'an adherence
to the probabilities of real life is an essential
requisite.' Such a 'melodrama,' it would seem, is more
of Menander than of Aristophanes. Mr. Eliot's staging of
nine characters simultaneously is defensible. His sup-
pression of a separate chorus in favour of duets replete
with tambo and bones is excusable. But Aristophanic or
not, his melodrama has every appearance of being decidedly
dull. His choice of epigraphs would suggest that he is no
more in love with Sweeney to-day than he was in 1920.
But the terseness and compression of the Sweeney poems was
the most remarkable thing about them. Their tension was
more interesting than their content. But Sweeney in melodrama is rather less impressive than Sweeney in lyric.
Sweeney in melodrama, be it admitted, sprawls.

That the people he describes annoy Mr. Eliot intensely
we can well believe. But it is less the people described
than Mr. Eliot's description of them that annoys his
reader. To describe dullness in an interesting, even in
an amusing manner, is defensible as possible art. So Mr.
Eliot has done in many of his earlier poems. But to describe dullness accurately and in detail, fully and at
length, is a different matter.

[Quotes 'Sweeney Agonistes', CPP, p. 115, 'Dusty: How
about Pereira?' to 'Dusty: Well that's true'.]

Thus opens the 'Fragment of a Prologue.' It is all
very clever, all very cutting, all very true, and all
very futile, - as Mr. Eliot, no doubt, intended it to be.
In so far as he has achieved with it what he (apparently)
intended to achieve, the technique of the passage may
therefore be justified forthwith. But the value of the
passage remains suspect. The best way to satirise dullness is not, necessarily, to record it dully.

Klipstein and Krumpacker, two Americans over in London
on business, awake an expectancy (if only by their names)
for work of the Burbank and Bleistein order. But the
following remark of Klipstein is not very reassuring:-

Yes we did our bit, as you folks say,
I'll tell the world we got the Hun on the run.

It is rather more obvious, as humour, than we might
have desired. That Klipstein should be wearing Music-
hall horn-rimmed glasses and chewing Music-hall gum seems
inevitable.

Perhaps the easiest thing in the work to praise is its
rhythm. This is pure barrel-organ, and with its constant
repetition in Music-hall crosstalk, makes no bad medium
for the whole. The parodies of popular song are also well
enough in their way, but again rather obvious. A mildly
amusing feature of the dialogue, however, is its accurate
recording of inflexion. Snow remarks that he is very
interested in a tale of Sweeney's. Loot Sam Wauchope is
described as being 'at *home* in London.' A conversation by
telephone gives rise to this:-

Oh I'm *so* sorry. I *am* so sorry
But Doris came home with a terrible chill
No, just a chill
Oh I *think* it's only a chill
Yes indeed I hope so too -
Well I *hope* we shan't have to call a doctor....

Once again, we can suppose the humour very clever, very
cutting and very true. Once again it seems rather feeble.
It is not, perhaps, Aristophanic.

If 'Sweeney Agonistes' were completed, no doubt the
effect of the whole would be sufficient justification for
every fault we can find in these fragments. But that is
not sufficient justification for them in itself. That
they give a fair picture of banality is the most that can
be said for them. And this is not exactly the sort of
criticism we should prefer to pass on a work of so peculiar a genius as Mr. Eliot's. There are not many living
poets who could not have equalled the achievement, and we
may suspect that there are quite a number who could have
bettered it. Mr. Eliot has written no other work of which
this could be said.

72. GEORGE BARKER, FROM A REVIEW, 'ADELPHI'

January 1933, vol. v, 310-11

Barker (b. 1913), an English poet, is the author of

'Poems' (1935), 'Calamiterror' (1936) and 'Collected
Poems' (1957).

Swill, guzzle, and copulate: 'Birth, copulation, and
death' - equivalent terms. Eliot, for all I can see to
the contrary, wrote 'Sweeney Agonistes' with the coccyx
of that spine, fear. Of birth, of death, and of that
potent mobility in which birth and death find some kind
of union and some kind of interpretation. I am compelled
by my youthful respect of such elemental things, to refrain
from comment on the 'perfectly slick' texture and architecture of the verse: but I am correspondingly compelled
by that respect to state that in this poem (so far, for
me, his most *easily* admirable work) Eliot has got down to
the reservoirs of subject which lie nearer to exoteric
earth than his detached intelligence. By this I mean that
although the most unpoetic, everyday person might be
annoyed by the new Eliot idiom, such a person could not
but receive most of the inspiring emotion which, of
itself, informs the poem. To reduce that emotion to a
phrase, as near as one can, the queer shivering of a hand
in fear of performing its function as a hand. Sweeney,
afraid, sits describing his fear. Of birth, and copulation, and death.
    I feel that in 'Sweeney Agonistes', we observe poetry
dissolving into a condition of exquisite, and perfectly
lucid, decay. About it I perceive a pallor not only of
subject, but as well of treatment: Eliot has contrived as
deathly an elegy of his poetic decease, as he composed
triumphal ode of his birth, 'The Waste Land'. The loveliness, so proximate to inanition, of 'Ash-Wednesday', in
'Sweeney Agonistes' has become a sort of valediction from
death. Contemplate these words, with which the poem is
introduced:

Orestes: You don't see them, you don't - but *I* see
         them: they are hunting me down, I must move
         on. - *Choephoroi.*

Hence the soul cannot be possessed of the divine union,
until it has divested itself of the love of created
beings. - *St. John of the Cross.*

73. MORTON D. ZABEL, A MODERN PURGATORIO, 'COMMONWEAL'

19 April 1933, vol. xvii, 696-7

The quotation from Saint John of the Cross which Mr. Eliot
prefixes to his latest book of verse goes farther than the
hint of parody in his title or the apologetic compromise
of his sub-title to explain his motive in republishing
these two desultory fragments of satire from the 'Criterion.' 'Hence the soul cannot be possessed of the divine
union, until it has divested itself of the love of created
beings.' Mr. Eliot's portrayal of 'created beings' has in
the past been sufficiently scathing; its purpose must be
understood by anyone who wishes to grasp the nature and
process of his spiritual experience. In the desolation
and vacuity of 'A Cooking Egg,' 'The Hippopotamus,'
'Gerontion,' 'Prufrock' and 'The Waste Land,' he achieved
that ruthless notation of reality without mastering which
no knowledge of material fact may be gained and no renunciation of it justified. These were records of a self-
scrutiny bordering on spiritual masochism. They explored
with an ironic intensity unknown to most of Mr. Eliot's
contemporaries the material ambition and depravity of his
time. They found their climax in the empty monotony of
'The Hollow Men' and their justification in the regenera-
tive impulse of 'Ash-Wednesday.' It is difficult to see
how his new long poem (of which two sections have already
appeared: 'Triumphal March' and 'Difficulties of a Statesman') or the present operatic burlesque improves on the
earlier presentation, or, indeed, justifies a repetition
of what has already found its logical place in a remarkable personal and historical record.
     The method of Eliot remains his own; his imitators
cannot dispute that fact. A poet should also be granted
his diversions. These facts do not, however, improve the
dulness which 'Sweeney Agonistes' offers in fully twenty
of its thirty pages. The Aristophanic element is hardly
authentic enough to enliven a kind of satire already over-
exploited in recent years, whereas the use of 'jazz as a
medium for tragedy' attributed to these fragments by one
critic is not only a dubious venture, but a venture at
which Mr. Eliot, despite his mastery of topical accents
and banality, has not conspicuously succeeded. The fact
that he has already depicted that tragedy in classic
terms renders this book a tactical error to any reader who
has followed him into the beautiful and profound passages
of 'Ash-Wednesday.'

There is one purpose which may justify these poems,
however. Most modern readers require a great quantity of
repetition before an effect is achieved in their minds.
If Mr. Eliot still thinks it possible to reach this audience, there can be no question that even an obtuse reader
will leave these pages without admitting the emptiness,
tedium and depravity of the elements in contemporary life
which they describe. The renunciation of 'the love of
created beings' is not only a painful process, but a slow
one. Since the evidence guaranteeing Mr. Eliot's sincerity exists, he should doubtless be allowed not only the
amusement but the thoroughness by which he will achieve
that spiritual triumph. To those who cannot accept the
sterile horrors here presented, he offers another quotation, this time from the 'Oresteia': 'You don't see them,
you don't - but *I* see them: they are hunting me down, I
must move on.' The last phrase here contains, of course,
one of the most important declarations in modern poetry.

74. MARIANNE MOORE, REVIEW, 'POETRY'

May 1933, vol. xlii, 106-9

In 'Sweeney Agonistes' Mr. Eliot comes to us as the men of
the neighboring tribes came to Joshua under a camouflage
of frayed garments, with mouldy bread in the wallet. But
the point is not camouflaged. Mortal and sardonic victims though we are in this conflict called experience, we
may regard our victimage with calmness, the book says; not
because we don't know that our limitations of correctness
are tedious to a society which has its funny side to us,
as we have our slightly morbid side to it, but because
there is a moment for Orestes, for Ophelia, for Everyman,
when the ego and the figure it cuts, the favors you get
from it, the good cheer and customary encomium, are as the
insulting wigwaggery of the music-halls.
    Everyman is played by Pereira, an efficiently incon-
spicuous, decent, studious chap. Well, not so decent,
since he pays the rent for Doris and Dusty, who are an
unremarkable, balky, card-cutting pair of girls whose
names symbolize society's exasperating unanimity of
selfishness. Shakespeare's 'lecherous as a monkey' is
rather strong, but in a world of buncombe and the fidgets,
where you love-a me, I love-a you, 'One live as two,' 'Two

live as three' - and there is no privacy - under the bam-
boo tree, the pair of given names go well with the sur-
names of a laidly, shallow set of heroes from America,
London, Ireland, Canada, who became intimate at the time
they 'did' their 'bit' and 'got the Hun on the run.'
There is, as the author intended, an effect of Aristophanic melodrama about this London flat in which the visitors play with the idea of South Sea languor and luxury -
work annihilated, personality negatived, and conscience
suppressed; a monkey to milk the goat and pass the cock-
tails - woman in the cannibal-pot or at hand to serve.

It is correct and unnotorious for the race to perpetu-
ate itself; committing adultery and disclaiming obligation
is the suicide of personality, and the spirit wearies of
clarity in such matters. The Furies pursuing Orestes are
abler casuists than the King of Clubs and Queen of Hearts
of Dusty and Doris. 'They are hunting me down,' he said.

A stark crime would not be so difficult to commit as
the mood of moral conflict is difficult to satisfy. One
is dead in being born unless one's debts are forgiven;
and equipoise makes an idiot of one. The automatic
machinery of behavior undoes itself backwards, putting
sinister emphasis on wrong things, and no emphasis on the
right ones.

If he was alive then the milkman wasn't
            and the rent-collector wasn't,
And if they were alive then he was dead.

Death or life or life or death -
Death is life and life is death.

Is one to become a saint or go mad? - remain mad, we
should say. 'The soul cannot be possessed of the divine
union until it has divested itself of the love of created
beings,' St. John of the Cross says; as all saints have
said. If one chooses God as the friend of the spirit,
does not the coffin become the most appropriate friend for
the body? 'Cheer him up? Well here again that don't
apply,' says Sweeney. 'But I gotta use words when I talk
to you.' This plucky reproach has in it the core of the
drama. In their graveyard of sick love which is no love,
which is loneliness without solitude, the girls can't
understand what Pereira has to do with it and that it is
a lucky eclecticism which cuts him off from what the Krum-
packers and Horsfalls call a good time. A man should not
think himself a poor fish or go mad, Sweeney maintains,
because two girls are blockheads. He should answer a
question as often as they ask it and put in as good an

evening as possible with them. If by saying, 'I gotta
use words when I talk to you,' he insults them and they
don't know they've been insulted, they, not he, should go
mad.

When the spirit expands and the animal part of one
sinks, one is not sardonic, and the bleak lesson here set
forth is not uncheerful to those who are serious in the
desire to satisfy justice. The cheer resides in admitting
that it is normal to be abnormal. When one is not the
only one who thinks that, one is freed of a certain
tension.

Mr. Eliot is not showy nor hard, and is capable at
times of too much patience; but here the truculent commonplace of the vernacular obscures care of arrangement, and
the deliberate concise rhythm that is characteristic of
him seems less intentional than it is. Upon scrutiny,
however, the effect of an unhoodwinked self-control is
apparent. The high time half a dozen people of unfasti-
dious personality can seem to be having together, is
juxtaposed with the successful flight of the pursued son
of Agamemnon, and it is implied, perhaps, that 'he who
wonders shall reign, he who reigns shall have rest.' One
is obliged to say 'perhaps' - since Sweeney in conflict is
not synonymous with Sweeney victorious.

'The Rock'

First performed at Sadler's Wells Theatre, 28 May - 9 June 1934; first published, London, 31 May 1934, and New York, 23 August 1934

75. UNSIGNED REVIEW, 'LISTENER'

6 June 1934, vol. xi, 945

The immediate object of 'The Rock', the pageant play now being performed at Sadler's Wells, for which Mr. T.S. Eliot has written the words, is to raise money for the Forty Five Churches fund of the Diocese of London - a purpose which dictates the main theme of the play, the building of a church, against which are shown certain 'experiments in time' which illustrate the growth of the churches in London from the time of the conversion of the Anglo-Saxons. But beyond this main object, which deserves all support, the play raises the whole issue of dramatic poetry to-day, an issue which the author himself has discussed as thoroughly as any contemporary critic. In the course of a dialogue on that subject, written a few years ago, Mr. Eliot put forward certain general propositions with which his dramatic poetry in this 'Rock' can now be compared. One was the necessity for something more than pure entertainment. 'The Rock' most certainly does entertain; as well as its choruses and historical pictures, it has Cockney backchat, topical references to Redshirts and Blackshirts and the Douglas Credit Scheme, a music-hall song and dance, and even a ballet (of Whittington and his Cat). But the energy which carries through its diverse scenes and gives the whole performance shape is (as it was in Mr. Auden's 'Dance of Death') the writer's conviction of the importance of his theme. The fault with poetic dramatists of the Stephen Phillips kind was that they never seemed to care two pins about their subject; but Mr. Eliot obviously does have very strong feelings about those

who 'stray, in high-powered cars, on a by-pass way', and
does care very much about 'A Church for us all and work for
us all and God's world for us all even unto this last'.   A
second observation, that 'Drama springs from religious
liturgy and cannot afford to depart far from religious
liturgy' is amply illustrated, not only by the actual
introduction of parts of the Church service (in the scene
showing the blessing of the Crusaders, and in the climax
where the Bishop of London blesses the audience) as by the
use of the rhythms of the liturgy in certain of the choruses.   And this links up with the third proposition, the
necessity of providing a verse that will be as satisfactory
for us as blank verse was for the Elizabethans.   There is
no one form of verse in 'The Rock'; it comprehends a
variety, from the measures of the Psalms to those of the
music hall; but the point is that they are familiar
rhythms, to which the audience's ear is attuned.   And so,
either sung, or spoken with beautiful clearness by the
Chorus which links up the scenes, they present no difficulty in acceptance.   Those to whom Mr. Eliot's name is
synonymous with 'modernist' and 'difficult' poetry may
be surprised that audiences of bishops, aldermen, church
workers, school children and 'general public', most of
whom are probably unfamiliar with his other works, should
be able to join in anything written by him as they do in
the last chorus of all.   Those, however, who remember the
smart rhythms of 'Sweeney Agonistes', or the clear lines
of the 'Journey of the Magi', will not be in the least
surprised; but simply pleased that a great contemporary
poet should have been given the opportunity of writing
directly for a popular audience.

76. UNSIGNED REVIEW, MR. ELIOT'S PAGEANT PLAY, 'TIMES
LITERARY SUPPLEMENT'

7 June 1934, no. 1688, 404

Evidently Mr. Eliot has prepared, step by step, to enter
the theatre.   'The Rock' is not actually a drama, being
first a pageant; but it is a work for the stage, and may
be regarded - Mr. Eliot having advanced so far - as a
notable demonstration of possibilities.   That his approach
has been deliberate, preceded by much critical examination, is apparent from previous writings.

The contemporary theatre presented him with two obstacles: first, the dislike or fear of poetry on the stage; second, the lack of a recognized morality either on the stage or in the audience. The dramatists of to-day mostly write for 'plutocratic St. Moritzers.' The regular theatre therefore did not provide an immediate objective: for without poetry or traditional morals he could not work. Perhaps, in order to seek guidance for his advance, he made his study of former dramatists, especially the Elizabethan; and within recent years enunciated his discovery that poetry and drama are not contradictory, as this century assumes: the best drama is in fact that which comes nearest to poetry, and *vice versa*. This declaration gave confidence for experiment, and he wrote several fragments. But now the request to write for a church audience, in support of a church extension campaign, solved for him the second problem – at least for the occasion: Christianity was present on both sides of the curtain.

Mr. Eliot is not alone among modern writers in desiring a poetic drama. And internal evidence shows him sensitive to what others are doing, to the ground won, the methods employed. His genius, indeed, might be said to rest on a careful regard of other artists, predecessors and contemporaries. He balances two forms of awareness, which might be described as horizontal and vertical, more nicely than anyone to-day. In this play the vertical (or past) influences are obvious and gloried in. Liturgy, which gave birth to English drama, is a model; there is antiphonal use of choric speaking; and many scenes, which are all linked on the theme of church-building, contain portions of actual liturgy. The Latin ritual for taking the Cross for the Crusades is bodily inserted. There are also bits of sermons. Early moralities authorize comic relief to the most serious intentions; and that relief, naturally enough, is expressed in terms of the music-hall and pantomime we know. The cockney builders of a church, which is gradually erected as the pageant proceeds, are ready to indulge in jokes, arguments, songs and humble reverence, as required. Each difficulty in church-building is illustrated by a scene showing a similar (or worse) difficulty overcome in the past. Liturgical chanting and mime are used in these scenes, which include such occasions as Mellitus's conversion of London, Rahere's building of St. Bartholomew's, the rebuilding of Jerusalem and the Danish invasion of England.

As already suggested, awareness of present writers is shown. With them, what might be called the modest or non-sublime approach to poetic drama has become almost a convention. They take the popular stage forms to-day (the

modern 'folk' forms), such as musical comedy or *revue*, and
use them as a basis. There was recently Mr. O'Casey's
'Within the Gates'; and echoes of its sing-song choruses,
its pervasive harping on modern down-and-outs find their
way into 'The Rock,' as:

> In this land
> There shall be one cigarette to two men,
> To two women one half pint of bitter
> Ale.

Mr. W.H. Auden is another experimenter; he is marked by
strangeness and an arrogant threatening of a doomed
society, as he sees it. Him, too, Mr. Eliot recalls on
occasion:-

> Though you forget the way to the Temple
> There is one who remembers the way to your door.

His gift of parody may unconsciously lead him to this.
But conscious parody appears elsewhere, as in the Commu-
nists' verses - typographically parodied also.
   The scene where this occurs, set in 1934, is most
characteristic of the Eliot known through his poems. (It
should be made clear that the scenario is by another
hand, Mr. E. Martin Browne; Mr. Eliot is author 'only of
the words.' As he explains, 'Of only one scene am I
literally the author,' and this modern scene is presumably
the one.) The chorus, despondent, wonder if the young
offer hope of better things. Bands of Redshirts and
Blackshirts are questioned. Their replies are, with
exaggeration, unsatisfactory. The chorus says: 'There
seems no hope from those who march in step.' A Plutocrat
enters, criticizes the Church and, instead, offers to the
crowd a golden calf, for which they fight. As a comment
on our modern situation, it cannot be said that in this
the pessimism of 'The Waste Land' has been abandoned.
   Mr. Eliot takes a hard view of the Christian stuggle.
The emphasis of his chorus counters the optimistic scenario, an emphasis such as is expressed in:-

> The desert is not remote in southern tropics,
> The desert is not only around the corner,
> The desert is squeezed in the tube-train next to you,
> Squeezed like tooth-paste in the tube-train next to
>   you.

These choruses, as the publisher points out, exceed in
length any of his previous poetry; and on the stage at

Sadler's Wells they prove the most vital part of the performance, being excellently spoken. They combine the
sweep of psalmody with the exact employment of colloquial
words. They are lightly written, as though whispered to
the paper, yet are forcible to enunciate.

[Quotes 'The Rock', Chorus III, CPP, p. 155, 'Where My
Word' to 'lost golf balls'.]

In 'The Rock' Mr. Eliot's success is certainly lyrical;
the action scenes have immaturities and faults, for which,
on account of collaborators, he may not be entirely blame-
worthy. The cockney humour is often curiously feeble;
sometimes alien points of view, such as the Agitator's are
thinly projected. But with his use of the chous he has
regained a lost territory for the drama. Nor is it only
satiric, as the tender music of the closing scene may
exemplify:-

> In our rhythm of earthly life we tire of light. We are
>   glad when the day ends, when the play ends; and
>   ecstasy is too much pain.
> We are children quickly tired: children who are up in
>   the night and fall asleep as the rocket is fired;
>   and the day is long for work or play.
> We tire of distraction or concentration, we sleep and
>   are glad to sleep.

Mr. Eliot, having at last entered the theatre, may well
continue towards a proper play in verse. There is exhibited here a command of novel and musical dramatic speech
which, considered alone, is an exceptional achievement.

77. MICHAEL SAYERS, MR. T.S. ELIOT'S 'THE ROCK', 'NEW
ENGLISH WEEKLY'

21 June 1934, vol. v, 230-1

Sayers, a theatre critic, wrote book reviews and drama
criticism for the 'Criterion'.

Before attending at the theatre to see this Pageant

performed, I read the text carefully; and it seemed to me
then, that though the book contained many passages of
poetic worth, interest and beauty, yet on the whole the
verse was of such strained lucidity, that it would provide
an extremely thin, flat or lymphatic dialogue when spoken
aloud in the process of dramatic action.

I speak from the point of view of a critic of stage
entertainments. I believe that Mr. Eliot's poetry is the
best of its kind, but also that Mr. Eliot's poetic style,
if it is to be adopted generally for dramatic purposes
(which, fortunately, is unlikely), will result in a vitia-
tion of the serious stage comparable only to that brought
about by the *Scribe-and-Dumas-fils* - adorers of the last
generation.

French influence has rarely improved our English drama.
Concerning the literature of the stage, at least, it is
true to say that the Entente exemplifies little more than
a reciprocal exchange of misunderstandings. Modern or
fairly modern French criticism and poetry, I learn, have
impressed Mr. Eliot to the extent of reproduction; and
certainly they have led him to dispense as far as possible
with the essentially English poetic device which, by a
combination of precise communications and evocative suggestions, yields a language continuously creative. Mr.
Eliot has struggled nobly and brilliantly against the
deterioration, imprecision and misuse of language in our
time; but, not satisfied by this excellent work, he went
on to elevate his negative critical principles into a
theory of poetry, and to practise his own teaching. He
commenced by deliberately smothering those magnificent
sonorities, (Even when our poetry snored it was magnificent!) which has become the test of good poetry; and substituted in their place the witty café-table rattle, the
morbid whine and the mere boudoir coo characteristic of
his favourite French verses. Consequently, even when most
earnest, much of Mr. Eliot's poetical writing still
strikes the eye more forcibly than the ear. These lines
from the text under review are a case in point. The
reference is to a Temple:-

> And the lamp thereof is the Lamb.
> And there with us is night no more, but only
> Light
> Light
> Light of the Light.

The passage looks more interesting than it sounds.
Nevertheless this poet is capable of producing at times
extremely lovely-sounding lines, as those beginning:-

O greater light we praise thee for the less,

And that he is well aware of what might be a deficiency in
his work may account for his frequent use of liturgical
movements, with rather monotonous results.

For my purposes, then, Mr. Eliot's verses lack that
precipitation of the spirit without which stage dialogue
is tedious and flat. His verse 'stays on the ground';
it walks, with irregular steps, in a circle. It does not
stir us by a bold advance, though it may disappoint us by
a feeble recession (or Tchekovian anti-climax); at best it
keeps steadily to an improgressive circumambulation. Its
emotional gamut is restricted, dropping from satiric lev-
ity down to hopeless despondency, but reaching neither
really comic impetuosity on the one hand, nor tragic con-
templativeness on the other hand. And in this play 'The
Rock,' at any rate, the content is equally as uninspiring
as the form.

Mr. Eliot allows certain limits to be set to his
thought and feelings by his beliefs. He does not seek to
justify the ways of his God to us; this, it appears, he
would consider a piece of impertinence to attempt. He
does not concern himself very deeply with the mystery of
our existence; this, it appears, would be contrary to his
orthodoxy. Not to phrase it irreverently, Mr. Eliot's
dramatic verse, in its most moving expressions, is the in-
cantation of a Dean manqué, who would call strayed Chris-
tians into the Catholic Church of England.

Again, these beliefs of Mr. Eliot cause him to voice
in most melodramatic utterances (which too often, in this
book, take the place of intense feeling), a series of
mediaeval platitudes decked out in canonicals; as, for
instance, when he expresses his horror at the hygienic
practice of brushing the teeth; and also when he declares
that our culture is decadent because it ignores the Church,
though it is more probable that the Church is degenerate
because it has lost touch with our culture. One can only
share the lament, of the other critics, upon the passage
of this great literary gentleman into 'the Wasteland of
Futile Superstition'; and murmur, in the words of the Tal-
mudic funeral oration pronounced upon Rabbi Hillel: 'Alas,
the humble and pious man, the disciple of Ezra!'

I know that there is a tendency among modern critics
to desire to confine the subject-matter of art to an
accepted number of abstractions from common experience.
Just as we speak in our debates of Communism, instead of
the different disciples of Karl Marx; and of Social Credit,
instead of individual exponents of Major Douglas's Theory;
so, if we wish to make a play or novel about 'love,' to

take a lively example, we shall no longer create a Romeo
and Juliet, a David and Agnes, a Lady Chatterley and the
Gamekeeper, embodying our particular experiences and
observations of the sexual impulse; but rather choose to
deal with universal affections; and write, as it might be,
the tragedy of Lingham and Yoni, where only whatever is
common to collective experience of sex is allowed. It
seems to me that this modern inclination to restrict the
field of artistic enquiry would reduce our Western art to
the static condition of Chinese aesthetics, which we might
call the science of trifling; and we should come to agree
with Voltaire that Shakespeare was altogether a barbarian.
If, however, some of our dramatists welcome this limitation of material, then in that case they may find Mr.
Eliot's forms of verse to be indicative of the sort of
vehicle necessary for the conveyance of mass emotions.
I think that these verse-forms might be suitable for
Comedy, but a very specialised kind of comedy: - a Collective Comedy of Manners - e.g., the Calf of Gold episode in
the play under review. The tragic experience, like that
of the mystic, the poet and the lover, will remain an individual revelation; and the experiments going forward in
the Soviet Russian Theatre appear to bear me out in this
speculation.

As a special kind of comedic poet, then, Mr. Eliot indicates in a few passages in 'The Rock' how talent, insight, wit, information, chastened sentiment and proper
dignity may be put to use in the modern drama, although
it still remains to be done. Yet it may be that an
adequate dramatic poetry will result from the impact between this collective or mass consciousness and, what I
might call, the Shakespearian apprehension of particulars; a new Drama combining the grim, intellectual can-
dour of the first with the human plentitude of the
latter.

Mr. Eliot's pageant-play was performed at Sadler's
Wells by a number of amateur players. They acted admirably
at the one or two opportunities provided for them by the
author. I shall never be able to follow the thought-
processes of stage costumiers, and I have no explanation
to offer why The Rock, one of the characters in the play,
appeared to carry a set of organ-pipes upon his back, or
maybe a hot-water central-heating radiator. Both may here
be represented in order to supply music and heat to the
frequently flat and frigid dialogue. As my kindly colleagues say, 'it would be invidious to single out any one
actor from so great a number' (and then proceed to select
the friends of their friends); but I might mention Rev.
Vincent Howson, part author of the prose dialogue, who

brought the house down, or, to speak with more exactness, woke the house up, with his rendering of an excellent bur-lesque upon an old-time Variety duet and dance: 'When I was a lad what 'ad almost no sense'; together with Miss Phyllis Woodcliffe, who was delightful, complete with bonnet and boa and boots.

The leaders of the Chorus, Miss Janet Lewis and Mr. Stewart Cooper, delivered their lines with intelligence and grace, in spite of their whitewashed faces, which made them resemble an ensainted Nigger Minstrel Troupe, with skins washed whiter than snow!

The production was under-rehearsed; and the scenes of pageantry, like all spectacles when the onlookers are in no other relation except that of passive submission to the proceedings, distressed the intelligent members of the audience by their dullness, and bored everybody by their protraction.

78. UNSIGNED EDITORIAL ON 'THE ROCK', 'THEOLOGY'

July 1934, vol. xxix, 4-5

The text of the Sadler's Wells London Church Pageant, 'The Rock', by T.S. Eliot, is now available, and very good reading it is. Our only criticisms are that it is diffi-cult to grasp at a single hearing, and that the modern London working-man does not speak as he is here made to do. Ethelbert, Alfred and young Edwin are at once too intelligent and too illiterate. But what a blessed re-lief, after the Wardour Street lamb-doodle sometimes put forward as the language of Church-plays, to have words with a bite in them, full of wit, satire and poetry. It is a genuine modern exposition of belief in the Church, as an ancient, unpopular, hard-pressed, conquering, divine society. It is modern in that it is aware of the modern situation (we even have the Douglas scheme of Social Credit - 'that bein' the case, I say: to 'ell with money'), and of Red Shirts, Black Shirts and so forth, but in a deeper sense it is modern in that we have in it the *confessio fidei* of a modern Churchman, a real faith ex-pressed in the language of to-day. Above all it is a pageant, with Mellitus, Rahere and even Nehemiah to re-assure the builders of to-day. The time-series is used with freedom. Bishop Blomfield comforts the leader of the

Chorus with a reminder of the Crusades, and we at once see
a mediaeval Bishop giving the Cross, with Latin prayers
and benediction, to two young Crusaders, and the next
moment the twentieth-century builders are patting one
another on the back because the difficulties have miracu-
lously vanished. We congratulate the diocese of London
on having secured Mr. Eliot to write their book.

79. UNSIGNED REVIEW, 'TABLET'

4 August 1934, vol. clxiv, 138

If we had been among the spectators of the 'Pageant-play'
recently presented by our Anglican friends at Sadlers
Wells we might be able to write more favourably of 'The
Rock' by T.S. Eliot in which the full text of the play is
printed. As the performances were in aid of the Protestant Bishop of London's 'Forty-five Churches Fund,' Mr.
Eliot and his collaborator, Mr. Martin Browne, have used
the notion of three cockney bricklayers in colloquy with
one another; with contemporaries (including an anti-God
agitator); and with ghostly visitants from the past, such
as Mellitus, Bishop of London, and Rahere, the founder of
St. Bartholomew's. The scanty action and copious talk
are expressed partly in not very successful *vers libre* and
partly in a cockney dialect with the omitted aspirates so
laboriously indicated as to make the very long speeches
of the bricklayers exceedingly tiresome to read. Unhappily, there is little freshness and beauty of thought to
mollify the exacerbating diction.

80. UNSIGNED REVIEW, 'EVERYMAN'

17 August 1934, 189

One may guess, impertinently perhaps, that Mr. Eliot has
chosen a hard path to tread in coming out into the open to
assist in the production of a pageant play meant to raise
funds for London churches. The admiration of the honesty

and courage needed to emerge from the study to engage in
such a broil must condition all criticism of 'The Rock'
considered as pure poetry and he himself, by the admission
of clerical collaborators with embarrassingly fertile
pens, has provided a loophole for a more cautious criticism than if he had presented his piece as an individual
achievement. Many of the choruses of 'The Rock' are of a
moving solemnity, and the gusts of strangulated song bear
witness that a force which he has never yet allowed to
move with its own momentum still exists, though now subdued to a direction which, it is to be feared, will range
him with a secondary Herbert rather than a primary Smart
or Crashaw. The trappings of a doctrinal humility do not
at all become a poet of Mr. Eliot's standard. We ask for
at least a dash of purple. Well, he understands his own
genius best, and the ways of a serious experimenter are
always worth watching, even when they give the impression
of being wrong ones.

81. A.M., REVIEW, 'BLACKFRIARS'

September 1934, vol. xv, 642-3

Mr. Eliot has come out of the Waste Land.
     His sojourn in the desert was not, as his less intelli-
gent disciples seem to have thought, an intellectual
antic: it was a necessary asceticism, and an asceticism
for poetry. Analogous renunciations are observable in
other arts. All are stripping to structure in order to
regain tradition. But the desert is a dangerous place:
there are devils in it as well as God. *Surréalist* paintings suggest that it is the devil whom the painters have
met in the desert.
     Mr. Eliot has come out of the Waste Land a Christian.
This play, which ran for a fortnight at Sadler's Wells,
with crammed audiences (and was reported in 'Blackfriars'), is an explicitly Christian play, it is vulgar
propaganda, it is to collect cash for Church extension.
It is a phenomenon to be noted when the greatest living
English poet finds it an honour for poetry to be an
ancilla Fidei.
     The play is built on several planes. In the fore-
ground two Cockney bricklayers are trying to build a
church in a swamp. On another plane are the appearances

of great church-builders of the past who come to encourage
the workmen - Rahere, Nehemiah, Blomfield. Then there is
the contemporary 'world,' with its aimlessness and lucre
lust, and its panaceas of Fascism and Communism. And behind all is the mysterious figure of the Rock. The Rock
is Peter.

Mr. Eliot has always claimed that the poet should be in
organic relation with the community: in this play he has
achieved that relation, and without any loss to his
poetry, for the great choruses which weld the play together contain some of the noblest poetry he has written.
Only the language of the Cockneys is a little uninterest-
ing: Cockney is more than misplaced h's, and Mr. Eliot
would do well to rely on his own judgment in this matter,
since the advice he says he has taken seems not to have
been very helpful. But this is to carp at a work which as
a whole is a magnificent and thrilling success. The temptation to quote is furious, but we must be content to conclude with the refrain which is the 'motive' of the entire
play: 'A Church for us all and work for us all and God's
world for us all even unto this last.'

82. UNSIGNED REVIEW, 'SUNDAY TIMES'

30 September 1934, 12

Mr. Eliot's previous fragments of dramatic dialogue have
now blossomed into a pageant play, though he is careful
to explain that he has supplied nothing but the text for
the scenario by Mr. E. Martin Browne.

The pageant is a succession of scenes, some historical, some contemporary, in which the builders of a new
church figure or which they are inspired to see. Some
of the dialogue is in prose, some in verse, and both are
interlinked with choruses. The rhythm of these choruses,
in which the author can be most directly heard, is haunted
by the whimper already familiar, as if even now he was
unable to get away from the futility against which he has
reacted so bitterly and to give his verse the joy of the
old affirmations that his intelligence has rediscovered.
Such drama as there is is that of the erection of the new
church in spite of every difficulty, a work accomplished
under the inspiration of previous builders, such as
Rahere, who return to remind the workmen that they had
similar difficulties in their own time. The talk of the

workmen is so consistently aitchless as to read like a
literary convention, but here, we are told, the dialogue
has been 're-written' by another hand.

'The Rock' is more interesting for its promise than for
its performance, and it appears that Mr. Eliot is trying
for much the same effect as that which Mr. Sean O'Casey
achieved by 'Within the Gates' triumphantly. Let us hope
this example will continue to spread.

83. D.W. HARDING, 'THE ROCK', 'SCRUTINY'

September 1934, vol. iii, 180-3

Harding (b. 1906), Emeritus Professor of Psychology, University of London, was a member of the editorial board of
'Scrutiny' from 1933 to 1947. He has written a number of
important works of literary criticism, including 'Experience into Words' (1963) and 'Words into Rhythm' (1976).

'The view that what we need in this tempestuous turmoil of
change is a Rock to shelter under or to cling to, rather
than an efficient aeroplane in which to ride it, is comprehensible but mistaken.' The attitude expressed by Dr.
Richards here is one that many people now find less allur-
ing than once they did, and to them the general theme of
'The Rock' will be welcome. The whole book bears witness
to the conviction that the only possible advance at the
present time is a 'spiritual' one and has little to do
with anything specifically modern, nor any appeal for
those who

> ...constantly try to escape
> From the darkness outside and within
> By dreaming of systems so perfect that no one will need
>   to be good.

Mr. Eliot's subtle tone of humble and yet militant contempt
could hardly be improved upon. What is not convincing,
however, is his suggestion that the Church is the only
alternative, for his pleading relies upon false antitheses.
It puts the plight of the uncultured vividly but it does
not show what the Church would do for them. A description

of the breakdown of social and particularly of family life
ends

>   But every son would have his motor cycle,
>   And daughters ride away on casual pillions.

But the alternative to the pillion is not suggested. As
far as we can judge from the time when such families were
more stable, it would be the horsehair sofa, in a front
parlour left vacant by the rest of the family with appropriate pleasantries. The only alternatives to godless
restlessness that this book gives are the rough diamond
piety of the builder's foreman, and more impressive, the
satisfactions of the highly cultured who happen to be
within the Church:

>   Shall we not bring to Your service all our powers
>   For life, for dignity, grace and order,
>   And intellectual pleasures of the senses?

But the plight of people capable of appreciating such culture and still outside the Church is not put. In so far
as 'The Rock' is pleading for certain attitudes which the
Church at its best supports it is undoubtedly effective,
but as an assertion of the necessity of the Church to the
establishing or maintenance of those attitudes it is in-
validated by its false antitheses. Undoubtedly it is
more effective in its denunciatory description of things
as they are, of the misery of the poor and the spiritual
vacuity of the well-to-do, than in the remedy it proffers.
And it is in the choruses where these descriptions occur
that the greatest intrinsic value of the work is to be
found.
     The prose dialogue which maintains the action of the
pageant is distressing. It is difficult to believe that
the spinsterish Cockney of the builders was written by the
author of the public house scene in 'The Waste Land', and
the speeches of the Agitator and the fashionable visitors
to the Church are just the usual middle-class caricatures
of a reality that has never been accurately observed.
They are the caricatures of a class by a class, and well-
worn and blurred they are, inevitably. The reach-me-down
character of the dialogue is partly responsible for and
partly derived from - in fact is one with - the banal and
sentimental treatment of a scene like The Crusaders' Fare-
well, which offers so painful a contrast to the dignity
of the liturgical Latin that comes next. Only in some
of the ingenious pastiches of archaic styles which Mr.
Eliot introduces from time to time is the prose readable

with even mild pleasure.

The verse is altogether more interesting. Naturally
in a work written to order and presumably in a limited
time there is included some which is not as fine as most
of what Mr. Eliot has published. Necessarily, too, this
verse cannot have the concentration and subtlety of a
short poem intended for many attentive readings. Its interest lies rather in its experimentation with a tone of
address. Innovations of 'tone' (in Richards' sense) are
at least as significant as innovations of 'technique' in
the restricted sense, and in the addresses of the Chorus
and The Rock to the decent heathen and the ineffectual
devout, who are taken as forming the audience, Mr. Eliot
achieves a tone that is new to contemporary verse. Its
peculiar kind of sermonizing is especially welcome in contrast to the kind the young communist poets offer us: in
particular it succeeds in upbraiding those it addresses
while still remaining humble and *impersonally* superior to
them:

> The Word of the Lord came unto me, saying:
> O miserable cities of designing men,
> O wretched generation of enlightened men,
>
> Will you build me a house of plaster, with corrugated
>   roofing,
> To be filled with a litter of Sunday newspapers?

And again:

> Do you need to be told that even such modest attain-
>   ments
> As you can boast in the way of polite society
> Will hardly survive the Faith to which they owe their
>   significance?

Just occasionally the tone verges on the sententious:

> The lot of man is ceaseless labour,
> Or ceaseless idleness, which is still harder...;

but usually its poise is perfect.

Closely bound up with the tone of address is the texture of the language. The idiom Mr. Eliot has developed
here is admirably suited to, and has evidently emerged
from pressure of, the practical circumstances of the work:
its dramatic presentation before an audience whose muzzy
respect for the devotional had to be welded to a concern
for contemporary realities. A particularly successful and

characteristic trick of idiom is the quick transition from
vaguely Biblical language to the contemporary colloquial.
It can be seen in this:

> I have trodden the wine-press alone, and I know
> That it is hard to be really useful

and in this:

> And they write innumerable books; being too vain and
>   distracted for silence; seeking every one after his
>   own elevation, and dodging his emptiness.

This passage also illustrates the dominant feeling of
the denunciatory choruses, a dry contempt which has passed
beyond the stage of tiredness and now has a tough springi-
ness:

> O weariness of men who turn from God
> To the grandeur of your mind and the glory of your
>   action,
>
> Engaged in devising the perfect refrigerator,
> Engaged in working out a rational morality,
> Engaged in printing as many books as possible,
> Plotting of happiness and flinging empty bottles,
> Turning from your vacancy to fevered enthusiasm
> For nation or race or what you call humanity;...

'The Rock' is in many ways typical of Mr. Eliot's later
work. Far less concentrated, far less perfect, far more
easy-going than the earlier work, it has an increased
breadth of contact with the world which takes the place
of intensity of contact at a few typical points. The
change is not one that can be described briefly. It can
be roughly indicated by saying that the earlier work
seemed to be produced by the ideal type of a generation,
and asked for Mr. Eliot to be looked upon almost as an
institution, whereas this later work, though not more
individual, is far more personal. What seems certain is
that it forms a transition to a stage of Mr. Eliot's work
which has not yet fully defined itself.

84. CONRAD AIKEN, AFTER 'ASH-WEDNESDAY', 'POETRY'

December 1934, vol. xlv, 161-5

Aiken considered not only 'The Rock' but also 'After
Strange Gods' (London, 22 February 1934; New York, 19
April 1934).

To read these two new books of Mr. Eliot's together is to
be made more than ever uncomfortable about his present
predicament, his present position and direction. It is
unfair to examine a lecture as closely as one would an
essay in criticism, and 'After Strange Gods' consists, of
course, of three lectures delivered at the University of
Virginia. It is equally unfair to judge the printed text
of a pageant, a pageant written in co-operation with
others and for performance on a special occasion, as one
would judge a new book of poems presented in the ordinary
way. In other words, one must begin by discounting both
books as not quite 'pure' Eliot. Nevertheless, there they
are, they must be fitted into the Eliot tradition, they
fall into line, and Mr. Eliot himself invites the comparison by publishing them; and it must be confessed that they
leave one with a feeling of dissatisfaction and uncertainty.
    The lectures consist chiefly of an extension and
elaboration of the now famous essay in 'The Sacred Wood'
- Tradition and the Individual Talent. It is difficult to
see that they add much of importance, whether in refinement of perception, or in division or addition; if anything, they are a dilution of the earlier work, they seem
a little thin. Of course, as we all know, Mr. Eliot has
turned to religion in the interval of thirteen years between 'The Sacred Wood' and 'After Strange Gods,' and it
is not without a melancholy interest to consider the later
book in this special light. From 'tradition' to 'orthodoxy' was, in the circumstances, a natural semantic and
mantic step to take; Mr. Eliot takes it, and is at no
pains to conceal it. Everywhere here is the implication
that not only is it of vital importance for the artist (as
individual) to remain in a sort of conscious connection
with the tradition from which he springs, but also that if
this contact can be further or more deeply extended to
include a connection with the Church he will be safer
still. Leaving aside, as one must, the whole question of

religious belief, or of orthodox religion, nevertheless
one is at once aware that the change in Mr. Eliot's critical attitude is decidedly in the direction of limitation.
Already, in Tradition and the Individual Talent, his
emphasis was not so much on the *freedom* offered the artist
by tradition as on the *restrictions*; the use of tradition
was rather to hold one back than to release one for a
forward step of exploration; in short, the position was a
cautious one. The effect of orthodoxy is not unnaturally
to deepen this timidity. If little room was then left for
the individual's 'free play,' there is now very much less.
As a mother of the arts, Mr. Eliot's 'tradition' would be
a very anxious and possessive one indeed; and (one is
afraid) very crippling. Individualism must go by the
board - if such a program should become universal - and
the creative renewal of the arts fall to so low a level as
to lead inevitably to stagnation. With the death of the
individual would come the death of tradition; and art
would be simply a history.
     A curious state of things, a curious attitude in one
who has himself been one of the most pronouncedly and
creatively 'individual' of contemporary writers, and himself therefore a pretty violent *creator* of tradition; and
one immediately begins to wonder what effect his doctrines will have on his own poetry. 'The Rock' alone cannot give us much of an answer, for as observed above, it
is not a 'pure' offering, but an amalgam. In conjunction,
however, with the handful of poems which Mr. Eliot has
given us in the twelve years since he published 'The Waste
Land,' it is enough to make one uneasy. Without in any
way detracting from the extraordinary beauty of 'Ash-
Wednesday' or 'Marina,' or from the occasional brilliance
of other of the later poems, one cannot fail to notice a
contraction both of interest and power in the recent
work. 'Ash-Wednesday,' let it be said at once, is perhaps
the most beautiful of all Mr. Eliot's poems: it seems not
unlikely that its 'value' will outlast that of 'The Waste
Land.' It is purer and less violent; it depends less on
shock, though elements of shock are still there, enough of
them to give energy; in Mr. Eliot's own sense, it is more
absolutely a poem, has a new being and constitutes a new
experience, and is so much more without 'reference,' or
conscious reference, and so much more heavily weighted
with *un*conscious reference (or *affect*) as to approach the
kind of heavenly meaninglessness which we call pure
poetry. But, though we can like it better than 'The Waste
Land,' or feel it to be finer, we also feel it to mark the
beginning of a diminution of vigor and variousness: the
circle has narrowed, and it has gone on narrowing.

We cannot, of course, argue that this change is due to
the change in Mr. Eliot's views, any more than we can
argue that some deeper diminution of energy led to the
change of view; all we can do is observe that the two
things have gone together. In 'The Rock,' the choruses
are not the very best Eliot, though they are skilful and
beautiful; they are admirably calculated for declamation;
they have an excellent hardness and plainness; but at
times one feels the cunning of the rhetoric and the rhythm
to be almost too glib and easy, and as if usurping the
place of what would formerly have been a richer and more
natural inventiveness.

Mr. Eliot remarks, in 'After Strange Gods,' that to
write religious poetry is one of the most difficult of all
things. *Orthodox* religious poetry, yes: for that is merely
to state, or to state by referring, or to argue: which is
propaganda, or something very like it, as long as it remains within that given frame of traditional or taught conviction, as it must. It is this that makes one uneasy
about Mr. Eliot's future: this and his converse belief
that poetry, or the poetic genius, cannot be a substitute
for religion. To many of us it must appear that 'orthodox
religion,' on the one hand, and 'tradition,' on the other,
are simply nothing but a temporary conservatism, or freez-
ing in formula, of the initial poetic impulse. Beyond a
certain point, or for more than a given time, it *cannot* be
formalized: along comes a poet who reaches through it to
the thing itself. Perhaps Mr. Eliot's experiment with
dramatic form in 'The Rock,' which must have been as highly
suggestive to himself as to his auditors and readers, will
release him once more in ways which neither he nor ourselves can foresee.

'Murder in the Cathedral'

First performed in the chapter house, Canterbury Cathedral,
on the evening of 15 June 1935;
first (acting) edition, London, 10 May 1935;
first complete edition, London, 13 June 1935;
first American edition, New York, 19 September 1935

85. UNSIGNED REVIEW, MR. ELIOT'S NEW PLAY, 'TIMES LITERARY
SUPPLEMENT'

13 June 1935, no. 1741, 376

Mr. Eliot's new work of poetic drama has moved farther
from the theatre than his previous attempts and come
nearer to the Church. It is written for production in
Canterbury Cathedral this week. Its conventions have more
in common with ritual than with the stage, as in the
earliest English drama; and these conventions which he
has adopted, including strong use of a chorus, are well
assimilated to the whole texture. In 'The Rock' they were
often self-conscious, but here they have become subordinate, natural, appropriate. The play might be described
as a poem for several voices used liturgically.

The subject covered by a title that echoes detective
fiction is Thomas Becket's assassination. It is told
without an obvious propagandist intention, which was not
the case with 'The Rock.' We open with Becket returning
after seven years abroad, to a scene which has been prepared by a chorus of Canterbury women, who speak in
strikingly simple language:-

[Quotes CPP, p. 243, 'Here is no continuing city' to
'return to France'.]

But Becket, who is shown throughout as one ready for death,
will not accept any warning. Tempters appear. One tempter
would have him revive the worldly pleasures of his youth,
and when rejected remarks:- 'I leave you to the pleasures
of your higher vices.' Another tempter would have him

313

re-seek the power he once held as Chancellor.   To whom
Becket replies:-

> Those who put their faith in worldly order
> Not controlled by the order of God,
> In confident ignorance, but arrest disorder,
> Make it fast, breed fatal disease,
> Degrade what they exalt.

A third tempter would have him lead rebellion against the
king; a fourth makes a subtler appeal - to triumph over
his enemies by martyrdom:-

> Think, Thomas, think of enemies dismayed,
> Creeping in penance, frightened by a shade..,
> Think of miracles, by God's grace,
> And think of your enemies in another place.

But Becket is aware of the danger of this last temptation:
'to do the right deed for the wrong reason.'
    As an interlude we see him preaching in the cathedral
on Christmas morning, 1170, when he pronounces his view
that a Christian martyrdom is not the effect of man's will
to become a saint. He says:-

> A martyr, a saint, is always made by the design of
> God, for His love of men, to warn them and to lead them,
> to bring them back to His ways ... the true martyr is he
> who has become the instrument of God, who has lost his
> will in the will of God, not lost it but found it, for
> he has found freedom in submission to God. The martyr
> no longer desires anything for himself, not even the
> glory of martyrdom.

He concludes his sermon by saying he does not think he will
ever preach to them again.
    In Part II, the murder takes place. First, the four
knights accuse Becket. The priests try to persuade him to
take sanctuary, but he is more than ready for death: 'I
have had a tremor of bliss, a wink of heaven, a whisper,
And I would no longer be denied.' When the priests carry
him by force into the cathedral, he makes them unbar the
doors. The knights enter, slightly tipsy, and kill him.
They then, in mock-elaborate prose, justify themselves,
urging that their act is disinterested, that Becket's
crime was his failure to unite temporal and spiritual
office (Chancellor and Archbishop), 'an almost ideal
State,' and that by his attitude he more or less killed
himself.

All through the play the two main notes are of Becket
with his *idée fixe* of fulfilment in death and of the
chorus exhibiting a sense of approaching death. Mr.
Eliot's talent seems to be most effective in this second
note, of imminent desolation:-

> The forms take shape in the dark air:
> Puss-purr of leopard, footfall of padding bear,
> Palm-pat of nodding ape, square hyena waiting
> For laughter, laughter, laughter.

Or, again, a recurrence of the undersea imagery of his
early work:-

> I have lain on the floor of the sea and breathed
> with the breathing of the sea-anemone, swallowed with
> ingurgitation of the sponge. I have lain in the soil
> and criticized the worm.

But those former contradictions which were the special
surprise of Mr. Eliot's verse are here fused. This is his
most unified writing. He has admirably brought to maturity his long experimenting for a dramatic style, the chief
merit of which lies in his writing for a chorus.

86. I.M. PARSONS, FROM POETRY, DRAMA AND SATIRE, 'SPECTATOR'

28 June 1935, vol. cliv, 1112

Parsons (1906-80) was chairman of Chatto & Windus from
1954 to 1974. He is known particularly for his anthology
of First World War poetry, 'Men Who March Away' (1965).
In the 'Spectator' for 22 October 1932, he entered into
controversy with Rebecca West over Eliot's 'Selected
Essays 1917-1932', which he had reviewed and defended
against her in the 'Spectator' on 8 October.
     In this review Parsons also considered Auden and Isher-
wood's 'The Dog Beneath the Skin', which he found 'a
shoddy affair, a half-baked little satire which gets
nowhere'.

Artists, it has been said, usually know what is best for
themselves. And certainly Mr. Eliot's preoccupation with
religion, in which many critics saw the end of his poetry
and the stultification of his criticism, wears a different
aspect in the light of his latest work. 'Murder in the
Cathedral' is an historical episode, or series of episodes, dealing with the life and death of Thomas à Becket.
The action takes place alternately in the Archbishop's
Hall and in the Cathedral at Canterbury, and covers the
last few weeks of Becket's life. The episodes are linked
by a chorus of Women of Canterbury, and divided into two
parts by a prose interlude in which Becket preaches in the
Cathedral on Christmas Day, 1170. So much for the frame
of the piece. To suggest its essential quality is not so
simple. One might begin by referring to the choruses,
used in the Greek manner to create an atmosphere of
impending evil, among an audience expectantly acquainted
with the outcome of the plot.

> Some presage of an act
>   Which our eyes are compelled to witness, has forced our
>   feet
>   Towards the Cathedral. We are forced to bear witness.

Or to Becket's tempters, advocates in turn of luxury,
temporal power, and spiritual glory through martyrdom,
whose arguments are used both to reveal Thomas's character
and to introduce relevant details of his past life:

>   If you will remember me, my Lord, at your prayers,
>   I'll remember you at kissing-time below the stairs.

Or to the Christmas sermon, Becket's final affirmation of
his position, which acts as a bridge between the psychological action of Part I and the physical action of Part
II. All these are important to the play's effectiveness,
contribute to its atmosphere, construction and presentation of character. But equally one might mention those
passages of the chorus in which the stress is not on the
fate that is foreboded, but on the fate that is the portion of the common man:

>   Of the men and women who shut the door and sit by the
>   fire,

passages in which Mr. Eliot's particular touch is most
revealing and most assured. Or to the skilful variety of
tone and modulations of rhythm in the Tempter's speeches;
or to the scene immediately following the murder when the

four knights advance and address the audience in justification of their act: a scene whose satire gives point to
the main theme of the play, while relieving the tension
created by the climax and providing a smooth elision to
the exaltation of the final chorus. All these again are
part of the play's quality, though still only part. Its
main quality is bound up inextricably with the written
word, which cannot be paraphrased. And if one were to
start quoting it would be hard to know where to begin or
where to stop. For the play is a dramatic poem, and has
an imaginative unity which does not lend itself to brief
quotation. An imaginative unity ... there perhaps is the
essence of the matter. Many people could have made a play
out of Becket's murder – an instructive play, a witty
play, a good thriller or a moral tale. Mr. Eliot has done
more: he has reanimated a literary form which in England
has been dead or dormant for nearly three hundred years,
and in doing so he has found himself anew as a poet, only
with an added ease, lucidity and objectiveness.

87. JAMES LAUGHLIN, MR. ELIOT ON HOLY GROUND, 'NEW
ENGLISH WEEKLY'

11 July 1935, vol. vii, 250-1

Laughlin (b. 1914) founded New Directions in 1936, and
became the leading American publisher of the avant-
garde.

> ...wherever a martyr has
> given his blood for the blood of Christ,
> There is holy ground, and the sanctity shall not depart
> from it
> Though armies trample over it, though sightseers come
> with guide-books looking over it ...

However you want to feel about Mr. Eliot's 'position,'
'Murder in the Cathedral' proves that he is still a great
master of metric and that he knows how to put together a
play. These new lines do not sparkle as do those of 'The
Waste Land,' but in their quiet way they are perfect.
   The mind jumps at once to the problem of poetry and

belief, but I don't want to get myself entangled in that.
Mr. Eliot himself has treated it quite adequately in his
essay on Dante. It is enough to say that although an
Anglican vicar will naturally feel more excited about this
play than others would, agnostics and heretics need not
abstain, as it contains enough intellectual pabulum to
hold all their attention. For example, you can do a lot
of thinking about Mr. Eliot's blending of Aristotelian
tragedy with Christian dogma.
    The play begins in the best Greek manner with a Chorus
(of the women of Canterbury) chanting of bad things to
come and a Herald ushering in the Protagonist. But with
A'Becket's first speech you realize that here is no Oedipus about to be battered from all sides by blind fate, but
a Christian martyr forging his own destiny with eyes open
to the forces moving against him.

Thomas: (to the priests who have rebuked the women for
         their 'croaking like frogs in the tree-tops.')

[Quotes CPP, p. 245, 'Peace. And let them be' to 'forever
still'.]

    These lines deserve your careful analysis, for they
are not only the principle motif of the play, but as well,
I think, a deliberate expression of the poet's philosophy.
Roughly I interpret them as orthodox Thomism; in any case
they indicate the intellectual nature of Eliot's faith.
    Reading Sophocles I always get the impression of fly-
swatting - of a superhuman hand suddenly reaching down
from nowhere to crush a bewildered little animal. Thus
in the Greek frame such a line as

    And which all must suffer that they may will it...

is all out of drawing. What is Eliot's purpose in this
distortion?
    An examination of the psychological angle provides the
clue. Aristotle's criteria call for pity and terror to
induce the catharsis. But the fall of A'Becket produces
neither; he forsees his doom and declines escape though
it is offered - hence no terror; he is obviously ready for
death and glad to fulfill his faith - and so no pity. And
yet the play's action does release emotion within the
observer. Of what kind? The same, I think, as is aroused
by a Medieval Mystery or Miracle, one of religious exaltation, of completion of faith. It is clear then that
Eliot has attempted a fusion of the Classic and Medieval
dramatic formulae. Perhaps this will offend the purist,

but for me it is curious and thought-provoking.

Is this fusion purely a technical matter, or does Eliot intend a deeper meaning? Does he wish to indicate a fundamental affinity between the Classic and Christian tempers? Does this duality reflect a similar tendency in his own thought? Or is he, in blending an act of faith with tragedy, merely recalling that Greek drama had its origin in the religious ritual of the Goat Song, in which masked priests induced a mystic ecstasy in the celebrants by their chant and pantomime? I guess you would have to ask him.

To make his work completely solid Eliot presents through the assassins' after-murder speeches a clear analysis of the historical forces conditioning the event. A'Becket would not compromise between Church and State and was put on the spot. The knights speak in prose.

Throughout 'Murder in the Cathedral' the versification is of a high and even quality. There are few lines which will catch in your memory and stick there, as do so many of those of the 'Waste Land,' and the poems in 'Prufrock,' but neither is there a faulty line. There is no fixed metre, but there is, in the best sense, a fine free metric. Mr. Eliot has been to school and knows his language-tones and sound-lengths as few others do. He can cut a line of sound in time so that it comes off the page to you as a tangible design. His cadences are soft and cool and flowing, but there is never an unnecessary word. The language is highly charged with meaning, but there is no looseness of rhetoric. The craftsmanship of the verse is so unostentatious that you must look closely to see all the richness of detail.

[Quotes CPP, p. 257, 'We are not ignorant women' to 'drinking and laughter'.]

Yes, it's a long, long way to 'Prufrock,' it's a long long way from here. There has been much change, but I think it is in the nature of a fertile evolution and not a sterile decline.

And yet is the change so great? 'Murder in the Cathedral' ... hardly a title chosen by a religious recluse! And even back in 1917 (with apologies to the HIPPOPOTAMUS) we find that

the True Church can never fail
For it is based upon a rock.

88. EDWIN MUIR, NEW LITERATURE, 'LONDON MERCURY'

July 1935, vol. xxxii, 281-3

Muir (1887-1959) was a poet, critic and translator. In
1965, Faber & Faber published his 'Selected Poems', edited
and with a preface by Eliot.

Mr. Eliot's latest play is an interesting and moving piece
of work and, unlike 'The Rock', a unified one. The drama
is simple, direct and closely knit, and it proceeds within
an intellectual scheme which is stated quite early in the
play and is never forgotten during the rest of the action,
which in turn is circumscribed by it and takes its govern-
ing significance from it. The scheme of the action, that
is to say, is related to or rather becomes part of a
scheme of human action in general, seen timelessly. This
scheme of human action is tentatively stated in the first
chorus by the poor women of Canterbury with which the play
opens:

[Quotes CPP, p. 240, 'We wait, we wait' to 'pattern of
time'.]

It is stated more definitely by Thomas at his first
entrance, in a reply to one of the priests who had reproved the women for 'croaking like frogs in the tree-
tops':

[Quotes CPP, p. 245, 'Peace. And let them be' to 'forever still'.]

This image of the wheel recurs again in Thomas's reply to
the First Tempter:

[Quotes CPP, p. 247, 'Men learn little' to 'on which he
turns'.]

And a little farther on he says:

    You come twenty years too late.

This is Mr. Eliot's image of earthly life: the wheel that
turns and is forever still. But as man is a spirit he is
not completely bound to this wheel with every power; and

this is the other aspect of the intellectual scheme of the play. The first clear statement of it comes at the end of the first act, when Thomas deliberately embraces his martyrdom, which he sees is bound to follow:

[Quotes CPP, pp. 258-9, 'I know what yet remains' to 'the sword's end'.]

The last line is the crucial one, for it declares that Thomas, by purification of the will, has set himself free from the wheel. This mystery is dealt with more fully in the sermon which follows, forming an interlude between the first and the second (and last) act, and dealing with martyrdom. 'Saints are not made by accident. Still less is a Christian martyrdom the effect of a man's will to become a Saint, as a man by willing and contriving may become a ruler of men.... A martyrdom is never the design of man; for the true martyr is he who has become the instrument of God, who has lost his will in the will of God, not lost it but found it, for he has found freedom in submission to God.' These quotations should make clear the main lines of the action, which is both earthly and transcendental, a matter therefore both for grief and rejoicing (part of the sermon deals with this question, how believers can sorrow and rejoice at the same action). The meaning of the whole play is summed up in a few lines spoken by Thomas before his death:

> I give my life
> To the Law of God above the Law of Man.
> Those who do not the same
> How should they know what I do?

That expresses both the nature of Thomas's action and the mystery implied in it. And this is what Mr. Eliot is mainly concerned with, and without bearing it in mind the drama loses most of its meaning.

It is not for a reviewer to agree or disagree with the intellectual scheme of a work of imagination; all that he need be concerned with is its consistency, and its imaginative and dramatic force. From the outline I have given I think it will be clear that the intellectual fabric of this play is quite unusually consistent and closely knit, and also imaginatively impressive. But it is the dramatic force that it conveys to the action that is perhaps most striking of all; for one might almost say that the action owes its ultimate force to the consistency with which Mr. Eliot's imagination has moved within the bounds of his general conception of human action, stated abstractly in the passages which I have quoted. It may be said, of

course, that every work of imagination moves within the
limits of its author's general conception of human action;
but here the conception is held far more clearly and consistently than in most dramatic works, and the result is
not only a greater intellectual, but a greater dramatic
intensity, for every utterance of the actors being given
its exact place in the scheme, is given also a more packed
and full meaning. Sometimes, it seems to me, Mr. Eliot
secures this precision at the expense of imaginative freedom, particularly in the figures of the four knights, who
represent the ordinary man of action. But the action itself as he conceives it is truly dramatic; the figure of
Thomas in particular is beautifully imagined: the scene
between him and the Tempters being probably the finest in
the play.

Obviously a play conceived on such terms as these must
have a number of meanings apart from or flowing from the
main one. 'I give my life To the Law of God above the Law
of Man' clearly expresses one of them and one which at present is of the utmost urgency: the rival claims of religion and politics. In this question one feels that Mr.
Eliot is on the same side as Thomas Becket; but what he
has written is a play, and so he has to state both sides.
In the first act both sides are finely balanced, and that
is what makes it so strong dramatically; in the second the
murderers of Becket are somewhat burlesqued and belittled,
and even though they may have been in themselves quite
commonplace or even ridiculous characters, Mr. Eliot by
making them actually so loses the feeling, which he catches
so finely in the scene of the Tempters, of the deep and
permanent worldly power which they represent: they have
not enough behind them. He holds the balance between the
two powers in the first act, but in the second he actually
gives the impression of making Becket's triumph too easy,
perhaps a strange complaint to make about a dramatic
representation of martyrdom. The Chorus immediately preceding the murder, on the other hand, is one of the finest
in the whole play. But this poetic drama, unlike 'The
Rock', does not depend on the choruses. It is a unified
work, and a work of great beauty.

89. MARK VAN DOREN, THE HOLY BLISFUL MARTIR, 'NA?
YORK)

9 October 1935, vol. cxli, 417

It is only in a minor sense that the action of Mr. Eliot's
play can be understood as taking place at Canterbury. The
stage directions put it there; the chorus is composed of
women from the town; the Archbishop stands and talks in
his own hall, and at the end is murdered by four English
knights while he prays before the cathedral altar; and the
date, 1170, is displayed with sufficient prominence. But
the peculiar merit of the poet has little to do with all
this. It has rather to do with the fact that Mr. Eliot
has confined himself with a strict and icy purity to the
one aspect of the story which he was equipped to treat.
This aspect is such as not even to suggest a comparison
with Shakespeare, whose kind of humanity Mr. Eliot nowhere attempts. It suggests only Mr. Eliot, who achieves
perfection here to the degree that he explores his own
mind and employs his own art.

He is concerned first and last with the morality, or
perhaps it is the theology, of martyrdom. Chaucer's 'holy
blisful martir' is so far from blissful in these pages as
to strike a kind of silent terror in the spectator's heart
through the spectacle of his bleak and puzzled loneliness.
And as for his holiness – ah, that is a question which Mr.
Eliot is unable to answer. Indeed the impossibility of
answering it is the theme of the play. For who can say
that Thomas Becket was without spiritual pride when he
determined to obey his instinct of martyrdom? Who can say
that he exposed himself to the swords for any better reason than a certain tempter gave him – this tempter being
the last of four, and the most deadly of them because he
urges 'the right deed,' namely martyrdom, for 'the wrong
reason,' namely glory? The point is plainly made that if
Thomas suffered death for the sake of power and glory he
was not holy; and there is abundant evidence, both before
and after the catastrophe at the altar, that most of England felt a fanaticism in his final act. But the point is
as plainly made that this particular martyrdom may have
been designed in heaven, where 'the Saints are most high,
having made themselves most low.' As for an earthly solution to the problem, there is and can be none; nor can
Thomas's own words to himself be taken as testimony, since
he dies a man and not a saint, and speaks accordingly – as
one, that is to say, who desires to know rather than knows.

'Murder in the Cathedral' has been compared with 'Saint
Joan,' but it is both higher and thinner than that; higher
because it rises above the merely political problem of
obedience to authority, and thinner because theology must
always be thin on any stage, even the stage to which Mr.
Eliot adapts himself with such dignity, simplicity, and
skill. Within its limits the play is a masterpiece, a
thing of crystal whose appearance of flawlessness is not
altered by the weird reality of the four speeches in
prose delivered by the murderers after their job is done.
For the irony which tinkles through those speeches is
merely the accompaniment of an irony pervading the whole,
and reaching its deepest tones in the last words of Becket.
Mr. Eliot has written no better poem than this, and none
which seems simpler. It is of course not simple; but that
is another of its ironies.

90. F.O. MATTHIESSEN, T.S. ELIOT'S DRAMA OF BECKET,
'SATURDAY REVIEW'

12 October 1935, vol. xii, 10-11

Matthiessen (1902-1950), an American critic, wrote extensively on American literature. 'The Achievement of T.S.
Eliot', first published in 1935, has since become a
standard work. H.A. Mason's review of it in 'Scrutiny'
(4 December 1935), iv, 311-12, gives a good sense of the
'Scrutiny' group's marked antipathy towards what was seen
as Eliot's appropriation by an 'academic' mentality. 'It
is this success in detail due to careful research (there
is a very neat chapter on the "influences"), and this failure in presenting a total valuation that I consider
academic.'

That 'Murder in the Cathedral' was produced at this
summer's Canterbury Festival with apparently considerable
success, should not surprise anyone who has tried reading
it aloud. For not only do its lines fall naturally into
spoken patterns, but, even more importantly, its structure
is dramatically conceived *as a whole*, each of its two
parts building strongly up to a climax. In this respect
it is in marked contrast with Eliot's two previous

experiments with drama. 'Sweeney Agonistes,' 1927, which
broke away from the packed intricacy of his former poetry
by attempting to utilize music-hall rhythms, was left as a
fragment. 'The Rock,' which was written for production at
Sadler's Wells last year, was more in the nature of a
ritualistic pageant than a play.

But in this play presenting the martyrdom of Becket,
the poet has worked out an original and effective form.
Its general construction and its choruses bear a kinship
to the kind of classical drama represented by Milton's
'Samson'; in its characterization by types, especially in
the four Tempters in the first part and the four Knights
in the second, it shows a relationship also to the medieval morality plays. But it is naturally far more supple
than these latter. The varied movement of its long lines
seems often to have sprung from the response of the poet's
ear to the cadences of the Bible and the Catholic Mass.
As a result it demonstrates at last the fruitfulness of
the belief that Eliot voiced in his Dialogue on Dramatic
Poetry in 1928, that the essentially dramatic quality of
church ritual might again furnish a stimulation and release for poetic drama.

Recent criticism has tended to insist that a poet should
should find his material in his immediate surroundings,
claiming that otherwise he takes refuge in a world of his
own fancy and fails to portray an authentic relation with
the urgent problems of society. And it is probably a
matter of considerable skepticism to many readers as to
wherein the career of a twelfth-century archbishop can
have much relevancy to existence as they know it. What
Eliot argued, in pointing out that Pound's translations
from the early Italian poets are often much more 'modern'
than his contemporary sketches, seems to me far more
searching: that 'it is irrelevant whether what you see,
really see, as a human being is Arnaut Daniel or your
greengrocer'; the important consideration is to grasp
the permanent elements in human nature. To what degree
Eliot has grasped and portrayed such elements in this
poem can be briefly suggested by a speech in which Thomas,
addressing one of his Priests, meditates on the lot of
the Chorus, the working women of Canterbury:

[Quotes CPP, p. 245, 'They speak better' to 'forever
still'.]

The full weight and meaning of such a passage can be
appreciated only in its context; but it is at once apparent how closely its assumptions relate to Eliot's long
absorption in the view of life that has been best

expressed in poetry by Dante. Here, in this speech of
Becket's, Eliot reveals an increased share of the depth
of understanding which also characterizes Dante, not
merely of an acute part of life but of its total pattern,
a pattern that embraces not only 'the eternal burden' but
'the perpetual glory' as well. Here is a voicing of the
subtle interweaving of suffering, striving, and acceptance
that unite to form the attitude that finds expression
in such a line in the 'Paradiso' as

la sua voluntade è nostra pace.

Here, in this mature reflection on the incalculably intricate relation between feeling and action, is the poetic
statement of what Eliot has in mind when, discussing the
relation of the individual to society, he refers to 'the
Catholic paradox: society is for the salvation of the
individual and the individual must be sacrificed to
society. Communism is merely a heresy, but a heresy is
better than nothing.'
    The dramatic conflict in the first part of the work is
an inner one, of a sort that shows Eliot even more clearly
than ever in the tradition of Henry James, and, more
especially here, of Hawthorne. For the conflict is
Becket's struggle against pride and his final transcendence over it. The last Tempter speaks to him insidi-
ously in words that had often been Becket's own thoughts,
luring him on to martyrdom not as a result of losing his
will in God's, but as an act of self-aggrandizement, as a
final overweening of his pride. Tortured by a dilemma in
which it seems to him that he can 'neither act nor suffer
without perdition,' and where all existence consequently
seems unreal, he fights his way through to his final resolve:

Now is my way clear, now is the meaning plain:
Temptation shall not come in this kind again.
The last temptation is the greatest treason:
To do the right deed for the wrong reason.

Thus fortified, his will at last made perfect in acceptance of God's will, he continues to maintain the supremacy
of the law of God above the law of man, and goes forward,
in the second part, to his death at the hands of the
Knights.
    It is upon his consecration to perseverance in his
career and the world's denial of its value that the dramatic conflict of the second part hinges. Immediately after
the murder, in the most effectively unexpected passage of

the play, the Knights themselves turn to the audience, and, speaking in prose, conduct a systematic defense of their act. The writing of their speeches is masterly in its wit and irony: the Knights fall naturally into all the clichés of an actual present day parliamentary debate.

The contrast between them and Becket is thoroughly presented. Becket argues throughout - in passages which illuminate Eliot's apprehension of human history - that the Knights, by judging only from results, by deferring always to the appearance of social circumstance, have blurred all distinction between good and evil. In consequence of their conception of deterministic process, no individual can be blamed for oppression, exploitation, or crime that he undertakes in the cause of the State. There are only social forces and expediency, the responsibility of a human will for its own actions has been utterly lost. But in opposing this doctrine with his life, in reasserting the value of the idea as rising above that of the fact, Becket's is never a plea for the individual without the deepest obligations to society. His most characteristic tones sound in his experienced thoughts, again concluding in the image of the turning wheel, on the inexorability of man's fate as part of a force far greater than himself:

[Quotes CPP, p. 247, 'We do not know' to 'on which he turns'.]

The samples of the verse that I have been able to include here by no means suggest its freedom and variety. Never departing in any of his variations far enough from the norm of blank verse to break down his formal pattern, Eliot reveals throughout the controlled mastery of technique that, among other living poets writing in English, only Yeats can rival.

The lines quoted are sufficient, however, to show this play's principal defect. Though the language is both sharp and precise, it is extremely bare. It avails itself very little of the new life that comes from sensuous imagery; and compared with Eliot's early work, many passages, particularly those spoken by the Priests, seem attenuated. A relative lack of density also emerges in comparing the play as a whole with 'The Waste Land.' This is partly owing to the fact that in 'The Waste Land' the poet employed symbols which maintained the action continually in the present at the same time that he was exploring analogies with the past. In the play, though centering throughout on problems that reveal the 'permanent in human nature,' he has not made that complete

fusion. His imagination has not created the illusion of
a four-dimensional world; the characters remain partly
abstractions. Putting it in terms of the usual objection
to historical fiction, one could say that the life represented is lacking something in immediacy and urgency, an
objection that is forgotten only in the face of a 'Corio-
lanus' or a 'Phèdre.' Nevertheless, this play – the title
of which, with its unfortunately smart suggestion of a
detective story I have done my best to avoid – even
though it does not reach the rank of Eliot's most nearly
perfect work of art, 'Ash-Wednesday,' demonstrates how
Eliot has survived both popularity and unpopularity,
both generously bestowed frequently for the wrong reasons.
He has gone on undistracted, cultivating and perfecting
his craft, and bringing to bear upon it his accruing
experience.

91. EDWARD SHILLITO, REVIEW, 'CHRISTIAN CENTURY'

2 October 1935, vol. lii, 1249-50

Shillito (1872-1948), an Anglican clergyman, and poet,
published a number of works of Christian apologetics,
including 'Man's Other Religion' (1933) and 'The Way of
the Witnesses' (1936).

At the Canterbury festival in June, Mr. T.S. Eliot's play,
'Murder in the Cathedral,' was produced. It marks an
advance in the work of this poet. Last year he wrote 'The
Rock,' but in his new play he has done what he could not
do in that; he has shaped a drama which has a unity
throughout, such as a Greek drama had. In his earlier
work it was chiefly in the choruses that the reader looked
for the mind of Mr. Eliot. The new drama, which deals
with the death of Archbishop Thomas Becket, is of one
piece and everywhere shows the same creative imagination.
Mr. T.S. Eliot in his new work has won for religious drama
a fresh hearing. Whether we admire it or not, we cannot
ignore it. In my judgment it is a noble drama of enduring
worth.
    Like other supposed revolutionaries in literature, Mr.
Eliot is in reality a reverent student of the great
traditions. His method is in many ways like that of the
Greek tragedians and yet it is new, since it is handled by
a new thinker living in new spiritual realms.

It is strictly historical and yet while all the time
the reader is in the Canterbury of 1170, he is haunted by
the thought that the conflict is still taking place. All
the great spiritual conflicts are never finally answered.
It belongs to the greatness of a play that, even when the
modern scene is not mentioned, it should be before the
reader's inner eye. While he thinks of Canterbury 1170,
he may be in Moscow or Munich 1935. There is still the
question before us how the two kingdoms are to be related,
the kingdom of nature and the kingdom of grace; the state
and the church; the prince and the spiritual ruler; the
law of man and the law of God.

The one supreme difficulty for the writer of religious
drama is to find a scene of action in which the spiritual
world shall find true and indeed inevitable expression.
The murder of Becket in the cathedral provides such an
action. It was no accident; the deed was not done by some
madmen with no intelligible purpose. As the poet tells the
story, it was a significant deed, taking its place as a
crisis in a drama, which deals with one of the great
issues for man, not in that age but in all ages. St.
Thomas himsels sees clearly what his death means:

It is not in time that my death shall be known;
It is out of time that my decision is taken
If you call that decision
To which my whole being gives entire consent.
I give my life
To the law of God above the law of Man.
Those who do not the same
How should they know what I do?

There had been times in the life of Becket, in which
the loyalties of his life had been disordered. He had
submitted himself to the temporal power to secure his
ends as a servant of God. Now he resists one by one the
tempters who call him back to this and other passages of
his life. He stands before us in the play not as a man
who has kept one way from youth. Thomas says of himself:

[Quotes CPP, p. 258, 'Thirty years ago' to 'equally
desirable'.]

And afterwards ambition had come to him to win power as
the servant of a king. But then the call had come to him
to serve God above all other services. It is with this
Thomas Becket we have to do. Tempters in the play call
him back to the easier ways of his past. But he scorns
them. One tempter alone makes an appeal to him and this
because he interprets to him the secret thoughts and
desires against which he has always to fight.

Why is he ready to die? What motive is moving him?

Why do martyrs die? The fourth tempter reveals the temptation which may come to the servant of God who is set in
a place where he may retreat or be faithful even unto
death. Thomas may win a kingly rule from his tomb; at his
glittering shrine men would bend the knee. The time would
come when that sanctuary would be pillaged; yet he would
be in a glory surpassing all that earth would give. Who
would not suffer the brief pain of death for this glory?
The tempter says:

> Seek the way of martyrdom, make yourself the lowest
> On earth, to be high in heaven.

Thomas knows what these voices mean. He knows that the
man who is faced by death for the sake of God may be tempted to do the right thing for the wrong motive. But in
the sermon which he preaches on Christmas morning he tells
what Christian martyrdom is and in the spirit of his own
words he makes perfect his will:

> Ambition fortifies the will of man to become ruler
> over other men; it operates with deception, cajolery
> and violence, it is the action of impurity upon impur-
> ity. Not so in Heaven. A martyr or saint is always
> made by the design of God, for His love of men, to warn
> them and to lead them, to bring them back to His ways.
> A martyrdom is never the design of man; for the true
> martyr is he who has become the instrument of God, who
> has lost his will in the will of God, not lost it but
> found it, for he has found freedom in submission to
> God. The martyr no longer desires anything for him-
> self, not even the glory of martyrdom.

In this faith the archbishop offers himself to God,
ready to suffer with his blood.

> This is the sign of the church always,
> The sign of blood. Blood for blood.
> His blood given to buy my life,
> My blood given to pay for His death,
> My death for His death.

It is not hard, even for those who have not seen the
drama, to imagine how impressive it must have been.
Not since 'St Joan' has there been any play on the English
stage in which such tremendous issues as this have been
treated with such mastery of thought, as well as dramatic
power.
The chorus consists of women of Canterbury; they use

the same splendid incantations which were used in 'The
Rock.' These women let the spectator see how the common
folk are involved in this murder. Every sorrow has a kind
of end, for there is no time in life to grieve long.

> But this, this is out of life, this is out of time
> An instant eternity of evil and wrong. It shows a
>   world that is 'wholly foul.'

But as the book is put down, the outstanding memory is
of the discussion of martyrdom and of the way in which the
martyr must bear himself if he is not to sin even in his
high calling. The higher the spiritual destiny the more
terrible is the sin of the man who does not make his
calling and election sure. The martyr has not the same
temptation as other men; he has his own; and that is a
more searching temptation than any other he has known
before.
Thomas Becket will die; but how will he die?
The question has a curiously modern value. In India
Mahatma Gandhi believes in martyrdom; but he believes in
seeking it as a way of winning the dull and listless
children of men to his cause. This is not martyrdom in
the Christian use of the word.
A Christian must be ready to die for his faith, and he
must die gladly, for this is the only way in which under
certain conditions he can serve. But he must not seek
death to win spiritual glory, nor must he die as a deliberate way of serving a cause. He must suffer in pure
love to God. If I give my body to be burned and have not
love, I am nothing.
Canterbury is a city in which no one can escape from
the memory of that hour in which the knights killed the
archbishop. It is fitting that such a martyr should be
remembered there. It is no less fitting when it is recalled through what stages Thomas Becket had passed before
he won his crown. The church of Christ rightly remembers
the last act into which the martyr puts his heart:

> For wherever a saint has dwelt, wherever a martyr has
>   given his blood for the blood of Christ,
> There is holy ground, and the sanctity shall not depart
>   from it
> Though armies trample over it, though sightseers come
>   with guide-books looking over it.

From such places the earth is forever renewed. Let us
praise the noble army of martyrs.
But it is also a true theme for drama to show how in

that last hour the soul of the martyr met and conquered
the last temptation, which is to do right from the wrong
motive.

92. FREDERICK A. POTTLE, FROM DRAMA OF ACTION, 'YALE
REVIEW'

December 1935, vol. xxv, 426-9

Pottle (b. 1897), an American academic, was Professor of
English at Yale from 1930 to 1966.

Drama in our days is struggling towards a new birth; the
change can best be described by saying that our most
gifted authors are deeply dissatisfied with drama of
character and are turning to drama of plot. Their lively
interest in Greek tragedy is symptomatic. Mr. MacLeish
studies Sophocles and Mr. O'Neill refers to Aeschylus.
But to write genuine drama of plot, of action, in our days
is not altogether a matter of choice. The essence of
Greek drama is religious certainty; an unshaken conviction
that there is an order of things in the universe more real
and more important than the individual hero. The difficulty which most modern playwrights face is that, lacking
religious certainty, they have to invent an equivalent -
to set up deliberately the external sanctions by which
alone drama of plot can be organized. They start with a
considerable - perhaps an insuperable - handicap. An
artist who really feels dogmatic Christianity will have
the advantage; and so also, it appears, will a convert to
that most striking of modern religions - communism.
   In June, 1934, Mr. T.S. Eliot published his first completed drama, 'The Rock,' a pageant-play written and produced in the interest of a London church fund. 'The Rock'
was admitted Anglican propaganda. A clergyman furnished
Mr. Eliot with a scenario for which he wrote words. The
internal evidence of collaboration is abundant. No one,
familiar with Eliot's earlier works, would expect him to
have chosen just that subject matter, not to have put it
together in just that way. Yet the foreign matter is, to
a remarkable extent, dominated by his astringent personality, and the overtones of the piece are so characteristic

that one wonders whether they may not have caused his
clerical sponsors some misgivings. He introduced a
chorus, and within the speeches of the chorus (which probably contain the best Christian poetry of our time) he
moved freely, reiterating that arid and austere Christian
faith which he had announced in 'Ash-Wednesday.' His
scenario, one fancies, must have tended towards a facile
optimism, but for him the air was still thoroughly small
and dry. He repudiated the notion of progress in the
Church Militant. Churches must be always building, not
as part of a slow but ultimately triumphant penetration of
the powers of darkness, but because churches are always
decaying and we must bear witness.

> If the blood of Martyrs is to flow on the steps
> We must first build the steps;
> And if the Temple is to be cast down
> We must first build the Temple.

Man's duty is simple and single: it is to 'make perfect
his will.'
     In 'Murder in the Cathedral' Eliot resumes that text
and founds an entire action upon it. The murder of
Thomas à Becket is only a terminus, clearly announced from
the very beginning of the piece. Far from striving to
escape martyrdom, Thomas welcomes it. His struggle is to
make perfect his will before the events; to purge himself
of the last and most deadly manifestation of pride, which
is 'to do the right thing for the wrong reason.' Parallel
with his struggle runs another, expressed in the speeches
of the chorus of poor Canterbury women: the struggle of
the ordinary unsaintly mortal to nerve himself for the
bloody working out of Destiny. The Archbishop is only too
eager for the consummation; the women in sick and shudder-
ing suspense beseech him to depart out of their coasts and
spare them the awful intrusion of the Divine Will into the
tolerable pattern of their lives. With this starkly
simple plot, Eliot achieves a drama perhaps more nearly
Greek in its method than anything hitherto written in
English.
     In dramatic writing Eliot deliberately avoids that
obscurity, both of style and sequence, which makes 'The
Waste Land' and 'Ash-Wednesday' such slow reading.
'Murder in the Cathedral' can be read rapidly, but like
other good verse tragedies it contains some lines which
give up their full content only after patient study and
some others concerning the meaning of which there will
always be difference of opinion. The method is completely unhistorical and unrealistic: Thomas's Four

Tempters instance 'The Catherine wheel, the pantomime cat,
The prizes given at the children's party, The prize
awarded for the English Essay' as examples of life's dis-
appointments; and the Third Knight, justifying himself to
the audience for the murder, shows that he has heard of
the execution of Archbishop Laud and the humiliation of
Archbishop Davidson in the rejection of the Revised
Prayer-Book. Some of the lines assigned to the chorus
have no dramatic propriety - as, for example, that
extremely powerful and metaphysical passage in which the
women proclaim the identity of their flesh with the worms
of the soil and the living creatures of the deep. In this
it may be thought that Mr. Eliot has been too clever. The
chorus which follows immediately after the murder is peculiarly in character for the 'scrubbers and sweepers of
Canterbury,' and seems to gain tremendously thereby:

> Clean the air! clean the sky! wash the wind! take stone
>   from stone and wash them.
> The land is foul, the water is foul, our beasts and
>   ourselves defiled with blood.

The verse shows Eliot's curious and inexhaustible
resourcefulness in both rhymed and unrhymed measures, and
he reveals in addition a fertility of dramatic invention
which will surprise those who have not read 'Sweeney
Agonistes' and 'The Rock' with attention. To devote an
entire scene to a Christmas sermon preached by Thomas in
the cathedral four days before his death was daring, but
the device succeeds. Even more audacious is that of
having the Four Knights, after the murder, step forward
in turn and justify their deed in Shavian prose - a device
for bringing various modern historical judgments of Thomas
into the framework of the play. But to my mind the most
impressive of all Eliot's feats are his liturgical adap-
tations in the Second Part of the play: the three introits
at the beginning; the parody of the 'Dies Irae' spoken by
the chorus outside the cathedral against the singing of
the hymn inside; the concentration of blasphemy achieved
just before the murder by having the Four Knights,
slightly tipsy, speak in turn lines from a revivalist
hymn and a negro spiritual....

'Collected Poems 1909-1935'

London, 2 April 1936; New York, 21 May 1936

93. JOHN HAYWARD, LONDON LETTER, 'NEW YORK SUN'

28 March 1936, 19

Hayward (1905-65) was editorial adviser to the Cresset
Press, vice-president of the Bibliographical Society and
editorial director of the 'Book Collector'. He edited
Eliot's 'Selected Prose' in 1953. For a sympathetic
account of his life and friendship with Eliot, see Helen
Gardner, 'The Composition of "Four Quartets"' (London,
1978), pp. 5-13.

...If you are as tired as I sometimes feel of the twitter-
ings of the fledgling poets about whom so much has been
written in the last year or so, you will turn eagerly to
Eliot's new volume. To those who are already familiar
with his work, this volume offers three things. In the
first place it enables one to trace the evolution of his
poetry over a period of twenty-five years, from 'Prufrock'
(1917), to the beautiful mystical poem, 'Burnt Norton,'
which was completed only a month or so ago. Secondly,
it provides, for the first time, a collection of a number
of pieces that have hitherto been scattered in various,
not always easily accessible places - notably the 'Ariel
Poems,' which originally appeared separately as Christmas
pamphlets, and the Choruses from 'The Rock,' which lose
nothing, indeed gain from being isolated from the text of
the pageant-play in which they were incorporated. And
finally, it contains besides 'Burnt Norton' - the longest
and most important poem Eliot has written, apart from the

dramatic choruses in 'The Rock' and 'Murder in the Cathedral,' since the sequence 'Ash Wednesday' (1930) - a number of short lyrics, which have only been privately printed. Here is 'Usk,' the third of five 'Landscapes' (The Usk, by the way, is an English river, in Monmouthshire on the border of Wales, which Eliot visited last summer).

[Quotes 'Usk', CPP, p. 140.]

What I think must strike anyone who reads, or rather rereads Eliot's poems is the fact that so much that once seemed obscure now presents only occasional difficulties. I remember so well the frenzied discussions at Cambridge when 'The Waste Land' was published. And now I cannot help wondering what they were all about. I do not deny that difficulties still exist - 'Burnt Norton' with its allusions to St. John of the Cross and the London Underground is not a 'simple' poem - but they do not seriously interfere with one's enjoyment. The beauty of Eliot's poetry is apparent; but its beauty is not surface deep. The more one turns it over in one's mind the richer it becomes. For this is no dross lightly sprinkled with gold, but the ore itself.

94. EDWIN MUIR, MR. ELIOT'S POETRY, 'SPECTATOR'

3 April 1936, vol. clvi, 622

The first eighty pages in this volume are taken up by the poems which have already appeared in 'Poems 1909-1925'; the remaining hundred pages contain Mr. Eliot's poetic production for the last ten years, except for 'Murder in the Cathedral,' which is not included. This second part begins with 'Ash-Wednesday,' embraces two unfinished poems, 'Sweeney Agonistes' and 'Coriolan,' ten choruses from 'The Rock,' four 'Ariel Poems,' thirteen 'Minor Poems,' and ends with 'Burnt Norton,' which is in some ways different from any of Mr. Eliot's other poems, and is one of the most remarkable, I think, that he has yet written.

It will be seen from this that Mr. Eliot has been considerably more productive during the last ten years than during the sixteen years before; but it is very difficult to judge whether he has been productive on the same level,

firstly because a writer of such individuality as his
changes the taste of his readers, and they come to his
later work with a different mind, and secondly because his
style has altered. The alteration has been towards a
greater explicitness of statement; 'Ash-Wednesday' is far
more explicit than any poetry that Mr. Eliot wrote before
it, and it represents, I think, a turning point in his
development. 'The Waste Land' is no doubt his greatest
work, but there is in it, compared with his later work, a
certain blindness both in the despair it expresses and in
turning away from despair at the end. Since 'The Hollow
Men,' where that despair reached its lowest depths, Mr.
Eliot has never expressed it again; he has taken it as a
theme, certainly, in 'Sweeney Agonistes' and other poems;
but though he is still in the midst of it, he is no longer
within it. That is to say that he is not so firmly under
the influence of his time and is more deliberately concerned with permanent things. The difference may be seen
by setting side by side:

These fragments I have shored against my ruins

from 'The Waste Land,' and

Redeem the time, redeem the dream
The token of the word unheard, unspoken

from 'Ash-Wednesday.' This difference, the difference
between despair and faith, is so great that it is very
hard to compare the two kinds of poetry that derive from
it. A good deal of the second kind is obscure, like the
first, but with a different obscurity: not the obscurity
of deep darkness, but rather that of darkness against
light. It is consequently less heavily charged and more
easy to understand, more finally comprehensible. This
must be admitted to be in its favour, unless we are to
regard obscurity in itself, deep and total obscurity, as
a poetic virtue.

The second half of the volume is nevertheless more unequal than the first. 'Sweeney Agonistes,' brilliant as
it is, is definitely in a lower class of poetry than the
rest, and doubtless is intended to be. The choruses from
'The Rock' are first of all choruses, that is compositions
intended to be spoken and to be comprehensible as soon as
spoken. They contain some beautiful poetry, they are
original in form, but they naturally lack the condensation
which Mr. Eliot's poetry has at its best. On the other
hand, almost all the shorter poems have intense concentration and perfect clarity at the same time; 'Ash-Wednesday'

and the four 'Ariel Poems' are works of great beauty; and
'Burnt Norton' is surely one of the best poems that Mr.
Eliot has ever written. Its subject is Time and its main
text a quotation from Herakleitos to the effect that the
road upwards and downwards is one and the same road.
This poem is different from the others inasmuch as it is
not at all dramatic, being a pure intellectual enquiry
into the nature and forms of Time. It alternates between
the most close argument and the most vivid imagery expressing the contradiction of Time, a contradiction implicit in the recurring phrase, 'At the still point of the
turning world.' It contains lines of great beauty:

> We move above the moving tree
> In light upon the figured leaf
> And hear upon the sodden floor
> Below, the boarhound and the boar
> Pursue their pattern as before.

That is a far more rarefied poetry than

> In the juvescence of the year
> Came Christ the tiger
> In depraved May, dogwood and chestnut, flowering judas,

but it has something in common with it, a sense of the
fabulous; the difference is that the second kind is very
much more figured and patterned (to use words that recur
frequently in it), which means that it is more thoroughly
worked out. Imagery which is thoroughly worked out often
becomes mechanical and lifeless; but in this poem both the
thought and the imagery are intensely concentrated, and
gain immensely from the development. Whether this poem
owes anything to Dante I do not know, but one might chance
the guess that Mr. Eliot's later development as a poet
has been away from the Elizabethans, by whom he was so
much influenced at the beginning, towards Dante.

   Mr. Eliot's position as a poet is established, and his
work has been more thoroughly discussed than that of any
of his contemporaries. His influence on poetry has been
decisive. That influence was due chiefly to his genius
for poetry, but it was due also to certain qualities which
he held in common with some other men in his age. He has
had an influence on the form and on the attitude of poetry.
By this I do not mean that he has encouraged a kind of
poetry in which all sorts of poetical quotations and
reminiscences alternate with realistic descriptions of
contemporary life. This method was employed very effectively in 'The Waste Land' because it was a natural part

of the scheme; it has not been employed successfully by
any of Mr. Eliot's imitators, and as a set poetic method
it is obviously ridiculous. Mr. Eliot's dramatic approach
has influenced the form of poetry away from the purely
lyrical, and his exercise of the historical sense has
influenced the attitude of poetry. The first influence
has been entirely salutary; it has led to a necessary reform of poetic language and a spirit of objectivity which
had been buried in the degeneration of Romanticism. The
reliance on the historical sense Mr. Eliot himself seems
to have lost in his later work; it does not go with religious poetry; it cannot survive the vision of 'the still
point of the turning world.' But even in 'The Waste Land'
he used it conditionally, for there too, if less explicitly, he was concerned with permanent things, which are
not affected by history. When the historical sense is
employed without reference to these permanent things it
leads to a shallowness of the imaginative faculty, for it
robs the individual existence of meaning and can in itself
give no meaning to society, since society is still in becoming, and by the laws of history will always be. Where
the historical sense has been used in this way, the
responsibility is not Mr. Eliot's; but it partly explains
why his influence should be so great with poets who do not
hold his beliefs.

95. PETER QUENNELL, MR. T.S. ELIOT, 'NEW STATESMAN'

18 April 1936, vol. xi, 603-4

Quennell (b. 1905), an English poet and critic, wrote quite
frequently for the 'Criterion', especially on the poetry
of the French Symbolists.
    This review also contains a discussion of Eliot's
'Essays Ancient and Modern', published in London on 5
March 1936.

Were a bibliography to be composed of the various critical
studies that have been devoted to Mr. T.S. Eliot during
the last ten or fifteen years, it would make up a fairly
considerable volume. For almost every modern critic has
had his say. There are, indeed, very few literary

undergraduates who have not, at one time or another, voiced their appreciation of his poems; and, even in the Far East, solemn spectacled faces are earnestly bent, and round shaven skulls dolorously scratched, over 'The Waste Land', 'Prufrock' or 'Ash-Wednesday'. At Oxford, ten years ago, admiration of 'The Waste Land' had given rise to a new and, now and then, extremely tiresome form of intellectual snobbism. The intelligentsia were as knowledgeable and talkative about the relationship and precise significance of Mr. Eugenides and Phlebas the Phoenician as their Bullingdon equivalent about the genealogical complications of the Stud Book; 'La Figlia Che Piange' provided the *leit-motif* of a dozen adolescent love-affairs. And yet, although the mass of writing around Mr. T.S. Eliot is by now probably much more voluminous than the whole corpus of his published verse and prose, it is still possible to retrace one's steps through his poems, experiencing as one reads a continuous movement of pleasure, interest and surprise. Perhaps surprise is the final criterion of poetic excellence. However hackneyed it may have become, no poem of real quality can quite lose the power of administering that kind of salutary emotional shock which, if only for a few minutes, possesses the brain and shows us the familiar universe in a refreshing light. 'Collected Poems' embraces Mr. T.S. Eliot's entire poetic output between 1909 and 1935. It covers the same ground as 'Poems', published several years back, but includes 'Ash-Wednesday', four poems published in the Ariel Series, a quantity of minor and unfinished work, as well as a new and remarkably accomplished poem, 'Burnt Norton'.

Here is a panorama of Mr. Eliot's poetic achievement. Beginning with the section headed 'Prufrock', 1917, one is at first startled by the brilliance and liveliness of those early poems – we know them so well; yet, even today, how well they stand re-reading! – then a little puzzled and disconcerted because, although certain elements in 'Prufrock' have continued to develop until we reach the uncommon rhythmic virtuosity of 'Burnt Norton' (written nearly twenty years later) they contain another element that has very largely disappeared. In 'The Love Song of J. Alfred Prufrock', Mr. Eliot displays a gaiety, energy and satirical versatility that he has long since discarded. The influence of Jules Laforgue is extremely strong; but this is a Laforgue with additions and, I think, at least from the Anglo-Saxon point of view, very definite improvements. He has Laforgue's wit and dexterity without his fragility – Laforgue's skill without the touch of flatness and thinness that gives so many of La-. forgue's *vers libre* essays a slightly consumptive and

debilitated air. For there is a background of something
we can best describe as *gusto* - a sense of enjoyment that
may co-exist with a knowledge of human suffering, a love
of life not incompatible with the horror of humanity; and
from more recent works that element of gusto proved
strangely lacking. The *peur de vivre* had broken down his
poetic defences; the poet was in full retreat through 'The
Waste Land'.

Having entered it, he was obliged to find an issue. If
the influence of Laforgue had done much to shape 'Prufrock'
and 'Poems', 1920, even to the extent of suggesting
images, lines and whole passages, Baudelaire (with Tristan
Corbière as a secondary influence) was the presiding
spirit of that extraordinary poem which burst, like an
organ cactus dominating an herbaceous border, from among
the pleasant flower-beds and meandering grass-walks of
Georgian poetry. But now compare the methods of master
and disciple. When I ventured to observe that Eliot
lacked gusto, I did not, of course, mean to complain that
he lacked optimism, that he was a perverse and atrabilious
highbrow malcontent. No poet has ever expressed a deeper
or more unrelieved despair, a more uncompromising and
embittered attitude towards contemporary society, than the
author of 'Les Fleurs du Mal'. And yet how solid, sensuous and - in spite of condemnation, disgust and disenchant-
ment - how almost *appreciative* is his rendering of the real
world! The nightmare metropolis of 'Tableaux Parisiens'
reveals a depth of light and shade, hints at a beauty,
cruelty and oddity, that evoke the mingled squalor and
splendour of a modern industrial city, as they have been
evoked by no other poet or novelist. Nineteenth-century
Paris, with the old struggling against the new, as Hauss-
mann ploughed his way, amid dust and rubble, through the
labyrinth of ancient quarters, was a city full of phan-
toms and stalking memories:

> Fourmillante cité, cité pleine de rêves,
> Où le spectre en plein jour raccroche le passant ...

There was no end to the emotions of wonder and horror that
it aroused; it was intensely real to the poet, even though
its reality may have been intensely unpleasing; whereas
the landscape of twentieth-century London, glimpsed in
'The Waste Land', seems, by comparison, as drab, low-
toned and shadowily inconsequent as the stream of spirit-
less human automata trudging to their work over London
Bridge:

[Quotes 'The Waste Land', CPP, p. 62, 'Unreal City' to

'stroke of nine'.]

For Mr. Eliot shares the malady of his epoch; and that
malady - at any rate, among intellectuals- comes not so
much from a positive misdirection of energy as from a mere
lack of vitality, not so much from any failure of sensitiveness as from a general lowering of temperature that
leaves us face to face with a world where the good is
flavourless, the bad insignificant, where our values,
slowly and quietly, seem to be crumbling away to form part
of a general desert-level of indifference and ill-will.
Such is the predominant mood of 'The Waste Land'. And a
historian of the future may find that the poem affords him
interesting material for a study of the period, noting,
moreover, that when Mr. Eliot escaped from the wilderness
he did so by taking refuge in a narrow and sectarian, but
evidently absorbing and satisfying, faith, and that, under
the influence of this new faith, he was to achieve some
of his most exquisite and finely balanced later poems. We
may regret that the gaiety and gusto of 'Prufrock' should
already have begun to disappear in 'The Waste Land', and
we may regret that, on emerging from 'The Waste Land',
he should have limited himself to a smaller poetic field;
but a poet, after all, can only progress along the lines
that his individual temperament lays down; and, by
remaining faithful to his temperament - one of Protestant
and transatlantic puritanism, exasperated by contact with
an alien culture - Mr. Eliot has continued to perfect his
gift. 'Collected Poems', then, is a valuable and
fascinating book because it gives a bird's-eye view of his
poetic progress, from his early, brilliant but derivative
excursions, right up to the present day. It is particularly interesting, for example, to see the admirable
choruses of 'The Rock' divorced from their somewhat less
stumbling context, and to be able to trace Mr. Eliot's
link with the main tradition of English devotional verse.
About the poems in 'Ash-Wednesday' there was an occasional
touch of almost pre-Raphaelite prettiness; and, personally, I prefer the choruses; since Mr. Eliot must be
numbered among the very few modern poets who have learned
to combine eloquence and simplicity of statement with a
feeling for poetic expression in its more allusive form:

[Quotes 'The Rock', Chorus III, CPP, pp. 154-5, 'A Cry
from the North' to 'lost golf balls'.]

Nor is 'Burnt Norton' disappointing. In harmony and
flexibility it is the equal of Mr. Eliot's earlier poems;
and, though the first section opens in a style rather too

reminiscent of the text-book:

> Time present and time past
> Are both perhaps present in time future,
> And time future contained in time past.
> If all time is eternally present
> All time is unredeemable.

it closes with a long passage of remarkable felicity, to
which quotation and abbreviation do less than justice:

[Quotes 'Burnt Norton', CPP, pp. 171-2, 'What might have
been' to 'in your mind', 'Other echoes' to 'are looked at'
and 'Go, said the bird' to 'is always present'.]

   But, if the acquisition of faith has added to the delicacy – while detracting, I believe, from the breadth and
variety – of Mr. Eliot's poetic method, it has had another
effect on his discursive and critical work. 'The Sacred
Wood' and 'Homage to John Dryden', though often abused
by academic journalists, were among the most exciting and
illuminating critical products of their time. 'For Lancelot Andrewes', which contained a suggestion that
Andrewes was a finer stylist than John Donne (apparently
because he was the more orthodox theologian) struck a sad
shock through the heart of many a hopeful reader, who
expected something as good as Mr. Eliot's essays on the
Elizabethan dramatists and seventeenth-century poets.
'Essays Ancient and Modern' is 'Lancelot Andrewes'
revised, corrected and brought up to date. The all-too-
famous foreword – plumping for classicism in literature,
royalism in politics and Anglo-catholicism in religion –
is now judged to have served its purpose and has been
removed. Studies of Machiavelli and Crashaw, which their
author considers unsatisfactory, have also been deleted;
while a paper on Middleton does not appear since it has
found a place in 'Elizabethan Essays'. To fill the gap,
we have two articles written round religious or semi-
religious themes, Religion and Literature and Catholicism and International Order, an essay – sound, but not
particularly exciting – entitled Modern Education and
the Classics, an introduction to 'The "Pensées" of
Pascal' (in which Mr. Eliot explains the dangerous fascination of Montaigne by comparing that unfortunate sage to
'a fog, a gas, a fluid, insidious element') and a note,
in his best manner, on the poetry of Tennyson. Here the
critic uses only aesthetic arguments; and the result is
wise, sensitive and brilliantly expounded.

96. CYRIL CONNOLLY, A MAJOR POET.   THE INFLUENCE OF
MR ELIOT, 'SUNDAY TIMES'

3 May 1936, 8

Connolly (1903-74), a well-known English critic and man of
letters, was founder-editor of 'Horizon' from 1939 until
1950.

A good way to gauge the importance of a writer is to try
to imagine what his subject would have been like without
him. Let us suppose Mr. Eliot had never existed, what
would English poetry be like to-day? I think it would
have advanced no further from the Georgian poets than they
had progressed from the 'nineties. There would be Yeats,
of course, but otherwise we would still be reading
Flecker and Housman and Ralph Hodgson, and writing like
them. They would have been the intellectual poets, themselves in advance of the other Georgians, with Sassoon
and the Sitwells as the last word in youthful and fero-
cious opposition. Pound, without Eliot's appreciation
and adaptation of him, would not be important. Auden
would have been no more than a young Kipling of the Left
(which he may yet become), Spender a deflated Rupert
Brooke, Day Lewis a baby W.J. Turner, while MacNeice and
Barker could not have existed at all.

Dignity and Distinction

   The theme of poetry would still be the lyrical expression of simple nostalgia; Babylon, Popacatapetl, Innis-
free, Grantchester, Sussex - 'The meadows of England
shining in the rain' - we would not have got beyond them,
and the best poetry would still consist of exercises in
homesickness and be written by old laureates or young
medallists, or by imitative and large-hearted women.
Eliot, in fact, has brought to English poetry dignity and
intellectual distinction, without which it might well have
gone the way of most modern English music, novel-writing,
and architecture. But he has brought to it as well an
exquisite lyrical gift: that real beauty of diction which
provides the aesthetic reader with a unique emotion, and
to which hardly any other modern poet, except Yeats, can
lay claim.

How many single lines, for instance, can you remember
from Auden, Spender, and Day Lewis, or, for that matter,
from more conservative poets? Yet Eliot is packed with
them. 'There will be time to murder and create,' 'The
troubled midnight and the noon's repose,' 'Supine on the
floor of a narrow canoe,' 'The infirm glory of the positive hour,' 'The awful daring of a moment's surrender.'
     I often think what an experience it must have been,
during the second year of the war, to have come upon that
small paper-covered, biscuit-coloured volume with the odd
title, 'Prufrock,' and to have opened it at the first
poem:-

         Let us go then, you and I,
     When the evening is spread out against the sky
     Like a patient etherised upon a table;

It must have provided one or two people with the fine
shock of discovering a new talent, such as a Roman must
have had from another opening couplet:-

     Cynthia prima suis miserum me cepit ocellis
         Contactum nullis ante cupidinibus.

                The Maker of Mysteries

     Unfortunately, the extraordinary freshness, the
special gaiety of 'Prufrock,' a gaiety partly due to the
influence of Laforgue, from which much is imitated, and
partly to the dandyism of those young men of 1913 (we
find it also in 'Crome Yellow' and in Ronald Firbank) disappears from the later Eliot. This is largely due to the
influence of Pound, who brings, after the 'clever' period
of the 'Sweeney' poems, in which his dandyism is finally
stifled by his horror for life, two new features into
Eliot. They are the introduction of unassimilated quotations into the body of his work, and the more serious
introduction of a mystical, but also rather muddy and
disingenuous bardic quality into his thought. He is no
longer the pleasant young man who confides in the reader,
but the prophet, the maker of myseries, descending only
to tell us, as of Shantih, for instance, that 'The Peace
which passeth understanding is a feeble translation of
this word.' Through the despair of the 'cactus' poems,
the hopefulness of 'Ash-Wednesday,' and the severity of
the choruses from 'The Rock,' the same lyrical power persists however, and it is found in equal purity in the
long new poem, 'Burnt Norton,' a philosophical meditation

on Time, with which this book closes,

> The Eagle soars in the summit of heaven,
> The Hunter with his dogs pursues his circuit,
> O perpetual revolution of configured stars,
> O perpetual recurrence of determined seasons
> O world of spring and autumn, birth and dying.
>
> — From 'The Rock.'

> Time and the bell have buried the day,
> The black cloud carries the sun away,
> Will the sunflower turn to us, will the clematis
> Stray down, bend to us; tendril and spray clutch and
>   cling?
> Chill
> Fingers of yew be curled
> Down on us? After the kingfisher's wing
> Has answered light to light, and is silent, the light is
>   still
> At the still point of the turning world.
>
> — From 'Burnt Norton.'

The Next Station

The work of any great writer is like a train running
through various stations. At each station some admirers
get out and begin to say, 'Such a pity the train ever went
on to the next station.' Sometimes if they say this loud
enough they do actually stop the train from going any further, and then all is over with it. This is particularly
true of Eliot, who has one lot of passengers still waiting
at the terminus of the Waste Land, and another which is
not willing to follow him into the Drama, with his two
Church of England plays, 'Murder in the Cathedral' and
'The Rock.'
It is obvious, however, that the art of Mr. Eliot is
still a living spiritual force, anything may happen to it,
and whatever happens will be vastly interesting. There is
no reason even, now that he has found peace of mind in
religion, why his early lyrical and ironical high spirits,
driven out by post-war depression, should not return, or
else why his mastery of language, and his incessant and
conscientious experiment and adaptation (for Mr. Eliot is
one of the few writers who deliberately imitate, yet are
able to absorb and give, unlike Pound, an added power and
meaning to the thing imitated) should not lead him into
unpredictable discoveries. For he is gifted with that
great rarity of these days: an imaginative and emotional
staying power, poetical long-life.

97. MALCOLM COWLEY, AFTERTHOUGHTS ON T.S. ELIOT, 'NEW
REPUBLIC'

20 May 1936, vol. lxxxvii, 49

Cowley (b. 1898), American critic and poet, was a member
of the staff of 'New Republic' from 1929 to 1944.
    In 'New Republic' (3 January 1934), lxxvii, 216-18, he
described the reaction of some of the younger writers
against Eliot after 'The Waste Land', because it seemed to
them as though Eliot considered the present inferior to
the past. The essay was reprinted in 'Exile's Return'
(1934) and in Unger, pp. 30-3. In the review printed
below Cowley developed his earlier doubts about the nature
of Eliot's lasting importance.

T.S. Eliot's early poems are beginning to seem less cos-
mically important than they did in 1925, when they first
appeared in a collected volume. It is harder now to
admire their deliberate obscurity, and this is particularly true in the case of 'The Waste Land,' which has been
discussed and elucidated at greater length than any other
modern poem, without answering half the questions that it
raises. Just what is the function in it of the drowned
man, Phlebas the Phoenician? Why are we told in a note
that he suggests the Western asceticism of St. Augustine?
Are we meant to identify Eliot himself with the Fisher
King - that is, with the legendary monarch of a country
that had been rendered waterless and desolate at the very
moment when its king was struck with impotence for the sin
of falling in love with a pagan maid? In that case, has
the pagan any connection with the Russian noblewoman
remembered longingly by Eliot in the first episode? The
more I study the poem as a whole, the more it seems personal and arbitrary, not so much the embodiment of a
great contemporary problem as a private diary written in
rebuses.
    On the other hand, it is quite possible that both 'The
Waste Land' and other poems of the same period have been
partly spoiled for me by all the imitations they have
called forth. Some of these are actually better than
Eliot's own work, in the sense of being more sustained in
mood and richer in images: he is beginning to suffer by
comparison with his ablest followers. Moreover, I am beginning to doubt whether his enormous influence over his

contemporaries is a just or accurate measure of his own
poetical achievement. Some of the very greatest poets –
Shakespeare, Milton, for example – have had a less tangible effect on other writers than anyone would judge from
their personal eminence. A possible explanation is that
they did their job too well: nobody else was impelled to
do it again or felt sure of doing it better. Eliot, with
his habit of making suggestions that he never developed
and of changing every subject without exhausting it, has
tempted others to continue his work. In the past, his
very faults have attracted disciples.

The poems he has written since 1930, which occupy more
than half of the new collected edition, have been much
less widely imitated. Most of them are devotional poems,
a fact which many critics might assume to be connected
with their indifferent quality as verse. But the connection here, which really exists, is a result of Eliot's
personal reaction to his new faith. He has developed into
a peculiarly doleful type of Christian, given more to describing the sorrows of this world than to celebrating the
joys of the next. Even when he writes a Christmas poem,
'Journey of the Magi,' he fills it with lamentations – it
was the worst time of the year for such a long trip, the
camel men were mutinous, the inns were dirty and expensive, and the very birth of the Christ Child was 'hard and
bitter agony for us, like Death, our death.' Yet this is
one of Eliot's happier and more factual pieces; elsewhere
he loses himself in a mist of abstract sorrows. During
the last half-century there have been several distinguished Catholic poets in France, but their best works
have been poems of repentance, of pity, or of abuse
directed against the infidels. Eliot has simply not
sinned enough to make his repentance interesting as
literature. He writes poems of pity for nobody but himself, and he is too frigidly polite to abuse his enemies.
His Anglo-Catholicism has so far been intellectual rather
than emotional or sensuous, with the result that his religious poems have no more color than a New England sermon.
As compensation for this lack of appeal to eye and touch
and taste, he has tried to give his verse a more complicated music, but in achieving this effect he depends too
much on simple repetition:

Only through time time is conquered ...
Distracted from distraction by distraction ...
World not world but that which is not world ...

But 'Murder in the Cathedral' – his latest work and the
only one not included in this volume – seems to show that

his talents are being revived. There are still too many
repeated words, too many abstract words; there is an almost
terrifying absence of sensuous impressions; but there is
also more energy and more deftness in meter than he has
shown since 'The Waste Land.' The murder of Thomas Becket,
which is the central incident of the play, is handled with
a sequence of surprising effects. First the chorus chants
while the Archbishop is being killed, then the four murderers come forward and excuse themselves to the audience
in the language of modern politicians (and the satire here
is exceptionally keen), then the First Priest asks who
shall guide us now that the Church lies bereft, then finally the Third Priest, after answering that the Church is
only fortified by persecution, thunders a malediction
against the assassins:

> Go, weak sad men, lost erring souls, homeless in earth
>   or heaven.
> Go where the sunset reddens the last gray rock
> Of Brittany, or the Gates of Hercules ...
> Or sit and bite your nails in Aquitaine.

It is a magnificent curse, yet it forces comparison
with another passage that I vastly prefer to it, the passage in 'Femmes Damnées' where Baudelaire, after reporting
the courtship of two Lesbians, suddenly rises in his own
person and thunders against them:

> O lamentable victims, go ye down,
> Down, down the pathway to eternal hell –

In Baudelaire's passage there is no mechanical listing of
countries to which the culprits might flee: Gibraltar,
Morocco, Norway, Aquitaine. Instead there is indignation
bursting forth in sometimes extravagant and sometimes
homely metaphors; there is a warmth of feeling that makes
the climax of Eliot's poetic drama seem chilly and academic. Yet 'Murder in the Cathedral' is the best verse
that he has written since 1922. The shorter pieces collected in this new volume make me feel for the first time
that Eliot is a minor poet; that his apparent greatness
was forced upon him by the weakness of his contemporaries
and their yearning for a leader.

98. MARIANNE MOORE, IT IS NOT FORBIDDEN TO THINK,
'NATION' (NEW YORK)

27 May 1936, vol. cxlii, 680-1

A fuller version of this review was published in 'Predilections' (London, 1956), pp. 47-51.

The grouping of these poems - chronological through 1930,
and inclusive except for 'Murder in the Cathedral' - seems
to point to a mental chronology of evolvement and deepening technique. But two tendencies mark them all: the instinct for order and certitude, and 'contempt for sham.'
'I am not sure,' Mr. Eliot says in 'The Uses of Poetry,'
'that we can judge and enjoy a man's poetry while leaving
wholly out of account all the things for which he cared
deeply, and on behalf of which he turned his poetry to
account.' He detests a conscience, a politics, a rhetoric,
which is neither one thing nor the other. For him hell is
hell in its awareness of heaven; good is good in its distinctness from evil; precision is precision as triumphing
over vagueness. In 'The Rock' he says, 'Our age is an age
of moderate virtue And of moderate vice.' Among Peter the
Hermit's hearers were 'a few good men Many who were evil
And most who were neither.' Although as a critic, con-
fronted by apparent misapprehension, he manifests what
seems at times an almost pugnacious sincerity, by doing
his fighting in prose he is perhaps the more free to do
his feeling in verse. But in his verse, also, judgment
remains awake. His inability to be untormented by 'the
Demon of Thought' as action, in Prufrock, posits an overwhelming question:

    Oh, do not ask what is it,
    Let us go and make our visit;

and as writing is satirized in 'Lines for Cuscuscaraway
and Mirza Murad Ali Beg':

    How unpleasant to meet Mr. Eliot!
    With his features of clerical cut,

    And his conversation, so nicely
    Restricted to What Precisely
    And If and Perhaps and But.

One sees in this collected work conscience - directed
toward 'things that other people have desired,' asking
'are these things right or wrong' - and an art which from
the beginning has tended toward drama. 'The Waste Land'
(1922) characterizes a first period. In 'Ash-Wednesday'
and later Mr. Eliot is not warily considering 'matters
that I with myself too much discuss Too much explain'; he
is *in* them; and 'Ash-Wednesday' is perhaps the poem of the
book, as submitting in theme and technique to something
greater than itself.

> And spirit of the river, spirit of the sea,
> Suffer me not to be separated

> And let my cry come unto Thee.

This is a summit; an instance, as well, of increased pli-
ancy in rhythm, the lengthened phrase and gathered force
of rhymes suddenly collided being characteristic of the
later poems.
Mr. Eliot's aptitude for mythology and theology sometimes pays us the compliment of expecting our reading to
be more thorough than it is; but correspondences of allusion provide an unmistakable logic: stillness, intellectual beauty, spiritual exaltation, the white dress, 'the
glory of the humming bird,' childhood, concentration and
wholeness of personality - in contrast with noise, darkness, drugs, dreams, drowning, dust on the rosebowl,
Dusty the makeshift enchantress, cards, clairvoyants,
serpents, evasiveness, aimlessness, fog, intrusiveness,
temptation, unlogic, scattered bones, broken pride, rats,
drafts under the door, distortion, 'the sty of content-
ment.' Horror, which is unbelief, is the opposite of
ecstasy; and wholeness, which is the condition of ecstasy,
is to be 'accepted and accepting.' That is to say, we are
of a world in which light and darkness, 'appearance and
reality,' 'is and seem,' are ineludable alternatives.
And there are words of special meaning which recur
with the force of a theme: 'hidden,' referring to poetry
as the revelation of a hidden life; 'the pattern' continuing the Aristotelian concept of 'form' as the soul, the
invisible actuality of which the body is the outward
manifestation. Fire, the devourer, can be a purifier;
water has in it the thought of drowning or of drought
ended by inundation; as God's light is for man, the sun is
life for the natural world. Concepts and images are
toothed together and the poems are so consistently intri-
cated that one rests on another and is involved with what
was earlier; the musical theme at times being separated by

a stanza, as the argument sometimes is continued from the
preceding poem - 'O hidden' in 'Difficulties of a Statesman' completing the 'O hidden' in 'Triumphal March.' The
period containing 'Ash-Wednesday,' concerned with 'the infirm glory of the positive hour,' is succeeded by the
affirmative one to which 'Murder in the Cathedral'
belongs; also 'Burnt Norton,' a new poem which is concerned with the thought of control ('The high road and the
low are one and the same') embodied in Deity and in human
equipoise, its temporal counterpart:

[Quotes 'Burnt Norton', II, CPP, p. 172, 'We move above'
to 'among the stars'.]

In 'Usk', also, Mr. Eliot expresses the conviction that the
via media of discipline and self-control is the valuable
one:

> Where the roads dip and where the roads rise
> Seek only there
> Where the gray light meets the green air
> The hermit's chapel, the pilgrim's prayer.

One notices here the compactness, four thoughts in one -
the visible, the invisible, the indoors, the outdoors; and
that in the later poems, although statement is simpler,
the rhythm is more complex.
    Mr. Eliot has tried 'to write poetry which should be
essentially poetry, with nothing poetic about it, poetry
standing naked in its bare bones, or ... so transparent
that in reading it we are intent on what the poem *points
at* and not on the poetry.' He has not dishonored 'the
deepest terrors and desires,' depths of 'degradation' and
heights of 'exaltation,' or the fact that it is possible
to have 'walked in hell' and 'been rapt to heaven.'
    Those who have power to renounce life are those whose
lives are valuable to a community; one who attains equi-
librium in spite of opposition to himself from within is
in a stronger position than if there had been no oppos-
tion to overcome; and in art, freedom evolving from a
liberated constraint is stronger than if it had not by
nature been cramped. Indigenous skepticism, also constraint are part of Mr. Eliot's temperament; but at its
apex art is able to conceal the artist while it exhibits
his 'angel'; like the unanticipatedly limber florescence
of fireworks as they expand into trees or bouquets with
the abandon of 'unbroke horses'; and this effect we have
in 'Cape Ann' - denominated a minor poem, perhaps as being
a mood or aspect rather than part of a thought-related

sequence:

[Quotes 'Cape Ann', CPP, p. 142.]

99. MORTON D. ZABEL, FROM POETS OF FIVE DECADES, 'SOUTHERN REVIEW'

Summer 1936, vol. ii, 168-71

The review opens with a consideration of 'Selected Poems' by AE (George E. Russell), a *fin de siècle* poet associated with Yeats.

When Eliot began to write, the moment for this kind of spiritual illusion had passed from the serious poets of the English scene. He subtitles his 'Collected Poems' with the dates '1909-1935,' and by 1909 whatever heroic assumptions remained among the older poets (Swinburne, Meredith, or Moody) passed with the deaths of those men. It had in any case been long reproved by the tragic sarcasm of Hardy, Housman, and Robinson, or - for Eliot more forcibly - by the withering irony of the later Symbolists. There was no further opportunity to lean toward dreams and visions, or upon the ennobling humility of public confession and absolution. If the heroic emerged from the past it did not console the poet either when he borrowed its language or adapted its legends. It diminished to further frailty his dispossession and mediocrity. But curiously, where the promise of oblivion and oneness in 'the Dream' deceived AE into making ineffectual splendor of his own destiny, the extreme contempt of human meanness in a poet like Eliot led to a tangible grasp of what there was in him to be exalted. This produced in the end an illumination of selfhood which achieved the hard and concrete performance of a legend. It is to legend that Prufrock and Sweeney belong. They cleanse the conscience of modern man by a species of critical purgation. Long as we have read and pondered them, they still give the pleasure of severe epitomes of the meaning of experience.
    But as everyone knows, Eliot has moved far from the

style and spirit of those poems. 'The Waste Land' showed
his transition toward a less personal idiom, and a less
sympathetic participation in the modern problem. 'The
Hollow Men' marked a release from, and a disintegration of
the critical intelligence of the earlier verse, showing
this not only by its greater flexibility of structure and
cadence, but by the words employed. These words begin to
modify the sharp epithet and accent of the satires, and to
weave around the sensibility within the poems a subtle web
of logical complexity and the casuistries of dialectic
argument. It is not too much to claim that this development in Eliot's style reveals the exchange of his powers
of introspection for something superior to and beyond personality. His themes change from the dramatic situation
of 'The Love Song,' and 'Portrait of a Lady,' where self-
scrutiny is remorseless and laconic, to the delirium of
'The Hollow Men,' the self-effacing abnegation of 'Ash-
Wednesday,' and finally to the abstract considerations on
the nature and meaning of Time in his latest long poem,
'Burnt Norton.' Here also is a growth away from the
meagerness of personal agony toward the freedom of impersonal speculation. But the best quality of 'Burnt Norton'
resides in its reminders of how severe, strenuous, and
practical was the poet's approach toward the present en-
largement of his philosophic vision.

Eliot's poems show remarkably changes in these two
hundred pages. While they have become more abstract and
intricate in their ideas, they have grown simpler and more
expository in method. They have exchanged the pithy
terseness of the early allegories for the sinuous devices
of metaphysical search. Their language has almost entirely lost the colloquial formality of the 'Prufrock'
volume. Where this persists, and where he still employs
the contrasts of cheap modernity with past greatness (as
in the two 'fragments of an Aristophanic melodrama' or
the two poems - 'Triumphal March' and 'Difficulties of a
Statesman' - now grouped as parts of an unfinished work
called 'Coriolan'), the yoking seems to have the obvious
violence of a patented device. By contrast this gives a
superior effect to later poems that avoid such conjunction, 'Ash-Wednesday' and 'Marina.' Oblique humor has
also disappeared from the later work (though not entirely
from the volume, for Eliot here prints a number of nonsense pieces, 'Five-Finger Exercises,' which hardly impress
as important.) He has become on the whole a more patient
and explicit - that is, a more popular - poet. No doubt
there are derivations concealed in his later work which
will enlist the services of future Williamsons and
Matthiessens. I have not traced them far; 'Burnt Norton'

seems to derive its Time-theme as much from speculators
like Whitehead and Dunne as from the lines of Heraclitus
printed below the title. But these poems, like the
choruses from 'The Rock' and 'Murder in the Cathedral,'
impose no such task of identification on the studious
reader as was demanded by every line and page of 'The
Waste Land.' Their subtleties are organic to themselves;
the poem's whole problem is contained within the poem and
does not fly off at the tangent of each literary echo or
historical reference. And at times, as in 'Animula' and
'Marina,' the feeling and utterance of the poet concentrate into passages of superb lyric vision.

When Eliot stood isolated and dispossessed among the
ruins of a familiar universe, every nerve and sensation
quivered with its own life. The antennae of his intelligence were alive with nervous vitality. This resulted in
images and allegories of great focal sharpness. In more
recent years, approaching stranger territory, this grip on
identity is no longer held, and with its relaxation the
nervous sensibility of his diction and cadence has less-
ened. He writes either a more relaxed and speculative
verse, or a sort of argument which attempts to extend his
intellectual problems beyond their own limits. He has become a poet of more public qualities, of religious respon-
sibilities, and even (in 'The Rock') of social concerns.
These have entailed a change from a style of cryptic historical reference and erudition to one of dialectic lucidity, or even of popular simplification. He also has
doubtless felt 'a drift in the times.' He has been compelled, as churchman and citizen, toward popularizing and
clarifying his language, even though he has not descended
to simplifying his metaphysical vision. But that his
address has broadened is obvious. One has only to recol-
lect his essays on poetic drama in 'The Sacred Wood,' or
his remarks on poetic popularity in the study of Tennyson
in his new book 'Essays Ancient and Modern,' to be aware
of his long-standing inclination to enlist the moral support and affirmation of a wide human public.

There remains the question of which of these two kinds
of poetry - the personal and allegorical or the more human
and explicit - he shows greater mastery in. 'Ash-
Wednesday' and 'Murder in the Cathedral' are brilliant
achievements. They may bear the more lasting signs of
poetic authority. They rise above that poetic value which
is restricted to the circle of initiates. But Eliot's
creative temperament still stands in its original and
fundamental quality in the poems before 1925, and is cor-
roborated there by the essays of the same period. Moreover, those earlier poems were in their way primary

creations. They embodied a specific poetic method, and
the form of the poems exactly conveyed the matter presented and the kind of experience defined. In later works
the hortatory or penitential style is often weakened by
such pastiche of his own earlier manner as mars the pages
of 'The Rock.' Humor and skepticism now seem to sprout
artificially from the thicker stem of religious faith, and
we are left uncertain of just what is essential and what
is not....

100. ROLFE HUMPHRIES, ELIOT'S POETRY, 'NEW MASSES'

18 August 1936, vol. xx, 25-6

Humphries (b. 1894), an American poet, edited, in 1936,
a collection of poems entitled 'And Spain Sings'.

Half this book is a reprint of Eliot's 'Poems: 1909-1925.'
That work formed the basis of the finest Marxist criticism
of poetry in this reviewer's experience, D.S. Mirsky's
essay on T.S. Eliot and the End of Bourgeois Poetry.
Concerning this half of the present collection, it is
sufficient here to refer the reader to the version of
Mirsky's essay which appeared in the 'New Masses' (November 13, 1934), or, if he knows French, to the fuller
statement in the files of the Paris magazine 'Echanges.'
     'What distinguishes Eliot,' Mirsky sums it up, 'is that
with him a rare poetic gift is allied with a social theme
of real significance, with indeed the sole historically
valid and sincere theme accessible to a bourgeois poet of
today. His contemporaries are but manifestations of the
death of bourgeois poetry and civilization; he alone has
been able to create a poetry of this death.'
     The risk run by such a poet is that of exposing himself
to the infection of his material. Eliot, who has created
a poetry of death, may survive to demonstrate, in his personal history, the death of poetry. In the poems from
'Ash-Wednesday' on, there is perceptible evidence of the
fatal trend. There is repetition, if not self-imitation:
the minor poems, 'Eyes That Last I Saw in Tears,' and 'The
Wind Sprang up at Four O'Clock,' for instance, contain
phrases that seem like scraps left over from their use in

'The Hollow Men' or 'The Waste Land.' There is doggerel
and triviality: Items IV and V of 'Five-Finger Exercises,'
for instance, seem a bit unworthy of one who may aspire to
saintliness, and the spectacle of an ascete copying the
attitudes of Edward Lear is ghastly incongruous rather
than genuinely comic or edifying. The much-admired choruses from 'The Rock' seem to me to contain, rather than to
be, poetry; taken as wholes, they illustrate what Eliot
was talking about (in his introduction to Perse's 'Ana-
base') when he told us we needed a term to complete the
series verse, poetry, prose.

    If we elevate Eliot above his contemporaries and en-
title him the ideal classical poet of an age in break-up,
we do not thereby intend to accept his own valuation of
himself as classicist - a romantic and pathetic gesture in
the teeth of his time. But his genius, unusually sensitive to an atmosphere of disintegration, has contrived to
resist its attraction by his art, to make aesthetic use
of the phenomena of dissolution. He has a power of dealing with fragments; both in their invention and synthesis,
Eliot has elevated the status of the fragmentary from
accident to design. 'These fragments I have shored
against my ruins' runs the last completely intelligible
sentence of 'The Waste Land'; and in subsequent work he
seems to take comfort in their creation as well as in
their use. Thus we have before us fragments of an agon,
fragments of a prologue, unfinished poems, five-finger
exercises as such; 'Ash-Wednesday' includes scraps of the
litany, the choruses from 'The Rock' of the 'Te Deum.'
'A Song for Simeon of the Nunc Dimittis'; and elsewhere
can be found, as mentioned, lumps of Edward Lear, or
Gertrude Stein.

[Quotes 'Ash-Wednesday', V, CPP, p. 96, 'Where shall the
word' to 'deny the voice'.]

Here, too, there are signs of a reduction of temperature
from the white-hot fervor of energy which fused and
smelted the scrap-metal in 'The Waste-Land' to a durable
poetic amalgam. Or, to vary the metaphor, what we are
permitted to see at times now in Eliot is the undigested
substance in the crop of the dissected bird rather than
its conversion to formal discharge of energy in poetic
flight.

    There is more light and less heat in Eliot now, more
radiance and less candor, but whatever details of weakness
appear in his work are in it, rather than of it. They are
there as tendencies which will perhaps be magnified and
accelerated as Eliot attains to that state of senile

blessedness to which he professes to aspire; at present
they reside in him only in the same sense that a man in
the prime of life houses, barring accident, his own peculiar dissolution, predictable enough by the expert in
prognosis.

'Little by little we see rising against the Laforguian
atmosphere that pervades the verse of the young Eliot a
poetry altogether different, freed from the vacillating
ambiguity of the decadent, a poetry in which irony cedes
before the tragic, and the sexual ambivalence of the consumptive is replaced by the renunciation of the aesthete.'
Eliot's later work confirms the accuracy of Mirsky's prediction. We are not yet beyond earshot of ambivalence:
the 'Sweeney' fragments in the present collection, placed
after the 'Ash-Wednesday' and 'Ariel' sequences, testify
to the temptations assailing the soul, which 'cannot be
possessed of the divine union, until is has divested
itself of the love of created beings.' This, curiously,
is the same note that sounds in the central philosophy of
the American poet Jeffers - 'Humanity needs to fall in
love outward'; the same philosophy that Shaw puts in the
mouth of his Ancients in 'Back to Methuselah' applies to
the aspirations of Eliot's art - 'on towards a religion
of pure mind, free from all vitalism, a religion purely
spiritual, mystic in the strictest sense of the term, and
also rigorously intellectual.' Reaching the final impasse, bourgeois aestheticism is compelled to make the
desperate attempt to transcend the inexorable laws of
material considerations. In Eliot's case, as the attrac-
tions of high austerity and low vulgarity make war on
each other, out of their conflict he achieves his finest
poetry; his spirit announces 'the completion of its partial ecstasy, the resolution of its partial horror' in the
beautiful musical despair of the final poem, 'Burnt Norton.'

'All the arts,' Eliot has quoted Pater to us, 'aspire
to the condition of music and their meaning reaches us
through ways not directly traceable by the understanding.'
More than ever, Eliot seems to feel that words fail him;
more than ever, he grows in his capacity to make them
assume the functions of music. There is a sense in which
the Collected Poems are one whole - a symphony, with
deliberately introduced dissonances, with studied repetitions of theme and phrase (as, for example, the cry,
'Resign, resign!' appears both in the political satire
'Difficulties of a Statesman' and the simple nature lyric
'Cape Ann'). How beautifully, in 'Burnt Norton,' Eliot
winds the theme, from the simple statement that perhaps
any dialectical materialist would accept:

Time present and time past
Are both perhaps present in time future,
And time future contained in time past.

to the conclusion that any revolutionist might find difficulty in understanding:

[Quotes 'Burnt Norton', V, CPP, pp. 175-6, 'Words move'
to 'before and after'.]

How beautifully it is done!
    We must not let ourselves become insensitive to this
means of communication, no matter how thoroughly we are
bent on understanding that the apparent motions of Eliot's
art and the real motions are by no means identical.   It
would be too easy to let Eliot's sense of moral resignation conduce to our sense of moral outrage, and declare a
boycott on all his works: but if Marxist criticism of
poetry is presumed to partake of the nature of economic
science, it would be poor economics. To that science,
wrote Engels, 'moral indignation, however, justifiable,
cannot serve as an argument, but only as a symptom.'
Eliot is not a proletarian poet, nor has he urged a class-
less society even in heaven.   Still, he is a prophet of
revolution; he has written, with poetic authority too
great to be questioned, the elegy of an age that is passing.   Let us not be so boisterous shouting our war songs
that we fail to hear from the citadel of our enemies the
cry of capitulation.

101. D.W. HARDING, T.S. ELIOT, 1925-1935, 'SCRUTINY'

September 1936, vol. v, 171-6

This review was reprinted in 'The Importance of Scrutiny',
edited by Eric Bentley (New York, 1948), pp. 262-6.

This new volume is an opportunity, not for a review - for
'The Poetry of T.S. Eliot' begins to have the intimidat-
ing sound of a Tripos question - but for asking whether
anything in the development of the poetry accounts for the
change in attitude that has made Mr. Eliot's work less

chic now than it was ten years ago. Perhaps the ten years
are a sufficient explanation - obvious changes in fashionable feeling have helped to make the sort-of-communist
poets popular. But on the other hand it may be that these
poets gratify some taste that Mr. Eliot also gratified in
his earlier work but not in his later. If so it is surely
a taste for evocations of the sense of protest that our
circumstances set up in us; for it seems likely that at
the present time it is expressions of protest in some
form or other that most readily gain a poet popular
sympathy. And up to 'The Waste Land' and 'The Hollow Men'
this protest - whether distressed, disgusted, or ironical
- was still the dominant note of Mr. Eliot's work, through
all the subtlety and sensitiveness of the forms it took.
Yet already in these two poems the suggestion was creeping
in that the sufferers were also failures. We are the
hollow men, but there are, besides,

>   Those who have crossed
>   With direct eyes, to death's other Kingdom

And in all the later work the stress tends to fall on
the regret or suffering that arises from our own choices
or our inherent limitations, or on the resignation that
they make necessary. Without at the moment trying to define the change more closely one can point out certain
characteristics of the later work which are likely to
displease those who create the fashions of taste in
poetry to-day, and which also contrast with Mr. Eliot's
earlier work. First it is true that in some of the
poems (most obviously in the 'Choruses from "The Rock"')
there are denunciation and preaching, both of which
people like just now. But there is a vital difference
between the denunciation here and that, say, in 'The Dog
Beneath the Skin': Mr. Eliot doesn't invite you to step
across a dividing line and join him in guaranteed rightness - he suggests at the most that you and he should
both try, in familiar and difficult ways, not to live so
badly. Failing to make it sound easy, and not putting
much stress on the fellowship of the just, he offers no
satisfaction to the craving for a life that is ethically
and emotionally *simpler*.

And this characteristic goes with a deeper change of
attitude that separates the later work from the earlier.
Besides displaying little faith in a revolt against anything outside himself, Mr. Eliot in his recent work never
invites you to believe that everything undesirable in you

is due to outside influences that can be blamed for
tampering with your original rightness. Not even in the
perhaps over-simple 'Animula' is there any suggestion that
the 'simple soul' has suffered an avoidable wrong for
which someone else can be given the blame. Mr. Eliot declines to sanction an implicit belief, almost universally
held, which lies behind an immense amount of rationalization, self-pity and childish protest - the belief that the
very fact of being alive ought to ensure your being a
satisfactory object in your own sight. He is nearer the
more rational view that the process of living is at its
best one of progressive dissatisfaction.

Throughout the earlier poems there are traces of what,
if it were cruder and without irony and impersonality,
would be felt at once as self-pity or futile protest: for
example,

> Put your shoes at the door, sleep, prepare for life.
> The last twist of the knife.

or,

> Wipe your hand across your mouth, and laugh;
> The worlds revolve like ancient women
> Gathering fuel in vacant lots.

or again,

> The nightingales are singing near
> The Convent of the Sacred Heart,
>
> And sang within the bloody wood
> When Agamemnon cried aloud,
> And let their liquid siftings fall
> To stain the stiff dishonoured shroud.

Obviously this is only one aspect of the early poetry,
and to lay much stress on it without qualification would
be grotesquely unfair to 'Gerontion' especially and to
other poems of that phase. But it is a prominent enough
aspect of the work to have made critics, one might have
thought, more liable to underrate the earlier poems than,
with fashionable taste, the later ones. For there can be
no doubt of the greater maturity of feeling in the later
work:

> And I pray that I may forget
> These matters that with myself I too much discuss
> Too much explain

> Because I do not hope to turn again
> Let these words answer
> For what is done, not to be done again
> May the judgment not be too heavy upon us

This may be called religious submission, but essentially
it is the submission of maturity.

What is peculiar to Mr. Eliot in the tone of his work,
and not inherent in maturity or in religion, is that he
does *submit* to what he knows rather than welcoming it. To
say that his is a depressed poetry isn't true, because of
the extraordinary toughness and resilience that always
underlie it. They show, for instance, in the quality of
the scorn he expresses for those who have tried to overlook what he sees:

> ... the strained time-ridden faces
> Distracted from distraction by distraction
> Filled with fancies and empty of meaning
> Tumid apathy with no concentration
> Men and bits of paper ...

But to insist on the depression yields a half-truth. For
though acceptance and understanding have taken the place
of protest the underlying experience remains one of suffering, and the renunciation is much more vividly communicated than the advance for the sake of which it was
made. It is summed up in the ending of 'Ash-Wednesday':

[Quotes 'Ash-Wednesday', VI, CPP, pp. 98-9, 'Blessèd
sister' to 'come unto Thee'.]

This is the cry of the weaned child, I suppose the ana-
lysts might say; and without acquiescing in the genetic
view that they would imply one can agree that weaning
stands as a type-experience of much that Mr. Eliot is
interested in as a poet. It seems to be the clearer and
more direct realization of this kind of experience that
makes the later poems at the same time more personal and
more mature. And in the presence of these poems many who
liked saying they liked the earlier work feel both
embarrassed and snubbed.

However, all of this might be said about a volume of
collected sermons instead of poems. It ignores Mr. Eliot's
amazing genius in the use of words and rhythms and his
extraordinary fertility in styles of writing, each 'manner'
apparently perfected from the first and often used only
once (only once, that is, by Mr. Eliot, though most are
like comets with a string of poetasters laboriously

tailing after them). One aspect of his mastery of language may perhaps be commented on here because it reaches
its most remarkable expression in the latest of the poems,
'Burnt Norton.' Here most obviously the poetry is a
linguistic achievement, in this case an achievement in
the creation of concepts.

Ordinarily our abstract ideas are over-comprehensive
and include too wide a range of feeling to be of much use
by themselves. If our words 'regret' and 'eternity' were
exact bits of mosaic with which to build patterns much of
'Burnt Norton' would not have had to be written. But

> ...Words strain,
> Crack and sometimes break, under the burden
> Under the tension, slip, slide, perish,
> Decay with imprecision, will not stay in place,
> Will not stay still.

One could say, perhaps, that the poem takes the place of
the ideas of 'regret' and 'eternity.' Where in ordinary
speech we should have to use those words, and hope by conversational trial-and-error to obviate the grosser misunderstandings, this poem is a newly-created concept,
equally abstract but vastly more exact and rich in meaning. It makes no statement. It is no more 'about' anything than an abstract term like 'love' is about anything: it is a linguistic creation. And the creation of
a new concept, with all the assimilation and communication of experience that that involves, is perhaps the
greatest of linguistic achievements.

In this poem the new meaning is approached by two
methods. The first is the presentation of concrete
images and definite events, each of which is checked and
passes over into another before it has developed far
enough to stand meaningfully by itself. This is, of
course, an extension of a familiar language process. If
you try to observe introspectively how the meaning of an
abstract term - say 'trade' - exists in your mind, you
find that after a moment of blankness, in which there
seems to be only imageless 'meaning,' concrete images of
objects and events begin to occur to you; but none by
itself carries the full meaning of the word 'trade,' and
each is faded out and replaced by another. The abstract
concept, in fact, seems like a space surrounded and defined by a more or less rich collection of latent ideas.
It is this kind of definition that Mr. Eliot sets about
here - in the magnificent first section for instance -
with every subtlety of verbal and rhythmical suggestion.

And the complementary method is to make pseudo-

statements in highly abstract language, for the purpose,
essentially, of putting forward and immediately rejecting
ready-made concepts that might have seemed to approximate
to the concept he is creating. For instance:

> Neither from nor towards; at the still point, there
>   the dance is
> But neither arrest nor movement. And do not call it
>   fixity,
> Where past and future are gathered. Neither movement
>   from nor towards,
> Neither ascent nor decline.

Or

> Not the stillness of the violin, while the note lasts,
> Not that only, but the co-existence,
> Or say that the end precedes the beginning,
> And the end and the beginning were always there
> Before the beginning and after the end.
> And all is always now.

In neither of these methods is there any attempt to
state the meaning by taking existing abstract ideas and
piecing them together in the ordinary way. Where something approaching this more usual method is attempted, in
the passage beginning 'The inner freedom from the practical desire,' it seems a little less successful; admirable
for the plays, where the audience is prominent, it fails
to combine quite perfectly with the other methods of this
poem. But it is Mr. Eliot himself who, by the closeness
of his approach to technical perfection, provides a background against which such faint flaws can be seen.

102. LOUIS UNTERMEYER, FROM NEW POETRY, 'YALE REVIEW'

September 1936, vol. xxvi, 165-6

T.S. Eliot has become a symbol of all that is advanced in
poetry, and yet he is an anachronism in the sense that he
is both futurist and *fin de siècle*. No one, as far as I
know, has compared him to the aesthetes of the Nineties;
yet his course and theirs are curiously similar. They
mixed Anglican intellectuality and Parnassian

impressionism; he combined academic erudition and French symbolism. They found their own times ugly, and retreated into the remote and exotic; he, equally horrified by his world, pitted a beautiful past against an evil present, and explored an unreal limbo where even the brutal was bizarre. They - Lionel Johnson, Ernest Dowson, Oscar Wilde, Aubrey Beardsley - could no longer face their own distortions and turned to the Catholic church, which supplied them with new color as well as a new impetus; he, unable to dwell in his Waste Land, with its nightmares of vulgarity, has found an Anglo-Catholic haven, and in return, the church has given him another kind of subsistence as well as fresh subject matter. With their desperate audacities they marked the end of the century; with his confused desperation he marks the end of an epoch.

Eliot's 'Collected Poems,' including all the poetic work he wished to print with the exception of 'Murder in the Cathedral,' his simplest and most moving creation, presents a still further paradox. The early poems - the poems of contempt, frustration, and horror, - are more compelling than the later penitences and salvations. Eliot communicates his aversions through Sweeney and Bleistein far more successfully than his resignations through Burnt Norton. 'The Love Song of J. Alfred Prufrock,' that remarkable study of futility, written when Eliot was an undergraduate, scarcely depended on abstractions. Here, and in the poems that immediately succeeded it, Eliot expressed his hatred of his times in biting, if bewildering, stanzas. 'The Waste Land,' with its sequential 'The Hollow Men,' was the impasse; the poet could descend no further into boredom, emptiness, drought. 'Ash-Wednesday' points the way out; 'A Song for Simeon' and the choruses from 'The Rock' define it.

And what is the sum of the contrasts and shiftings now they are collected in one volume? Is the final effect a growth or incongruity? It is an uncertain mixture of all. Eliot can be the most solemn of poets; there are times when his solemnities are sillier than his purposeful nonsense. The burlesque of third-rate comic opera in 'Sweeney Agonistes' is mildly amusing, but prefixing his absurdities with a quotation from St. John of the Cross is both pretentious and funny. There is no fusion, not even a 'lunar synthesis.' There are remarkable images, strange and exciting juxtapositions, sweet and acidulous discords, bleak hope matched with no final faith, the words of other men shaped into new cadences. Eliot's very idiom - and there can be no doubt of its individuality - is a paradox, being largely composed of idioms not originally his own.

His lines are a mosaic of fragments from poets as incongruously joined as Browning and Paul Dresser (Theodore
Dreiser's brother and composer of 'On the Banks of the
Wabash'), Shakespeare and the Upanishads, Ovid and Verlaine, Dante and Edward Lear. Certain borrowed lines,
often without benefit of quotation, appear again and
again; for example Dante's 'At the still point of the
turning world' occurs in 'Triumphal March' and the still
more recent and seemingly autobiographical 'Burnt Norton.'
   Yet there is no questioning Eliot's influence or his
authority. The authority, however, lies not so much in
what Eliot says as in his manner of saying it, even in his
manner of making others say it. It lies in the very amalgam of accents, in his timely sense of confusion, and his
peculiarly persuasive techniques of escape. In spite of
major sonorities and an often exalted pitch, Eliot is not
a major poet, but a new kind of minor poet - a minor poet
in the grand manner.

103. R.P. BLACKMUR, THE WHOLE POET, 'POETRY'

April 1937, vol. 1, 48-51

Blackmur (1904-65), an American literary critic, wrote a
number of essays on Eliot, among the most important being
T.S. Eliot: From 'Ash-Wednesday' to 'Murder in the
Cathedral' in 'The Double Agent' (New York, 1935),
pp. 184-218, reprinted in Unger, pp. 236-62.

It is always a pleasant exercise, with a poet of any
scope, to run over the bulk of his work all at once, and
especially if, as is the case with Mr. Eliot's present
collection, there is a small quantity of new or relatively
unfamiliar work to add to the old stock as a fresh ferment. A man's poems act upon each other specifically as
the works of different poets act upon each other generally. From the whole body of poetry we get an idea - a
fading or quickening image - of what poetry is like; not
a demonstrable idea but an idea of which we are perfectly
possessed however we may come to alter it. From the
works of one poet, as we increase our ability of response,
we get similarly an indestructible haunting idea of what

his work is about. Shakespeare is about all his plays,
sonnets, and poems. Eliot is about all his poems and
plays. There is a fundamental limited, or stretched,
habit of response, of objective expression of that response, which is the actual subject of a man's work. It
is by no legerdemain but by a deep absorptive process of
the intelligence that we come to speak most satisfyingly
of a man's work by the mere abstract handle of his name.
With the name, as we are able, we put on the power; forgetting the name we sometimes come on the glory; or
again, if we can enough divest ourselves, come on both
the ignominy and the glory.

It is astonishing, generally, how much the poems here
collected tell about each other in the way of prediction
and illumination, of obsession and insight, of the
strength of form and the agony of formulation, of poverty,
of means and of the riches secured and even predetermined
by those means. The unity of the work taken together as
a form of response is indefeasible, and creates, among the
fragments of the separate poems, a kind of inevitable
involvement which is a virtual unity of substance. It is
the more astonishing, specifically, how much the latest
poem in the book, 'Burnt Norton', both depends on all the
earlier poems as their inalienable product and adds to
them critically and emphatically. 'Burnt Norton' makes
the earlier poems grow and diminish, as it illuminates
them or shows them up. Yet it is not easy to say what the
poem is about as a matter of fact. There is a central
image, the whole of part III, of a number of people riding
in a subway train; it is an image of a spiritual, or non-
spiritual, condition of which inescapable analogues
assault us all. Associated with this image is an image
of a rose garden with a pool, various flowers, singing
birds and laughing children. Superimposed throughout are
Eliot's intense and elaborated meditated versions of the
two fragments of Heraclitus which form his epigraph, one
about words and the other about the identity of the soul
in change. Thus we get a great deal about time, a great
deal in one place about the pattern or form of words (the
problem of the imagination faced with actuality), and a
great deal about the still point of the turning world.
The poem is what happens when these elements and others
not easy to name unite under the impact of the most Eliot
is able to apply of the auditory imagination: that imagination which reaches down into the syllables of words,
into the roots both of meaning and sound, and brings the
words up newly alive.

I do not know how far, on this new level of abstraction, Mr. Eliot has made his words new and how far he has

been compelled to use words worn, or moribund, or plainly
dead; there are passages which read like emptied formulae
from other poems; time will tell the responsive ear and
the waiting intelligence. Meanwhile, it seems to me conspicuously important to say that the frames of the words
used, the specific symbols, the obsessive feelings, the
whole apparatus of Eliot's *private* clues to reality are
the same here as in the earlier poems. It is the same
material throughout that the poetic process is meant to
make actual. I do not mean that Eliot is re-working 'Ash-
Wednesday' or that 'Ash-Wednesday' re-worked 'The Waste
Land', or that 'Lear' re-worked 'Hamlet'. I mean that the
identity of poetic means shows a fundamental response to
identic material made on different levels of a unifying
sensibility. A different level is secured by the incor-
poration of a different or *specific* approach into the
poetic process. Here Eliot attempts to incorporate the
approach of the abstracting, schematizing intellect into
a process essentially dramatic and concrete. The question
is how far the abstract can reach into the realm of the
concrete without benefit of a driving or dramatic form –
which is here absent; and the specific difficulty would
seem to be to make the outline or regimen of such a meditation clear without that benefit. 'Burnt Norton' will
seem successful, perhaps, if the earlier poems supply the
lack; it will fail if it remains a mere appended commentary upon the material of the other poems.

Select Index

The index is divided into three parts: I Works by Eliot; II Themes and Thematic Groupings; III General Index.

I WORKS BY ELIOT

II   THEMES AND THEMATIC GROUPINGS

III   GENERAL INDEX